ALL THINGS RESTORED

Confirming the Authenticity of LDS Beliefs

ALSO BY MATTHEW B. BROWN

Symbols in Stone: Symbolism on the Early Temples of the Restoration
(with Paul Thomas Smith)

The Gate of Heaven: Insights on the Doctrines and Symbols of the Temple

* * * *

available in book
or book on cassette format
from Covenant

ALL THINGS RESTORED

Confirming the Authenticity of LDS Beliefs

MATTHEW B. BROWN

Covenant Communications, Inc.

Covenant

For my parents

Lee and Sheryll Brown

Published by Covenant Communications, Inc.
American Fork, Utah

Printed in the United States of America
First Printing: October 2000

07 06 05 04 03 02 01 00 10 9 8 7 6 5 4 3 2 1

ISBN 1-57734-712-9

CONTENTS

ABBREVIATIONS

In citing works in the notes, short titles have generally been used. Works frequently cited have been identified by the following abbreviations:

BYUS	*Brigham Young University Studies*
CR	*Conference Report*
D&C	Doctrine and Covenants
DS	*Doctrines of Salvation*
EM	*Encyclopedia of Mormonism*
HC	*History of the Church*
JBMS	*Journal of Book of Mormon Studies*
JD	*Journal of Discourses*
JS–H	Joseph Smith–History
JST	Joseph Smith Translation
MD	*Mormon Doctrine*
MS	*Millennial Star*
TPJS	*Teachings of the Prophet Joseph Smith*
TS	*Times and Seasons*
WJS	*Words of Joseph Smith*

INTRODUCTION

On a beautiful spring morning in the year 1820, a fourteen-year-old boy named Joseph Smith entered into a grove of trees near his home in Palmyra, New York, so he could pray in solitude.[1] Trusting the scriptural promise that God would answer the petitions of those who humbly sought wisdom at his hand,[2] young Joseph asked the Lord which of all the various denominations was the true Church of Jesus Christ, for they all taught different doctrines.

In response to this boy's simple prayer, the adversary of all righteousness became enraged. "I was seized upon by some power which entirely overcame me," relates Joseph Smith, "and had such an astonishing influence over me as to bind my tongue so that I could not speak. Thick darkness gathered around me, and it seemed to me for a time as if I were doomed to sudden destruction." In great alarm over his dire circumstances, Joseph exerted all his power to call upon God for deliverance. At the very moment when he was about to abandon himself to certain destruction, a bright pillar of light appeared exactly over his head, and his enemy quickly departed. "When the light rested upon me," Joseph relates, "I saw two Personages, whose brightness and glory defy all description, standing above me in the air. One of them

FIGURE 1. President Joseph F. Smith in the Sacred Grove in Palmyra, New York. President Smith is standing nearest to the spot where the First Vision took place.

spake unto me, calling me by name and said, pointing to the other—*This is My Beloved Son. Hear Him!*"[3]

As soon as Joseph was able to get possession of his faculties, he asked the Father and the Son which of all the divergent Christian sects was right, so that he might join himself with it. In response, he was told that the Christian faith had fallen into a serious state of apostasy.[4] "They told me," said the Prophet, "that all religious denominations were believing in incorrect doctrines, and that none of them was acknowledged of God as His Church and kingdom: and I was expressly commanded to 'go not after them,' at the same time receiving a promise that the fullness of the gospel should at some future time be made known unto me."[5]

Several years after this marvelous manifestation, the Lord sent a series of heavenly messengers to Joseph Smith to teach him about the nature of the Restoration of true Christianity, to instruct him in the pure doctrines and ordinances of the gospel, to confer the holy Priesthood upon him, and to give him all the keys, rights, and powers that belong to the dispensation of the fullness of times.[6]

The Lord Jesus Christ has proclaimed to all the world that The Church of Jesus Christ of Latter-day Saints is "the only true and living Church upon the face of the whole earth."[7] This is an extraordinary statement, one that is worthy of the consideration of all those who profess to be disciples of the Savior or who seek for religious truth. The purpose of this book is to examine some of the numerous spiritual, physical, and intellectual evidences that support the claim that the religion of the Latter-day Saints is a true restoration of Christ's everlasting gospel.

Evidence plays a vital role in the creation and preservation of faith. Elder Orson Pratt explained that "faith or belief is the result of evidence presented to the mind. Without evidence, the mind cannot have faith in anything. . . . Faith in every fact, statement, truth, or proposition which we have confidence in is, in all cases whatsoever, derived from evidence. Therefore, without evidence, faith can have no existence."[8] When Jesus Christ dwelt among mortals He utilized three different types of evidence in order to create and nourish faith in Him—spiritual evidence, physical evidence, and intellectual evidence.

Spiritual Evidence: The Savior once asked His twelve apostles a profoundly important question: "Whom say ye that I am?" Peter, the chief apostle, answered and said, "Thou art the Christ, the Son of the living God." Then Jesus pointed out that Peter's faith was built upon a spiritual testimony. "Flesh and blood hath not revealed it unto thee, but my Father which is in heaven."[9] John the Baptist also received a heavenly witness, or evidence, that Jesus was the Christ when he saw the sign of the dove at the Savior's baptism. Because of this spiritual manifestation John was able to testify, without a doubt, that he knew Jesus was the Son of God. Jesus, in turn, reminded the Jews that they had been supplied with an evidence of His true identity when they heard John's testimony.[10]

Physical Evidence: The Savior appeared unto His disciples after His resurrection to supply them with "many infallible proofs" that He was, indeed, the risen Redeemer.[11] So important was the presentation of this physical evidence that the Lord made a special appearance to Thomas so that his faith could become solidified, even as it had among the other apostles.[12] Christ's miracles also served as physical evidence of the truthfulness of His claims. Even though Jesus performed many miracles in private, there were several occasions when He performed them publicly so that there was absolutely no doubt among the children of Israel that He possessed the power of God.[13]

Intellectual Evidence: Jesus Christ not only taught the Israelites that the scriptures bore witness of Him[14] but on occasion He actually pointed out the very scriptures that bore such a witness.[15] The early Saints, following their Master's lead, drew upon various evidences from scriptural texts to demonstrate that Jesus was truly the Son of God. Not only did they quote from the scriptures, but they also "reasoned" from them and "persuaded" their listeners that their message was true.[16] Why are such intellectual exercises necessary? It was Austin Farrer who taught that even "though argument does not create conviction, lack of it destroys belief. What seems to be proved may not be embraced; but what no one shows the ability to defend is quickly abandoned. Rational argument does not create belief, but it maintains a climate in which belief may flourish."[17]

Just as spiritual, physical, and intellectual evidences served as tools for establishing the divine authenticity of Christ's work in the meridian of time, so too they can serve in the dispensation of the fullness of times. Elder Neal A. Maxwell has predicted that eventually "there will be a convergence of discoveries to make plain and plausible what the modern prophets have been saying all along." But even though these evidences may confirm and strengthen our faith, Elder Maxwell reminds us that they will never be enough to remove the need for faith.[18]

The material in this book has been divided into eight chapters. The first, called "Evidences of Apostasy," demonstrates that the early Christian leaders not only predicted an apostasy from the pure religion of Jesus Christ, but they also documented its progress in many New Testament texts. In this chapter, readers will learn about some of the causes and consequences of the Great Apostasy and will discover that the Christians who lived during the meridian of time knew there would be a "restoration" before the Second Coming of Jesus Christ.

The second chapter of this book is about "The Divine Calling of Joseph Smith." Upon these pages, the reader will find numerous evidences that Joseph Smith was a true prophet of God. Subjects covered here include the fulfillment of Joseph Smith's prophecies, independent witnesses to some of the Prophet's visions, and ancient Jewish legends about an Israelite leader who would arise in the last days, restore the true religion of Jehovah, gather the tribes of Israel, reinstate true temple worship, and die as a martyr.

The third chapter, entitled "The Restoration of the Church," compares some of the unique practices, priesthoods, ordinances, and organizational structures of the LDS Church and shows that while they do not match those of modern Christianity, they do match those of the Christians who lived shortly after the time of the Messiah.

In the chapter called "The Restoration of Doctrine," the reader will be shown that many of the unique beliefs of the Latter-day Saints are the same as those of the early Christian Church. The doctrines discussed here include the nature of God, the nature of the Godhead, the nature of man, premortal life, the creation, the fall, continuous revelation, three degrees of glory, and man's potential to attain godhood.

The next chapter is about "The Restoration of Spiritual Gifts" and is designed to demonstrate that the gifts of the Spirit manifested so prominently among the early Christians are now manifested within the LDS Church. These gifts include speaking in tongues, healings, prophecy, visions, inspired dreams, the beholding of angels, the performance of miracles, casting out evil spirits, and raising the dead.

The following chapter, called "The Restoration of Biblical Texts," draws upon non-LDS scholarship to confirm Joseph Smith's claim that the texts of the Bible have been tampered with over the centuries. Non-LDS scholars are also called upon in this section of the book to verify some of the corrections that were made by the Prophet in the Joseph Smith Translation of the Old and New Testaments.

In the chapter entitled "Book of Mormon Evidences," the reader will learn how modern research is providing support for the claim that the Book of Mormon is an authentic, ancient Hebrew text. Subjects covered in this part of the volume include the miraculous production of the Book of Mormon, the historical plausibility of various elements within the text, literary evidences, archeological evidences, ancient patterns, and internal complexity.

The last chapter of this book is called "Witnesses of the Restoration." Upon its pages, the reader will find the testimonies of Latter-day Saints who have discovered for themselves, by means of heavenly manifestations, that Joseph Smith was a prophet of God and that his work was divinely directed. This chapter ends with a discussion on how one may obtain a personal witness of the reality of the Restoration through the power of the Holy Ghost.

There are two things that readers should be made aware of before they continue. It should be noted that even though this book covers an extensive amount of material, it should not be considered exhaustive, either in its scope or its detail. Readers should also be made aware that some of the quotations in this work have been standardized for modern spelling, punctuation, and grammar.

Although I am solely responsible for the content of this book, I would like to express my appreciation to all of the readers who critiqued various versions of the manuscript and to the editors who helped to transform this work into a readable publication. Special recognition is due to graphic artist Jessica A. Warner of Covenant Communications, Inc. for creating the magnificent cover for this volume.

It is my sincere hope that the evidences presented in this book will justify the faith of those who already believe, fortify the faith of those who may have doubts, and create faith in those who are searching for the truth. "For there are many yet on the earth among all sects, parties, and denominations . . . who are only kept from the truth because they know not where to find it."[19]

NOTES

1. "It is very probable that the [First] Vision came to the Prophet on the Paschal day of that year, although no date has been kept for us, but it was on the Paschal day when the Church was organized [6 April 1830], when Elijah visited the Prophet in the temple at Kirtland [3 April 1836], and when, strange to say, the Prophet organized the Relief Society. That day, the 17th of March, 1842, was the opening of the Paschal season for the year 1842. It was the day celebrated as the fast day of Queen Esther, by the Jews" (*Relief Society Magazine*, vol. 7, no. 4, April 1920, 189).
2. "If any of you lack wisdom, let him ask of God, that giveth to all men liberally, and upbraideth not; and it shall be given him. But let him ask in faith, nothing wavering" (James 1:5–6).
3. JS–H 1:15–17. The same phraseology that was used by the Father during the First Vision is found in Matthew 3:17; 17:5.
4. The Prophet recounts: "I asked the Personages who stood above me in the light, which of all the sects was right (for at this time it had never entered into my heart that all were wrong)—and which I should join. I was answered that I must join none of them, for they were all wrong; and the Personage who addressed me said that all their creeds were an abomination in his sight; that those professors were all corrupt; that: 'they draw near to me with their lips, but their hearts are far from me, they teach for doctrines the commandments of men, having a form of godliness, but they deny the power thereof'" (JS–H 1:18–19; cf. Isaiah 29:13; 2 Timothy 3:5; Mark 7:6–7). The Prophet reports that he "saw many angels in this vision" (Milton V. Backman, Jr., *Joseph Smith's First Vision*, 2d ed. [Salt Lake City: Bookcraft, 1980], 159).
5. *HC*, 4:536. In accordance with divine law the Lord has permitted at least one other person to witness the First Vision. On 3 April 1893, at the dedication of the Salt Lake Temple, a member of the Tabernacle Choir named Bardella Curtis saw "the veil between mortality and high heaven drawn aside." During this manifestation she was shown several events of the past, including the appearance of the Father and the Son to Joseph Smith in the Spring of 1820 (Bardella S. Curtis, *Autobiography 1874–1957*, LDS Church Archives, Salt Lake City, Utah). For further reading on the First Vision, see Richard L. Anderson, "Circumstantial Confirmation of the First Vision Through Reminiscences," *Brigham Young University Studies*, vol. 9, no. 3, Spring 1969, 373–404; Milton V. Backman, Jr., "Did Brigham Young Confirm or Expound on Joseph Smith's First Vision?" *Ensign*, April 1992, 59–60; Richard L. Anderson, "Joseph Smith's Testimony of the First Vision," *Ensign*, April 1996, 10–21.
6. See JS–H 1:30–49, 68–72; D&C 27:12–13; 110:1–16; 128:20–21. The Lord states in modern revelation that the Restoration was necessary so that He could establish His everlasting covenant once more among mortals and facilitate the proclamation of the fullness of His gospel to the ends of the earth (see D&C 1:17–23).
7. D&C 1:30. By the time of Joseph Smith, the Christian faith had become severely fragmented and seriously degenerated. The Lord said of those churches that claimed to represent Him: "they have strayed from mine ordinances, and have broken mine everlasting covenant; they seek not the Lord

to establish his righteousness, but every man walketh in his own way, and after the image of his own god, whose image is in the likeness of the world, and whose substance is that of an idol" (D&C 1:15–16).

8. Nels B. Lundwall, comp., *Lectures on Faith* (Salt Lake City: N. B. Lundwall, 1943), 70.
9. Matthew 16:15–17.
10. See John 1:15–36; 5:33.
11. Acts 1:1–3; see also Luke 24:36–43. The Greek word translated as "infallible proofs" in Acts 1:3 is a derivative of *tekmērion* which means "a sure sign," "a mark," "a token" (William E. Vine, Merrill F. Unger, and William White, Jr., *Vine's Complete Expository Dictionary of Old and New Testament Words* [Nashville: Thomas Nelson Publishers, 1996], part 2, 492; James Strong, *The New Strong's Exhaustive Concordance of the Bible* [Nashville: Thomas Nelson Publishers, 1996], Greek Dictionary of the New Testament, 89, word #5039).
12. See John 20:24–29.
13. See Matthew 4:23–25; 9:32–35; 11:2–5; Luke 7:11–17; 13:10–17; 14:1–6; John 6:5–14; 11:1–45; see also John 5:36; 10:23–25; 20:30–31. On page 732 of the LDS Bible Dictionary, we read that the Lord's miracles "were intended to be a *proof* to the Jews that Jesus was the Christ" (emphasis added).
14. See John 5:39, 46–47.
15. See Luke 4:16–21.
16. Acts 17:2–4; 18:4, 28; 28:23.
17. Quotation found in Neal A. Maxwell, "Discipleship and Scholarship," *BYUS*, vol. 32, no. 3, Summer 1992, 5. Elder Maxwell has admonished the Saints: "Let us be articulate, for while our defense of the kingdom may not stir all hearers, the absence of thoughtful response may cause fledglings among the faithful to falter. What we assert may not be accepted, but unasserted convictions soon become deserted convictions" (Neal A. Maxwell, "'All Hell is Moved,'" in *BYU Devotional and Fireside Addresses* [Provo, Utah: Brigham Young University Press, 1977], 179).
18. Neal A. Maxwell, *Deposition of a Disciple* (Salt Lake City: Deseret Book, 1976), 48–49. For further reading see John W. Welch, "The Power of Evidence in the Nurturing of Faith," in *Nurturing Faith Through the Book of Mormon* (Salt Lake City: Deseret Book, 1995), 149–86.
19. D&C 123:12.

CHAPTER 1

Evidences of Apostasy

One fundamental teaching of The Church of Jesus Christ of Latter-day Saints is that the Savior's gospel has been on the earth "from the beginning" (D&C 20:21–26; cf. Moses 5:58–59; JST John 1:1) and has thus been proclaimed by all of God's prophets. President Lorenzo Snow expounded upon this doctrine in the following manner:

> Mormonism, a nickname for the real religion of the Latter-day Saints, does not profess to be a new thing, except to this generation. It proclaims itself as the original plan of salvation, instituted in the heavens before the world was, and revealed from God to man in different ages. That Adam, Enoch, Noah, Abraham, Moses, and other ancient worthies had this religion successively, in a series of dispensations, we, as a people, verily believe. To us, the gospel taught by the Redeemer in the meridian of time was a restored gospel, of which, however, He was the author, in His pre[mortal] state. Mormonism, in short, is the primitive Christian faith restored, the ancient gospel brought back again—this time to usher in the last dispensation, introduce the Millennium, and wind up the work of redemption as pertaining to this planet.[1]

The apostle Paul likewise taught that the gospel of Jesus Christ was known by mortals before the meridian of time. For instance, in Galatians 3:8, he says that "God . . . preached . . . the gospel unto Abraham." And in Hebrews 4:2, Paul just as explicitly states that the "gospel" was preached unto the Israelites who were led out of Egypt by Moses (see also Hebrews 3:6–17; 1 Corinthians 10:1–4).

Some Christian leaders who lived shortly after the apostolic age declared the same truth. Eusebius, who served as bishop of Caesarea in A.D. 339, said that "it is obvious that [the biblical patriarchs] knew God's Christ Himself, since He appeared to

Abraham, instructed Isaac, spoke to [Jacob], and conversed freely with Moses and the prophets who came later. . . . Obviously we must regard the religion proclaimed in recent years to all nations through Christ's teaching as none other than the first, most ancient, and most primitive of all religions, discovered by Abraham and his followers."[2] Many of the early Christian writers such as Tatian (ca. A.D. 150), Justin Martyr (A.D. 165), Tertullian (ca. A.D. 200), Irenaeus (ca. A.D. 115–202), Clement of Alexandria (ca. A.D. 160–215), Theophilus of Antioch (ca. A.D. 100–200), and Origen (ca. A.D. 185–251) also taught that Jesus Christ was the divine being who appeared unto mortals in the Old Testament. Therefore, Christianity was "not a new religion" but was "connected with the birth of mankind."[3]

THE APOSTASY FORETOLD

Periodic apostasies from the precepts of the gospel are recorded in Old Testament texts. A prime example is the generation of Noah. During that time, all the inhabitants of the earth had become "corrupt before God" (Genesis 6:11–13) and only eight souls were considered righteous enough to be saved from destruction (Genesis 7:1). Apostasy was also a constant problem among the children of Israel as evidenced by such scriptural passages as Deuteronomy 9:7, 29:24–25; Judges 3:7; 1 Kings 14:22–23; 2 Kings 17:7–8; Psalms 106:32–43; Isaiah 2:6–8, 24:5, 29:13–14; Jeremiah 7:8–11, 35:15; Ezekiel 2:3–4, 11:12, 22:23–29; and Micah 3:11. Indeed, the apostle Paul informs us that the Law of Moses was "added" to the gospel of Jesus Christ because of the apostasy of the Israelites in Moses' day (Galatians 3:19).

When Jesus Christ came to dwell upon the earth, He told His contemporaries that they were in a state of apostasy. "Ye hypocrites, well did [Isaiah] prophesy of you, saying, 'This people draweth nigh unto [God] with their mouth, and honoureth [God] with their lips; but their heart is far from [Him]. But in vain they do worship [Him], teaching for doctrines the commandments of men" (Matthew 15:7–9). Thus, Jesus Christ reintroduced the gospel among the Israelites so that they could understand correct doctrine and worship God in the proper manner.

According to the Prophet Joseph Smith, the Saints of Christ's dispensation fell into apostasy like their predecessors because they eventually departed from the true faith, became high-minded and unbelieving, transgressed the laws of God, changed the ordinances of the gospel, and broke the everlasting covenant. As a result, said the

Prophet, they lost the companionship of the Spirit and the gifts, signs, and powers of the gospel.[4] And this is precisely why the gospel of Jesus Christ had to be restored, once again, in the latter days.

Is there any biblical evidence to support Joseph Smith's claim that the early Christians apostatized from the true faith? Yes, there most certainly is. To begin with, there are many New Testament texts that predict an apostasy that was to occur among the followers of Christ.[5] Let us briefly examine these passages.

Matthew 24:5–11, 23–24

The Lord's apostles asked Him when the Jerusalem Temple would be destroyed and also when His Second Coming would occur. The Lord, speaking of the future, replied: "*many* shall come in my name, saying, 'I am Christ'; and shall deceive *many*" (v. 5, emphasis added). The Savior then stated that before the end came, there would be wars, famines, pestilences, and earthquakes. He also said that His disciples would be afflicted, hated, and killed for His name's sake. "And then shall *many* be offended [*skandalisthēsontai*, enticed to apostasy],[6] and shall betray one another, and shall hate one another. And *many* false prophets shall rise, and shall deceive *many*" (vv. 10–11, emphasis added). The Lord said yet again: "there shall arise false Christs, and false prophets, and shall show great signs and wonders; insomuch that, if . . . possible, they shall deceive the very elect" (v. 24).[7]

Acts 20:29–31

In speaking to a group of "the elders of the church" (v. 17) who were "overseers" (v. 28), the apostle Paul prophesied and warned them that apostasy would occur from within the Church: "after my departing shall grievous wolves enter in among you, not sparing the flock. Also *of your own selves shall men arise*, speaking perverse [*diestrammena*, distorted, twisted, corrupted] things, to draw away disciples after them" (vv. 29–30, emphasis added).

1 Timothy 4:1–3

This passage is especially important because it informs us that Paul had received a revelation from the Holy Ghost regarding apostasy in the "latter times." All of the statements in this section should, therefore, be taken in the same context (i.e., information about the coming apostasy was a divine revelation). "Now the Spirit speaketh expressly [*rhētōs*, distinctly], that in the latter times some shall depart [*apostēsontai*, apostatize][8] from the faith, giving heed to seducing [*planois*, deceitful] spirits, and doctrines of devils. Speaking lies in hypocrisy; having their conscience seared with a hot iron; forbidding to marry, and commanding to abstain from meats [*brōmatōn*, food],[9] which God hath created to be received with thanksgiving of them which believe and know the truth" (cf. Acts 10:9–16; 11:2–10).

2 Timothy 3:1–5; 4:3–4

"This know also, that in the *last days* perilous times shall come. For men shall be lovers of their own selves, covetous, boasters, proud, blasphemers, disobedient to parents, unthankful, unholy, without natural affection, trucebreakers, false accusers, incontinent [without self-control], fierce, despisers of those that are good, traitors, heady [reckless], high-minded, lovers of pleasures more than lovers of God; having a form of godliness, but denying the power thereof: from such turn away" (emphasis added).

"Preach the word . . . exhort with all longsuffering and doctrine. For the time will come when they [i.e., the Saints] will not endure [*anexontai*, bear, put up with] sound doctrine; but after their own lusts [*epithumias*, desires] shall they heap [*epiaōreusousi*, accumulate] to themselves teachers, having itching ears; and they shall turn away their ears from the truth, and shall be turned unto fables [*muthous*, myths]."

2 Peter 2:1–2

"There shall be false teachers among you [i.e., the Saints], who privily [*pareisaxousin*, secretly] shall bring in damnable [*apōleias*, destructive] heresies. . . . And *many* shall follow their pernicious ways; by reason of whom the way of truth shall be evil spoken of" (emphasis added).

Revelation 13:1–8

In the apostle John's symbolic vision of the future (see 4:1), he was shown the image of a blasphemous beast that received its power from Satan or the dragon (see 13:2, 4). "And it was given unto him [the beast] to make war with the saints, and to overcome [*nikēsai*, conquer] them: and power was given him over *all kindreds, and tongues, and nations.*" The Joseph Smith Translation of this passage clarifies that this beast was a "sign" or symbol of "the kingdoms of the earth." It is most interesting that directly after John's vision of the beast conquering the Saints, he saw an "angel fly in the midst of heaven, having the everlasting gospel to preach unto them that dwell on the earth, and to *every nation, and kindred, and tongue*" (14:6, emphasis added). Taken together, these passages imply that the gospel had to be restored in its purity because the kingdoms of the earth had somehow corrupted it when they "conquered" the Saints.

2 Thessalonians 2:1–5

In the King James translation of 2 Thessalonians 2:1–5, we find the apostle Paul reminding the Thessalonian Saints that the Second Coming of Jesus Christ would not occur until after there was "a falling away." The words "falling away" are translated from only a single Greek word, *apostasía*. This word is more properly rendered as "apostasy" in English.[10] In the Greek manuscripts of this passage, the word *apostasía* is preceded by the definite article, thus indicating that the phrase should be translated as "the apostasy."[11]

In the King James rendition of verse 3, the words "falling away" imply a gradual drifting of sorts. But the Greek word *apostasía* carries a much more aggressive meaning like "rebellion,"[12] "revolt,"[13] "defection,"[14] "abandonment,"[15] or "mutiny."[16] These words suggest that "the apostasy" spoken of by the apostle Paul in 2 Thessalonians would originate from within the early Christian church. This conclusion is strengthened by the fact that in several texts of the Septuagint (or Greek Old Testament) the word *apostasía* is employed to refer to "rebellion against God."[17] Hendriksen and Kistemaker inform us that this prophesied apostasy was not simply the falling away of a few of Christ's disciples.

> What the apostle Paul is . . . saying . . . in 2 Thessalonians 2:3, amounts to this: Just like the first coming of Christ was preceded by a period of apostasy, so also the Second Coming will not occur until a similar apostasy has taken place. . . . It will be a defection on the part of those who have been reached by the gospel (cf. 1 Peter 4:17; Ezekiel 9:6), and it will be on a large scale: "many shall stumble . . . many false prophets shall arise and shall lead many astray . . . ." (Matthew 24:10–13). The use of the term apostasy here in 2 Thessalonians 2:3 without an accompanying adjective points to the fact that, by and large, the visible Church will forsake the true faith.[18]

NEW TESTAMENT EVIDENCES OF APOSTASY

Not only do New Testament texts prophesy of a future apostasy among the early Saints, but they also provide ample evidence that the destructive forces of defection were beginning to spread while Christ was still among them (see John 6:47–71). The following section lays out the deterioration of the Church, chronologically, after the Lord's ascension.

1 Thessalonians (ca. A.D. 50–51)

Incorrect ideas were circulating among the Saints about the Second Coming of Jesus Christ and how it would affect the living and the dead.

James (ca. A.D. mid-50s)

Some of the Saints had a mistaken understanding about the relationship between faith and works. They also had "wars [*polemoi*, quarrels] and fightings [*machai*, strifes]" among them (4:1).

1 Corinthians (ca. A.D. 56)

Factions or divisions were developing among the Saints. Doctrinal heresies were arising, orthodox doctrines were being rejected, and severe moral problems were going unpunished.

2 Corinthians (ca. A.D. 57)

Paul feared that the Corinthian Saints might be corrupted if they were beguiled like Eve and accepted "another gospel" that preached "another Jesus" in opposition to that which he had delivered unto them. He also warned the Saints of "false apostles, deceitful workers, transforming themselves into the apostles of Christ" and referred to them as Satan's "ministers" (11:3–4, 13–15).

Galatians (ca. A.D. 58)

There were some who caused "trouble" among the Galatian Saints. These trouble-makers "pervert[ed] the gospel of Christ" and had thereby turned the Saints to "another gospel" (1:6–12). Those who were teaching this "other gospel" were probably Judaizers who still accepted the Law of Moses, observed Jewish holidays, and advocated the practice of circumcision (see 3:1–5; 4:10; 5:2–4). Such did "not obey the truth" (3:1).

Colossians (ca. A.D. 61)

Paul warned the Colossian Saints not to be beguiled by the false worship of the *gnostics* (see 2:18). Paul also warned them not to let any man lead them astray "through philosophy and vain deceit, after the tradition of men, after the rudiments of the world" (2:8).

1 Timothy (ca. A.D. 63)

Paul warned Timothy not to give heed to certain "fables" [*muthois*, myths] that were current (1:4) and also to avoid the "profane and vain babblings, and disputations of what is falsely called *gnosis*" or knowledge (6:20, see ftnt. b). Some had "swerved" [*astochēsantes*, deviated] from correct doctrine and had been "turned aside" to empty babblings that even they themselves did not understand (1:3–7).

Titus (ca. A.D. 63)

There were "gainsayers" among the Saints in Crete. There were "*many* unruly and vain talkers and deceivers," especially among the Jewish converts; they taught "Jewish fables" and the "commandments of men"; they raised "foolish questions" and taught "things which they ought not"; their false ideas had caused entire households to lose their faith. Paul considered these people to be abominable, disobedient reprobates (1:9–16). Paul warned Titus to "avoid [their] foolish questions . . . and contentions, and strivings about the law" of Moses. Paul further instructed Titus to reject those heretics who wouldn't repent because they had become subverted and sinful (3:9–11).

2 Timothy (ca. A.D. 67)

Paul lamented to Timothy: "*all* they which are in Asia be turned away from me" (1:15, emphasis added). Even among the Ephesian Saints, Paul noted that there were those who had erred concerning the truth. They spouted "profane and vain babblings" and their false teachings had overthrown the faith of some believers. They had "erred" concerning the truth (2:14–18).

Jude (ca. A.D. 80)

Certain "ungodly men" had infiltrated the Church (1:4). They were separatists (1:19); they were rebellious against authority (see 1:8); they were "murmurers [and] complainers" (1:16); they spoke "great swelling words" (1:16) and also spoke evil of things that they did not understand (see 1:10); they were immoral (see 1:4, 8, 16, 18, 19); they were spiritually "dead" (1:12, 19); they were comparable to some of history's worst apostates (see 1:5–7, 11–13). Because of the potential damage that these infiltrators could inflict upon the Church, Jude admonished the faithful Saints to "earnestly contend for the faith" that had been delivered unto them by the authorized servants of God (1:3). Yet, with it all, Jude acknowledged that it was "the last time [*chronō*]," predicted by the Lord's apostles, when the "mockers" would appear (1:18).

Revelation (ca. A.D. 96)

In a revelation given through the apostle John, the Lord rebuked the churches of Asia and commanded them to repent of a variety of grievous sins or they would be rejected and destroyed. False apostles (see 2:2), false prophets (see 2:20), evil persons (see 2:2), and liars (see 2:2) had arisen in the Asian churches. False doctrines were being openly taught (see 2:14–15) and immoral behavior was being advocated (see 2:14, 20–22). The Lord referred to one church as "wretched, and miserable, and poor, and blind, and naked" (3:17) and stated that another of the churches was in a "fallen" condition (2:5). One of the Asian churches was so far gone into apostasy that it was "dead" as far as the Lord was concerned (3:1–2).

1 John (ca. A.D. 98)

The apostle John declared: "it is the last [*hōra*, hour]" (2:18). He spoke these words because the sign had come to pass—there were now "*many* antichrists" in the world who had originated from within the Christian Church (2:18–19, emphasis added). The antichrists were teaching *docetism*, a false set of beliefs about the physical nature of Jesus Christ (see 4:1–6). John labeled these antichrists as "false prophets" and, once again, emphasized that there were *many* of them (4:1).

2 John (ca. A.D. 98)

John stated again that there were "*many* deceivers" in the world who were teaching the "anti-Christ" precepts of *docetism* (1:7, emphasis added). John directed the Saints to turn away any who did not teach the true "doctrine of Christ" (1:9–10).

3 John (ca. A.D. 98)

John records that even before the end of the first century A.D. some of the Church *leaders* were apostatizing. One church official named Diotrephes, who loved to have preeminence among the Saints, rejected the apostles and "the brethren" outright and spoke against them "with malicious words." He even forbade the members of his congregation from receiving any of the Church authorities and excommunicated those who did (see 1:9–11).

TESTIMONY OF THE EARLY CHRISTIANS

Some of the Christians who lived shortly after the time of the apostles also testified that apostasy was taking place among the Saints. The Christian writer Hegesippus (ca. A.D. 110–180), in

> relating the events of the times [of the Roman emperor Trajan (A.D. 98–117)], . . . says that the Church continued until then as a pure and uncorrupt virgin; whilst if there were any at all that attempted to pervert the sound doctrine of the saving gospel, they were yet skulking in dark retreats; but when the sacred choir of apostles became extinct, and the generation of those that had been privileged to hear their inspired wisdom had passed away, then also the combinations of impious error arose by the fraud and delusions of false teachers. These also, as there were none of the apostles left, henceforth attempted, without shame, to preach their false doctrine against the gospel of truth.[19]

Cyril, who served as the bishop of Jerusalem between A.D. 349 and 387, places the apostasy predicted by the apostles squarely within his own time. After quoting 2 Thessalonians 2:3–10, Cyril said:

> Thus wrote Paul, and *now is the falling away.* For men have fallen away from the right faith; and some preach the identity of the Son with the Father, and others dare to say that Christ was brought into being out of nothing. And formerly the heretics were manifest [openly]; but *now the Church is filled with heretics* in disguise. For men have fallen away from the truth, and have itching ears [see 2 Timothy 4:3–4]. . . . *Most* have departed from right words, and rather choose the evil, than desire the good. This, therefore, is the falling away.[20]

We also have the testimony of Cyprian, the bishop of Carthage, North Africa, who served from A.D. 248–258. Cyprian paints a stark and disturbing picture of apostasy among the Christians of his day. Bishops, he said, had lost their devotion to God's service (some even abandoning their congregations) and the clergy had lost their integrity. The Saints had become insatiably greedy, had lost their compassion for the needy, had become proud, and behaved in undisciplined ways. Christians were marrying pagans, practicing perjury, committing fraud, displaying contempt for authority, and even betraying their faith. Cyprian argued that since the Saints had sunk to such low levels of depravity they rightly deserved the harsh judgments of a just God.[21]

Several non-LDS scholars agree with the LDS view that apostasy changed the original form and function of the Christian Church. "The sad truth is," laments Philip Smith, "that as soon as Christianity was generally diffused, it began to absorb corruptions from all the lands in which it was planted, and to reflect the complexion of all their systems of religion and philosophy."[22] The result of this transformation, says William Smith, is that "we must not expect to see the Church of holy scripture actually existing in its perfection on earth. It is not to be found, thus perfect, either in the collected fragments of Christendom, or still less in any one of these fragments."[23] As Stuart Hall contends, "fourth-century orthodoxy is not the same as what Peter and Paul believed, any more than modern Roman Catholicism or Anglicanism is."[24]

SCRIPTURAL OBJECTIONS TO THE APOSTASY

There are those who believe that Jesus Christ would never allow His Church to degenerate into a state of apostasy and they believe that several New Testament scriptures support their view. It is therefore appropriate to examine these scriptural passages in order to determine whether or not they support the argument that the Church of Jesus Christ could never fall.

Jude 1:3

This passage of scripture speaks of "the faith which was *once* delivered unto the saints" (emphasis added). Some non-LDS commentators have interpreted this verse to mean that since the gospel was delivered only "once" (i.e., at the time of Jesus Christ's ministry) it has perpetual validity and, therefore, does not require repetition (i.e., a restoration). The scriptures, however, tell a different story. According to Galatians 3:8, "God . . . preached before the gospel unto Abraham." Hebrews 4:2 also informs us that "the gospel [was] preached . . . unto [the Israelites at the time of Moses] but the word preached did not profit them, not being mixed with faith in them that heard it." Thus, to claim that the gospel was only delivered "once" to humankind would be inaccurate since it is evident that it has been imparted on several different occasions (see also Revelation 14:6). This perspective helps considerably in determining the correct translation of the passage under examination. The Greek word translated as "once" in Jude 1:3 is *hapax*. It is the same word that is found in

Jude 1:5. Even though the King James translators also rendered the *hapax* of verse 5 as "once," it is clear from the word's context that it means "already"—which is how the New International Version translates the word in verse 5. Thus, the *hapax* of verse 3 could correctly be rendered as "already," "before," "previously," or "in the past."

Matthew 16:15–18

Some biblical scholars are of the opinion that this is the most controversial passage in the entire Bible.[25] The Savior "saith unto them, 'But whom say ye that I am?' And Simon Peter answered and said, 'Thou art the Christ, the Son of the living God.' And Jesus answered and said unto him, 'Blessed art thou, Simon [son of] Jona: for flesh and blood hath not revealed it unto thee, but my Father which is in heaven. And I say also unto thee, that thou art Peter, and upon this rock I will build my Church; and the gates of hell shall not prevail against it.'"

Many Christians believe that in this passage Jesus Christ declared that His Church would never be destroyed. If this is the correct interpretation, they reason, then there is no need for the "restoration" that the LDS Church proclaims. As the material presented earlier in this chapter clearly indicates, the Savior and the early leaders of His Church knew that an apostasy would take place, they prophesied of it and even recorded its progress. The Protestant Reformation bears forceful witness to the fact that the apostasy eventually overwhelmed the Church established by the Savior.

There are those who believe that the phrase "the gates of hell shall not prevail against it," refers to the "Church." But those who champion such an interpretation must keep in mind that the word used here for "Church" [*ekklēsian*] means "the whole company" of the Saints. They must then account for the fact that the powers of hell *did* prevail against that company. After His resurrection and ascension, the Lord Jesus Christ showed the apostle John, by vision, that Satan would not only wage war against the Saints of the Most High God but he would also "overcome" [*nikēsai*, conquer] them (Revelation 13:7).

The Prophet Joseph Smith offered an interpretation of Matthew 16:18 that focuses on the fact that Peter received a "revealed" testimony from heaven that Jesus was the Christ. "Jesus in His teachings says, 'Upon this rock I will build my Church, and the gates of hell shall not prevail against it.' What rock? Revelation."[26] There are several non-LDS scholars who agree with this interpretation, choosing to read the passage as "Upon this rock of revealed truth I will build my Church."[27] The Joseph Smith Translation of John 1:42 adds an interesting dimension to this verse. It reads: "And when Jesus beheld [Peter], he said, 'Thou art Simon the son of Jona: thou shalt be called Cephas, which is, by interpretation, *a seer*, or a stone." Certainly a seerstone can be symbolically seen as the "rock of revelation" (see Mosiah 8:13–18). Non-LDS scholars have noted that in John 1:42 the Lord is bestowing a new name upon Peter. The themes of the new name, the white stone, and divine revelation are tied closely together in D&C 130:6–11.

Matthew 28:20

In this passage, Jesus Christ says to His apostles: "I am with you alway[s], even unto the end of the world." Critics of the LDS view of Apostasy and Restoration see this as an iron-clad declaration that the Lord would never suffer His Church to fall. But this is not the case. The Greek word translated in this verse as "world" is *aiōnos* and can be properly rendered as "age," "period of time," "space of time," "segment of time," "epoch," "era" or "generation."[28] One scholarly translation of this verse reads: "I am with you all the days until the completion of the age."[29] Latter-day Saints might phrase this as "I am with you all the days until the end of the dispensation."

Thus, Jesus Christ is not saying here that the Church will endure till the end of the world. Instead, it is possible to interpret this passage to mean that the Lord would guide the leaders of the Church for a predetermined period of time. But there are no promises beyond that point.

CAUSES AND CONSEQUENCES OF APOSTASY

Several factors contributed to the early Christian apostasy; some of them were causes while others were consequences. As the evidence in this chapter clearly suggests, the apostasy was well under way before the close of the first century A.D. Causes of the apostasy included private interpretation of scripture and other teachings, open rebellion against established authority, the acceptance of heretical ideas, and the moral and ethical decay of Church leaders. Consequences of the apostasy would include the willingness of the early Christians to embrace worldly thought systems such as Greek philosophy (end of second century A.D.), the acceptance of pagan influences, and the acceptance of political interference.

Private Interpretation

The apostle Peter made it known that even in his own day there were "unlearned and unstable" Christians who twisted [*streblousin*] the meaning of Paul's epistles and "other scriptures" as well. Peter said that such people were "being led away with the error of the wicked [*athesmōn*, lawless]" (2 Peter 3:15–17). This implies that there was a lawful method for interpreting scripture (see 2 Peter 1:20–21).

The apostle Peter is also represented, in a very early letter, as complaining that some Christians were taking great liberties with his teachings. "They think they are able to interpret my own words better than I can, telling their hearers that they are conveying my very thoughts to them, while the fact is that such things never entered my mind. If they take such outrageous liberties while I am alive, what will they do after I am gone?"[30]

Gnostic Heresies

As seen in the New Testament texts cited above, *gnosticism* fueled the fire of apostate thinking. "O Timothy, keep that which is committed to thy trust, avoiding profane [*bebēlous*, unhallowed] and vain babblings [*kenophōnias*, empty discussions], and oppositions [*antitheseis*, opposing theories] of science [*gnōseōs*, knowledge] falsely so called: which some professing have erred concerning the faith" (1 Timothy 6:20–21). In reference to this very passage of scripture Eusebius, bishop of Caesarea (ca. A.D. 260–339), said that once Christ's apostles and their generation had passed away, "then the league of godless error took its rise as a result of the folly of heretical teachers, who, because none of the apostles was still living, attempted henceforth, with a bold face, to proclaim, in opposition to the preaching of the truth, the 'knowledge [*gnōsis*] which is falsely so-called.'"[31]

In 1 John 4:1–3 and also in 2 John 1:7, the apostle John obliquely refers to the *gnostics*, calling them "deceivers," "false prophets," and "antichrists" because they teach false doctrine about the Savior's sojourn in the flesh. *Gnostic* teachings were a strange mixture of "oriental mythologies, astrological doctrines, Iranian theology, elements of Jewish tradition, . . . Christian salvation-eschatology, [and also] Platonic terms and concepts."[32]

As an example of how *gnosticism* corrupted the doctrines of Christ, we need only turn our attention to one of the most influential early Christian theologians. Augustine (A.D. 354–430), the bishop of Hippo in North Africa, popularized the concept of original sin. Modern scholars have argued that original sin was derived from Augustine's *gnostic* background and that, instead of being the orthodox view of the Christian faith, it was actually a *heresy* that was popularized by Augustine.[33]

Greek Philosophy

When the apostle Paul tried to teach the doctrines of Christ's gospel to the Greeks at Mars Hill in Athens, they "mocked" his teachings because they were at variance with Greek philosophy (Acts 17:22–32). Paul taught the Saints: "Beware lest any man spoil [*sulagōgōn*, lead away captive] you through philosophy and vain deceit, after the tradition of men, after the rudiments [*stoicheia*, principles, speculations] of the world, and not after Christ" (Colossians 2:8). The Greeks sought after "wisdom," said Paul, but they looked upon the gospel of Jesus Christ as "foolishness" (1 Corinthians 1:22–23).

Harnack has pointed out that neither the gospel of Jesus Christ nor the "earliest Christian writings" show "the presence of a Greek element" to any considerable extent.[34] Yet, over a relatively short period of time we find "a reversed situation. The religious message is now framed in philosopher's language, reminiscent at every turn of Heraclitus or Plato or Aristotle . . . Indeed, the Christian religion is now occasionally called a philosophy and its founder described as a philosopher."[35] Edwin Hatch claims that "a large part of what are sometimes called Christian doctrines, and many usages which have prevailed and continue to prevail in the Christian Church, are in reality Greek theories and Greek usages changed in form and colour by the influence of primitive Christianity, but in their essence Greek still."[36]

Mosheim writes of "the eagerness of certain learned men to bring about a union between the doctrines of Christianity and the opinions of the philosophers; for they thought it a very fine accomplishment, to be able to express the precepts of Christ in the language of the *philosophers*, *civilians*, and *rabbis*." As a consequence of this mingling together of scripture and the philosophies of men, "perplexity and confusion" were produced and "genuine Christianity almost disappeared."[37]

The Christian philosophers of the second century A.D. borrowed the ideas of Middle Platonic philosophers such as Plutarch. By doing so, they radically reshaped the Christian view of who and what, God was.[38] It is acknowledged that "the Bible does not teach the doctrine of the Trinity. Neither the word 'trinity' itself, nor such language as 'one-in-three,' 'three-in-one,' one 'essence' or 'substance,' or three 'persons' is biblical language. The language of the doctrine is the language of the ancient Church, taken not from the Bible but from classical Greek philosophy."[39]

Pagan Influences

According to the assessment of historian Will Durant, "Christianity did not destroy paganism; it adopted it." The Greek mind gained new life "in the theology and liturgy of the Church; the Greek language, having reigned for centuries over philosophy, became the vehicle of Christian literature and ritual; the Greek mysteries passed down into the impressive mystery of the Mass." Durant concludes that "Christianity was the last great creation of the ancient pagan world."[40]

Evidence to support these statements can be found in the cult of Saints and Martyrs. Scholars have long recognized that the Catholic Saint/Martyr cult is a continuation of the pagan hero cult. In both instances shrines were built, relics were venerated, and forms of worship were offered to the deceased. The oracle of Delphi prescribed that if a dead man's relics appeared to possess supernatural power, then a cult was to be devoted to him. In a truly ironic twist, there were pagans in the ancient world who pointed out that there was no warrant whatsoever for the cult of Saints and Martyrs in the Christian gospels. It was a novelty, they said.

The arts of pagan divination were also absorbed by the Christian Empire. Books that were used by pagan diviners were modified for Christian use, old pagan oracular techniques were practiced among the monks, and astrology took root despite strong opposition in some quarters. "By the sixth century," writes Robin Fox, "the debris of pagan oracles and pagan *epiphaneia* was Christian property, maintained on sufferance in Christian books."[41]

There were also subtle ways whereby early Christianity became more like the heathen religions. Protestant historian Adolf Harnack notes that "certain influential teachers—teachers, in fact, who founded the whole theology of the Christian Church—felt a strong impulse, and made it their definite aim, to get some *rational* conception of the Christian religion and to present it as the reasonable religion of mankind. . . . [As] these discussions were carried on in a purely rational spirit . . . vital Christian truths were either abandoned or at any rate neglected. This meant a certain impoverishment, and a serious dilution, of the Christian faith."[42]

Political Interference

When Constantine the Great became emperor of the Roman empire in A.D. 312, he put a stop to state-sanctioned persecution of the Christians. But at the same time, he also began a fatal melding of the Christian Church and the pagan state.

Even though Constantine was a non-Christian he took the leading role in determining what would be considered official Christian doctrine. It was Constantine who ordered a large body of Christian leaders to meet at Nicaea in order to take a vote upon what would come to be the officially accepted doctrine of the nature of God (now known as the Nicene Creed). It was Constantine who oversaw the contentious debate and the taking of a vote to settle a religious controversy regarding the Godhead. It was Constantine who issued an edict that branded the losers of the vote with an extremely bad reputation. It was Constantine who decreed that books written by the losers of the vote were to be burned, and anyone found possessing them put to death. It was Constantine who pronounced banishment upon those Christian leaders who would not subscribe themselves to the dogmas of the Nicene Creed.[43]

With the axe of imperial authority hanging over their heads, Christian leaders had little choice but to accept the vote of the majority on this important theological issue. Nineteenth-century Church historian Augustus Neander notes that "it was nothing but the influence of the emperor Constantine which induced the eastern bishops, at the council of Nicaea, to suffer the imposition of a doctrinal formula which they detested, and from which, indeed, they sought immediately to rid themselves."[44]

In all of this, Constantine, the pagan emperor of Rome, imposed his political will upon the revealed religion of Jesus Christ. And by the imposition of that will, he solidified a central religious creed that the Savior Himself has called "an abomination in his sight," professed by those who have become spiritually "corrupt."[45] The "creeds of the [early Christian] fathers," taught Joseph Smith, were founded upon "lies," and they have, therefore, "filled the world with confusion." The Prophet also stated that the "spirit" that had riveted these creeds upon the hearts of the children of men originated in hell and was "the very mainspring of all corruption" (D&C 123:7–8).

Instances of political interference in the vital affairs of the Christian Church are too numerous to list. We will, however, bring the reader's attention to one that illustrates how politics can corrupt a religious system. Ambrose of Milan, Italy, became a leading bishop in the Christian Church in the beginning of the fourth century A.D. The only problem was, Ambrose was not a Christian when he was elected to be a bishop. Ambrose was a government official who was supervising the election of the new bishop of Milan when a child shouted from the balcony of the meeting hall, "Ambrose is bishop." The crowd took up the chant and Ambrose, by acclamation, was elected as the ecclesiastical overseer of Milan, Italy. Shortly thereafter, Ambrose was baptized and consecrated into office.[46] Thus, a non-Christian became a bishop at the suggestion of a child and the chanting of a crowd. This type of political interference is a far cry from the words of Jesus: "Ye have not chosen me, but I have chosen you, and ordained you" (John 15:16).

Moral and Ethical Corruption of Leadership

After the Lord's apostles (except John) had all been murdered in various ways, a struggle ensued among some of the Christian bishops for control of Church government. Eventually, the bishop of Rome gained control over many of the Christian congregations and was acclaimed as the "pope," or head of the Roman Catholic confederation. This branch of Christianity claimed to be the one true Church of Jesus Christ, and the pope was alleged to be Christ's official earthly representative.[47] However, the immoral and unethical behavior of *some* of the popes is a clear indication that they could not retain legitimate authority from Jesus Christ who taught, in metaphorical language, that trees bringing forth degenerate fruit were only good to be "hewn down, and cast into the fire." The Savior stated plainly that even though such persons professed to be his disciples he would *not* recognize them but would command them to "depart" (see Matthew 7:17–23; cf. 1 Corinthians 5:9–13).[48]

Some of the popes became so morally destitute that they allowed Christians to purchase "indulgences" or pardons for their sins. These pardons came with the promise that no penalty would have to be endured either here or hereafter, as long as the requisite price was paid. This abhorrent practice degenerated to the point of indulgences being sold before sins had even been committed, thus granting the purchaser a virtual license to sin.[49]

Over time, the corporate Church began taking aggressive measures against those Christians who would not conform to its teachings. Those who were unfortunate enough to be labeled as "heretics" were in danger of being fined, persecuted, imprisoned, tortured, or even publicly executed.[50]

THE PROTESTANT REFORMATION

With all of the above in mind, it is little wonder that the voice of the Reformation began to be heard. Courageous men such as Wycliffe, Hus, Luther, Tyndale, Zwingli, Knox, and Calvin all declared that since the Mother Church had become abusive and corrupt, it desperately needed to be reformed. Some of these protestors were excommunicated for their views, some were banished from society, and some were burned at the stake.

The great good of the Reformation was that it offered new options of worship to the Christian faithful. "Perhaps the greatest legacy of the Reformation was the increased attention to freedom, one's own freedom more than that of others. This concern eventually grew into religious toleration and the desire for greater political self-determination. The ending of the single, 'universal' church and the proliferation of new churches and sects had echoes in the political arena, most notably in the independence of the United States of America."[51]

Joseph Fielding Smith acknowledged the fact that the Protestant reformers played an important role in the historical and religious drama of mankind.

> In preparation for [the] Restoration the Lord raised up noble men, such as Luther, Calvin, Knox, and others whom we call reformers, and gave them power to break the shackles which bound the people and denied them the sacred right to worship God according to the dictates of conscience. . . .
>
> Latter-day Saints pay all honor to these great and fearless reformers, who shattered the fetters which bound the religious world. The Lord was their Protector in this mission, which was fraught with many perils. In that day, however, the time had not come for the Restoration of the fullness of the gospel. The work of the Reformers was of great importance, but it was a preparatory work.[52]

The Reformation, for all of its good, had several crippling limitations. First, it did not restore any legitimate priesthood authority. Instead, it necessitated the creation of the non-scriptural belief in a "priesthood of all believers." Neither did the Reformation restore a unified system of doctrine and ordinances, as evidenced by the widely divergent beliefs and practices that it helped to flourish. And finally, the Reformation did not open the heavens and provide divine guidance in ecclesiastical affairs. The Reformers believed that the heavens were forever sealed and that the final, and complete, word of God was to be found in the Bible. Without divine guidance, the Reformation churches were as sterile as the church that they had broken away from. The Prophet Joseph Smith emphasized this point.

> Here is a principle of logic that most men have no more sense than to adopt. I will illustrate it by an old apple tree. Here jumps off a branch and says, "I am the true tree, and you are corrupt." If the whole tree is corrupt, are not its branches corrupt [see Matthew 7:17–18]? If the Catholic religion is a false religion, how can any true religion come out of it? . . . All men are liars who say they are of the true Church

> without the revelations of Jesus Christ and the Priesthood of Melchizedek, which is after the order of the Son of God.
>
> It is in the order of heavenly things that God should always send a new dispensation into the world when men have apostatized from the truth and lost the Priesthood. But when men come out and build upon other men's foundations, they do it on their own responsibility, without authority from God . . . . Did I build on any other man's foundation? I have got all the truth which the Christian world possessed, and an independent revelation in the bargain, and God will bear me off triumphant.[53]

The Reformation also created a serious problem. The Reformed sects of Christianity began to splinter into still other Reformed sects of Christianity until there were numerous Christian denominations, each teaching divergent doctrines from the very same Bible. Without the guidance of God, there is only speculation and opinion, not unity and salvation.

THE RESTITUTION OF ALL THINGS

The early Christians were well-acquainted with the doctrine of "restoration." Just as the apostle Paul testified that the Second Coming of Jesus Christ would not occur until after "the apostasy" had taken place (2 Thessalonians 2:1–5), so too did the apostle Peter testify that Christ would remain in the heavenly realms "until the times of restitution of all things." This restitution, Peter explained, had been foretold by "all" of God's holy prophets "since the world began" and would be coupled with fixed or definite periods [*kairoi*] of revival [*anapsuxeōs*] that would come "from the presence of the Lord" (Acts 3:19–21). The Greek word translated in this passage as "restitution" [*apokatastaseōs*] can also be properly rendered as "restoration."[54] An almost identical Greek word [*apokatestathē*] is translated as "restored" in Matthew 12:10–13 and is used to describe something that had once deteriorated but was then returned to its proper function.

The early Christians, believing that Jesus was the Christ coming into the world for the first time, would have understood Malachi 4:5–6 to mean that the Second Coming would not occur until after the Lord had sent the prophet Elijah once more to the earth. Elijah's premillennial mission could be understood as one of restoration according to the Hebrew text of Malachi 4:6. In the King James Version, the word "turn" comes from the Hebrew *shûwb* which can be rendered as "restore."[55] In the

Greek Septuagint version of this verse, the underlying word is *apokatastēsei*, the same word that is used in Matthew 17:11 to indicate that the ancient Israelites expected Elijah to come and "restore [*apokatastēsei*] all things."

And finally, the apostle John learned during a symbolic vision of the future (see Revelation 4:1) that prior to the battle of Armageddon (see Revelation 16:16) and the binding of Satan at the beginning of the Millennium (see Revelation 20:1–3) an angel of God would descend–flying through the midst of heaven–to preach "the everlasting gospel . . . unto them that dwell on the earth" (Revelation 14:6–7). Since the gospel was already being preached on the earth when John saw this vision, the obvious implication would be that before the Second Coming of Christ, it would need to be brought down to the earth once more.[56] On 3 November 1831 the Lord stated in a revelation: "I have sent forth mine angel flying through the midst of heaven, having the everlasting gospel, who hath appeared unto some and hath committed [the everlasting gospel] unto man, who shall appear unto many that dwell on the earth." Directly after making this declaration the Lord paraphrased the words found in Revelation 14:6–7 (D&C 133:36–39).[57]

From the information contained in the preceding pages we can deduce that the New Testament Saints believed that prior to the Second Coming of Jesus Christ:

1. "The apostasy" would take place (2 Thessalonians 2:1–5).
2. There would be a foreordained "restitution of all things" (Acts 3:19–21).
3. An angel of God would descend from heaven and deliver "the everlasting gospel" to those dwelling upon the earth (Revelation 14:6–7).
4. The prophet Elijah would return to the earth and participate in the restoration of "all things" (Malachi 4:5–6; Matthew 17:11).

SUMMARY

The Church of Jesus Christ of Latter-day Saints teaches that the gospel of Jesus Christ is eternal and has been taught by all of God's prophets, beginning with Adam. This doctrine is sustained both by the Bible and also by the writings of the early Christians. The LDS Church further declares that the Church that was set up by the Savior in the meridian of time fell into a severe state of apostasy. This doctrine is also supported by biblical records and the testimony of the early Saints. Finally, the LDS Church proclaims that in the premortal councils of heaven, God foreordained that in the last days the Church of Jesus Christ would be restored in its purity in order to prepare the inhabitants of the earth for the Second Coming of the Messiah. The scriptures of Christianity bear witness to this point.

With all of this evidence at hand, it is difficult to deny that Joseph Smith's story rings true.

NOTES

1. *MS*, vol. 64, no. 1, 2 January 1902, 1–2. Joseph Smith observed: "Perhaps our friends will say that the gospel and its ordinances were not known till the days of John [the Baptist]. . . . But we will here look at this point. For our own part we cannot believe that the ancients in all ages were so ignorant of the system of heaven as many suppose, since all that were ever saved, were saved through the power of this great plan of redemption, as much before the coming of Christ as since. If not, God has had different plans in operation (if we may so express it), to bring men back to dwell with Himself. And this we cannot believe, since there has been no change in the constitution of man since he fell. . . . It will be noticed that, according to Paul [in Galatians 3:8] the gospel was preached to Abraham. We would like to be informed in what name the gospel was then preached, whether it was in the name of Christ or some other name. If in any other name, was it the gospel? And if it was the gospel, and [was] preached in the name of Christ, had it any ordinances? If not, was it the gospel?" (*TPJS*, 59–60). President Brigham Young taught the very same doctrine espoused by the Prophet Joseph Smith. "We are safe in saying that from the day that Adam was created and placed in the Garden of Eden to this day, the plan of salvation and the revelations of the will of God to man are unchanged, although mankind have not for many ages been favored therewith, in consequence of apostasy and wickedness. There is no evidence to be found in the Bible that the gospel should be one thing in the days of the Israelites, another in the days of Christ and his apostles, and another in the nineteenth century but, on the contrary, we are instructed that God is the same in every age [see Hebrews 13:8], and that His plan of saving His children is the same. . . . The plan of salvation is one, from the beginning of the world to the end thereof" (*JD*, 10:324). On other occasions President Young taught: "The doctrines of salvation are the same now as they were in the days of Adam, or Elijah, or Jesus when he was upon the earth" (*JD*, 5:229); "the gospel was among the children of men from the days of Adam until the coming of the Messiah; this gospel of Christ is from the beginning to the end" (*JD*, 13:269).
2. Geoffrey A. Williamson, trans., *Eusebius: The History of the Church from Christ to Constantine* (New York: Dorset Press, 1984), 47–48. Eusebius also said that the "religion of Abraham" had "reappeared" in his day and was being practiced solely by the Christians. He proclaimed: "we who are of Christ practice one and the same mode of life and have one and the same religion as those divinely favored men of old . . . [T]he perfect religion committed to us by the teaching of Jesus is not new; . . . it is the first and true religion" (*Church History*, 4.14–15 cited in Philip Schaff and Henry Wace, eds., *Nicene and Post-Nicene Fathers* [Peabody, Massachusetts: Hendrickson Publishers, 1994], 1:88).
3. Fernand Mourret, *A History of the Catholic Church* (St. Louis: B. Herder Book Co., 1931), 1:352; see also Kirsopp Lake, trans., *Eusebius: The Ecclesiastical History* (Cambridge, Massachusetts: Harvard University Press, 1926), 1:xv–xvi; *Address of Tatian to the Greeks*, 31, cited in Alexander Roberts and James Donaldson, eds., *Ante-Nicene Fathers* (Peabody, Massachusetts: Hendrickson Publishers, 1994), 2:77.

4. See *TPJS*, 15.
5. The following two sections are formatted after the material presented in Kent P. Jackson, "'Watch and Remember': The New Testament and the Great Apostasy," in John M. Lundquist and Stephen D. Ricks, eds., *By Study and Also By Faith* (Salt Lake City: Deseret Book and FARMS, 1990), 1:81–117. A shorter version of this article has been published as Kent P. Jackson, "Early Signs of the Apostasy," *Ensign*, December 1984, 8–16. For further reading see also the article by S. Kent Brown, "Whither the Early Church?" *Ensign*, October 1988, 7–10.
6. James Strong, *The New Strong's Exhaustive Concordance of the Bible* (Nashville: Thomas Nelson Publishers, 1996), Greek Dictionary of the New Testament, 81, word #4624.
7. The reason for the ellipses in this verse is that the italicized words "it were" are not present in the Greek text but have been added by the translators. In fact, the JST eliminates them (see Joseph Smith–Matthew 1:22). Without the italicized words it is clear that even "the elect" can be deceived by false prophets and false Christs. Joseph Smith–Matthew 1:44 places these occurrences "in the last days."
8. See William E. Vine, Merrill F. Unger, and William White, Jr., *Vine's Complete Expository Dictionary of Old and New Testament Words* (Nashville: Thomas Nelson Publishers, 1996), part 2, 160.
9. These foods are "especially articles . . . forbidden by the Jewish law" (Strong, *The New Strong's Exhaustive Concordance of the Bible*, Greek Dictionary of the New Testament, 18, word #1033).
10. See for example Walter Bauer, William F. Arndt, and F. Wilbur Gingrich, eds., *A Greek-English Lexicon of the New Testament and Other Early Christian Literature*, 2d ed. (Chicago: The University of Chicago Press, 1979), 98; Joseph H. Thayer, *Thayer's Greek-English Lexicon of the New Testament*, rev. ed. (Grand Rapids, Michigan: Baker Book House, 1987), 67; William D. Mounce, *The Analytical Lexicon to the Greek New Testament* (Grand Rapids, Michigan: Zondervan, 1993), 94; James Strong, *The New Strong's Exhaustive Concordance of the Bible* (Nashville: Thomas Nelson Publishers, 1996), Greek Dictionary of the New Testament, 12, word #646. This word means "'a defection, revolt, apostasy' [and] is used in the New Testament of religious apostasy. In Acts 21:21, it is translated 'to forsake' . . . . In 2 Thessalonians 2:3 'the falling away' signifies apostasy from the faith. In papyri documents it is used politically of rebels" (William E. Vine, Merrill F. Unger, and William White, Jr., *Vine's Complete Expository Dictionary of Old and New Testament Words* [Nashville: Thomas Nelson Publishers, 1996], part 2, 223).
11. "Paul does not speak of 'a' rebellion, as though introducing the topic for the first time, but of 'the' rebellion, i.e., the well-known rebellion, that one about which he had already instructed them" (Leon Morris, *The First and Second Epistles to the Thessalonians* [Grand Rapids, Michigan: Eerdmans, 1989], 219). "English argues that the [definite] article ἡ marks the αποστασία out as something about which the readers were already informed" (F. F. Bruce, *1 & 2 Thessalonians* [Waco, Texas: Word Books, 1982], 167). "The apostasy (αποστασία with the definite article [ἡ]) is clearly a term already known to the Thessalonians" (Ernest Best, *A Commentary on the First and Second Epistles to the Thessalonians* [New York: Harper and Row, 1972], 281). "ἡ αποστασία. The [definite] article [ἡ] suggests that 'the apostasy' or 'the religious revolt' is something well-

known to the readers" (James E. Frame, *A Critical and Exegetical Commentary on the Epistles of St. Paul to the Thessalonians* [New York: Charles Scribner's Sons, 1912], 250). The New American Bible translates the Greek as "the apostasy," the Twentieth Century New Testament renders it as "the Great Apostasy," in the Jerusalem Bible we find "the Great Revolt," and in the New Revised Standard Version we have "the rebellion."

12. Mounce, *The Analytical Lexicon to the Greek New Testament,* 94. Liddell and Scott note that "in a religious sense [this word means] *rebellion against God, apostasy*" (Henry G. Liddell and Robert Scott, *A Greek-English Lexicon*, rev. ed. [Oxford: Clarendon Press, 1968], 218, emphasis in original).
13. The word *apostasia* is found in late Greek "in the sense of political defection or revolt" (George Milligan, *St. Paul's Epistles to the Thessalonians* [London: Macmillan and Co., 1908], 98).
14. Thayer, *Thayer's Greek-English Lexicon of the New Testament*, 67.
15. Bauer, Arndt, and Gingrich, eds., *A Greek-English Lexicon of the New Testament and Other Early Christian Literature*, 98. "In secular Greek [*apostasía*] meant 'desertion,' often associated with *treason* and *rebellion against a lawful ruler*. In the Greek Old Testament, including the deuterocanonical books (the Apocrypha), the word [*apostasía*] is used to describe unfaithfulness to God or the denial of God. This is the meaning of the closely related word 'apostasy.' Acts 21:21, the only other place in the New Testament where this term [*apostasía*] is used, speaks of those who 'abandon the Law of Moses'" (Paul Ellingworth and Eugene A. Nida, *A Translator's Handbook on Paul's Letters to the Thessalonians* [New York: United Bible Societies, 1976], 162–63, emphasis added).
16. "The Greek word *apostasía* . . . means *rebellion* or *revolution*. It conveys the sense of an internal takeover by factions hostile to the intentions of the previous leaders. I personally prefer the translation *mutiny*, as it suggests that unauthorized members commandeer a ship and take it where the ship is not supposed to go. Since early Christians often thought of the church as a ship, I think *mutiny* conveys the sense of what Paul and others meant by the term *apostasía*" (Stephen E. Robinson, "Warring Against the Saints of God," *Ensign*, January 1988, 34, emphasis in original).
17. I. Howard Marshall, *1 and 2 Thessalonians* (Grand Rapids, Michigan: Eerdmans, 1983), 188. In the Septuagint see Joshua 22:22 and Jeremiah 2:19. "Thus in Joshua 22:22 the word [*apostasía*] is directly applied to rebellion *against the Lord*" (Milligan, *St. Paul's Epistles to the Thessalonians*, 98, emphasis in original).
18. William Hendriksen and Simon J. Kistemaker, *New Testament Commentary: Exposition of Thessalonians, the Pastorals, and Hebrews* (Grand Rapids, Michigan: Baker Books, 1995), 169–70, emphasis in original. "From the time of the Maccabean revolt (1 Maccabees 1:11, 15, 43; 2:15) [the word *apostasía*] was used in relation to attempts by [the Jews'] oppressors to make [them] forsake their God and certainly some strands of Jewish thought believed that at the End there would be a great apostasy when many of the people of God would defect (cf. Jubilees 23:14ff; 4 Ezra 5:1ff; 1 QpHab 2:1ff; cf. 2 Timothy 3:1–9; Jude 1:17ff; see also Billerbeck, III, p. 637; IV, pp. 977ff). . . . Has the apostasy then been simply transferred by the Christians to themselves, the new people of God? [And] was an apostasy of the Church expected as a prelude to the [Second Coming]? This is possible (cf. Matthew 24:11ff; 1 Timothy 4:1ff)" (Best, *A Commentary on the First and Second Epistles to the Thessalonians*, 281–82).

19. Paraphrase of Hegesippus by Eusebius (*Church History*, 3.32.7–8) cited in Christian F. Cruse, trans., *The Ecclesiastical History of Eusebius Pamphilus* (Grand Rapids, Michigan: Baker Book House, 1955), 118.
20. *Catechetical Lectures*, 15.9 cited in Philip Schaff and Henry Wace, eds., *Nicene and Post-Nicene Fathers* (Peabody, Massachusetts: Hendrickson Publishers, 1994), 7:106–107, emphasis added. The editors of this volume note that "Cyril in this passage regards the heresies of his time as the apostasy in general" (ibid., 106, n. 2).
21. See Maurice Bévenot, trans., *Ancient Christian Writers: St. Cyprian* (New York: Newman Press, 1957), 16–19.
22. Philip Smith, *The History of the Christian Church During the First Ten Centuries* (London: John Murray, 1882), 1:49.
23. William Smith, *Dictionary of the Bible* (Boston: Houghton, Mifflin and Co., 1896), 1:458.
24. Stuart G. Hall, *Doctrine and Practice in the Early Church* (Grand Rapids, Michigan: Eerdmans, 1991), 36.
25. The Catholic Church utilizes this passage to bolster its claim to exclusive authority. This claim, however, cannot be sustained. See especially the article by J. Massingberd Ford, "'Thou Art Abraham' and Upon this Rock . . .," *The Heythrop Journal*, vol. 6, no. 3, July 1965, 289–301. Compare the imagery of Matthew 16:18 with D&C 6:34; 10:69; 11:16, 23–24; 18:1–5, 17; 33:12–13; 50:44.
26. *TPJS*, 274.
27. Cleon L. Rogers, Jr. and Cleon L. Rogers III, *The New Linguistic and Exegetical Key to the Greek New Testament* (Grand Rapids, Michigan: Zondervan, 1998), 37.
28. Bauer, Arndt, and Gingrich, *A Greek-English Lexicon of the New Testament and Other Early Christian Literature*, 27–28; Liddell and Scott, *A Greek-English Lexicon*, 45; Mounce, *The Analytical Lexicon to the Greek New Testament*, 57; Vine, Unger, and White, Jr., *Vine's Complete Expository Dictionary of Old and New Testament Words*, 685.
29. Jay P. Green, Sr., ed., *Interlinear Greek-English New Testament*, 3d ed. (Grand Rapids, Michigan: Baker Books, 1996), 104.
30. *Patrilogia Graecae*, 2:28, cited in Hugh W. Nibley, *The World and the Prophets* (Salt Lake City: Deseret Book, 1987), 28.
31. *Church History*, 3.32.8 cited in Philip Schaff and Henry Wace, eds., *Nicene and Post-Nicene Fathers* (Peabody, Massachusetts: Hendrickson Publishers, 1994), 1:164.
32. Hans Jonas, *The Gnostic Religion* (Boston: Beacon Press, 1958), 25.
33. See William E. Phipps, "The Heresiarch: Pelagius or Augustine?" *Anglican Theological Review*, vol. 62, no. 2, April 1980, 124–33. The practice of infant baptism goes hand in hand with the concept of "Original Sin." In fact, Augustine referred to the practice of infant baptism as justification for belief in the concept of "Original Sin." But "the earliest explicit reference to infant baptism occurs ca. 200 [A.D.] in Tertullian, *On Baptism* 18, a passage that opposes what appears to be a relatively new practice. . . . The great church leaders, including those born to strong Christian parents (Basil, Gregory of Nyssa, Gregory of Nazianzus, John Chrysostom, Ephraem the Syrian,

Jerome, Rufinus, Augustine), were not baptized until the end of their student days. . . . Early Christian documents . . . contain frequent reference to the sinlessness of children (Hermas, *Sim.* 9.29.1–3; *Barn.* 6; Aristides, *Apol.* 15.11; Athenagoras, *Res.* 14)" (Everett Ferguson, ed., *Encyclopedia of Early Christianity*, 2d ed. [New York: Garland Publishing, 1997], 1:162). "Pedobaptism, in the more modern sense, meaning thereby baptism of newborn infants, with the vicarious promises of parents or other sponsors, was utterly unknown to the early Church; not only down to the second, but indeed to the middle of the third century. . . . Towards the close of the second century, this practice originated in the baptism of children of a more advanced age." Both new converts and Christian children in this era had to do three things during the baptismal process: (1) be instructed, (2) be examined as to their faith, and (3) take a vow. All of these, of course, were an impossibility for infants (Wolfred N. Cote, *The Archaeology of Baptism* [London: Yates and Alexander, 1876], 82; cf. Moroni 8:8–26; D&C 18:42; 20:71; 68:25–28; 93:40; 137:10). "The sins of the parents cannot be answered upon the heads of the children, for they are whole from the foundation of the world" (Moses 6:54). "We believe that men will be punished for their own sins, and not for Adam's transgression" (Article of Faith #2). Gregory of Nyssa (A.D. 331–395), Gregory of Nazianzus (A.D. 329–389), and John Chrysostom (A.D. 345–407), all Greek Christian Fathers, taught that "newly born children are exempt from sin" (J. N. D. Kelly, *Early Christian Doctrines* [New York: Harper and Brothers, 1958], 349). According to Tertullian, children should not be baptized "until they reach years of discretion" (ibid., 209). "Tertullian appears as a zealous opponent of infant baptism; a proof that the practice had not as yet come to be regarded as an apostolic institution; for otherwise, he would hardly have ventured to express himself so strongly against it" (Augustus Neander, *General History of the Christian Religion and Church*, rev. ed. [Boston: Houghton, Mifflin and Co., 1871], 1:312). Instead of baptizing children, Latter-day Saints are to bless them in the name of the Lord. "Every member of the Church of Christ having children is to bring them unto the elders before the Church, who are to lay their hands upon them in the name of Jesus Christ, and bless them in His name" (D&C 20:70). Compare this with the name and blessing given to Israelite children as cited in Alfred Edersheim, *Life and Times of Jesus the Messiah* (Grand Rapids, Michigan: Eerdmans, 1950), 1:157–58, 227. In Mark 10:13–16 we read that when young children were brought to the Savior, "he took them up in His arms, put [*titheis*, laid] His hands upon them, and blessed them."

34. Adolf Harnack, *What is Christianity?* (New York: Harper and Brothers, 1957), 200.
35. James Shiel, *Greek Thought and the Rise of Christianity* (London: Longmans, Green and Co., 1968), 1.
36. Edwin Hatch, *The Influence of Greek Ideas on Christianity* (Gloucester, Massachusetts: Peter Smith, 1970), 350.
37. John L. Mosheim, *An Ecclesiastical History, Ancient and Modern* (New York: Harper and Brothers, 1856), 1:61, emphasis in original.
38. See Kelly, *Early Christian Doctrines*, 83–136, 252–79.
39. Shirley C. Guthrie, Jr., *Christian Doctrine: Teachings of the Christian Church* (Richmond, Virginia: CLC Press, 1968), 92.

40. Will Durant, *Caesar and Christ* (New York: Simon and Schuster, 1944), 595.
41. Robin L. Fox, *Pagans and Christians* (New York: Penguin Books, 1986), 672–81, emphasis in original; see also Peter Brown, *The Cult of the Saints* (Chicago: University of Chicago Press, 1981), 4–7; Martin P. Nilsson, *Greek Folk Religion* (New York: Harper and Brothers, 1961), 20–21.
42. Adolf Harnack, *The Mission and Expansion of Christianity in the First Three Centuries* (New York: Harper and Brothers, 1962), 234–35, emphasis in original.
43. In regard to the early Christian creeds, Hatch observes that "one who accepted them received immunity and privileges." On the other hand, "one who did not was liable to confiscation, to banishment, [and] to death" (Hatch, *The Influence of Greek Ideas on Christianity*, 347). He also notes that the darkest pages of Christian history "record the story of its endeavoring to force its transformed Greek metaphysics upon men or upon races to whom they were alien" (ibid., 349).
44. Neander, *General History of the Christian Religion and Church*, 2:164.
45. JS–H 1:19.
46. A. Burt Horsley, *Peter and the Popes* (Provo, Utah: BYU Religious Studies Center, 1989), 39–40. Acts 20:28 indicates that in the proper order of things it is the Holy Ghost who chooses men as "overseers" [*episkopous*, bishops] in the "Church of God."
47. For refutations of the claim that Peter was the first pope and the bishops of Rome are his legitimate successors see Brigham H. Roberts, *The Falling Away* (Salt Lake City: Deseret Book, 1950), 33–39; James L. Barker, *Apostasy from the Divine Church* (Salt Lake City: Deseret News Press, 1960), 627–57; James E. Talmage, *The Great Apostasy* (Salt Lake City: Deseret Book, 1968), 132–33.
48. The following quotation from historian John W. Draper, though disturbing in its content, indicates what kind of fruit was being produced by some of the popes between the eighth and eleventh centuries.

> On the death of Pope Paul I, who had attained the pontificate A.D. 757, the Duke of Nepi compelled some bishops to consecrate Constantine, one of his brothers, as pope; but more legitimate electors subsequently, A.D. 768, [chose] Stephen IV [and] the usurper and his adherents were severely punished; the eyes of Constantine were put out; the tongue of the Bishop Theodorus was amputated, and he was left in a dungeon to expire in the agonies of thirst. The nephews of Pope Adrian seized his successor, Pope Leo III, A.D. 795, in the street and, forcing him into a neighboring church, attempted to put out his eyes and cut out his tongue; at a later period, this pontiff [tried] to suppress a conspiracy to depose him [and] Rome became the scene of rebellion, murder, and conflagration.
>
> His successor, Stephen V, A.D. 816, was ignominiously driven from the city; his successor, Paschal I, was accused of blinding and murdering two ecclesiastics in the Lateran Palace; it was necessary that imperial commissioners should investigate the matter, but the pope died, after having [declared his innocence] by oath before thirty bishops.

John VIII, A.D. 872, unable to resist the Mohammedans, was compelled to pay them tribute; the Bishop of Naples, maintaining a secret alliance with them, received his share of the plunder they collected. Him John excommunicated, nor would he give him absolution unless he would betray the chief Mohammedans and assassinate others himself. There was an ecclesiastical conspiracy to murder the pope; some of the treasures of the church were seized; and the gate of St. Pancrazia was opened with false keys to admit the Saracens into the city. Formosus, who had been engaged in these transactions, and excommunicated as a conspirator for the murder of John, was subsequently elected pope, A.D. 891.

He was succeeded by Boniface VI, A.D. 896, who had been deposed from the diaconate, and again from the priesthood, for his immoral and lewd life.

By Stephen VII, who followed, the dead body of Formosus was taken from the grave, clothed in the papal habiliments, propped up in a chair, tried before a council, and the preposterous and indecent scene completed by cutting off three of the fingers of the corpse and casting it into the Tiber [river]; but Stephen himself was destined to exemplify how low the papacy had fallen: he was thrown into prison and strangled.

In the course of five years, from A.D. 896 to A.D. 900, five popes were consecrated.

Leo V, who succeeded in A.D. 904, was in less than two months thrown into prison by Christopher, one of his chaplains, who usurped his place and who, in his turn, was shortly expelled from Rome by Sergius III who, by the aid of a military force, seized the pontificate, A.D. 905. This man, according to the testimony of the times, lived in criminal intercourse with the [well-known] prostitute Theodora who, with her daughters Marozia and Theodora, also prostitutes, exercised an extraordinary control over him.

The love of Theodora was also shared by John X: she gave him first the archbishopric of Ravenna and then translated him to Rome, A.D. 915, as pope. John was not unsuited to the times; he organized a confederacy which perhaps prevented Rome from being captured by the Saracens, and the world was astonished and edified by the appearance of this war-like pontiff at the head of his troops. By the love of Theodora, as was said, he had maintained himself in the papacy for fourteen years; by the intrigues and hatred of her daughter Marozia he was overthrown. She surprised him in the Lateran Palace, killed his brother Peter before his face, [and] threw him into prison where he soon died smothered, as was asserted, with a pillow.

After a short interval Marozia made her own son pope as John XI, A.D. 931. Many affirmed that Pope Sergius was his father, but she herself inclined to attribute him to her husband Alberic, whose brother Guido she subsequently married. Another of her sons, Alberic, so called from his supposed father, jealous of his brother John, cast him and their mother Marozia into prison. After a time Alberic's son was elected pope, A.D. 956; he assumed the title of John XII, the amorous Marozia thus having given a son and a grandson to the papacy.

John was only nineteen years old when he thus became the head of Christendom. His reign was characterized by the most shocking immoralities, so that the Emperor Otho I was compelled by the German clergy to interfere. A synod was summoned for his trial in the Church of St. Peter, before which it [was charged] that John had received bribes for the consecration of bishops; that he had ordained one who was but ten years old, and had performed that ceremony over another in a stable; he was charged with [having relations] with one of his father's concubines, and with so many adulteries that the Lateran Palace had become a brothel; he put out the eyes of one ecclesiastic and castrated another, both dying in consequence of their injuries. He was given to drunkenness, gambling, and the invocation of Jupiter and Venus. When cited to appear before the council he sent word that "he had gone out hunting;" and to the fathers who [argued] with him he threateningly remarked "that Judas, as well as the other disciples, received from his Master the power of binding and loosing, but that as soon as he proved a traitor to the common cause the only power he retained was that of binding his own neck." Hereupon he was deposed and Leo VIII elected in his stead, A.D. 963; but subsequently getting the upper hand he seized his antagonists, cut off the hand of one [and] the nose, finger, [and] tongue of others. His life was eventually brought to an end by the vengeance of a man whose wife he had seduced.

After such details it is almost needless to allude to the annals of succeeding popes: to relate that John XIII was strangled in prison; that Boniface VII imprisoned Benedict VII and killed him by starvation; that John XIV was secretly put to death in the dungeons of the Castle of St. Angelo; that the corpse of Boniface was dragged by the populace through the streets.

The sentiment of reverence for the sovereign pontiff, nay, even of respect, had become extinct in Rome; throughout Europe the clergy were so shocked at the state of things that, in their indignation, they began to look with approbation on the intention of the Emperor Otho to take from the Italians their privilege of appointing the successor of St. Peter, and confine it to his own family. But his kinsman, Gregory V, whom he placed on the pontifical throne, was very soon compelled by the Romans to fly; his excommunications and religious thunders were turned into derision by them; they were too well acquainted with the true nature of those terrors; they were living behind the scenes.

A terrible punishment awaited the anti-pope John XVI. [Emperor] Otho returned to Italy, seized him, put out his eyes, cut off his nose and tongue, and sent him through the streets mounted on an ass, with his face to the tail, and a wine-bladder on his head. It seemed impossible that things could become worse; yet Rome had still to see Benedict IX, A.D. 1033, a boy of less than twelve years, raised to the apostolic throne. Of this pontiff, one of his successors, Victor III, declared that his life was so shameful, so foul, so [utterly detestable], that he shuddered to describe it. He ruled like a captain of banditti rather than a prelate. The people at last, unable to bear his adulteries, homicides, and abominations any longer, rose against him. In despair of maintaining his position, he put up the papacy to auction. It was bought by a presbyter named John, who became [pope] Gregory VI, A.D. 1045.

More than a thousand years had elapsed since the birth of our Savior, and such was the condition of Rome. Well may the historian shut the annals of those times in disgust; well may the heart of the Christian sink within him at such a catalogue of hideous crimes. Well may we ask, "Were these the [representatives] of God upon earth–these, who had truly reached that goal beyond which the last effort of human wickedness cannot pass?"

Not until several centuries after these events did public opinion come to the true and philosophical conclusion—the total rejection of the divine claims of the papacy. For a time the evils were attributed to the manner of the pontifical election, as if that could by any possibility influence the descent of a power which claimed to be supernatural and under the immediate care of God. The manner of election was this. The Roman ecclesiastics recommended a candidate to the college of cardinals; their choice had to be ratified by the populace of Rome and, after that, the emperor must give his approval. There were thus to be brought into agreement the machinations of the lower ecclesiastics, the intrigues of the cardinals, the clamors of the rabble of Rome, and the policy of the emperor. Such a system must inevitably break [into] pieces with its own incongruities. Though we may wonder that men failed to see that it was merely a human device, we cannot wonder that the emperors perceived the necessity of taking the appointments into their own hands, and that Gregory VII was resolved to confine it to the college of cardinals to the exclusion of the emperor, the Roman people, and even the rest of Christendom–an attempt in which he succeeded.

No one can study the development of the Italian ecclesiastical power without discovering how completely it depended on human agency, too often on human passion and intrigues; how completely wanting it was of any mark of the Divine construction and care–the offspring of man, not of God, and therefore bearing upon it the [features] of human passions, human virtues, and human sins (John W. Draper, *History of the Intellectual Development of Europe*, rev. ed. [New York: Harper and Brothers, 1876], 1:378–82). On page 378 of this source Draper notes that, in consideration of his religious audience, he deliberately refrained from reporting some profoundly shocking cases of papal infamy.

49. For general reading on the practice of issuing "indulgences" see F. L. Cross, ed., *The Oxford Dictionary of the Christian Church*, 3d ed. (New York: Oxford University Press, 1997), 829–30.

This practice did not begin until the eleventh century A.D. For a medieval depiction of clergymen and bankers' agents collecting money "in return for absolving the purchaser of his sins," under the authoritative banner of the pope, see Tim Dowley, ed., *Eerdmans Handbook to the History of Christianity* (Grand Rapids, Michigan: Eerdmans, 1977), 360.

50. For general reading on the atrocities of the Inquisition, see James B. Given, *Inquisition and Medieval Society* (Ithaca, New York: Cornell University Press, 1997); Henry C. Lea, *The Inquisition of the Middle Ages: Its Organization and Operation* (New York: The Citadel Press, 1954).

51. *EM*, 3:1171. For further reading see Arnold K. Garr, "A Great and Marvelous Work. Part One: 1350–1805, Preparing for the Restoration," *Ensign*, June 1999, 34–45.

52. Joseph Fielding Smith, *Doctrines of Salvation*, ed., Bruce R. McConkie (Salt Lake City: Bookcraft, 1954), 1:174–75.

53. *TPJS*, 375–76.

54. Bauer, Arndt, and Gingrich, A *Greek-English Lexicon of the New Testament and Other Early Christian Literature*, 92; Liddell and Scott, *A Greek-English Lexicon*, 201.

55. Strong, *The New Strong's Exhaustive Concordance of the Bible*, Hebrew and Aramaic Dictionary of the Old Testament, 138, word #7725.

56. The restoration of the gospel was necessary because it had become badly damaged during the Great Apostasy. The damage that occurred can be summed up in the following ten categories.
    (1) Loss of Central Authority (quorum of the twelve apostles, Aaronic and Melchizedek Priesthoods)
    (2) Loss of Church Offices (apostles, prophets, seventies)
    (3) Loss of Doctrines (three degrees of glory, deification)
    (4) Loss of Practices (baptism by immersion, temple rituals, non-clerics forbidden to study and explain the scriptures).
    (5) Mixing of Orthodox and Pagan Beliefs (trinitarianism, transubstantiation, asceticism, creation ex nihilo).
    (6) Unauthorized Tampering with Ordinances (baptism by pouring and sprinkling, age necessary for baptism changed)
    (7) Unauthorized Introduction of Practices (infant baptism, celibacy, mass, selling of indulgences)
    (8) Unauthorized Alteration of Church Organization (introduction of popes, monks, nuns, sub-deacons, abbots, friars, exorcists, acolytes, cardinals, etc.)
    (9) Formal Discarding of Doctrines (baptism for the dead, premortal life)
    (10) Fabrication of Doctrines (supererogation, assumption of Mary, papal infallibility, predestination, purgatory, praying to individuals other than God, bestowal of sainthood)

57. Since the Book of Mormon contains the "fullness of the everlasting gospel" (D&C 135:3; see also 27:5), some scriptural interpreters have concluded that the angel Moroni is the heavenly messenger spoken of in Revelation 14:6–7 and D&C 133:36–39. Even though some writers have countered this argument by pointing out that several angels participated in the restoration of keys, powers, and knowledge to Joseph Smith, D&C 133:36 cannot be logically applied to them since it

only speaks of a single "angel" ("Angel" in the original manuscript of the revelation). It is also not logical to apply D&C 133:36 to angels who participated in the Restoration after D&C 133 was recorded on 3 November 1831 (i.e., Moses, Noah, and Elijah who appeared in the Kirtland Temple in 1836). In speaking of the angel of Revelation 14:6–7, Elder Rudger Clawson said: "We believe and claim as a people, that that angel has come to the earth and appeared to Joseph Smith, in the person of Moroni, who delivered to the youthful Prophet a record familiarly known as the Book of Mormon, a record containing the fullness of the gospel, with a message that said the gospel must be preached in every nation under the heavens before the end should come" (*CR,* April 1909, 92). In the *Encyclopedia of Mormonism* we read: "Because of the angel Moroni's role in restoring the everlasting gospel to be preached to all the world (cf. Revelation 14:6–7; D&C 133:31–39), the Church placed a statue depicting him as a herald of the Restoration atop the Salt Lake Temple, and later on the hill Cumorah near Palmyra, New York, where anciently he had buried the Book of Mormon plates. Copies of the statue have also been placed atop several other LDS temples" (*EM*, 2:953). The footnoting system of the Doctrine and Covenants also lends support to the idea that Moroni is the "angel flying through the midst of heaven." D&C 133:36 note *a* sends the reader to D&C 20:6, which clearly refers to Moroni (see JS-H 1:30–33).

CHAPTER 2

The Divine Calling of Joseph Smith

Brigham Young declared that Joseph Smith was foreordained to stand as the leading prophet in the dispensation of the fullness of times. "It was decreed in the councils of eternity," said President Young, "long before the foundations of the earth were laid, that [Joseph Smith] should be the man, in the last dispensation of this world, to bring forth the word of God to the people, and receive the fullness of the keys and powers of the Priesthood of the Son of God."[1]

FIGURE 2. Joseph Smith was chosen in the premortal councils of heaven to be the prophet who would usher in the dispensation of the fullness of times and restore the fullness of the gospel.

Joseph's grandfather, Asael Smith, had a premonition that a prominent religious leader would someday be born into his family. He said, "It has been borne in upon my soul that one of my descendants will promulgate a work to revolutionize the world of religious faith."[2] In speaking of this premonition, Joseph Smith stated: "My grandfather, Asael Smith, long ago predicted that there would be a prophet raised up in his family, and my grandmother was fully satisfied that it was fulfilled in me. My grandfather Asael died in East

Stockholm, St. Lawrence county, New York, after having received the Book of Mormon, and read it nearly through; and he declared that I was the very prophet that he had long known would come in his family."[3]

Joseph Smith bore this simple witness of his life's mission. "I was called of my Heavenly Father to lay the foundation of this great work and kingdom in this dispensation, and [to] testify of His revealed will to scattered Israel."[4] Those who were not of the LDS faith were continually asking the Prophet if there was any evidence to back up his claim to be a legitimate representative of the Almighty. The Prophet responded, "'What signs does Joseph Smith give of his divine mission?' The signs which God is pleased to let him give, according as His wisdom thinks best."[5] In the pages that follow the reader will be introduced to some of the "signs" that substantiate Joseph Smith's claim to be a true prophet of God.

THE LEGEND OF MESSIAH BEN JOSEPH

Ancient Hebrew traditions speak of two separate *messiahs*[6] that were foreordained to arise among the covenant people of the Lord—one from the tribe of Judah (the *Messiah ben David* or "son of" David) and one from the tribe of Joseph (the *Messiah ben Joseph/Ephraim*). According to Jewish lore the *Messiah ben Joseph* concept first arose when Rachel, the mother of Joseph of Egypt, prophesied that Joseph would be the ancestor of a *messiah* who would "arise at the end of days."[7] Scholars who have studied this legend have determined that it was "a standard article of faith, early and firmly established and universally accepted."[8]

The *Messiah ben Joseph* legends hold special interest for Latter-day Saints for two main reasons. First, these Jewish legends claim that Joseph of Egypt uttered prophecies about the *Messiah ben Joseph*[9] while prophecies by Joseph of Egypt found in the Book of Mormon and JST speak of a latter-day seer who would be named "Joseph" (see 2 Nephi 3:6–15; JST Genesis 50:26–33). Second, there are several elements found in the *Messiah ben Joseph* legends that closely correspond to the life of the Prophet Joseph Smith. Following are ten points of correspondence:

1. The *Messiah ben Joseph* is to be held in reserve to live on the earth in the "last days."[10]

In Doctrine and Covenants section 132 verse 7 the Lord states that He had appointed Joseph Smith to hold the keys of the sealing power of the Priesthood "in the last days."

2. The *Messiah ben Joseph* is to be born through the lineage of Joseph of Egypt's birthright son Ephraim.[11]

In a meeting held in Nauvoo, Illinois, on 8 January 1845, President Brigham Young stated that Joseph Smith's "descent from Joseph that was sold into Egypt was direct, and the blood was pure in him. That is why the Lord chose him."[12] On a later occasion President Young stated that "Joseph Smith was a pure Ephraimite."[13]

3. The *Messiah ben Joseph* is to live upon the earth prior to "when Messiah ben David [i.e., Jesus Christ] appears in all his glory"[14] and is to act as His "forerunner."[15]

"President [Lorenzo] Snow reported that on one occasion Joseph Smith was . . . asked who he was. The Prophet smiled kindly upon his interlocutor and replied, 'Noah came before the flood. I have come before the fire'"[16]—meaning the fire that will accompany the Second Coming of Christ (see D&C 29:12; 133:40–41).

The Prophet taught the following about the "Elias" principle. "The spirit of Elias is to prepare the way for a greater revelation of God . . . . When God sends a man into the world to prepare for a greater work, holding the keys of the power of Elias, it [is] called the doctrine of Elias . . . . That person who holds the keys of Elias [has] a preparatory work."[17] According to Parley P. Pratt, "Joseph Smith was the Elias, the Restorer, the presiding Messenger, holding the keys of the Dispensation of the fullness of times . . . to prepare the way of the Lord."[18]

4. The *Messiah ben Joseph* is to be "the revealer of the true faith" of Jehovah.[19] In one Jewish legend Joseph of Egypt prophesies that the *Messiah ben Joseph* will cause some erroneous elements of religious worship that have crept in among the Israelite tribes to "vanish."[20] Thus, he will perform his work after a period of apostasy.

The Lord Jesus Christ has declared: "I have sent forth the fullness of my gospel by the hand of my servant Joseph" (D&C 35:17). The Lord has also indicated in a modern revelation that the religious system He revealed through Joseph Smith constitutes "the only true and living Church upon the face of the whole earth" (D&C 1:30).

5. The prophet Elijah is to return to the earth, as foretold in Malachi 4:5–6, during the days of the *Messiah ben Joseph*.[21]

D&C 110:13–16 records the fulfillment of this expectation. In verses 14–15 of this passage, Elijah is represented as saying that his arrival in the Kirtland Temple fulfilled the prophecy of Malachi 4:5–6.

6. The *Messiah ben Joseph* is to "rebuild the temple" of Israel and restore its "true worship."[22]

Just as the Lord revealed the pattern for the Tabernacle to Moses (see Exodus 25:9) and the pattern of the Jerusalem Temple to David and Solomon (see 1 Chronicles 28:11–19), He also revealed the patterns for the Kirtland Temple (see D&C 94:5–6) and the Nauvoo Temple (see D&C 124:42) to the Prophet Joseph Smith.

On 19 January 1841, the Lord told Joseph Smith that the ordinances to be performed in the Nauvoo Temple were previously performed in the Tabernacle of Moses and in the Temple of Solomon (see D&C 124:37–38). Hence, the Nauvoo Temple ordinances qualify as "restored" rituals. The Lord said He would reveal "all things pertaining to" the Nauvoo Temple "and the priesthood thereof" to the Prophet Joseph Smith (v. 42). This revelation of "the fullness of the priesthood" (v. 28) was to include certain "keys of the holy priesthood" (v. 34) which were "the keys whereby [one] may ask and receive" the blessings of the Lord (vv. 95, 97). In addition, the Lord would reveal to the Prophet such "ordinances" as baptism for the dead, washings, anointings, and memorials of Levitical sacrifices. The Lord would also teach Joseph Smith of solemn assemblies, statutes, judgments, oracles in most holy places, and revelations for establishing the foundation of Zion (vv. 39–40). Altogether, these ritual elements were to serve as an "endowment" that would bestow "glory and honor" upon its recipients (v. 39).[23]

7. The *Messiah ben Joseph* is to gather the children of Israel around him, including a portion of the lost ten tribes.[24]

Joseph Smith's father spoke the following words while administering a patriarchal blessing to his son. "A marvelous work and a wonder has the Lord wrought by thy hand, even that which shall prepare the way for the remnants of His people to come in among the Gentiles, with their fullness, as the tribes of Israel are restored."[25] In the Kirtland Temple on 3 April 1836, Joseph Smith received the keys for the gathering of the twelve tribes of Israel. "The heavens were again opened unto us; and Moses appeared before us, and committed unto us the keys of the gathering of Israel from the four parts of the earth, and the leading of the ten tribes from the land of the north" (D&C 110:11).

8. The *Messiah ben Joseph* is to be a warrior.[26]

On 10 March 1841 Thomas Carlin, Governor of the state of Illinois, commissioned Joseph Smith to the rank of Lieutenant General over the Nauvoo Legion.[27] By 1844 the Nauvoo Legion is estimated to have been about 5,000 men strong. The

FIGURE 3. Joseph Smith served as Lieutenant General of the Nauvoo Legion, a military unit that was second only in size to the United States Army.

Legion was not only the largest military unit in the state of Illinois but it was second only in size to the United States Army.

9. The *Messiah ben Joseph* is to be a king.[28]

William Clayton relates that during a Council of Fifty meeting held on 11 April 1844 in Nauvoo, Illinois, "President Joseph [Smith was] chosen [as] our Prophet, Priest and King by hosannas."[29] George A. Smith likewise recorded in his diary, under the date of 9 May 1844, that Joseph Smith had been installed as "King over the immediate House of Israel" by the Council of Fifty.[30] A revelation from the Lord to the Council of Fifty on 27 June 1882 verified that Joseph Smith had been called "to be a Prophet, Seer and Revelator to my Church and Kingdom; and to be a King and Ruler over Israel."[31]

Once when the Prophet was "preaching from Daniel 2nd chapter, 44th verse, [he] said that the kingdom referred to was already set up, and that he was the king over it."[32] Joseph Smith served in the capacity of a substitute sovereign over God's earthly kingdom, just as the kings of ancient Israel did (see 1 Chronicles 29:23).[33]

10. The *Messiah ben Joseph* is to die as a martyr.[34]

John Taylor informs us that "when Joseph [Smith] went to Carthage to deliver himself up to the pretended requirements of the law, two or three days previous to his assassination, he said: 'I am going like a lamb to the slaughter; but I am calm as a summer's morning; I have a conscience void of offense towards God, and towards all men. I shall die innocent, and it shall be said of me—he was murdered in cold blood'" (D&C 135:4).

While it cannot be stated with certainty that Joseph Smith and the *Messiah ben Joseph* are one and the same person, it cannot be denied that the parallels between

JST GENESIS 50

24 And Joseph said unto his brethren . . . .

26 A seer shall the Lord my God raise up, who shall be a choice seer unto the fruit of my loins.

27 Thus saith the Lord God of my fathers unto me, "A choice seer will I raise up out of the fruit of thy loins, and he shall be esteemed highly among the fruit of thy loins; and unto him will I give commandment that he shall do a work for the fruit of thy loins, his brethren.

28 And he shall bring them to the knowledge of the covenants which I have made with thy fathers; and he shall do whatsoever work I shall command him.

29 And I will make him great in mine eyes, for he shall do my work; and he shall be great like unto him whom I have said I would raise up unto you, to deliver my people, O house of Israel, out of the land of Egypt . . . [who] shall be called Moses. . . .

30 And again, a seer will I raise up out of the fruit of thy loins, and unto him will I give power to bring forth my word unto the seed of thy loins; and not to the bringing forth of my word only, saith the Lord, but to the convincing them of my word, which shall have already gone forth among them in the last days.

31 Wherefore the fruit of thy loins shall write, and the fruit of the loins of Judah shall write; and that which shall be written by the fruit of thy loins, and also that which shall be written by the fruit of the loins of Judah, shall grow together unto the confounding of false doctrines, and laying down of contentions, and establishing peace among the fruit of thy loins, and bringing them to a knowledge of their fathers in the last days; and also to the knowledge of my covenants, saith the Lord.

32 And out of weakness shall he be made strong, in that day when my work shall go forth among all my people, which shall restore them, who are of the house of Israel, in the last days.

33 And that seer will I bless, and they that seek to destroy him shall be confounded; for this promise I give unto you; for I will remember you from generation to generation; and his name shall be called Joseph, and it shall be after the name of his father; and he shall be like unto you; for the thing which the Lord shall bring forth by his hand shall bring my people to salvation."

2 NEPHI 3

6 For Joseph truly testified, saying: "A seer shall the Lord my God raise up, who shall be a choice seer unto the fruit of my loins."

7 Yea, Joseph truly said: "Thus saith the Lord unto me: 'A choice seer will I raise up out of the fruit of thy loins; and he shall be esteemed highly among the fruit of thy loins. And unto him will I give commandment that he shall do a work for the fruit of thy loins, his brethren, which shall be of great worth unto them, even to the bringing of them to the knowledge of the covenants which I have made with thy fathers.

8 And I will give unto him a commandment that he shall do none other work, save the work which I shall command him. And I will make him great in mine eyes; for he shall do my work.

9 And he shall be great like unto Moses, whom I have said I would raise up unto you, to deliver my people, O house of Israel.

10 And Moses will I raise up, to deliver thy people out of the land of Egypt.

11 But a seer will I raise up out of the fruit of thy loins; and unto him will I give power to bring forth my word unto the seed of thy loins–and not to the bringing forth my word only, saith the Lord, but to the convincing them of my word, which shall have already gone forth among them.

12 Wherefore, the fruit of thy loins shall write; and the fruit of the loins of Judah shall write; and that which shall be written by the fruit of thy loins, and also that which shall be written by the fruit of the loins of Judah, shall grow together, unto the confounding of false doctrines and laying down of contentions, and establishing peace among the fruit of thy loins, and bringing them to the knowledge of their fathers in the last days, and also to the knowledge of my covenants, saith the Lord.

13 And out of weakness he shall be made strong, in that day when my work shall commence among all my people, unto the restoring thee, O house of Israel, saith the Lord.'"

14 And thus prophesied Joseph, saying: "Behold, that seer will the Lord bless; and they that seek to destroy him shall be confounded; for this promise, which I have obtained of the Lord, of the fruit of my loins, shall be fulfilled. Behold, I am sure of the fulfilling of this promise.

15 And his name shall be called after me; and it shall be after the name of his father. And he shall be like unto me; for the thing, which the Lord shall bring forth by his hand, by the power of the Lord shall bring my people unto salvation."

FIGURE 4. These columns display the prophecies of Joseph of Egypt as they are recorded in the Book of Mormon and the Joseph Smith Translation of the Bible. Joseph of Egypt was shown by vision that in the last days a choice seer would be raised up out of his lineage and would be called "Joseph," after the name of his father (2 Nephi 3:15).

Parallels Between the *Messiah ben Joseph* Legend and Restoration Scriptures		
Element of Legend	**JST Genesis 50:24–33**	**2 Nephi 3:6–15**
Descendant of Joseph	JST Genesis 50:27	2 Nephi 3:7
Live in the Last Days	JST Genesis 50:30–32	2 Nephi 3:12
Gather Tribes of Israel	JST Genesis 50:32	2 Nephi 3:13
Reveal the True Faith*	JST Genesis 50:33	2 Nephi 3:15
Restore the Temple**	JST Genesis 50:28, 31	2 Nephi 3:7, 12

* The Joseph Smith material speaks of Joseph of Egypt's descendant bringing the Lord's people to *salvation* through the power of the Lord.
** The Joseph Smith material speaks of Joseph of Egypt's descendant bringing his fellow Israelites to a knowledge of the *covenants* that God made with Abraham, Isaac, and Jacob.

FIGURE 5. This chart illustrates five parallels between the ancient Jewish legends of the *Messiah ben Joseph* and scriptural literature that was produced by the Prophet Joseph Smith.

them are striking. It is also of great interest that some of the *Messiah ben Joseph* legendary elements are present in revealed scriptural texts that clearly *do* refer to the Prophet (see 2 Nephi 3:6–15; JST Genesis 50:26–33).

HEAVENLY TEACHERS

Joseph Smith was eminently qualified to teach the world about religious truth since he had been personally tutored by some of the most prominent figures of religious history. The Prophet indicates that between 21 September 1823 (when Moroni first appeared to him) and 22 September 1827 (when he actually took possession of the golden plates of the Book of Mormon) he "received many visits from the angels of God." The mission of these angels, said Joseph, was "unfolding the *majesty and glory* of the events *that should transpire* in the last days."[35] This is probably what D&C 128:21 refers to. In this verse the Prophet reveals that he was visited by "divers angels, from Michael or Adam down to the present time, all declaring their dispensation, their rights, their keys, their honors, their *majesty and glory*, and the power of their priesthood; giving line upon line, precept upon precept; here a little, and there a little; giving us consolation by *holding forth that which is to come*." Orson Pratt verified that "during these four years [1823–1827, Joseph Smith] was often ministered to by the angels of God, and received instruction concerning the work that was to be performed in the latter days."[36]

President John Taylor taught that Joseph Smith saw in vision, "the things that are to transpire in the latter-days associated with the dispensation that he was called upon by the Almighty to introduce." In addition, said President Taylor, the Prophet "understood things that were past, and comprehended the various dispensations and the designs of those dispensations." And furthermore, "he was conversant with the parties who officiated as the leading men of those dispensations, and from a number of them he received authority and keys and priesthood and power for the carrying out of the great purposes of the Lord in the last days, who were sent and commissioned specifically by the Almighty to confer upon him those keys and this authority."[37]

Following is a list of the heavenly beings that are known to have made personal appearances to the Prophet Joseph Smith at various times during his ministry. God the Father,[38] Jesus Christ,[39] Adam,[40] Eve,[41] Seth,[42] Enoch,[43] Noah (Elias),[44] Abraham,[45] Isaac,[46] Jacob,[47] Moses,[48] Elijah,[49] John the Baptist,[50] Peter,[51] James,[52] John,[53] Lehi,[54] Nephi,[55] Mormon,[56] Moroni,[57] and the Three Nephites.[58] In addition to these identifiable visitors, history records that several unidentified angels also appeared to the Prophet. For instance, an unnamed angel of God appeared to Joseph Smith in order to teach him about the sacrament.[59] An unnamed angel of God also appeared to the Prophet to teach him about the endowment ceremonies that were to be practiced in the Nauvoo Temple.[60] An unnamed angel of God made an appearance to Joseph to warn him of the consequences of delaying the introduction of plural marriage after the Lord had commanded it to be done.[61] Many unnamed angels were seen by the Prophet during the First Vision[62] and many unnamed angels were also seen by the Prophet inside the Kirtland Temple.[63]

Critics of Joseph Smith might accuse him of simply fabricating the account of visitations by heavenly beings in order to build up his importance in the eyes of the people. But the student of Church history knows that this argument falls apart for two reasons. (1) The Prophet was reluctant to speak of these experiences; some were not even known among the general membership of the Church. This is hardly what one would expect from someone who was only interested in promoting his own fame. (2) There were witnesses to some of these visitations. Some of the stories of these eyewitnesses are reproduced in the pages that follow and also in other sections of this book.

THE DOCTRINE AND COVENANTS REVELATIONS

One of the more subtle evidences of Joseph Smith's divine calling can be found in the revelations he produced. In D&C 24:5 the Lord commanded Joseph Smith to write down the revelations which were given to him. Parley P. Pratt was one of the witnesses who was present when some of the Doctrine and Covenants revelations were received and recorded. Pratt stated in May of 1831 that:

> . . . each sentence was uttered slowly and very distinctly, and with a pause between each, sufficiently long for it to be recorded, by an ordinary writer, in long hand. This was the manner in which all his written revelations were dictated and written. There was never any hesitation, reviewing, or reading back in order to keep the run of the subject; neither did any of these communications undergo revisions, interlinings, or corrections. As he dictated them so they stood, so far as I have witnessed; and I was present to witness the dictation of several communications of several pages each.[64]

William E. McLellin provides a similar testimony.

> I, as scribe, have written revelations from the mouth of [Joseph Smith]. And I have been present many times when others wrote for Joseph; therefore, I speak as one having experience. The scribe seats himself at a desk or table, with pen, ink, and paper. The subject of enquiry being understood, the Prophet and Revelator enquires of God. He spiritually sees, hears, and feels, and then speaks as he is moved upon by the Holy Ghost, the 'thus saith the Lord,' sentence after sentence, and waits for his [scribes] to write and then read aloud each sentence. Thus they proceed until the revelator says 'Amen,' at the close of what is then communicated. I have known [the Prophet], . . . without premeditation, to thus deliver in broken sentences, some of the most sublime pieces of composition which I ever perused in any book.[65]

All of this is even more fascinating when one considers that LDS researchers have discovered that the Doctrine and Covenants revelations are filled with an ancient literary form known as chiasmus.[66] If Joseph Smith was just a fraud, then how did this uneducated farmboy dictate several hundred pages of text in an ancient, and complex, literary style that was not generally recognized in the Bible until long after his death?

PROPHECIES FULFILLED

The Lord has stated that one can distinguish between true and false prophets by whether or not their prophecies, spoken in His name, actually come to pass (see Deuteronomy 18:20–22). Since Joseph Smith claimed to be a legitimate prophet of God, it is fair to ask, "Did he ever utter prophecies that were fulfilled?" The answer is yes, he certainly did. Following are ten prophecies that serve to establish Joseph Smith's prophetic abilities.

The Aspirations of Stephen A. Douglas

On 18 May 1843, Joseph Smith dined with Judge Stephen A. Douglas of Illinois. The Prophet told Douglas about the persecutions the Church had suffered at the hands of some lawless Missourians, the Saints' petition for redress to President Martin Van Buren, and the President's refusal to intervene in the matter. Judge Douglas agreed that the mobs of Missouri should be brought to justice for their heinous crimes. The Prophet then said to Douglas: "I prophesy in the name of the Lord of Israel . . . you will aspire to the Presidency of the United States; and if you ever turn your hand against me or the Latter-day Saints, you will feel the weight of the hand of the Almighty upon you; and you will live to see and know that I have testified the truth to you."

This prophecy is of particular interest because it was published on 24 September 1856 in the *Deseret News* in Utah. This was about one year before Douglas publicly turned against the Saints in a railing speech given at the Illinois state capitol (12 June 1857). During this speech Douglas perpetuated the lies of the Missouri mobs even though he knew they were false—the Prophet had told him so. He even went so far, in this speech, as to call Latter-day Saints a "cancer," "enemies and outlaws," and he strongly insinuated that the leaders of the Church should be "hanged for their crimes." On 2 September 1857, the Utah Saints responded to the speech by publishing an article in the *Deseret News* wherein they informed Douglas that because of his actions he had sealed his fate and lost his chance for the U. S. Presidency. Douglas was indeed nominated as the Democratic candidate for the Presidency on 23 June 1860, but in the popular vote Douglas carried only one state—Missouri. He lost the election to Abraham Lincoln. On 3 June 1861, less than one year after his nomination, Stephen A. Douglas died in Chicago at the age of 48.[67]

Rainstorm to Abate

Mary C. Westover remembered an unusual incident that occurred in Nauvoo, Illinois, on 7 April 1844.

> The most striking thing I remember of [Joseph Smith] was a prophecy he made, which I saw fulfilled immediately. I was at the funeral service of King Follett, which was held in the Nauvoo Grove. There was a heavy thunderstorm [that] arose and as it increased the people became frightened and started to go home; but before anyone left the Prophet arose and told the multitude if they would remain still and pray in their hearts the storm would not molest them in their services.
>
> They did as they were bidden, the storm divided over the grove. I well remember how it was storming on all sides of the grove, yet it was as calm around us as if there was no sign of a storm so nearby.[68]

Sidney Rigdon to be Buffeted

Shortly after Joseph Smith and Sidney Rigdon had been dragged, poisoned, and tarred and feathered by a mob in Hiram, Ohio, Rigdon began to exhibit apostate behaviors. With the Prophet still in the town of Hiram, Sidney openly challenged the authority of the Church by claiming, in the name of the Lord, that the keys of God's kingdom had been taken from the Church. This statement caused a great deal of disturbance and commotion among the Kirtland Saints. Hyrum Smith, who was infuriated by Rigdon's nonsense, immediately rode off to Hiram, Ohio, to inform the Prophet of the circumstances. When Joseph Smith arrived back in Kirtland, he stood before a gathering of Saints and stated that no power could take away the keys of the kingdom except the power that bestowed those keys, and this had *not* occurred. The next day Rigdon was tried before a council for lying in the name of the Lord and was delivered over to the buffetings of Satan. The Prophet then prophesied that "for what Sidney has done, the devil shall handle him as one man handles another."

Philo Dibble records the literal fulfillment of this prophecy. "About three weeks after this, Sidney was lying on his bed alone. An unseen power lifted him from his bed, threw him across the room, and tossed him from one side of the room to the other. The noise being heard in the adjoining room, his family went in to see what was the matter, and found him going from one side of the room to the other, from the effects of which Sidney was laid up for five or six weeks. Thus was Joseph's prediction in regard to him verified."[69]

Zion's Camp to Be Scourged

On 3 June 1834, the Prophet called the members of Zion's Camp together in order to "deliver a prophecy." Some of the men in the camp had been disobedient and rebellious. After giving the brethren some advice and exhorting them to be faithful, the Prophet issued a stark declaration. "I said the Lord had revealed to me that a scourge would come upon the camp in consequence of the fractious and unruly spirits that appeared among them, and they should die like sheep with the rot; still, if they would repent and humble themselves before the Lord, the scourge, in a great measure, might be turned away; but, as the Lord lives, the members of this camp will suffer for giving way to their unruly temper."[70] The Prophet even apologized. He said he "was sorry, but could not help it. The scourge must come; repentance and humility may mitigate the chastisement, but cannot altogether avert" the decreed punishment.[71]

On 24 June 1834, a sudden epidemic of cholera broke out in the camp. "At the commencement," says the Prophet, "I attempted to lay on hands for their recovery, but I quickly learned by painful experience, that when the great Jehovah decrees destruction upon any people, and makes known His determination, man must not attempt to stay His hand. The moment I attempted to rebuke the disease I was attacked, and had I not desisted in my attempt to save the life of a brother, I would have sacrificed my own."[72]

Preaching in Jackson County, Missouri

The Prophet tells of an interesting incident that occurred on 4 November 1838 while he was being held as a prisoner by military troops.

> We were visited by some ladies and gentlemen. One of the women came up, and very candidly enquired of the troops which of the prisoners was the Lord whom the "Mormons" worshiped. One of the guard pointed to me with a significant smile and said, "This is he." The woman then turning to me enquired whether I professed to be the Lord and Savior. I replied that I professed to be nothing but a man, and a minister of salvation, sent by Jesus Christ to preach the gospel.
>
> This answer so surprised the woman that she began to enquire into our doctrine, and I preached a discourse, both to her and her companions, and to the wondering soldiers, who listened with almost breathless attention while I set forth the doctrine of faith in Jesus Christ, and repentance, and baptism for the remission of sins, with the promise of the Holy Ghost, as recorded in the second chapter of the Acts of the Apostles.

> The woman was satisfied, and praised God in the hearing of the soldiers, and went away, praying that God would protect and deliver us. Thus was fulfilled a prophecy which had been spoken publicly by me, a few months previous—that a sermon should be preached in Jackson County by one of the Elders, before the close of 1838.[73]

Missionary Not to Return

Elder Erastus Snow, in writing to George A. Smith on 3 September 1865, related that in 1839 the Prophet had uttered a prophecy as he pronounced a blessing upon Andrew L. Lamoreaux, who was about to depart on a mission within the United States. The Prophet "laid his hands on Elder Lamoreaux and blessed him, and prophesied upon his head, that he would go on a mission to France, learn another tongue and do much good." This did, in fact, occur when Andrew was called as the President of the French Mission on 15 September 1852.

But Joseph Smith also said something during this blessing that caused him great sadness. The Prophet stated that Andrew "would not live to return to his family." Upon saying these words Joseph wept, but he said that "it was pressed upon him and he could not refrain from giving utterance to it. Elder Lamoreaux talked with his family about [the prophecy] when he left them in 1852, and endeavored to persuade them that this was not the time and mission upon which he should fall, but to believe that he would at this time be permitted to return again. When the [Church periodical called the] *Luminary* brought the tidings of his death [on 13 June 1855 from cholera], they exclaimed, 'Surely, Brother Joseph was a prophet, for all his words have come to pass.'"[74]

Willard Richards to Remain Unharmed

The Prophet Joseph Smith told Willard Richards that he would someday be involved in a scene of gunfire. This prediction became all too real at Carthage jail on the day that Joseph Smith was murdered. "Dr. Richards' escape was miraculous; he being a very large man, and in the midst of a shower of balls, yet he stood unscathed, with the exception of a ball which grazed the tip end of the lower part of his left ear. His escape fulfilled literally a prophecy which Joseph made over a year previously, that the time would come that the balls would fly around him like hail, and he would see his friends fall on the right and on the left, but that there should not be a hole in his garment."[75]

Dr. Richards' miraculous escape from harm is noted in the Doctrine and Covenants. Section 135 verse 2 states that "Willard Richards . . . through the providence of God, escaped, without even a hole in his robe."

The Prophet's Lifespan

While Joseph Smith was imprisoned in March of 1839, in a very small jail in Liberty, Missouri, the Lord spoke these words of comfort to him. "Thy days are known, and thy years shall not be numbered less; therefore, fear not what man can do, for God shall be with you forever and ever" (D&C 122:9).

After the Prophet was murdered, Elder Wilford Woodruff recorded in his journal: "Elder [Lyman] Wight said that Joseph told him, while in Liberty Jail, Missouri, in 1839, [that] he would not live to see forty years, but [Wight] was not to reveal it till [the Prophet] was dead."[76] The Prophet was 38 1/2 years old when he died in Carthage Jail on 27 June 1844.

Release from a Missouri Jail

Joseph Taylor tells of a prophecy that Joseph Smith uttered when Taylor approached him in faith.

> In February, 1841, my brother John was in jail, in the hands of the Missourians, about two hundred miles from home and my dear widowed mother was very much concerned about his safety. On one occasion she was crying and fretting about him.
>
> When I saw her in trouble, I asked what was the matter. She replied that she was afraid the Missourians would kill her dear son John and she would never see him again.
>
> I was strongly impressed to have her let me go to the Prophet Joseph and ask him if my brother would ever come home. She was very desirous for me to do so.
>
> As the Prophet lived only about three miles from our house, I got a horse and rode to his home. When I reached there, Sister Emma Smith said that he and his son Joseph had just gone up the river near Nauvoo. I rode up to them, when the Prophet enquired about my mother's welfare.
>
> I told him that mother was very sad and down-hearted about the safety of her son John; and she had requested me to come and ask him, as a man of God, whether my brother would ever return home.
>
> He bent his head for a moment as if in prayer or deep reflection. Then, with a beautiful beaming countenance, full of smiles, he looked up and told me to go and tell mother that her son would return in safety inside of a week. True to the words of the Prophet, he got home in six days after this occurrence.[77]

Saints in the Rocky Mountains

Wilford Woodruff reports that in April of 1834, in Kirtland, Ohio, Joseph Smith spoke of the Church's eventual presence in the Rocky Mountains. Said the Prophet to the priesthood bearers before him, "Brethren, I am very much edified and interested in listening to your testimony. But I want to tell you that you know no more concerning the result of this work and what lies before you as the Elders of Israel, and before this people, than a parcel of little children." The Prophet then told these brethren the restored Church of Jesus Christ would eventually fill the whole world and further remarked: "This work will fill the Rocky Mountains with tens of thousands of Latter-day Saints." President Woodruff recalled that when he heard these words he scarcely thought that he himself would live to see their fulfillment.[78]

As an indication that this was the Lord's plan, and not Joseph Smith's, we have the testimony of Lorenzo Dow Young. He relates that in Kirtland, Ohio, in 1836, Hyrum Smith gave him a blessing for his health. During this ministration "the Spirit rested mightily upon [Hyrum Smith]. He was full of blessing and prophecy. Among other things, he said that I should live to go with the Saints into the bosom of the Rocky Mountains, to build up a place there. . . . At that time, I had not heard about the Saints going to the Rocky Mountains; possibly Brother Smith had. After [Hyrum] had finished he seemed surprised at some things he had said, and wondered at the manifestations of the Spirit."[79]

In August of 1842, Joseph Smith repeated the prediction that the Saints would migrate to the West. "I prophesied that the Saints would continue to suffer much affliction and would be driven to the Rocky Mountains. Many would apostatize; others would be put to death by our persecutors or lose their lives in consequence of exposure or disease, and some of [them] will live to go and assist in making settlements, and build cities, and see the Saints become a mighty people in the midst of the Rocky Mountains."[80]

MANIFESTATIONS OF SPIRITUAL LIGHT

When Moses descended from Mount Sinai, after receiving the tablets of the ten commandments from Jehovah, "the skin of his face shone" with light (Exodus 34:29–35). This type of spiritual manifestation is also mentioned in the New

Testament. While Jesus Christ was on the Mount of Transfiguration "his face did shine as the sun, and his raiment was white as the light" (Matthew 17:2–3; see also Luke 9:29–31).

According to President Brigham Young,

> Those who were acquainted with [Joseph Smith] knew when the Spirit of revelation was upon him, for his countenance wore an expression peculiar to himself while under that influence. He preached by the Spirit of revelation, and taught in his council by it, and those who were acquainted with him could discover it at once, for at such times there was a peculiar clearness and transparency in his face.[81]

Several eyewitnesses testify that on various occasions they saw a spiritual light radiating from Joseph Smith. If Joseph Smith were not truly a man of God then how, one might ask, could he have faked such a spectacular phenomenon?

Harrison Burgess

On 30 March 1836, Harrison Burgess, a member of the Quorum of the Seventy, attended a meeting of the different Priesthood quorums in the Kirtland Temple. He relates an incident where he witnessed a spiritual light surrounding the Prophet.

> I will here relate a vision which was shown to me. It was near the close of the endowments. I was in a meeting for instruction in the upper part of the temple, with about a hundred of the High Priests, Seventies and Elders. The Saints felt to shout "Hosannah!" and the Spirit of God rested upon me in mighty power and I beheld the room lighted up with a peculiar light such as I had never seen before. It was soft and clear and the room looked to me as though it had neither roof nor floor . . . I beheld the Prophet Joseph and Hyrum Smith and Roger Orton enveloped in the light. Joseph exclaimed aloud, "I behold the Savior, the Son of God." Hyrum said, "I behold the angels of heaven." Brother Orton exclaimed, "I behold the chariots of Israel." All who were in the room felt the power of God to [the] degree that many prophesied, and the power of God was made manifest, the remembrance of which will remain with me while I live upon the earth.[82]

Wilford Woodruff

President Wilford Woodruff testified on several occasions that when Joseph Smith delivered his last charge to the Quorum of the Twelve Apostles, the room was filled with the Spirit of God. The feeling produced by this presence, said President Woodruff, was like a consuming, holy fire. The Prophet, said President Woodruff, was clothed upon with the power of God to such an accentuated degree that his face became "clear as amber" as he was "transfigured" before them.

In this heightened state of spirituality, the Prophet laid before the Apostles what the Lord required at his hand. He told the Twelve that God had sealed upon his head all of the priesthood, gifts, keys, powers, principles, and ordinances belonging to the dispensation of the fullness of times. He then said, "I have sealed upon your heads all those principles, priesthood, apostleship, and keys of the kingdom of God, and now you have got to round up your shoulders and bear off this kingdom."[83]

Oliver B. Huntington

Soon after the Saints settled in Nauvoo, Illinois, in 1839 some of the Church's enemies from Missouri kidnapped three citizens from Nauvoo, took them into Missouri, and tortured them until they escaped. One of the Missourians who had participated in this crime was caught wandering through the streets of Nauvoo in disguise. He was brought to trial and Joseph Smith, who was acting as the prosecuting attorney, suddenly stopped speaking of civil law and "declared the word of God with regard to the state of Missouri and its inhabitants." The servant of the Lord prophesied: "She shall drink out of the same cup, the same bitter dregs we have drunk, poured out, out, out! And that by the hand of an enemy—a race meaner than themselves."

Huntington records that "all the time he was delivering the word of the Lord his face shone as if there was a light within him and his flesh was translucent." After delivering this and two other prophecies, the Prophet stated that he did not know who the race was that would inflict such retribution upon the Missourians; but Oliver B. Huntington was satisfied that the prophesy was fulfilled by the ruthless guerilla warriors who decimated Missouri during the Civil War.[84]

Anson Call

On 6 August 1842 Anson Call was with Joseph Smith in Montrose, Iowa, when he saw the Prophet's face become illuminated. This occurred while the Prophet viewed a series of visions and uttered a prophecy about the Saints migrating to the Rocky Mountains. Call relates:

> I had before seen him in a vision, and now saw while he was talking his countenance change to white; not the deadly white of a bloodless face, but a living brilliant white. He seemed absorbed in gazing at something at a great distance, and said: "I am gazing upon the valleys of those mountains. . . . Oh, the beauty of those snow-

capped mountains! The cool, refreshing streams that are running down through those mountain gorges!" Then, gazing in another direction, as if there was a change of locality [the Prophet said], "Oh, the scenes that this people will pass through! The dead that will lay between here and there." Then turning in another direction as if the scene had again changed [the Prophet said,] "Oh, the apostasy that will take place before my brethren reach that land! But" he continued, "the Priesthood shall prevail over its enemies, triumph over the devil and be established upon the earth, never more to be thrown down!" He then charged us with great force and power, to be faithful to those things that had been and should be committed to our charge, with the promise of all the blessings that the Priesthood could bestow.[85]

Mary E. Lightner

The following incident occurred at the Smith family home at Kirtland, Ohio, in the Spring of 1831. The whole Smith family was present on this occasion, along with Martin Harris, Mary Lightner, and her mother. After the Prophet had decided that enough people were present to hold a meeting,

A board was put across two chairs to make seats. Martin Harris sat on a little box at Joseph's feet. They sang and prayed, then Joseph got up to speak. He began very solemnly and very earnestly. All at once his countenance changed and he stood mute. He turned so white, he seemed perfectly transparent. Those who looked at him that night said he looked like he had a searchlight within him. I never saw anything like it on earth. I could not take my eyes away from him. I remember I thought we could almost see the bones through the flesh of his face. I shall remember him as he looked then as long as I live.

He stood some moments looking over the congregation, as if to pierce each heart, then said, "Do you know who has been in your midst this night?"

One of the Smiths said, "An angel of the Lord."

Martin Harris said, "It was our Lord and Savior, Jesus Christ."

Joseph put his hand down on Martin's head and said, "The Spirit of God revealed that to [you]. Yes, brothers and sisters, the Savior has been in your midst this night and I want you all to remember it. There is a veil over your eyes, for you could not endure to look upon Him. You must be fed with milk not with strong meat. I want you all to remember this as if it were the last thing that escapes my lips. He has given you all to me, and commanded me to seal you up to Everlasting Life, that where He is there you may be also."[86]

Lydia B. Knight

This next incident to be related occurred on 20 October 1833 in the town of Mount Pleasant, which is situated in Brant County, Ontario, Canada. Freeman

Nickerson's parents had converted to the LDS faith and they requested Joseph Smith and Sidney Rigdon to meet with their children at Freeman's home to explain the precepts of the Restoration to them. Nickerson hoped their children might share in the blessings of the gospel with them.

Lydia Knight states, "the Prophet commenced by relating the scenes of his early life. He told how the angel [Moroni] visited him, of his finding the plates and the translation of them, and gave a short account of the matter contained in the Book of Mormon. As the Speaker continued his wonderful narrative," says Lydia, "I was listening and watching him intently. I saw his face become white and a shining glow seemed to beam from every feature. . . . The Prophet bore a faithful testimony that the priesthood was again restored to the earth, and that God and His Son had conferred upon him the keys of the Aaronic and Melchizedek Priesthoods."[87]

Sally Conrad

Sally H. Conrad lived in the David Whitmer home during the time when Joseph Smith and Oliver Cowdery were translating and transcribing the Book of Mormon in the upper level of the structure. Conrad relates that she "saw them come down from [the] translating room several times when they looked so exceedingly white and strange that she enquired of Mrs. Whitmer the cause of their unusual appearance, but Mrs. Whitmer was unwilling to tell [Conrad] the true cause as it was a sacred, holy event connected with a holy, sacred work which was opposed and persecuted by nearly everyone who heard of it."

Conrad was frightened by the appearance of these two men and insisted that she be told of its cause. "Sister Whitmer then told her what the men were doing in the room above and that the power of God was so great in the room that they could hardly endure it; at times angels were in the room in their glory which nearly consumed them."[88]

Philo Dibble

Philo Dibble was present during part of the time that the vision of the three degrees of glory was seen by Joseph Smith and Sidney Rigdon (see D&C 76). He saw the light and felt the power that attended the vision but did not see the vision itself. He made this note about the Prophet's appearance during this experience. "Joseph wore black clothes, but at this time seemed to be dressed in an element of glorious white, and his face shone as if it were transparent, but I did not see the same glory attending Sidney [Rigdon]."[89]

David Whitmer

In June of 1829, Joseph Smith was traveling with David Whitmer and Oliver Cowdery from Harmony, Pennsylvania, to Fayette, New York. As they crossed an open field in their wagon, an old man with a knapsack came walking alongside them and put his hand on the wagon bed. The Prophet was in the back of the wagon and Whitmer was driving the team. Whitmer asked the old man if he would like to ride along with them, but the stranger replied, "No . . . I am only going over to Cumorah" and then suddenly disappeared. Oliver and David "asked the Prophet to enquire of the Lord who this stranger was. Soon . . . they turned around and Joseph looked pale, almost transparent, and [he] said, 'That was one of the Nephites and he had the plates of the Book of Mormon in the knapsack.'"[90]

Edward Stevenson

This next incident occurred in 1834 in Pontiac, Michigan. The Prophet, his father Joseph Smith, Sr., Oliver Cowdery, David Whitmer and Martin Harris were visiting the Pontiac Branch of the Church. Martin Harris' sister, Sophia Kellog, lived in the Pontiac settlement. Stevenson informs us that:

> The meetings held were crowded to see and hear the testimonies given which were very powerful. I will here relate my own experience on the occasion of a meeting in our old log schoolhouse. The Prophet stood at a table for the pulpit where he began relating his vision and before he got through he was in the midst of the congregation with uplifted hand. I do believe that there was not one person present who [was] not, at the time being, convi[nced] of the truth of his vision, of an angel to him. His countenance seemed to me to assume a heavenly whiteness and his voice was so piercing and forcible. For my part, it so impressed me as to become indelibly imprinted on my mind. . . . The three witnesses bore their testimonies as to seeing the angel and hearing his voice.[91]

Orson Pratt

Orson Pratt testified that he "saw [Joseph Smith's] countenance lighted up as the inspiration of the Holy Ghost rested upon him, dictating the great and most precious revelations now printed for our guide" in the Doctrine and Covenants.[92] Pratt was present when the Prophet received the revelation that is now known as D&C 51. He indicated that "no great noise or physical manifestation was made; Joseph was as calm as the morning sun. But [Pratt] noticed a change in [the Prophet's] countenance that he had never noticed before, when a revelation was given to him. Joseph's face was exceedingly white, and seemed to shine."[93]

EVIDENCES OF SEERSHIP

Several historical documents record instances where Joseph Smith demonstrated that he possessed the gift of seership (see D&C 21:1; 107:91–92; 124:125; 127:12; 135:3). In the following story, related by David Whitmer, it is said that Joseph Smith was able to see and describe Whitmer's journey from Fayette, New York to Harmony, Pennsylvania, in minute detail.

> Joseph sent for me . . . to come to Harmony to get him and Oliver and bring them to my father's house. I did not know what to do, I was pressed with my work. I had some twenty acres to plow, so I concluded I would finish plowing and then go. I got up one morning to go to work as usual, and on going to the field, found between five and seven acres of my ground had been plowed during the night.
>
> I don't know who did it; but it was done just as I would have done it myself, and the plow was left standing in the furrow.
>
> This enabled me to start sooner. When I arrived at Harmony, Joseph and Oliver were coming toward me, and met me some distance from the house. Oliver told me that Joseph had informed him when I started from home, where I stopped the first night, how I read the sign at the tavern, where I stopped the next night, etc., and that I would be there that day before dinner, and this was why they had come out to meet me; all of which was exactly as Joseph had told Oliver, at which I was greatly astonished.[94]

Martin Harris relates an unusual incident that occurred in the early 1820s when the Prophet was challenged, on the spot, to demonstrate his ability to "see" with his seerstone.

> I was at the house of his father in Manchester, two miles south of Palmyra village, and was picking my teeth with a pin while sitting on the bars. The pin caught in my teeth and dropped from my fingers into shavings and straw. I jumped from the bars and looked for it. Joseph and Northrop Sweet also did the same. We could not find it. I then took Joseph on surprise, and said to him—I said, "Take your stone." I had never seen it, and did not know that he had it with him. He had it in his pocket. He took it and placed it in his hat—the old white hat—and placed his

> in his hat. I watched him closely to see that he did not look to one side; he reached out his hand beyond me on the right, and moved a little stick and there I saw the pin, which he picked up and gave to me. I know that he did not look out of the hat until after he picked up the pin.[95]

There is evidence that the Prophet had the ability to "see" things occurring even at a great distance. For instance: "The Prophet, it is said, while in the East, had seen [Newel and Elizabeth Whitney], in vision, praying for his coming to Kirtland."[96] When the Prophet had arrived by sleigh at Newel K. Whitney's store in Kirtland, Ohio, on 1 February 1831, he "alighted, and springing up the steps, walked into the store." Upon seeing the storekeeper, the Prophet exclaimed, "Newel K. Whitney! Thou art the man!" meaning that he was the person the Prophet had seen in vision. Whitney was completely caught off guard. Having never seen this person before, he enquired as to the stranger's identity. "I am Joseph," replied the Prophet. "You've prayed me here; now what do you want of me?"[97]

In a truly stunning demonstration of his ability to "see" Joseph Smith announced he had seen in vision that he and many other early Church leaders were related by a common ancestor. In speaking of this vision, and its relation to "the true aristocracy," Heber C. Kimball said:

> I have looked into the visions of eternity, and I know that I am true, and that I am of the true vine. I am one of the sons of those old veterans, and so is brother Brigham. . . . Now, I will refer to brother Brigham, brother Heber [C. Kimball], brother Joseph Smith, Oliver Cowdery, bishop N[ewel] K. Whitney, and lots of other men. Brother Joseph [Smith] actually saw those men in vision; he saw us in a day when we were all together. We have been separated by marriage and thrown apart; but he saw the day when we all came out of one stock, and that was out of the aristocracy. Yes, we came directly down through the prophets, and not only us, but lots of others—the whole Smith race. I could remember probably twenty or thirty that Joseph mentioned came down through that channel.
>
> My father's father and his brothers intermixed by marriage with the Smiths, and uncle John Smith was baptized [for the dead] in Nauvoo for upwards of twenty of my kindred. They mixed up in marriage, and in that way the names became changed; for they were the old veterans.
>
> There is another thing that brother Joseph said—viz., that we were positively heirs of the Priesthood; for he had seen us as such in his vision; yes, just as much so as my children are that have been born since I received my endowment. Our fathers were heirs to that Priesthood, which was handed down from father to son, and we came through that lineage[98] (see D&C 27:10; 86:8–11; 113:1–6; 132:30).

Elder Orson Pratt also mentioned the Prophet's vision of common ancestry to his brother, Parley P. Pratt, in 1853. "You will recall that Joseph had a vision in which he saw that our ancestral line and his had a common ancestor a few generations back."[99] Many years later, when the genealogical trees of all these men were sketched out, it was discovered that they were indeed related. It turns out that the common ancestor was John Lathropp, the English reformer who lived from A.D. 1584–1653. Some of the early Church leaders related through Lathropp included Joseph Smith, Oliver Cowdery, Willard Richards, Franklin D. Richards, Brigham Young, Heber C. Kimball, Newel K. Whitney, Orson F. Whitney, John Taylor, Wilford Woodruff, Lorenzo Snow, Heber J. Grant, Frederick G. Williams, Orson Pratt, Parley P. Pratt, George A. Smith, and Joseph F. Smith.[100]

WITNESSES TO THE PROPHET'S VISIONS

Among the other strong evidences that Joseph Smith was a genuine prophet of God are independent witnesses to some of his visions. If Joseph Smith were a fraud, he simply could not have produced such spiritual manifestations for the purpose of deception.

Three Degrees of Glory

On 16 February 1832, Joseph Smith and Sidney Rigdon both saw the vision of the Three Degrees of Glory now known as section 76 of the Doctrine and Covenants. Others who were present on this occasion saw a heavenly light and felt the glory that permeated the room where the manifestation took place. Philo Dibble relates the following:

> The vision which is recorded in the Book of Doctrine and Covenants [section 76] was given at the house of "Father Johnson" in Hyrum, Ohio, and during the time that Joseph and Sidney were in the Spirit and saw the heavens open. There were other men in the room, perhaps twelve, among whom I was one during a part of the time–probably two-thirds of the time. I saw the glory and felt the power, but did not see the vision.
>
> The events and conversation, while they were seeing what is written (and many things were seen and related that are not written), I will relate as minutely as is necessary.
>
> Joseph would, at intervals, say: "What do I see?" as one might say while looking out the window and beholding what all in the room could not see. Then he

> would relate what he had seen or what he was looking at. Then Sidney replied, "I see the same." Presently Sidney would say: "What do I see?" and would repeat what he had seen or was seeing, and Joseph would reply, "I see the same."
>
> This manner of conversation was repeated at short intervals to the end of the vision, and during the whole time not a word was spoken by any other person. Not a sound nor motion made by anyone but Joseph and Sidney, and it seemed to me that they never moved a joint or limb during the time I was there, which I think was over an hour, and to the end of the vision.
>
> Joseph sat firmly and calmly all the time in the midst of a magnificent glory, but Sidney sat limp and pale, apparently as limber as a rag, observing which Joseph remarked, smilingly, "Sidney is not [as] used to it as I am."[101]

The Father and the Son

On 18 March 1833 Joseph Smith, Zebedee Coltrin, and others who were gathered in the School of the Prophets (in the upper room of Newel K. Whitney's store) saw both God the Father and His Son Jesus Christ. Coltrin's account reads as follows:

> At one of these meetings after the organization of the school, [which occurred] on the 23rd of January 1833, when we were all together, Joseph having given instructions, and while engaged in silent prayer, kneeling, with our hands uplifted [and] each one praying in silence, no one whisper[ing] above his breath, a personage walked through the room from east to west, and Joseph asked if we saw him. I saw him and supposed the others did, and Joseph answered, "That is Jesus, the Son of God, our elder brother." Afterward Joseph told us to resume our former position in prayer, which we did. Another person came through; He was surrounded as with a flame of fire. I experienced a sensation that it might destroy the tabernacle as it was of consuming fire of great brightness. The Prophet said this was the Father of our Lord Jesus Christ. I saw Him. . . .
>
> I did not discover His clothing for He was surrounded as with a flame of fire, which was so brilliant that I could not discover anything else but His person. I saw His hands, His legs, His feet, His eyes, nose, mouth, head and body in the shape and form of a perfect man. He sat in a chair as a man would sit in a chair, but this appearance was so grand and overwhelming that it seemed I should melt down in His presence. And the sensation was so powerful that it thrilled [me] through my whole system and I felt it in the marrow of my bones. The Prophet Joseph said: "Brethren, now you are prepared to be the apostles of Jesus Christ, for you have seen both the Father and the Son, and know that they exist and that they are two separate personages."[102]

Kirtland Temple Pattern

On 1 June 1833, the Lord made it known that He would show the pattern for the Kirtland Temple to three people (see D&C 95:14). The three who were chosen to receive this revelation were the First Presidency of the Church consisting of Joseph Smith, Oliver Cowdery, and Frederick G. Williams. It was President Williams who left behind an account of the vision. "We went upon our knees, called on the Lord, and the building appeared within viewing distance, I being the first to discover it" said Williams. "Then all of us viewed it together. After we had taken a good look at the exterior, the building seemed to come right over us; and the make-up of this hall seemed to coincide with what I there saw to a minutia."[103]

Adam and Eve

On 18 April 1834 Joseph Smith, Oliver Cowdery, and Zebedee Coltrin all saw a vision of Adam and Eve.

> Once after returning from a mission [Zebedee Coltrin] met Brother Joseph in Kirtland, who asked him if he did not wish to go with him to a conference at New Portage. The party consisted of Presidents Joseph Smith, Sidney Rigdon, Oliver Cowdery and [Zebedee Coltrin]. Next morning at New Portage, [Zebedee] noticed that Joseph seemed to have a far off look in his eyes, or was looking at a distance and presently he, Joseph, stepped between Brothers Cowdery and Coltrin and taking them by the arm said, "Let's take a walk." They went to a place where there was some beautiful grass, and grapevines and swampbeech interlaced. President Joseph Smith then said, "Let us pray." They all three prayed in turn—Joseph, Oliver, Zebedee. Brother Joseph then said, "Now brethren, we will see some visions." Joseph lay down on the ground on his back and stretched out his arms and the two brethren lay on them. The heavens gradually opened, and they saw a golden throne, on a circular foundation, something like a lighthouse, and on the throne were two aged personages, having white hair and clothed in white garments. They were the two most beautiful and perfect specimens of mankind [Coltrin] ever saw. Joseph said, "They are our first parents Adam and Eve." Adam was a large broadshouldered man and Eve, as a woman, was as large in proportion.[104]

The Apostle John

Heber C. Kimball records that soon after the temple in Kirtland, Ohio, was dedicated, on 27 March 1836, the Prophet and several other people saw the ancient apostle John among them.

> When the Prophet Joseph had finished the endowments of the First Presidency, the Twelve and the Presiding Bishops, the First Presidency proceeded to lay hands upon each one of them to seal and confirm the anointing; and at the close of each blessing the whole of the quorums responded to it with a loud shout of Hosanna! Hosanna! etc. While these things were being attended to the beloved disciple John was seen in our midst by the Prophet Joseph, Oliver Cowdery and others.[105]

THE PROPHET'S LEGITIMATE SUCCESSOR

On the very first day he met Brigham Young, Joseph Smith prophesied that the time would come when Young would preside over the Church, though this statement was made in Young's absence.[106]

When Joseph Smith was martyred on 27 June 1844, there were several men who claimed to be his legitimate successor and each attempted to draw the membership of the Church after them. A meeting was held in Nauvoo, Illinois, on 8 August 1844 to discuss the question of who would succeed the Prophet as the leader of the people. Several thousand Saints were in attendance at this important meeting.

Sidney Rigdon made his best case for assuming "guardianship" of the Church and sat down. Then Brigham Young arose and began to speak. At this time a sizable portion of the congregation rose to their feet because they saw and heard something quite extraordinary. Brigham Young was transfigured before them; he looked like Joseph Smith and also spoke with the voice of the Prophet.

Some of the witnesses to this manifestation report that the transformation was so complete that Brigham Young's features, clothing, gestures, manner of reasoning, facial expressions, color of hair, and even physical stature were the same as the Prophet's. Other witnesses stated that even though the form of the Prophet shortly disappeared the voice of the Prophet remained speaking throughout Brigham Young's remarks.[107] George Laub said that Brigham Young's "voice was the voice of Brother Joseph and his face appeared as Joseph's face, and should I not have seen his face but heard his voice I should have declared that it was Joseph."[108] George Q. Cannon summarizes what happened on that day.

> If Joseph had risen from the dead and again spoken in their hearing, the effect could not have been more startling than it was to many present at that meeting. It was the voice of Joseph himself; and not only was it the voice of Joseph which was

> heard; but it seemed in the eyes of the people as though it was the very person of Joseph which stood before them. A more wonderful and miraculous event than was wrought that day in the presence of that congregation we never heard of. The Lord gave His people a testimony that left no room for doubt as to who was the man He had chosen to lead them. They both saw and heard with their natural eyes and ears, and then the words which were uttered came, accompanied by the convincing power of God, to their hearts, and they were filled with the Spirit and with great joy.[109]

The mechanism behind this transfiguration might be discernible in the accounts of several observers. Elizabeth H. Barlow saw the transfiguration as it occurred. "I saw a change come over him—saw him take on the form of Joseph Smith and heard his voice change to that of the Prophet's."[110] She also saw the reverse effects of the manifestation. "Shortly a mist seemed to pass from Brother Brigham's face and there stood Brother Young."[111] Orson Hyde made the interesting comment that "Joseph was there in the person of Brigham, speaking with an angel's voice."[112] Benjamin F. Johnson reports that he saw the form of Joseph Smith "clothed in a sheen of light, covering him to his feet."[113] The account of Edward Hunter may help to clarify what probably occurred during this manifestation. Hunter saw the countenance of Joseph Smith at first but then saw Brigham Young's face "gradually" return to its natural appearance. "Then beside Brother Brigham I saw the Prophet, who turned toward the speaker and smiled."[114]

FIGURE 6. Brigham Young succeeded Joseph Smith as the President of The Church of Jesus Christ of Latter-day Saints. Several different types of divine manifestations confirmed to the Saints that the Lord had chosen Brigham Young as the Prophet's legitimate successor.

To those who did not witness this spiritual event, and who thought that Brigham Young might have been simply trying to imitate the late Prophet's mannerisms, Elder Orson Hyde replied, "I would like to see the man who can mimic another in *stature* who was about *four or five inches higher than himself*."[115]

Those who saw Brigham Young take on the appearance of Joseph Smith include such well-known figures of Church history as Jacob Hamblin, Mosiah Hancock, Zina D. Huntington, Orson Hyde, Benjamin F. Johnson, George Laub, Wandle Mace, Abraham O. Smoot, Helen M. Whitney, and Wilford Woodruff. Even children were eyewitnesses to this miracle.[116] In all, the written accounts of over 100 witnesses to this event are known to exist.[117]

The Lord provided other people with different types of witnesses that Brigham Young was Joseph Smith's legitimate successor. Mariah Pulsipher writes: "The mobocrats were continually seeking Joseph Smith's life. He and Hyrum were finally slain. . . . That fall . . . I prayed . . . thinking of the situation of the Church, having to leave in the spring. I was not asleep. The room shone bright . . . [Then] a voice spoke [saying], 'I am your ministering spirit.'. . . I asked if Joseph Smith died a true prophet. He spoke, 'He died a true prophet; Brigham Young is now the man to lead the Church.'"[118]

Lorenzo Hatch, who was serving as a missionary in the state of Vermont when the martyrdom occurred, learned through spiritual means that Brigham Young was to succeed Joseph Smith. "I received the sad news of this awful affair [the martyrdom] in the town of Bristol, Addison County, Vermont. While I yet had the letter in my hand (this letter was written by my uncle who claimed that Sidney Rigdon was the man to lead the Church) a voice spoke to me and said, 'Brigham Young is the successor of Joseph Smith.'"[119]

Finally, we have the testimony of Elder Orson Hyde that the entire Quorum of the Twelve Apostles heard the voice of God proclaim that Brigham Young was to succeed Joseph Smith.

> In the month of February, 1848, the Twelve Apostles met at Hyde Park, Pottawattamie County, Iowa, where a small branch of the Church was established. . . . We were in prayer and council, communing together; and what took place on that occasion? The voice of God came from on high, and spake to the Council. Every latent feeling was aroused, and every heart melted. What did it say unto us? "Let my servant Brigham step forth and receive the full power of the presiding Priesthood in my Church and Kingdom." This was the voice of the Almighty unto us at Council Bluffs . . . It has been said by some that Brigham was appointed by the people, and not by the voice of God. I do not know that this testimony has

> often, if ever, been given to the masses of the people before; but I am one that was present, and there are others here that were also present on that occasion, and did hear and feel the voice from heaven, and we were filled with the power of God. . . . Men, women, and children came running together where we were, and asked us what was the matter. They said that their houses shook, and the ground trembled, and they did not know but that there was an earthquake. We told them that there was nothing the matter—not to be alarmed; the Lord was only whispering to us a little.[120]

Elder Hyde related this incident, in public, on 7 October 1860. On the same day Brigham Young verified the content of the story. "Brother Hyde, in his remarks, spoke about the voice of God at a certain time. I could tell many incidents relating to that circumstance, which he did not take time to relate. We were in his house, which was some ten or twelve feet square. The houses in the neighborhood shook, or, if they did not, the people thought they did, for they ran together and enquired whether there had been an earthquake. We told them that the voice of God had reached the earth–that they need not be afraid; it was the power of God."[121]

On 21 October 1860, Elder Hyde related this story once again. He "boldly declared that the Lord manifested himself to them, the (12) in council assembled at Hyde's Park, Pottowatomy Nation, on their return from the valley and said with a voice of thunder that made the earth tremble, 'This is my servant Brigham in whom I am well pleased, hear ye him, for he shall be the leader of my people and shall hold the keys of my kingdom as did my servant Joseph Smith.'"[122]

SUMMARY

There is ample evidence to support the belief that Joseph Smith was a genuine prophet of God. He prophesied in the name of the Lord and his prophecies were fulfilled. His visions and visitations were seen and experienced by independent witnesses. He possessed abilities that only God could grant. He exhibited a distinctive physical characteristic that is associated in the Bible with holy men. And finally, his life paralleled, in significant measure, the life of a person who was expected to arise from the tribe of Joseph in the last days and reveal the true religion after a period of apostasy.

NOTES

1. *JD*, 7:289. President Young further stated that "the Lord had his eye upon [Joseph Smith], and upon his father, and upon his father's father, and upon their progenitors clear back to Abraham, and from Abraham to the flood, from the flood to Enoch, and from Enoch to Adam. [The Lord] has watched that family and that blood as it has circulated from its fountain to the birth of that man. [Joseph Smith] was foreordained in eternity to preside over this last dispensation, as much so as . . . Jesus [was foreordained] to be the Savior of the world . . . . Joseph Smith, Jr. was foreordained to come through the loins of Abraham, Isaac, Jacob, Joseph [of Egypt], and so on down through the prophets and apostles" (ibid., 7:289–90). It appears from scriptural and historical texts that Joseph Smith's premortal identity is known. "I will prepare unto my servant Gazelem, a stone, which shall shine forth in darkness unto light," says Alma 37:23. "Gazelam" was the code-name for Joseph Smith in D&C 78:9; 82:11; 104:26, 43 up until late twentieth-century editions of the Doctrine and Covenants. Orson Pratt indicated that Gazelam referred to "a person to whom the Lord had given the Urim and Thummim" (*JD*, 16:156). At the Prophet's funeral, W. W. Phelps stated that Joseph Smith was Gazelam in the premortal spirit world and also spoke of the Prophet's high premortal status. "Surely, as one of the holy ones commissioned by his Father among the royal seventy, when the High Council of Heaven set them apart to come down and 'mutiply and replenish this earth,' he was the 'last,' and who knows but the 'greatest,' for he declared we knew not who he was! So, I may say, as the last is to be first, and the first last in eternal rotation, that Joseph Smith, who was Gazelam in the spirit world, was, and is, and will be in the endless progress of eternity–The Prince of Light. Tis so, and who can dispute it?" (*Brigham Young University Studies*, vol. 23, no. 1, Winter 1983, 12).
2. Joseph Fielding Smith, *Church History and Modern Revelation* (Salt Lake City: Deseret News Press, 1946), 1:4.
3. *HC*, 2:443.
4. *TPJS*, 315.
5. Ibid., 120.
6. "'Messiah' (*mashi'ah*) means 'anointed' and in the Bible can refer either to a king or a priest" (Cecil Roth, ed., *Encyclopaedia Judaica* [New York: Macmillan, 1972], 11:1411).
7. Louis Ginzberg, *The Legends of the Jews* (Philadelphia: The Jewish Publication Society of America, 1948), 5:299, n. 201; Raphael Patai, *The Messiah Texts* (New York: Avon Books, 1979), 165.
8. Charles C. Torrey, "The Messiah Son of Ephraim," *Journal of Biblical Literature*, vol. 66, 1947, 253.
9. See Ginzberg, *The Legends of the Jews*, 2:7.
10. Torrey, "The Messiah Son of Ephraim," 259. The *Messiah ben Joseph* will "arise at the end of days" (Ginzberg, *The Legends of the Jews*, 5:299, n. 201). The *Messiah ben Joseph* will live "in the latter days" (Joseph Klausner, *The Messianic Idea in Israel* [London: George Allen and Unwin Ltd., 1956], 496). In the Hebrew Book of Enoch (*3 Enoch* 45:5), rabbi Ishmael, who looked upon the

veil that was placed before the Holy of Holies of God's heavenly temple, saw "the events of the last times. The end of the course of the present world [was] marked by the appearance of Messiah ben Joseph and Messiah ben David" (Hugo Odeberg, ed., *3 Enoch or The Hebrew Book of Enoch* [New York: Ktav Publishing, 1973], 144).

11. Ginzberg, *The Legends of the Jews*, 5:299, n. 201; Klausner, *The Messianic Idea in Israel*, 483; Patai, *The Messiah Texts*, 165; Solomon Zeitlin, "The Essenes and Messianic Expectations," *Jewish Quarterly Review*, vol. 45, no. 2, October 1954, 107; Torrey, "The Messiah Son of Ephraim," 253; Aharon (Ronald E.) Agus, *The Binding of Isaac and Messiah* (Albany, New York: State University of New York Press, 1988), 208.
12. *Utah Genealogical and Historical Magazine*, vol. 11, July 1920, 107. President Young makes the same claim that Joseph Smith descended from Joseph of Egypt in *JD*, 7:290. The Prophet's descent through Joseph of Egypt is explicitly stated in his patriarchal blessing. The text of this blessing can be found in Archibald F. Bennett, *Saviors on Mount Zion* (Salt Lake City: Deseret News Press, 1950), 68.
13. *JD*, 2:269.
14. Klausner, *The Messianic Idea in Israel*, 497. "Messiah ben Joseph must precede Messiah ben David" (Agus, *The Binding of Isaac and Messiah*, 220). See also Dan Cohn-Sherbok, *The Jewish Messiah* (Edinburgh: T&T Clark, 1997), 47.
15. Klausner, *The Messianic Idea in Israel*, 486; Sigmund Mowinckel, *He That Cometh* (New York: Abingdon Press, 1954), 290; Cohn-Sherbok, *The Jewish Messiah*, xvii.
16. Abraham H. Cannon Journal, 1 January 1892, LDS Church Archives, Salt Lake City, Utah; see also D&C 133:63–64.
17. *TPJS*, 335–36.
18. Parley P. Pratt, *Key to the Science of Theology* (Salt Lake City: Deseret News Press, 1874), 78; see also D&C 77:9, 14.
19. Cohn-Sherbok, *The Jewish Messiah*, 139.
20. Ginzberg, *The Legends of the Jews*, 2:7.
21. Klausner, *The Messianic Idea in Israel*, 498.
22. Patai, *The Messiah Texts*, 170; Julius H. Greenstone, *The Messiah Idea in Jewish History* (Philadelphia: The Jewish Publication Society of America, 1906), 124; The *Messiah ben Joseph* "restores . . . the worship of the temple" (Torrey, "The Messiah Son of Ephraim," 269). The *Messiah ben Joseph* will "reintroduce the worship of the temple" (Isidore Singer, ed., *The Jewish Encyclopedia* [New York: Funk and Wagnalls, 1901], 1:683).
23. For further reading on the restoration of temple worship among the Latter-day Saints, see Matthew B. Brown, *The Gate of Heaven: Insights on the Doctrines and Symbols of the Temple* (American Fork, Utah: Covenant Communications, 1999), 205–47.
24. The *Messiah ben Joseph* "will gather Israelites around him, among whom . . . a part of the ten tribes will be found" (*Jewish Encyclopedia*, 1:683). "A part of the ten tribes will be found among those who will gather about his standard" (ibid., 8:512). The *Messiah ben Joseph* will "gather the remnants of the ten tribes" (Greenstone, *The Messiah Idea in Jewish History*, 211).

25. *Utah Genealogical and Historical Magazine*, vol. 23, October 1932, 175.
26. Torrey, "The Messiah Son of Ephraim," 267, 269. The *Messiah ben Joseph* is envisioned as "the first commander of the army of Israel" (Patai, *The Messiah Texts*, 165).
27. See *HC*, 4:309–10.
28. The *Messiah ben Joseph* will "establish his own dominion" (*Jewish Encyclopedia*, 1:683); he will "set up his own dominion" (ibid., 8:511).
29. William Clayton Journal, 1 January 1845, cited in *BYUS*, vol. 20, no. 3, Spring 1980, 268; cf. Matthew 21:1–11; Mark 11:1–10; John 12:12–15.
30. Diary of George A. Smith, 9 May 1844, cited in *BYUS*, vol. 8, no. 2, Winter 1968, 213.
31. Annie Taylor Hyde Notebook, 64, cited in *BYUS*, vol. 20, no. 2, Winter 1980, 186.
32. *HC*, 6:568–69. Compare this statement with Joseph Smith's own words: "I calculate to be one of the instruments of setting up the kingdom of Daniel by the word of the Lord" (*TPJS*, 366).
33. There is some evidence that Joseph Smith had a legitimate right to rule as a king over Israel. According to Elder Heber C. Kimball, the Prophet was "near kindred to . . . Jesus Christ" because he shared the same "lineage" (*JD*, 4:248). This would mean that Joseph Smith descended partly through the royal line of Jesse in the tribe of Judah. Several LDS authors have stated their belief that Joseph Smith is the "descendant of Jesse, as well as of Joseph," that is mentioned in D&C 113:5–6 (see George A. Horton, Jr., "Prophecies in the Bible about Joseph Smith," *Ensign*, January 1989, 22; Hoyt W. Brewster, Jr., *Doctrine and Covenants Encyclopedia* [Salt Lake City: Bookcraft, 1988], 477, 479–80; Kent P. Jackson, "Revelations Concerning Isaiah," in Robert L. Millet and Kent P. Jackson, eds., *Studies in Scripture: Volume One, The Doctrine and Covenants* [Salt Lake City: Randall Book, 1984], 330–33; Victor L. Ludlow, *Isaiah: Prophet, Seer, and Poet* [Salt Lake City: Deseret Book, 1982], 170–74).
34. The *Messiah ben Joseph* "stands heroically in 'battle' where it is *clear beforehand* that death *must* be the result. In other words, his death is a martyrdom" (Agus, *The Binding of Isaac and Messiah*, 209, emphasis in original).
35. *HC*, 4:537, emphasis added.
36. *JD*, 15:185.
37. Ibid., 20:174–75.
38. JS–H 1:17.
39. Ibid.
40. *JD*, 21:94. On 29 August 1972 Elder Mark E. Peterson asked the Saints at a Conference in Mexico City: "What power did Adam bring back to Joseph Smith? . . . Adam brought the keys of the First Presidency. Joseph Smith received the keys of the First Presidency from Adam, who came back and visited him" (Mexico Area Conference Report, August 1972, 61; cf. *TPJS*, 157–58, 169).
41. Merle Graffam, ed., *Salt Lake School of the Prophets Minute Book: 1883* (Salt Lake City: Pioneer Press, 1992), 64.
42. *JD*, 21:94.
43. Ibid., 21:65, 94. Elder Bruce R. McConkie believed that the angel Raphael, mentioned in D&C 128:21, may have been the patriarch Enoch (see Bruce R. McConkie, *Mormon Doctrine*, 2d ed. [Salt Lake City: Bookcraft, 1966], 618).

44. *JD*, 21:94; 23:48. Joseph Fielding Smith identified the "Elias" of D&C 110:12 as Noah (Joseph Fielding Smith, *Answers to Gospel Questions* [Salt Lake City: Deseret Book, 1975], 3:138–41).
45. *JD*, 21:94; 18:326; 23:48.
46. Ibid., 21:94.
47. Ibid., 21:94.
48. D&C 110:11.
49. Ibid., 110:13–16.
50. JS–H 1:68–72.
51. D&C 27:12.
52. Ibid.
53. Ibid.
54. *JD*, 16:266.
55. Ibid., 17:374; 16:266; Letter, Orson Pratt to John Christensen, 11 March 1876, Orson Pratt letter box, LDS Church Archives, Salt Lake City, Utah.
56. *JD*, 17:374.
57. JS–H 1:29–49. Historical records indicate that the angel Moroni appeared to the Prophet Joseph Smith on at least twenty-two different occasions (see H. Donl Peterson, "Moroni: Joseph Smith's Tutor," *Ensign*, January 1992, 22–29). For articles explaining what Moroni taught Joseph Smith during some of his visits see Kent P. Jackson, "Moroni's Message to Joseph Smith," *Ensign*, August 1990, 13–16; W. Jeffrey Marsh, "Training from the Old Testament: Moroni's Lessons for a Prophet," *Ensign*, August 1998, 10–17.
58. Letter, Orson Pratt to John Christensen, 11 March 1876, Orson Pratt letter box, LDS Church Archives, Salt Lake City, Utah.
59. See *HC*, 1:106.
60. "It was during the time we lived at the Brick Store that Joseph received the revelation pertaining to celestial marriage; also concerning the ordinances of the House of the Lord. He had been strictly charged by the angel who committed these precious things into his keeping that he should only reveal them to such persons as were pure, full of integrity to the truth, and worthy to be entrusted with divine messages" (*Woman's Exponent*, vol. 7, no. 14, 15 December 1878, 105). Elder Parley P. Pratt asked: "Who instructed [Joseph Smith] in the mysteries of the kingdom, and in all things pertaining to Priesthood, law, philosophy, sacred architecture, ordinances, sealings, anointings, baptisms for the dead, and in the mysteries of the first, second, and third heavens, many of which are unlawful to utter? Angels and spirits from the eternal worlds" (*JD*, 2:44).
61. See E. Dale LeBaron, *Benjamin F. Johnson: Friend to the Prophets* (Provo, Utah: Benjamin F. Johnson Family Organization, 1997), 227.
62. See Milton V. Backman, Jr., *Joseph Smith's First Vision*, 2d ed. (Salt Lake City: Bookcraft, 1980), 159.
63. See *HC*, 2:428.
64. Parley P. Pratt, *Autobiography of Parley P. Pratt*, ed., Parley P. Pratt, Jr. (Salt Lake City: Deseret Book, 1985), 48.

65. *Ensign of Liberty of the Church of Christ*, vol. 1, August 1849, Kirtland, Ohio, 98–99.
66. See H. Clay Gorton, *Language of the Lord* (Bountiful, Utah: Horizon Publishers, 1993); Charles F. King, Doctrine and Covenants*: Completely Structured Including Chiasmus* (Lindon, Utah: Alexander's Digital Printing, 2000); D. Lynn Johnson, "The Word of Wisdom," *This People*, Spring 1995, 49–54, 56. For further reading see John W. Welch, "Chiasmus in the Book of Mormon," *New Era*, February 1972, 6–11.
67. B. H. Roberts, *A Comprehensive History of the Church*, 2:183–89.
68. *Young Woman's Journal*, vol. 17, no. 12, December 1906, 545. A second witness to this prophetic event can be found on page 544 of this same source.
69. *Early Scenes in Church History: Eighth Book in the Faith-Promoting Series* (Salt Lake City: Juvenile Instructor Office, 1882), 80.
70. *HC*, 2:80.
71. Ibid., 2:107.
72. Ibid., 2:114.
73. Ibid., 3:200–201.
74. Andrew Jenson, *Latter-day Saint Biographical Encyclopedia* (Salt Lake City: Deseret News Press, 1901), 3:667.
75. *HC*, 6:619.
76. *Millennial Star*, vol. 25, no. 9, 28 February 1863, 135.
77. Edwin F. Parry, comp., *Stories about Joseph Smith the Prophet* (Salt Lake City: Deseret News Press, 1934), 98, 100.
78. *Millennial Star*, vol. 54, no. 38, 19 September 1892, 605.
79. *Fragments of Experience: Sixth Book of the Faith-Promoting Series* (Salt Lake City: Juvenile Instructor Office, 1882), 44.
80. *HC*, 5:85.
81. *JD*, 9:89.
82. *Labors in the Vineyard: Twelfth Book of the Faith-Promoting Series* (Salt Lake City: Juvenile Instructor Office, 1884), 67.
83. See Brian H. Stuy, ed., *Collected Discourses* (Burbank, California: B. H. S. Publishing, 1987), 2:383; 4:291; 5:188, 318.
84. *Young Woman's Journal*, vol. 2, no. 3, December 1890, 125.
85. *HC*, 5:86, ftnt.
86. *Young Woman's Journal*, vol. 16, no. 12, December 1905, 556–57.
87. Hyrum L. Andrus and Helen M. Andrus, *They Knew the Prophet* (Salt Lake City: Deseret Book, 1999), 48.
88. "History of Oliver B. Huntington," typescript, 49–50, Harold B. Lee Library, Special Collections, Brigham Young University, Provo, Utah.
89. *Early Scenes in Church History: Eighth Book in the Faith-Promoting Series* (Salt Lake City: Juvenile Instructor Office, 1882), 81.

90. Lyndon W. Cook, ed., *David Whitmer Interviews: A Restoration Witness* (Orem, Utah: Grandin Book, 1991), 181–82. Speaking of the same incident Whitmer "related many very interesting items [including one] of seeing one of the Nephites in company with the Prophet and Oliver, when Joseph's countenance became almost transparent" (ibid., 17). And again: "All felt very strange concerning this personage and the Prophet was besought to enquire of the Lord concerning him. Shortly afterwards . . . the Prophet looked very white but with a heavenly appearance" (ibid., 216).
91. Joseph G. Stevenson, ed., *Autobiography of Edward Stevenson 1820–1897* (Provo, Utah: Stevenson's Genealogical Center, 1986), 7.
92. *JD*, 7:176.
93. *Millennial Star*, vol. 36, no. 32, 11 August 1874, 498.
94. Ibid., vol. 40, no. 49, 9 December 1878, 772.
95. Joel Tiffany, "Mormonism–No. II," *Tiffany's Monthly*, vol. 5, June 1859, 164.
96. *HC*, 1:146, ftnt.
97. *Contributor*, vol. 6, no. 4, January 1885, 125.
98. *JD*, 5:215–16.
99. Letter, 1853, Orson Pratt to Parley P. Pratt, cited in Truman G. Madsen, *Joseph Smith the Prophet* (Salt Lake City: Bookcraft, 1989),107.
100. See *Church News*, 23 December 1984, 14. Elder Parley P. Pratt explained the importance of lineage, election, and heirship in this manner. "The prophets, kings, priests, patriarchs, apostles, and even Jesus Christ, were included in the election of Abraham, and of his seed, as manifested to him in an eternal covenant. . . . In the lineage of Abraham, Isaac, and Jacob, according to the flesh, was held the right of heirship to the keys of the Priesthood for the blessings and for the salvation of all nations. From this lineage sprang the prophets, John the Baptist, Jesus, and the apostles; and from this lineage sprang the great Prophet and restorer in modern times, and the apostles who hold the keys under his hand" (*JD*, 1:258, 261).
101. *Juvenile Instructor*, vol. 27, no. 10, 15 May 1892, 303–04.
102. Graffam, ed., *Salt Lake School of the Prophets Minute Book: 1883*, 54–55.
103. Letter, Truman O. Angell to John Taylor, 11 March 1885, John Taylor Papers, LDS Church Archives, Salt Lake City, Utah, cited in *Improvement Era*, October 1942, 630.
104. Graffam, ed., *Salt Lake School of the Prophets Minute Book: 1883*, 64. In a first-person recital of this vision on pages 102–03 of this same source, Coltrin adds, "Their heads were white as snow and their faces shown with immortal youth."
105. Orson F. Whitney, *Life of Heber C. Kimball*, 2d ed. (Salt Lake City: Stevens and Wallis, 1945), 91–92.
106. *Millennial Star*, vol. 25, no. 28, 11 July 1863, 439.
107. See the accounts gathered in Lynne W. Jorgensen and BYU Studies Staff, "The Mantle of the Prophet Joseph Passes to Brother Brigham: A Collective Spiritual Witness," *BYUS*, vol. 36, no. 4, 1996–97, 125–204.

108. George Laub Journal, 1845–46, cited in *BYUS*, vol. 18, no. 2, Winter 1978, 166.
109. *Juvenile Instructor*, vol. 5, no. 22, 29 October 1870, 174–75.
110. Pamela B. Thompson, "Biography of Elizabeth Haven Barlow," 6, Family History Library Archives, cited in Ora H. Barlow, *The Israel Barlow Story and Mormon Mores* (Salt Lake City: Ora H. Barlow, 1968), 204–05.
111. Letter, Eliza Ann Haven Westover to her son, 1918, 4, LDS Church Archives, Salt Lake City, Utah. George Morris records the reverse effect of the transfiguration as well. "The first thing I saw was Joseph—as plain as I ever saw him in my life—and the first words he uttered were, 'Right here is the authority to lead this Church' and at the same time striking his hand upon his bosom. And after uttering another sentence or two—it was Brigham Young" (George Morris, "Life Story of George Morris of the Seventeenth Ward, Salt Lake," holograph, unpaged, microfilm, Family History Library Archives). Edward Hunter also saw the reverse effect. "I heard a voice–the Prophet's voice as natural and true as I ever heard it. I raised up quickly, fully expecting to see the Prophet, and I did. There he stood and gradually changed to that of Brother Brigham, but the voice was not Brother Brigham's. It was still the Prophet's" (Janath R. Cannon, ed., *Edward Hunter: Faithful Steward* [n. p.: Mrs. William E. Hunter, 1970], 79).
112. *Deseret News Semi-Weekly*, vol. 4, no. 82, 16 November 1869, 2.
113. Letter, Benjamin F. Johnson to George S. Gibbs, 1903, LDS Church Archives, Salt Lake City, Utah.
114. Cannon, ed., *Edward Hunter: Faithful Steward*, 79.
115. *Deseret News Semi-Weekly*, vol. 4, no. 82, 16 November 1869, 2, emphasis in original.
116. See the account in Aurelia S. Rogers, *Life Sketches of Orson Spencer and Others* (Salt Lake City: George Q. Cannon and Sons, 1898), 331–32.
117. Brigham Young reports that after learning of Joseph Smith's death he returned to Nauvoo and there learned "by visions of the Spirit" that a new First Presidency would be chosen from among the Quorum of the Twelve Apostles (Miscellaneous Minutes, 12 February 1849, Brigham Young Collection, LDS Church Archives, Salt Lake City, Utah). For further reading on the succession of Brigham Young as President of the LDS Church see Ronald K. Esplin, "Joseph, Brigham and the Twelve: A Succession of Continuity," *BYUS*, vol. 21, no. 3, Summer 1981, 301–41.
118. Mariah Pulsipher, "Autobiography," cited in Milton V. Backman, Jr. and Keith W. Perkins, eds., *Writings of Early Latter-day Saints and Their Contemporaries: A Database Collection, Excerpts*, 2d ed. (Provo, Utah: BYU Religious Studies Center, 1996), 180.
119. Lorenzo Hill Hatch Journal, typescript, 282, cited in *BYUS*, vol. 36, no. 4, 1996–97, 149.
120. *JD*, 8:233–34.
121. Ibid., 8:196.
122. Robert G. Cleland and Juanita Brooks, eds., *A Mormon Chronicle: The Diaries of John D. Lee 1848–1876* (Salt Lake City: University of Utah Press, 1983), 1:278; cf. Matthew 3:17; John 12:29; Revelation 14:2; 2 Samuel 22:14; Job 37:5.

CHAPTER 3

The Restoration of the Church

It is a fundamental doctrine of the LDS faith that during the Savior's mortal ministry He established a formal Church with authoritative officers, specific ordinances, and set practices. The LDS Church proclaims it is an authentic, and divinely sanctioned, restoration of the Savior's ancient organization. The purpose of this chapter is to demonstrate that The Church of Jesus Christ of Latter-day Saints does have the same authority structure, organization, practices, and ordinances as the early Christian Church, thus qualifying it as a genuine restoration.

The apostle Paul taught that Jesus Christ is "the same yesterday, and today, and forever" (Hebrews 13:8). This statement logically applies to His Church and His gospel; they never change, even though countless Christian denominations put forward endless variations of them. Sidney Rigdon once observed that "whatever the gospel was, it now is, and ever will be . . . [I]t has not [changed] nor will it change; its laws are the same; its ordinances are the same; its institutions are the same; its commands are the same, and its regulations are the same."[1] In applying this principle to the Restoration, the Prophet Joseph Smith said that "all things [that were] had under the authority of the Priesthood at any former period shall be had again, bringing to pass the restoration spoken of by the mouth of all the holy prophets."[2]

ORGANIZATION

In the sixth Article of Faith Joseph Smith declared that Latter-day Saints "believe in the same organization that existed in the Primitive Church." There are some sectarian Christians, however, who deny that Jesus Christ established a formal ecclesiastical organization during His mortal ministry. To admit to such would be to agree that there was only one Church that was sanctioned and recognized by Him. The position that has been taken by the Latter-day Saints on this issue can be sustained by answering a series of simple questions.

Did the Christians of Christ's day belong to a formal "Church" organization?

New Testament texts clearly indicate that they did. Ephesians 1:17–22, for instance, informs us that God the Father assigned Jesus Christ to be the "head" of "the church [*ekklēsia*]." In Ephesians 5:23 we find something similar: "Christ is the head of the church [*ekklēsias*]." And, yet again, we are told in Colossians 1:18 that Christ "is the head of . . . the church [*ekklēsias*]." Thus, we find the Savior referring to "my church [*ekklēsian*]" in Matthew 16:18. New Testament scholars admit that, at least in the case of Matthew 16:18, "the term *ekklēsia* certainly means . . . the Church as a visible structure and society, having authoritative officials and authoritative functions."[3] In Acts 2:47 it is noted that "the Lord added to the church [*ekklēsia*] daily." Finally, the community of Saints is referred to as "the church of God" in Acts 20:28; Galatians 1:13; 1 Corinthians 10:32; 11:22; and 15:9.

Some may argue that there was no formal Church organization in New Testament times since the King James translation of Luke 17:21 says that the "kingdom of God is within you." The Joseph Smith Translation of this verse, however, indicates that the text has been tampered with and should read "the kingdom of God has already come unto you." In the footnotes of the LDS edition of the King James Bible, it is stated: "Many translations read 'among' because the pronoun 'you' is plural here in Greek." Modern translations that use the words "among you" include the Jerusalem Bible, New English Bible, New American Bible, New Revised Standard Version, and the New Living Translation. The Contemporary English Version reads "here with you." The New American Standard Bible has "in your midst." And finally, the Revised Standard Version reads "in the midst of you."

Did the early Christian leaders tolerate a diversity of doctrinal beliefs within Christ's Church?

No, they did not. As Paul so plainly taught, there is only "*one* faith" (Ephesians 4:5, emphasis added) and the Saints were continually admonished by the Lord's authorized representatives to be "all of *one* mind" (1 Peter 3:8, emphasis added; see also 2 Corinthians 13:11; Philippians 1:27; 2:2). Since "God is not the author of confusion" (1 Corinthians 14:33), early Church officials rejected, and ejected, those who espoused heretical views (see Titus 3:10).

Was the early Christian Church regulated by a code of conduct?

Yes, as is made clear in 1 Timothy 3:15. "But I tarry long," said the apostle Paul, "that ye mayest know how thou oughtest to behave [*anastrephesthai*, conduct] thyself in . . . the church [*ekklēsia*] of the living God."

Was the early Christian Church governed and directed by a formal group of leaders from a central location?

Yes, this was the case. Paul and Timothy "went through the cities, [and] they delivered [unto] them the decrees [*dogmata*, laws, authoritative judgments] . . . that were ordained of the *apostles and elders* which were at *Jerusalem*. And so were the churches established in the faith" (Acts 16:4–5, emphasis added). Once, when a serious doctrinal disputation arose among some of Christ's disciples, it was determined that Paul and Barnabas "should go up to *Jerusalem* unto the *apostles and elders* about this question. . . . And when they were come to *Jerusalem*, they were received of the church [*ekklēsias*], and of the *apostles and elders*" (Acts 15:2, 4, emphasis added). "Then pleased it the *apostles and elders*, with the whole church [*ekklēsia*], to send chosen men," says Acts 15:22 (emphasis added). It was God, says 1 Corinthians 12:28, who placed an hierarchy of "governments" [*kubernēseis*, guides] in the early Christian Church.

AUTHORITY AND OFFICES

"We believe," taught Joseph Smith in the fifth Article of Faith, "that a man must be called of God, by prophecy, and by the laying on of hands by those who are in authority, to preach the gospel and administer in the ordinances thereof." On another occasion the Prophet said: "We believe that no man can administer salvation through the gospel, to the souls of men, in the name of Jesus Christ, except he is authorized from God, by revelation, or by being ordained by someone whom God hath sent by revelation."[4] In other words, since "God is not the author of confusion" (1 Corinthians 14:33), He has established an orderly pattern whereby His legitimate priesthood authority is to be distributed among mortals and utilized by them.

Power and Authority

In Acts 10:38, it is stated that "God anointed Jesus of Nazareth with the Holy Ghost and with power [*dunamei*]." The basic Greek verb for "anoint" [*chriō*] means "to smear or rub with oil, i.e., (by implication) to consecrate to an office."[5] This is precisely the same procedure that was employed by the ancient Israelites when they conferred the Priesthood upon selected individuals (see Exodus 40:13–15). The implication of Acts 10:38, then, is that God the Father bestowed the Priesthood upon His Son Jesus Christ. This is confirmed explicitly by the apostle Paul in Hebrews 7:21 where he declares that God the Father said unto the Savior: "The Lord sware and will not repent, 'Thou art a priest forever after the order of Melchizedek.'"

It is recorded throughout the New Testament that Jesus Christ was able to perform two tasks with the power or *dunamis* that his Father had bestowed upon him–heal and command. The power to heal is more easily perceived by correcting several mistranslated biblical texts. First, we have the statement in Luke 6:19 that a "whole multitude sought to touch him [Christ]: for there went virtue [*dunamis*, power] out of him, and healed them all." This miraculous, and instantaneous, healing force is also mentioned in the story of the woman who had suffered from an issue of blood for twelve years.

> And a woman having an issue of blood twelve years, which had spent all her [savings] upon physicians, neither could be healed [by] any, came behind him [Christ], and touched the border of his garment: and immediately her issue of blood [ceased].
>
> And Jesus said, "Who touched me?" When all denied, Peter and they that were with him said, "Master, the multitude throng thee and press thee, and sayest thou, Who touched me?"
>
> And Jesus said, "Somebody hath touched me: for I perceive that virtue [*dunamin,* power] is gone out of me."
>
> And when the woman saw that she was not hid, she came trembling, and falling down before him, she declared unto him before all the people for what cause she had touched him, and how she was healed immediately.
>
> And he said unto her, "Daughter, be of good [cheer]: thy faith hath made thee whole; go in peace" (Luke 8:43–48; see also Mark 5:25–34).

Christ's power to issue commands, and be obeyed, is evidenced in a story that took place in a city of Galilee called Capernaum. In a synagogue of that city, the Savior cast an evil spirit out of a man. Those who witnessed this event were amazed and commented among themselves saying: "with authority [*exousia*] and power [*dunamei*] he commandeth the unclean spirits, and they come out" (Luke 4:36; see also Mark 1:27).

Jesus Christ bestowed this very same God-given power and authority upon His twelve apostles so that they could act in his name. Thus, in Luke 9:1 we read that the Lord "called his twelve disciples together, and gave them power [*dunamin*] and authority [*exousian*] over all devils, and to cure diseases" (see also Matthew 10:1; Mark 6:7). In another passage of the Bible we read that "Stephen, [being] full of faith and power [*dunameōs*], did great wonders and miracles among the people" (Acts 6:8).

How was authority transmitted among the early Christian Saints? There are two excellent examples found in the book of Acts. In Acts 6:5–6 it is stated that the apostles transmitted authority to seven men to conduct official Church business by laying their hands upon them. Likewise, in Acts 13:1–3 it is said that when the Holy Ghost revealed that Paul and Barnabas were to serve as missionaries they were set apart to their callings by the laying on of hands (cf. Numbers 8:9–11; 27:18–23; Deuteronomy 34:9). The Christians who lived shortly after the apostolic age continued the practice of ordaining Church officials by the laying on of hands.[6] In the *Apostolic Constitutions*, a Christian document originating in the fourth century A.D. but which may contain much older material, it is stated that among the functions "belonging to the priesthood . . . [is] the laying on of hands. . . . [But] 'no one taketh this honor to himself, but he that is called of God' [Hebrews 5:4]. For such sacred [functions] are conferred by the laying on of the hands of the bishop."[7]

THE AARONIC AND MELCHIZEDEK PRIESTHOOD ORDERS

Joseph Smith learned about the holy Priesthood of God during the first visit of the angel Moroni on the night of 21 September 1823. During this visitation, Joseph Smith was told of a future visit by Elijah the prophet who would somehow "*reveal* . . . the Priesthood" unto him (D&C 2:1–3, emphasis added).[8] Oliver Cowdery reports that the very next morning the angel Moroni informed the Prophet of the restoration of the Aaronic and Melchizedek Priesthoods, saying, "When [the golden plates] are interpreted the Lord will give the holy priesthood to some, and they shall begin to proclaim this gospel and baptize by water, and after that they shall have power to give the Holy Ghost by the laying on of their hands."[9]

On 18 December 1833, Joseph Smith gave Oliver Cowdery a patriarchal blessing in which he mentioned a fascinating prophecy that was uttered by Joseph of Egypt "in ancient days." According to this prophecy, reports Joseph Smith, "the seer of the last days and the scribe that should sit with him" would be ordained "by the hands of the angel in *the bush*" unto the "lesser priesthood" and afterwards to the "holy priesthood" by other angels of God.[10] Cowdery remarks: "we diligently sought for the . . . authority of the holy priesthood . . . Therefore we repaired to the woods, even as our father Joseph [of Egypt] said we should, that is, to *the bush*, and called upon the name of the Lord."[11]

How did Joseph and Oliver learn of this prophecy? Even though there are prophecies from Joseph of Egypt found in JST Genesis 50 and 2 Nephi 3 that mention the latter-day "seer," they do not speak of the "scribe" nor of the anticipated priesthood conferrals. It may be, therefore, that a more complete version of this prophecy was transcribed somewhere in the lost 116 pages of the Book of Mormon, also known as the Book of Lehi.[12] The Joseph of Egypt prophecies that are recorded in 2 Nephi 3:3–24 are reported by Lehi, but Nephi states that he only transcribed an abridged version of Lehi's book (see 1 Nephi 1:17). Since the prophecies of Joseph of Egypt, which were written on the Brass Plates, were quite extensive (see 2 Nephi 4:2), it would probably be safe to assume that only a small portion of them appear in current Book of Mormon texts.

In Doctrine and Covenants section 27 verses 7–8 and 12–13, the Lord confirms that he "sent" John the Baptist to Joseph Smith and Oliver Cowdery to "ordain" them to "the first priesthood" so that they "might be called and ordained even as Aaron." The Lord also confirms in this passage that he "sent" Peter, James, and John to ordain Joseph and Oliver as apostles and to commit unto them the keys of the kingdom of God.

Aaronic Order

The Aaronic order of the Holy Priesthood was restored to the earth in the following manner. While engaged in prayer on 15 May 1829, Joseph Smith and Oliver Cowdery suddenly heard the voice of Jesus Christ speak a message of peace unto them. After this message had been delivered, an angel of God descended in a cloud of light, laid his hands upon the Prophet's head and Oliver's head, in succession, and ordained them priests after the order of Aaron. The angel, who identified himself as John the Baptist, stated that the Priesthood he had given unto them did not have the power to bestow the gift of the Holy Ghost by the laying on of hands. But John also assured Joseph and Oliver that if they continued faithful, they would eventually receive the Melchizedek Priesthood, which possessed that additional power. The angel then commanded Joseph and Oliver to baptize each other and ordain each other to the Aaronic Priesthood by the laying on of hands.[13]

Sectarian Christians may take Hebrews 7:11–12 to mean that the Aaronic Priesthood was abolished among the early followers of Jesus Christ. This passage reads: "For the priesthood being changed [*metatithemēnes*], there is made of necessity a change [*metathesis*, disestablishment] also in the law." But the Greek verb translated in this passage as "changed" can be rendered as "to place differently."[14] Hebrews 7:11–12 could thus be interpreted as saying that since nobody could achieve "perfection" under "the order of Aaron" that Priesthood order took second place to "the order of Melchizedek" which *could* bring about the Saints' perfection.

It is hard to imagine that the earliest Christians (who were mostly Israelites) would abolish the Aaronic Priesthood since the God of Israel plainly stated that it was "an everlasting priesthood" (Exodus 40:15; Numbers 25:13). The continuation of the Aaronic Priesthood among the early Christians makes good sense when one considers that some ancient sources acknowledge there were "Levites" serving in the Church.[15] Of special interest to Latter-day Saints is the fact that the "deacons" were identified as the early Christian "Levites."[16]

In an apocryphal source known as the *Testament of Levi*,[17] the head of the tribe of Levi is told by an angel of God: "Levi, your posterity shall be divided into three offices." This may be a correspondence to the three offices of the Aaronic, or Levitical, Priesthood that Latter-day Saints are familiar with (deacons, teachers, priests).

Melchizedek Order

The Melchizedek Priesthood was conferred upon Joseph Smith and Oliver Cowdery by the ancient apostles Peter, James, and John on the banks of the Susquehanna river—somewhere between Colesville, New York, and Harmony, Pennsylvania. Some LDS scholars believe this restoration occurred between 16 May and 28 May 1829.[18] Oliver Cowdery testified: "I was . . . present with Joseph [Smith] when the Melchizedek Priesthood was conferred by the holy angels of God."[19] Cowdery also told Book of Mormon witness David Whitmer that Peter, James, and

John physically "laid their hands" on his head "and conferred the holy Melchizedek Priesthood" upon him.[20] During this manifestation Peter, James, and John ordained Joseph Smith and Oliver Cowdery as apostles of the Lord Jesus Christ (see D&C 27:12).

Joseph Smith taught that "all the prophets had the Melchizedek Priesthood."[21] Brigham Young likewise taught that the Melchizedek Priesthood "has been on the earth at various times. Adam had it, Seth had it, Enoch had it, Noah had it, Abraham and Lot had it, and it was handed down to the days of the prophets, long after the days of the ancients."[22] It is revealed in the Joseph Smith Translation of Hebrews 7:3 that early Christians were well aware of the Melchizedek Priesthood order. Is there any other evidence of a Melchizedek Priesthood order among the Saints of the New Testament? Yes, there is. Jesus Christ is designated as a "high priest after the *order* of Melchizedek" in Hebrews 5:6, 10; 6:20; 7:11, 17, 21. The word that is translated in all of these verses as "order" [*taxin*] is the same Greek word used in Hebrews 7:11 to speak of the "order of Aaron," a word that means "fixed succession."[23] Further evidence that the early Saints held the Melchizedek Priesthood can be seen in Peter's remarks in 1 Peter 2:9 where the chief apostle says they possessed a "royal priesthood." What Priesthood was connected with royalty in ancient Israel? The Melchizedek Priesthood (see Psalms 110:4). Finally, we should note that Melchizedek is identified as both a king and priest "of the most high God" in Genesis 14:18. What did Jesus Christ make his worthy followers? The apostle John states that the Savior made the Saints "kings and priests unto God" (Revelation 1:6; 5:10), thus intimating that they held the Melchizedek Priesthood.

Sectarian Christians, who hold to the nebulous notion of a "priesthood of all believers," often try to assert that when it is said in Hebrews 7:24 that Jesus Christ had an "unchangeable" priesthood, it really means that His priesthood was "untransferrable." Thus, in their view, the Melchizedek Priesthood was only held by the Savior. But some New Testament scholars disagree with this wrenched interpretation. The Greek word translated in Hebrews 7:24 as "unchangeable" is *aparabaton*. The idea that it means "'that [which] doth not pass from one to another' is not to be preferred. This active meaning is not only untenable, and contrary to the constant usage of the word, but does not adequately fit with either the preceding or the succeeding context" of Hebrews 7:24.[24]

Is there any evidence of the existence of a Melchizedek Priesthood order in the Old Testament? Yes, there is. There are several examples of people, living after the time of Moses, who were not from of the tribe of Levi or from among the "sons of Aaron" but who nevertheless performed priestly functions. First, there is Samuel (see 1 Samuel 7:9–10). Even though he was a member of the tribe of Levi, Samuel came through the line of Kohath (see 1 Chronicles 6:33–38), not through the priestly line of the sons of Aaron. Another example is seen in Ezra 8:23–24, where we read that there were "separated twelve of the chief of the priests," including Sherebiah and Hashabiah. These two priests were from the tribe of Levi; but since they were descendants of Merari (see Ezra 8:18–19), they were not qualified to be priests of the Aaronic order. That honor was only given, in accordance with divine decree, to the sons of Aaron (see Exodus 29:4–9). Next, there is Gideon (see Judges 6:24–28), who was a member of the tribe of Manasseh (see Judges 6:11–15). Then we read that king David, who came from the tribe of Judah, performed priestly functions (see 2 Samuel 6:12–18; 1 Chronicles 16:2–3). Solomon, who succeeded his father David as king of Israel, also performed priestly duties even though he was also of the tribe of Judah (see 1 Kings 8; 1 Chronicles 6–7). In the apocryphal work known as the *Odes of Solomon*,[25] King Solomon is represented as saying, "I am a priest of the Lord, and to Him I serve as a priest." In the cases of David and Solomon, their connection to the Melchizedek Priesthood is made explicit in Psalms 110, which is widely held by biblical scholars to be a royal coronation text. In verse four the king is told: "The Lord hath sworn, and will not repent, 'Thou art a priest forever after the order of Melchizedek.'"

OFFICES

In the sixth Article of Faith, it is stated that Latter-day Saints "believe in the same organization that existed in the Primitive Church, namely, apostles, prophets, pastors, teachers, evangelists, and so forth." Since it was God Himself who set these Priesthood offices within His Church (see 1 Corinthians 12:28), it follows that any denomination lacking them could not possibly qualify as God's true Church.

In the section below, the reader will find a New Testament reference for each priesthood office and then another reference for that same office as it exists in the restored Church. This will serve to demonstrate that the priesthood structure of The Church of Jesus Christ of Latter-day Saints follows the divine pattern.

Deacon: (Philippians 1:1; D&C 84:30)

The office of deacon appears to have its equivalent in the Old Testament. The single Hebrew word translated as "thine exactors" in Isaiah 60:17 is *nog^{e}sayik*. In reading from the Greek Septuagint, Clement of Rome translated the Greek equivalent of *nog^{e}sayik* as "deacons."[26] This tends to indicate that an office equivalent to that of "deacon" was had among the ancient Israelites. The Nethinim may qualify as the Old Testament "deacons" (see 1 Chronicles 9:2; Ezra 2:43; 7:7, 24; Nehemiah 10:28; 11:3). The Nethinim were "appointed for the service of the Levites" (Ezra 8:20). Thus, their standing would have been a step below that of the Levites. The Levites, in turn, were a step below the Priests. The correspondence between the Old Testament and LDS Aaronic Priesthood offices would thus run: Nethinim, Levite, Priest / Deacon, Teacher, Priest.

In the LDS Church, the deacons administer the emblems of the sacrament to the assembled Saints (see D&C 20:57–60).[27] Such was also the case among the early Christians. Justin Martyr reports: "Those who are called by us 'deacons' give to each of those present a portion of the . . . bread and wine . . . and they carry it away to those who are absent."[28]

Teacher: (Ephesians 4:11; D&C 84:30)

In 1 Corinthians 12:28, it is stated that God set the office of teacher in His Church. Notice that the Levites in Old Testament times served in the capacity of teachers (see 2 Chronicles 30:22; 35:3; Nehemiah 8:9).

Priest: (Acts 6:7; D&C 84:111)

In Acts 6:7, we read that "a great company of the priests were obedient to the faith." This passage of scripture clearly indicates that priests of the Aaronic order became members of the Christian Church. Did they lose their standing in the priesthood once they had joined with the followers of Jesus Christ? There is no New Testament scripture indicating that this was the case. In fact, the Lord states in the book of Exodus that the office of the Aaronic priest is meant to be "perpetual" (Exodus 29:9). Hence, we should not be surprised to find that "priests" are mentioned in an early Christian document that lists "those who attend upon the Church."[29]

Elder: (Acts 14:23; D&C 107:7)

The office of "elder" was known among the ancient Israelites (see Exodus 3:16; Deuteronomy 31:9; Joshua 8:33). The Talmud (*Yoma* 28b) claims that elders even existed as an institution in the time of Abraham.[30]

Seventy: (Luke 10:1; D&C 107:25)

The office of Seventy was known among the ancient Israelites (see Exodus 24:1, 9; Numbers 11:16; Ezekiel 8:11).

High Priest: (Hebrews 5:10; D&C 107:10)

The "high priest" of the Aaronic order could more properly be referred to as the presiding priest or "chief priest" (Ezra 7:5). In the LDS Church a "high priest" must hold the Melchizedek Priesthood. This is in accordance with Hebrews 5:10, where Jesus Christ is identified as a "high priest after the order of Melchizedek."

In the restored Church of Jesus Christ, a bishop must hold the office of "high priest." This practice finds a parallel in one ancient Christian ordination prayer that pleads, "Grant by thy name, O God . . . that this thy servant, whom thou hast chosen to be a bishop, may . . . discharge the office of an high priest to thee."[31]

Bishop: (Ephesians 4:11; D&C 84:29)

Ephesians 4:11 indicates that bishops [*poimenas*, shepherds] were established in the early Christian Church by divine decree. The Greek word translated in the New Testament as "bishop" [*episkopos*] means "overseer." This is precisely the task performed by an LDS bishop who oversees a ward or local congregation.

Clement of Rome informs us that "the office of bishop is no new thing. Many years ago it was written [in Isaiah 60:17] 'I shall establish their bishops in righteousness.'"[32] In this instance Clement is quoting from the Greek Septuagint (third century B.C.) where the word *episkopos* is translated as "bishops." The Hebrew word that underlies the King James translation of "officers" in Isaiah 60:17 is *p*^{e}*quddah*. This word is connected with the concept of "oversight."[33]

Patriarch: (Ephesians 4:11; D&C 124:91)

"Evangelists" are mentioned three times in the New Testament (see Acts 21:8; 2 Timothy 4:5; Ephesians 4:11). The Prophet Joseph Smith explained that "an

Evangelist is a Patriarch. . . . Whenever the Church of Christ is established [on] the earth, there should be a Patriarch for the benefit of the posterity of the Saints, as it was with Jacob in giving his patriarchal blessing unto his sons."[34] Scholars have discovered what appears to be an ancient Greek burial inscription for the high priest who lived on the island of Rhodes. In this inscription he is called an *euangelistēs* because it was his task to deliver "oracular sayings" to individuals who were seeking divine direction in regard to their personal lives.[35]

Apostle: (Ephesians 4:11; D&C 84:63)

Most sectarian Christians would argue that the quorum of twelve apostles was not meant to function in the Christian Church on a perpetual basis. 1 Corinthians 12:28, however, relates that it was God Himself who placed apostles in His earthly Church. Ephesians 2:20 declares that the apostles were part of the "foundation" of the Church of Jesus Christ and their function was to "perfect" the Saints and keep them from believing in false doctrines. One New Testament text indicates that the quorum of twelve apostles was meant to be perpetual. In Acts 1:23–26 we learn that soon after Judas died, he was replaced by Matthias. From this piece of evidence alone it is clear that the quorum of the twelve was meant to be perpetuated. The ancient historian Hegesippus stated that when James—the brother of Jesus Christ—became an apostle he "received the *succession* in the church."[36]

It should be remembered that during the time of Moses, the Lord directed that twelve men be chosen to represent the twelve tribes of Israel (see Numbers 1:4–16, 44; Joshua 4:4). Jesus Christ directly ties His twelve apostles to the twelve tribes of Israel in Matthew 19:28 and Luke 22:30. The apostolic quorum of Christ's day would thus appear to represent a restoration instead of an innovation.

Prophet: (Ephesians 4:11; D&C 88:127)

In 1 Corinthians 12:28, we are told that God placed prophets in His Church; and in Ephesians 2:20, prophets are classified as part of the "foundation" of Christ's Church. As Amos 3:7 explains: "the Lord God will do nothing, but he revealeth his secret unto his servants the prophets."

Priesthood Keys

Another point of parallel between the early Christian apostles and Latter-day Saint apostles is that the Lord bestowed sealing keys upon both groups. Compare the following scriptures. "Whatsoever thou shalt bind on earth shall be bound in heaven: and whatsoever thou shalt loose on earth shall be loosed in heaven" (Matthew 16:19; see also 18:18). "Whatsoever you bind on earth, may be bound in heaven; whatsoever you loose on earth, may be loosed in heaven" (D&C 127:7; see also 124:93; 128:8, 14; 132:46).

The prophet Elijah was involved in the delivery of sealing keys both in ancient and modern times. In the book of Matthew, we read that Jesus Christ promised the sealing keys to his apostles (16:19) then took Peter, James, and John up onto the Mount of Transfiguration where they saw the prophet Elijah (17:3). Shortly thereafter the Savior noted that the twelve apostles possessed the sealing keys (18:18). Joseph Smith and Oliver Cowdery stood in the presence of Elijah in the Kirtland Temple on 3 April 1836 (see D&C 110:13–16). Joseph Smith reported that on this occasion Elijah delivered the sealing keys of the priesthood unto Oliver and himself.[37] The day on which Elijah delivered these vital keys was significant in two different ways. First, 3 April 1836 was Passover day–a day on which Jews around the world anticipated, and prepared for, Elijah's return to the earth. Second, Elijah's return occurred on a rare Easter Sunday, astronomically speaking. This Sabbath day (3 April/16 Nisan) corresponded exactly with what some scholars believe was the actual date of the Savior's resurrection (cf. D&C 110:1–4).[38]

PRACTICES

In this section of the book, it will be demonstrated that the practices of the LDS Church are the same as those of the early Christian Church.

Identification of Disciples

In the restored Church of Jesus Christ, the disciples of the Lord are called "Saints" (see D&C 1:36). This was also the practice in the early Christian Church as evidenced by biblical passages such as Matthew 27:52; Romans 1:7; Ephesians 2:19; 4:12; 5:3; 1 Corinthians 1:1–2; 6:1–2; 14:33; 2 Corinthians 8:4; Philippians 4:21–22; and Jude 1:3.

The Saints of the restored Church address each other by the titles "brother" and "sister" (see D&C 42:88, 90). This was also the practice anciently. According to Mosheim "there reigned among the members of the Christian Church, however distinguished they were by worldly rank and titles, not only an amiable harmony, but also a perfect equality. This [was manifested] . . . by the names of 'brethren' and 'sisters,' with which they saluted each other."[39]

Common Consent

In a latter-day revelation, the Lord has specified that "all things shall be done by common consent in the Church" (D&C 26:2). In even more specific detail, we read that "no person is to be ordained to any office in [the] Church, where there is a regularly organized branch of the same, without the vote of that [branch]" (D&C 20:65; see also 28:13). We find a similar situation among early Christian congregations. "In those days the bishops gave to the people the names of those who were to be ordained, that if they had anything to object against them, they might attest it openly."[40]

The manner whereby this consent was given may possibly be indicated in the notes found at the end of the books of 2 Timothy and Titus. Timothy was "ordained [*cheirotoneō*] the first bishop of the church of the Ephesians" and Titus, likewise, was "ordained [*chierotoneō*] the first bishop of the church of the Cretians." The Greek word *chierotoneō* means "to be a hand-reacher, or voter (by raising the hand) . . . to select or appoint:–choose."[41]

Missionary Work

Missionary work is an integral part of the restored Church of Jesus Christ. LDS missionaries are formally ordained and sent out among the nations of the earth, by divine decree, to teach the everlasting gospel and bring souls unto Christ (see D&C 36:4–7; 133:8). In Matthew 28:19 we can see that this is the ancient pattern. In this verse the Lord tells his disciples: "Go ye therefore, and teach all nations, baptizing them in the name of the Father, and of the Son, and of the Holy Ghost" (see also Mark 16:15).

In New Testament times the Lord sent His missionaries out in pairs. "And he called unto Him the twelve, and began to send them forth two by two" (Mark 6:7). The Savior sent the "seventy also . . . two and two before His face into every city and place, whither He Himself would come" (Luke 10:1). There is no difference in the restored Church of Christ. The command has been given that latter-day missionaries are to go unto the nations of the earth two by two (see D&C 52:10; 61:33–35).

Tithing

As part of the Restoration of the gospel, the Lord reinstituted the law of tithing (see D&C 119:3–7; 64:23). Tithing has been a law among God's Covenant People in all dispensations of time. We have record of Abraham and Jacob paying the tithe (see Genesis 14:18–20; 28:22) and also the Israelites who lived between the times of Moses and the Messiah (see Leviticus 27:30–34; Deuteronomy 12:5–6; 14:22–23; 26:12–14; Malachi 3:8–10). The Master Himself insisted that the payment of tithing is a duty that should not be neglected (see Matthew 23:23; Luke 11:42).[42]

Since tithing did not originate with the Law of Moses, it continued to be practiced by the Christians after the Law had been abolished. Evidence that the early Christians paid tithing can be found in a variety of documents. In the early Christian text known as the *Apostolic Constitutions*, we read: "Let [the bishop] use those tenths and first-fruits, which are given according to the command of God, as a man of God; [and] also let him dispense in a right manner the free-will offerings which are brought in on account of the poor."[43] Again, in the same document: "You ought, therefore, brethren, to bring . . . your tithes, and your free-will offerings to [the bishop]. For he knows who they are that are in affliction."[44] Ambrose of Milan (A.D. 340–397), in one of his sermons, taught that "a good Christian pays tithes yearly to be given to the poor."[45]

Fasting

Another divinely instituted practice among the Latter-day Saints is fasting (see D&C 59:13; 88:119; 95:7). In ancient Israel there was a certain day set aside for fasting at the House of the Lord (see Jeremiah 36:6; cf. Luke 2:37). From Psalms 35:13 we learn that fasting engenders humility within the one who practices it. The prophet Isaiah mentions that when one fasts they are to impart of their substance to the poor and the needy (see Isaiah 58:3–7). Of special interest to Saints of the present day is the fact that a fast and testimony meeting of sorts is described in the book of Nehemiah chapter 9 verses 1–3.

Jesus Christ not only fasted (see Matthew 4:2; Luke 4:2) but He also instructed His disciples to participate in the practice (see Matthew 17:19–21; Mark 9:28–29). It is evident from the texts of the New Testament that the early Saints continued to engage in fasting even after the Lord had ascended into heaven (see Acts 13:2–3; 14:23; 27:33; 1 Corinthians 7:5).

One early Christian document, the *Pastor of Hermas*, preserves some of the instructions given to fasting Christians. "Having reckoned up the price of the dishes of that day which you intended to have eaten, you will give it to a widow, or an orphan, or to some person in want"[46] (cf. Isaiah 58:3–7).

Word of Wisdom

One of the practices that noticeably separates Latter-day Saints from other Christians is their adherence to a health code known as the Word of Wisdom. This code, which is a revelation from God, not only places restrictions upon what the Saints should take into their bodies but it also lists those things which they can freely consume (see D&C 89:1–21). The purpose of issuing this health code, said the Lord, was to ensure the "temporal salvation" of the Covenant People (v. 2).

A similar code can be found in the writings of the Old Testament. Those in ancient Israel who had been consecrated unto the Lord were considered by the Lord to be in a state of holiness. Because they were in such a state, these persons were restricted by the Lord from eating and drinking certain things so they did not become "unclean" or defiled before Him (see Numbers 6:1–4, 8; Judges 13:13–14; Leviticus 10:8–11; Daniel 1:8). The Lord not only provided a list of things the ancient Israelites should not eat but, like the Word of Wisdom, He also listed things they should eat (see Leviticus 11:1– 47).

The Saints of New Testament times were taught that their bodies were holy and, as such, they were not to be defiled (see 1 Corinthians 3:16–17). They, like their latter-day counterparts, had restrictions placed upon the substances that they were to consume (see 1 Corinthians 6:10; Ephesians 5:18; 1 Timothy 3:2–3; Titus 1:7; Galatians 5:21). The Lord also informed them about the types of foods that they could consume (see Acts 10:9–16).

Pattern of Meetings

The following is a summation by historian John L. Mosheim of the essential parts of divine worship that were observed in all Christian churches in ancient times.[47] These activities are remarkably similar to those that are practiced in the Sabbath services of Latter-day Saints.

1. Meetings were held on Sunday.
2. A bishop or an elder presided.

3. Scriptures were read.
4. Discourses were delivered.
5. Lessons were taught.
6. Exhortations were made.
7. Those moved upon by the Holy Ghost were permitted to speak in turn. The validity of their words was judged by the prophets who were present.
8. Hymns were sung.
9. Prayers were offered.
10. Offerings were made by all for the subsistence of the poor and church leaders.
11. Wine was mixed with water.
12. Bread was divided into several portions.
13. The bread and the wine were consecrated through a prayer that was offered by the presiding priesthood official. All of those who were present then said "Amen."
14. The bread and the wine were distributed by the deacons to those who were present. Part of the consecrated bread and wine were taken to the sick and to others who were absent.

ORDINANCES

The fourth Article of Faith declares that the Saints of the latter days "believe that the first . . . ordinances of the gospel are . . . baptism by immersion for the remission of sins [and the] laying on of hands for the gift of the Holy Ghost." But these ordinances cannot be administered by just anyone. "Whenever men can find out the will of God," said the Prophet Joseph Smith, "and find an administrator legally authorized from God, there is the kingdom of God; but where these are not, the kingdom of God is not. All the ordinances, systems, and administrations on the earth are of no use to the children of men, unless they are ordained and authorized of God; for nothing will save a man but a legal administrator; for none others will be acknowledged either by God or angels."[48]

The Prophet also taught that the ordinances of the gospel were divinely determined and "instituted in the heavens before the foundation of the world."[49] Therefore, if men change the ordinances of Christ's gospel, without divine approval, it is a sure sign they have fallen into a state of apostasy.

Baptism

According to the revealed scriptures of the LDS Church, baptism is as ancient as Adam. In Moses 6:52, we learn that the Lord Himself revealed the ordinance of baptism to Adam (see also vv. 64–65). In Moses 7:11 God commands the prophet Enoch to perform baptisms in the name of the Father, and of the Son, and of the Holy Ghost. In Moses 8:23–24 it is made known that Noah informed the people of his day that the "fathers" before them had been baptized. In the Joseph Smith Translation of Genesis 17:3–7, the Lord informs the patriarch Abraham that He had revealed "ordinances" to the ancient "fathers" which included "the burial, or baptism." As for the time of Moses, we read in the legends of the Jews that two days prior to the Lord's revelation at Mount Sinai the ordinance of baptism was imposed upon all of the children of Israel.[50]

In D&C 84:27–28, it is stated that John the Baptist was "baptized while he was yet in his childhood." The Joseph Smith Translation of Matthew 9:18 likewise puts forward the idea that the Jews who lived during the time of Jesus Christ were performing baptisms. This claim is verified in very old Jewish documents. "According to rabbinical teachings, which dominated even during the existence of the [Jerusalem] temple . . . baptism . . . was an absolutely necessary condition to be fulfilled by a proselyte to Judaism."[51] This ritual, according to the ancient Jews, accomplished three things. First, it was a "bath of purification."[52] Second, it permitted its recipient to "enter the Covenant of Israel."[53] Third, it enabled one to "receive the Spirit of God, or to be permitted to stand in the presence of God."[54] All of these points are readily recognizable to any Latter-day Saint who understands the doctrine of baptism.

The necessary nature of the baptismal rite is taught both by the early Christians and by the Latter-day Saints. In Luke 7:29–30 baptism is classified as "the counsel of God." Without this ordinance it is not possible to enter into God's heavenly kingdom (see John 3:5). With crystal clarity, the New Testament teaches that baptism is necessary for salvation (see 1 Peter 3:21; Acts 2:5, 37–38, 40; Mark 16:16; Titus 3:5). This same pattern is followed in modern revelations. The Lord has decreed that all who are accountable for their own actions must be baptized (see D&C 18:41–42). Baptism is a prerequisite for entering into the celestial glory (see D&C 76:51). This ordinance, according to latter-day revelation, is intricately interwoven with one's personal salvation (see D&C 20:25; 68:9; 112:29).

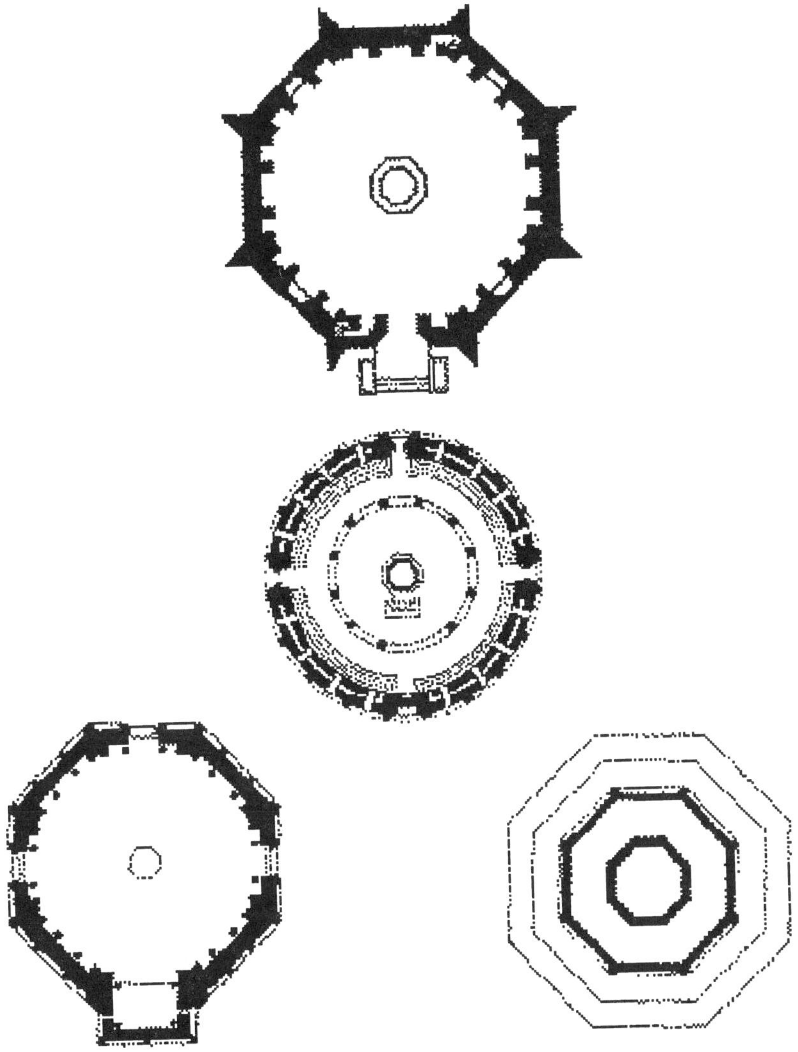

FIGURE 7. The number eight has been incorporated into these ancient Christian baptistries and baptismal fonts. This may have been done intentionally since the apostle Peter associated the number eight with baptism (see 1 Peter 3:20–21). Latter-day revelation indicates that children are not to be baptized until they are eight years old (see D&C 68:25; JST Genesis 17:3–7, 11).

The Lord has made it clear that children do not need to receive the ordinance of baptism until they have reached the age of accountability, which is eight years old (see JST Genesis 17:5–6, 11–12; D&C 18:42; 20:71; 68:25, 27; Moroni 8:5, 8, 10–15, 20–22). A hint of this doctrine can be seen in the writings of the apostle Peter. In his first epistle, Peter states that the number "eight . . . [is] the like figure whereunto even baptism doth also now save us" (1 Peter 3:20–21).

Latter-day Saints teach that no baptism is valid in the eyes of God unless it is performed by someone who holds legitimate priesthood authority. When Jesus Christ was baptized he went to John the Baptist to have the ordinance performed (see Matthew 3:13). Why did he go specifically to John? Because John the Baptist had legitimate priesthood authority in the eyes of God. John was the son of Zacharias the temple priest. John was, therefore, of the legitimate priestly lineage; one of the sons of Aaron from the tribe of Levi; a priest after the order of Aaron (see Exodus 28:41; cf. Hebrews 5:4). This same pattern is followed in the LDS Church. One must hold, at least, the office of a priest in the Aaronic Priesthood before he is allowed to perform baptisms (see D&C 20:46; see also 13:1).

The method of performing baptism is the same among the early Christians and the Latter-day Saints. The Lord's meridian disciples performed baptisms by full immersion. Several scriptures speak of those who were baptized "coming up out of the water" (see Matthew 3:16; Mark 1:5, 9–10; Acts 8:38). John the Baptist chose the place where he performed baptisms "because there was much water there" (John 3:23). "In the primitive Church, and down to the fourteenth century," says Wolfred Cote, "the ordinary mode of baptism was by the immersion of the whole body in water. The original [Greek] term *baptizo* conveys the meaning of immersion, and no other. On this point we have most valuable testimony from the Fathers of the Church, and other ecclesiastical writers. They invariably designate baptism as the act of dipping."[55] In the fourth Article of Faith, the Prophet Joseph Smith is specific in stating that the restored Church of Jesus Christ only practices "baptism by immersion." This is done according to the divine directive found in D&C 20:73–74 wherein the Lord says the person to be baptized is to "go down into the water . . . Then shall [the administrator of the ordinance] immerse him or her in the water, and [bring them] forth again out of the water."

The liturgical formula that accompanies the baptismal ordinance is the same among the early Christians and the Latter-day Saints. A hint of the early Christian baptismal formula can be seen in Matthew 28:19 where the Lord directs his disciples: "Go ye therefore, and teach all nations, baptizing them in the name of the Father, and of the Son, and of the Holy Ghost." The very same directive is given by the Lord in D&C 68:8: "Go ye into all the world, preach the gospel to every creature, acting in the authority which I have given you, baptizing in the name of the Father, and of the Son, and of the Holy Ghost." The exact wording of the baptismal prayer can be found in Doctrine and Covenants section 20 verse 73.

The purpose for baptism is the same among the early Christians and the Latter-day Saints. In Acts 22:16 Ananias says to Paul: "arise, and be baptized, and wash away thy sins." The same phraseology is employed by the Lord in D&C 39:10: "Arise and be baptized, and wash away your sins."

The symbolism behind the baptismal ordinance is the same among the early Christians and the Latter-day Saints. The apostle Paul asked: "Know ye not, that so many of us as were baptized into Jesus Christ were baptized into his death? Therefore we are buried with him by baptism into death: that like as Christ was raised up from the dead by the glory of the Father, even so we also should walk in newness of life. For if we have been planted together [*sumphutoi*, closely united] in the likeness of his death, we shall be also in the likeness of his resurrection" (Romans 6:3–5; see also Colossians 2:12). In the restored Church those who believe that Jesus Christ is the Son of God are "baptized after the manner of his burial, being buried in the water in his name" (D&C 76:51; see also 128:12–13; JST Genesis 17:3–7).

The penalty for failure to receive an authoritative baptism is the same among the early Christians and the Latter-day Saints. Jesus informed His meridian disciples: "He that believeth and is baptized shall be saved; but he that believeth not shall be damned" (Mark 16:16). In D&C 84:74 we read the very same thing. "Verily, verily, I say unto you, they who believe not on your words, and are not baptized in water in my name, for the remission of their sins, that they may receive the Holy Ghost, shall be damned, and shall not come into my Father's kingdom where my Father and I am."

The Gift of the Holy Ghost

LDS doctrine teaches that following baptism by immersion one must receive the gift of the Holy Ghost by the laying on of the hands of an authorized priesthood bearer.[56] This is in strict accordance with the pattern and sequence found in the New Testament. The gift of the Holy Ghost is to be given after the ordinance of baptism is performed (see Acts 2:38) and is to be bestowed by the laying on of the hands of an authorized servant of Christ (see Acts 19:1–6).

Only those who have received the gift of the Holy Ghost through an authorized channel of transmittal have the ability, and the legitimate right, to bestow it upon others. The authoritative line of transmittal for this gift is laid out in New Testament texts. God the Father bestowed the Holy Ghost upon His Son (see Acts 10:38) and then the Son, in turn, bestowed it upon His apostles and "sent" them out into the world (see John 20:21–22; Acts 1:5). The quorum of the twelve apostles then "sent"

Peter and John (authorized servants of Christ) to those who had "received the word of God" and had been "baptized in the name of the Lord Jesus." Peter and John "prayed for them, that they might receive the Holy Ghost. . . . Then they laid their hands on them, and they received the Holy Ghost" (Acts 8:14–17). Simon, who was a new convert to Christ's Church, "saw that through laying on of the apostles' hands the Holy Ghost was given" and he offered them money so that he too might have the authority [*exousian*] to bestow the gift of the Holy Ghost upon others. But Simon was rebuked and informed by Peter that the ability to bestow such a gift could not be purchased with money (vv. 18–20). Peter's words to Simon make it clear that only those whose hearts were "right in the sight of God" were to have the authority to distribute this gift (v. 21).

The proper method for bestowing the Holy Ghost continued to be practiced for several hundred years after Christ's mortal ministry. Tertullian (ca. A.D. 155–225), an elder living in Carthage, informs us: "In the water, under (the witness of) the angel, we are cleansed, and prepared for the Holy Spirit." Then, he says, "the hand is laid on us, invoking and inviting the Holy Spirit through benediction."[57] Cyprian (ca. A.D. 200–258), who served as the bishop of Carthage, said that "they who are baptized in the Church are brought to the [leaders] of the Church, and by our prayers and by the imposition of hands obtain the Holy Spirit, and are perfected with the Lord's seal."[58]

According to LDS theology the reception of the Holy Ghost is not an option but a requirement. The disciples of Christ "must be born again into the kingdom of heaven . . . of the Spirit" (Moses 6:59; see also D&C 5:16). This position is in complete agreement with the teaching of the Savior that all those who desire to "enter into the kingdom of God" must be "born of . . . the Spirit" (John 3:5).

Restoration scriptures compare the reception of the Holy Ghost to a baptism of fire (see 2 Nephi 31:13–14; 3 Nephi 9:20; 11:35; 12:1–2; 19:9–13; Mormon 7:10; Ether 12:14; D&C 19:31; 20:41; 33:11; 39:6; Moses 6:65–66). New Testament scriptures say Jesus Christ has power to "baptize . . . with the Holy Ghost, and with fire" (Matthew 3:11; see also Luke 3:16).

The Sacrament

The Lord has directed members of the restored Church to receive the sacrament each Sabbath day (see D&C 59:9–13). Among the early Christians the practice was the same. Justin Martyr, who died about A.D. 163, informs us that "on the day called Sunday, all who live in cities or in the country gather together to one place. . . . [Then] bread is brought and wine and water . . . and the [leader] . . . offers up prayers and thanksgivings to the best of his ability, and the people assent, saying the Amen; and the distribution . . . is to each, and to those who are absent a portion is sent by the deacons."[59]

Wine was originally utilized in the sacramental services of the LDS faith, but then a revelation was received that altered the way in which the Saints administered the sacrament. Newel Knight explains that during the first week of August in 1830 he and his wife met with the Prophet and his wife and it was decided that they would confirm the two women as members of the Church and also partake of the sacrament. Newel relates that "Brother Joseph set out to procure some wine for the occasion. But he had gone only a short distance when he was met by a heavenly messenger, and received the first four verses of the revelation" now known as section 27 of the Doctrine and Covenants.[60] These verses say: "Listen to the voice of Jesus Christ . . . For, behold, I say unto you, that it mattereth not what ye shall eat or what ye shall drink when ye partake of the sacrament, if it so be that ye do it with an eye single to my glory–remembering unto the Father my body which was laid down for you, and my blood which was shed for the remission of your sins" (D&C 27:1–2). Hence, Latter-day Saints now use water in the sacrament "in remembrance of the blood of [the] Son, which was shed for them" (D&C 20:79).

The Latter-day Saints are not alone in their use of water in the sacrament. Some of the early Christian congregations used water also. "An investigation . . . of such Jewish-Christian sects as the Ebionites, the Nazarenes, the Elkesaites, and the Encratites might provide considerable support for abstinence from fermented wine in the Apostolic Church. The fact that some of these sects went to the extreme of rejecting altogether both fermented and unfermented wine using only water, even in the celebration of the Lord's Supper, suggests the existence of a prevailing concern for abstinence in the Apostolic Church."[61]

The LDS practice of using water in the sacramental ordinance is in perfect harmony with its symbolic nature (see JST Matthew 26:22, 24–25) but is at variance with Christian denominations that claim there is a transformation of the sacramental emblems into the actual body and blood of the Redeemer. Hatch, however, has pointed out that "it is among the *gnostics* [i.e., early Christian heretics] that there appears for the first time an attempt to realize the change of the elements to the material body and blood of Christ."[62]

Baptism for the Dead

In a revelation dated 19 January 1841, the Lord Jesus Christ made it known to the Church that proxy baptisms would be performed in the Nauvoo Temple (see D&C 124:29–34; see also 128:12–13). The Prophet Joseph Smith pointed to the fact that this ordinance had previously been practiced by the early Christians since Paul refers to it in 1 Corinthains 15:29. This passage reads, "Else what shall they do which are baptized for the dead, if the dead rise not at all? Why are they then baptized for the dead?" Note *b* for this verse in the LDS edition of the King James Bible indicates that the Greek word translated as "for" [*huper*] could be rendered as "in behalf of, for the sake of." Biblical scholars admit that such a rendition is allowable.[63] And, indeed, this portion of the verse has been rendered in one scholarly translation as "those being baptized on behalf of the dead."[64] In the *Theological Dictionary of the New Testament* we read that:

> It has been shown already that the sense "on behalf of" is sometimes very close to "in the place of," "instead of," "in the name of." In all probability the word has the representative sense in Paul's saying about baptism for the dead. . . . None of the attempts to escape the theory of a vicarious baptism in primitive Christianity seems to be wholly successful. If one thus presupposes that there may be baptism "for the dead," this implies that the dead, probably relatives, were unbaptized at death. We thus have a kind of substitution even if, as one may suppose, the candidate was baptized for himself as well as with respect to someone who had died unbaptized.[65]

Ephesians 4:5 declares that there is only "one baptism" and John 3:5 plainly states that one must be baptized to enter into the Kingdom of God. Scriptural passages in the book of 1 Peter reveal that those who die without hearing the gospel of Jesus Christ are given that opportunity in the spirit world (see 1 Peter 3:19–20; 4:6). But since God is no respecter of persons (see Acts 10:34), the dead also must receive the baptismal ordinance to enter into God's Kingdom, just like their living counterparts. Hence, baptism for the dead was instituted during Jesus Christ's dispensation so that the divine requirement of baptism could be fulfilled.

Sectarian Christians who are critical of the LDS practice of baptism for the dead claim that Paul was not speaking of "orthodox" Christians engaging in this activity. But this stance does not square with the outlook of some eminent Christian scholars. Findlay, for example, notes that "in following up verse 29 with the words of verse 30 (τί και ήμεις κινδυνευομεν) *Paul associates himself with the action of* 'those bap-

FIGURE 8. This rare image of the Nauvoo Temple was probably produced around 1847. The ordinances that were performed inside this building were a restoration of the temple rituals of the ancient Israelites and early Christians.

tized for the dead,' indicating that they and he are engaged on the same behalf."[66] Wuest, emeritus teacher of New Testament Greek at the Moody Bible Institute, feels justified in translating 1 Corinthians 15:29 as follows: "Otherwise, what shall those do who are being baptized for the sake of those who are dead? Assuming that the dead are not actually raised up, why then are *we* being baptized for their sake?"[67] Then there is the opinion of Grosheide. "The objection that the apostle could not have meant anything like a baptism for the benefit of others is exegetically out of place. . . . [I]f Paul had disapproved of it he probably would have written more about it than what this one reference contains. In any case the apostle could hardly derive an argument for the resurrection of the body from a practice of which he did not approve."[68] Finally, we have Stendahl's point of view on this matter. He feels that "the text seems to speak plainly enough about a practice within the [early Christian] Church of vicarious baptism for the dead. This is the view of most contemporary critical exegetes" or biblical interpreters.[69]

Baptism for the dead was officially condemned at the Synod of Hippo in A.D. 393 and also at the third Council of Carthage in A.D. 397, thus indicating that this ordinance was practiced among Christian groups for almost 400 years after the death of Jesus Christ.

Baptism for the dead is just one of several ordinances that are practiced inside LDS temples. Joseph Smith claimed that the temple rituals he introduced into the Church were a genuine restoration of the sacred temple rites practiced among the ancient Israelites and early Christians. Abundant scholarly evidence supports this claim. In the paragraphs that follow, the reader will find brief descriptions of LDS temple ordinances from the *Encyclopedia of Mormonism*, and they will be directed to literature that confirms these rites were practiced in ancient times by the Lord's covenant people.

Washing and Anointing

In all LDS temples there are special "cubicles in which individuals are ritually washed and anointed before endowments can be performed."[70] The temple washings and anointings are "preparatory or initiatory ordinances. . . . They signify the cleansing and sanctifying power of Jesus Christ applied to the attributes of the person and the hallowing of all life. . . . Women are set apart to administer the ordinances to women, and men are set apart to administer the ordinances to men." The ceremonial words that are spoken during the washings and anointings include "inspiring promises."[71]

Ritual washings and anointing were received at the temple of the Lord by the kings and priests of ancient Israel (see Exodus 40:12, 15). Since the early Christians were "made . . . kings and priests" (Revelation 1:6; see also 5:10) it stands to reason that they would have also received these rites. And, indeed, there is plenty of historical evidence indicating that they did.[72]

Sacred Clothing

A white ceremonial garment is given to individuals who receive their washings and anointings.[73] This garment bears "several simple marks of orientation toward the gospel principles of obedience, truth, life, and discipleship in Christ." The garment is worn underneath a Saint's regular clothing for the remainder of their lives, "partially to remind them of the sacred covenants they have made with God" while in the temple.[74] Those Saints who engage in temple ordinances, or who act as temple administrators, dress themselves in white clothing.[75] In addition to this white clothing, all those who participate in the endowment ceremonies don white priestly robes.[76]

Those who are familiar with the Old Testament are well aware that those who served in Jehovah's temple were required by the Lord to wear special clothing made of white linen (see Exodus 39:27–29; Leviticus 16:4). The kings of ancient Israel

FIGURE 9. The early Christians wore ritual clothing that was similar to the vestments worn by the ancient Israelite temple priests. The robes that are worn by these Saints bear simple geometric markings.

were invested with sacred vestments when they received the rites of coronation in the temple. Some of these items of clothing were the same as those worn by the temple priests (see 1 Chronicles 15:27). The early Christians participated in initiation rituals wherein they donned clothing similar to that worn by ancient Israel's kings and priests.[77]

The Endowment

The temple endowment consists of a course of instruction that is given, in endowment rooms, through a series of lectures and representations. Some of the instruction is presented in the form of a drama which includes:

1. Recital of the creation story.
2. Recital of the story of Adam and Eve including their creation, entry into the Garden of Eden, expulsion, and reception of the plan of salvation.
3. Reception of information regarding the laws and ordinances that are required for one to become reconciled through the atonement of Jesus Christ and thus able to return to the presence of God.
4. Entry into covenants to live according to the laws of the new and everlasting covenant.
5. Reception of promises and blessings.[78]

Each of the elements that are listed above can be found in the initiation rituals of the ancient Israelites and the early Christians.[79]

Prayer Circle

"The prayer circle is a part of Latter-day Saint temple worship, usually associated with the endowment ceremony. Participants, an equal number of men and women dressed in temple clothing, surround an altar in a circle formation to participate unitedly in prayer. . . . Participants [affirm] that they bear no negative feelings toward other members of the circle . . .[and then there is a] unison repetition of the words of the leader. The prayer has no set text, but is, among other things, an occasion for seeking the Lord's blessings upon those with particular needs whose names have been submitted for collective entreaty."[80] In sum, the Saints petition the Lord for His blessings upon mankind, the Church,[81] the sick, the afflicted, and those who are seeking inspiration or guidance.[82]

In both the Old and New Testaments, the House of the Lord is referred to as a house of prayer (see Isaiah 56:7; Matthew 21:13; Mark 11:17; Luke 19:46). Some scholars have noted that Psalms 24:6 and 26:6–7, in the Hebrew language, may refer to prayer circles in connection with the Lord's sanctuary.[83]

Eternal Marriage

In regard to temple or celestial marriages the *Encyclopedia of Mormonism* says: "Kneeling opposite each other at the altar, the bride and groom are placed under mutual covenants to each other, and are married through the sealing power of Jesus Christ . . . [They] are sealed in the temple under the new and everlasting covenant. . . . By apostolic authority, the blessings of Abraham, Isaac, and Jacob are explicitly invoked upon all marriages."[84]

The eternal marriage ceremony, as understood by Latter-day Saints, can be discerned upon the pages of the Bible (see Genesis 2:18, 21–24; Ezekiel 16:8, 10–13; Isaiah 61:10) and also in the coronation rites of ancient Near Eastern royalty.[85]

SUMMARY

The material that has been presented in this chapter clearly demonstrates four things. (1) The organizational structure of The Church of Jesus Christ of Latter-day Saints matches that of the New Testament Church. (2) The authoritative offices that once governed the Savior's meridian flock are now found, in their fullness, in the LDS Church. (3) The unique practices of Christ's early Church organization exist today among the Latter-day Saints. (4) The rituals of the Restoration are the same as those once known to Moses, Aaron, Peter, and Paul. In all of these respects, the LDS Church qualifies as a genuine restoration of the ancient Church of Jesus Christ.

NOTES

1. *Messenger and Advocate*, vol. 1, no. 8, May 1835, 118.
2. *WJS*, 42.
3. Raymond E. Brown and John P. Meier, *Antioch and Rome* (New York: Paulist Press, 1983), 66.
4. *Times and Seasons*, vol. 1, no. 4, February 1840, 54. Directly after this quotation, Joseph Smith cites Romans 10:14–15 and Hebrews 5:4 to support his point.
5. James Strong, *The New Strong's Exhaustive Concordance of the Bible* (Nashville: Thomas Nelson Publishers, 1996), Greek Dictionary of the New Testament, 99, word #5548.
6. See Everett Ferguson, ed., *Encyclopedia of Early Christianity*, 2d ed. (New York: Garland Publishing, 1997), 2:669–71, 832–34. "This gesture signified a transfer from one to another or the creating of a substitute" (ibid., 669). "The Syriac Church saw ordination by the laying on of hands as transmitting the priesthood from the Old Testament" (ibid., 834). According to John Chrysostom "the hand of man is laid on, but God performs everything, and it is His hand that touches the head of the one being ordained, if he truly is ordained" (ibid., 833). Compare this concept with D&C 36:2 wherein the Lord says: "And I will lay my hand upon you by the hand of my servant."
7. Alexander Roberts and James Donaldson, eds., *Ante-Nicene Fathers* (Peabody, Massachusetts: Hendrickson Publishers, 1994), 7:429, *Apostolic Constitutions* (3.1.10).
8. When the angel Moroni first visited Joseph Smith on 21 September 1823, he quoted Malachi 4:5–6 and explained its meaning to the Prophet (see Kent P. Jackson, "Moroni's Message to Joseph Smith," *Ensign*, August 1990, 16; JS–H 1:41).
9. *Messenger and Advocate*, vol. 2, no. 1, October 1835, 199.
10. *Patriarchal Blessings*, Book 1, 1835, 12, LDS Church Archives, Salt Lake City, Utah, cited in *Improvement Era*, October 1904, 943, emphasis added.
11. *Patriarchal Blessings*, Book 1, 1835, 8–9, emphasis added.
12. See the introduction to section 3 of the Doctrine and Covenants.
13. See JS–H 1:68–72; *WJS*, 327, 332–33; Dean C. Jessee, ed., *The Papers of Joseph Smith* (Salt Lake City: Deseret Book, 1989), 1:238–39; *Messenger and Advocate*, vol. 1, no. 1, October 1834, 15–16.
14. William E. Vine, Merrill F. Unger, and William White, Jr., *Vine's Complete Expository Dictionary of Old and New Testament Words* (Nashville: Thomas Nelson Publishers, 1996), part 2, 95.
15. Roberts and Donaldson, eds., *Ante-Nicene Fathers*, 7:409, *Apostolic Constitutions* (2.4.25).
16. Samuel Cheetham, *A History of the Christian Church During the First Six Centuries* (New York: Macmillan, 1894), 129.
17. James H. Charlesworth, ed., *The Old Testament Pseudepigrapha* (Garden City, New York: Doubleday, 1985), 1:791.
18. See Larry C. Porter, "The Restoration of the Aaronic and Melchizedek Priesthoods," *Ensign*, December 1996, 30–47; Brian Q. Cannon and BYU Studies Staff, "Priesthood Restoration Documents," *Brigham Young University Studies*, vol. 35, no. 4, 1995–96, 163–207.

19. Reuben Miller Journal, 21 October 1848, 14.
20. David H. Cannon, Autobiography, 13 March 1917, 5, cited in Larry C. Porter, "The Restoration of the Priesthood," *Religious Studies Center Newsletter*, vol. 9, no. 3, 3 May 1995, 10.
21. *TPJS*, 181.
22. *JD*, 9:87.
23. Strong, *The New Strong's Exhaustive Concordance of the Bible*, Greek Dictionary of the New Testament, 89, word #5010; Vine, Unger, and White, Jr., *Vine's Complete Expository Dictionary of Old and New Testament Words*, part 2, 450.
24. Vine, Unger, and White, Jr., *Vine's Complete Expository Dictionary of Old and New Testament Words*, part 2, 649; see also Henry G. Liddell and Robert Scott, *A Greek-English Lexicon* (Oxford: Clarendon Press, 1968), 178. Despite the fact that the Greek word *aparabatos* in Hebrews 7:24 "is usually interpreted [as] *without a successor* . . . this meaning is found nowhere else. [*Aparabatos*] rather has the sense *permanent, unchangeable*" (Walter Bauer, William F. Arndt, and F. Wilbur Gingrich, *A Greek-English Lexicon of the New Testament and Other Early Christian Literature* [Chicago: The University of Chicago Press, 1979], 80, emphasis in original). Those who adhere to the "priesthood of all believers" theory often turn to 1 Peter 2:9 for support. It must be remembered, however, that in this verse Peter is paraphrasing Exodus 19:6. Even though Jehovah referred, in a corporate sense, to the Israelite nation as "a kingdom of priests," they still had a strictly defined priesthood structure among them. Only divinely approved individuals were allowed to be initiated into the Priesthood and such initiations could only be carried out by those who had direct authority from Jehovah (see Exodus 40:12–16).
25. Charlesworth, ed., *The Old Testament Pseudepigrapha*, 2:753.
26. See the comments in John A. Tvedtnes, *The Church of the Old Testament* (Salt Lake City: Deseret Book, 1980), 38–39.
27. See also Joseph Fielding Smith, *Doctrines of Salvation*, ed., Bruce R. McConkie (Salt Lake City: Bookcraft, 1956), 3:111–14.
28. Leslie W. Barnard, trans., *St. Justin Martyr: The First and Second Apologies* (New York: Paulist Press, 1997), 70, *First Apology* (65).
29. Roberts and Donaldson, eds., *Ante-Nicene Fathers*, 7:409, *Apostolic Constitutions* (2.4.25).
30. See Isidore Singer, ed., *The Jewish Encyclopedia* (New York: Funk and Wagnalls Co., 1902), 5:92.
31. Roberts and Donaldson, eds., *Ante-Nicene Fathers*, 7:482, *Apostolic Constitutions* (8.2.5).
32. 1 Clement, sect. 72, as cited in Tvedtnes, *The Church of the Old Testament*, 38.
33. See Strong, *The New Strong's Exhaustive Concordance of the Bible*, Hebrew and Aramaic Dictionary of the Old Testament, 116, word #6486.
34. *TPJS*, 151.
35. See Gerhard Kittel, ed., *Theological Dictionary of the New Testament* (Grand Rapids, Michigan: Eerdmans, 1964), 2:736–37.
36. Robert M. Grant, *Second-Century Christianity* (London: Society for Promoting Christian Knowledge, 1946), 58, emphasis added.
37. See *TPJS*, 337–38.

38. See John P. Pratt, "The Restoration of Priesthood Keys on Easter 1836, Part 2: Symbolism of Passover and of Elijah's Return," *Ensign*, July 1985, 55–64.
39. John L. Mosheim, *An Ecclesiastical History, Ancient and Modern* (New York: Harper and Brothers, 1856), 1:38.
40. Valesius in his note on Eusebius, *H. E.* bk, 6, ch. 43, cited in Ariel L. Crowley, *Statement of Beliefs of The Church of Jesus Christ of Latter-day Saints: Doctrines and Practices* (Salt Lake City: Deseret News Press, 1961), 9.
41. Strong, *The New Strong's Exhaustive Concordance of the Bible*, Greek Dictionary of the New Testament, 98, word #5500.
42. Even though some people have taken this passage to mean that Christ condemned the practice of tithing, this is simply not the case (see Paul J. Achtemeier, ed., *Harper's Bible Dictionary* [San Francisco: Harper, 1985], 1079).
43. Roberts and Donaldson, eds., *Ante-Nicene Fathers*, 7:408, *Apostolic Constitutions* (2.4.25); see also ibid., 7:494, *Apostolic Constitutions* (8.4.30).
44. Ibid., 7:410, *Apostolic Constitutions* (2.4.27).
45. Cited in Arthur V. Babbs, *The Law of the Tithe* (New York: Fleming H. Revell Co., 1912), 117.
46. Roberts and Donaldson, eds., *Ante-Nicene Fathers*, 2:34, *Pastor of Hermas* (3.5.3).
47. Mosheim, *An Ecclesiastical History, Ancient and Modern*, 1:45–46, 69.
48. *TPJS*, 274.
49. *HC*, 5:423.
50. See Louis Ginzberg, *The Legends of the Jews* (Philadelphia: The Jewish Publication Society of America, 1939), 3:88.
51. Singer, ed., *Jewish Encyclopedia*, 2:499. Baptism is necessary, in part, so that those who are not of Abraham's lineage can become his "seed" by adoption and, therefore, rightful heirs to the promises Jehovah made unto him—including the promise of eternal life (see Galatians 3:16, 27–29; 4:4–7; Titus 3:5–7).
52. Singer, ed., *Jewish Encyclopedia*, 10:222; Jewish baptism is also referred to as a "purificatory consecration" in James Hastings, ed., *Encyclopaedia of Religion and Ethics* (New York: Charles Scribner's Sons, 1951), 2:377.
53. Hastings, ed., *Encyclopaedia of Religion and Ethics*, 2:376.
54. Singer, ed., *Jewish Encyclopedia*, 2:499.
55. Wolfred N. Cote, *The Archaeology of Baptism* (London: Yates and Alexander, 1876), 16. On page 80 of this same source we read: "At an early period of the Church, certain persons were required to be present at the baptism of its members, who should serve as witnesses of the due performance and reception of the rite."
56. See the fourth Article of Faith; see also *HC*, 4:42; D&C 20:41, 43.
57. Roberts and Donaldson, eds., *Ante-Nicene Fathers*, 3:672, *On Baptism* (6).
58. Ibid., 5:381, *Epistle* (72.9).
59. Barnard, trans., *St. Justin Martyr: The First and Second Apologies*, 71, *First Apology* (67).

60. *Scraps of Biography: Tenth Book of the Faith-Promoting Series* (Salt Lake City: Juvenile Instructor Office, 1883), 62.
61. Samuele Bacchiocchi, *Wine in the Bible* (Berrien Springs, Michigan: Biblical Perspectives, 1989), 181. The practice of using water for the sacrament is traced back to apostolic times in the apocryphal *Acts of Thomas* (121). There we read: "And when [Mygdonia] was baptized and clad, [Thomas] brake bread and took a cup of water and made her a partaker in the body of Christ and the cup of the Son of God" (Montague R. James, *The Apocryphal New Testament* [Oxford: Clarendon Press, 1975], 418). Cyprian, the bishop of Carthage, acknowledged in 253 A.D. that some of the orthodox Christian congregations were using water exclusively in their sacramental services (see G. W. Clarke, trans., *The Letters of St. Cyprian of Carthage* [New York: Newman Press, 1986], 3:98–99, 288–90). Brigham Young relates that "the Lord told Joseph [Smith] that he would accept of water" instead of wine in the sacrament (*JD*, 10:245; see also ibid., 19:92).
62. Edwin Hatch, *The Influence of Greek Ideas on Christianity* (Gloucester, Massachusetts: Peter Smith, 1970), 308.
63. See Strong, *The New Strong's Exhaustive Concordance of the Bible*, Greek Dictionary of the New Testament, 93, word #5228.
64. Jay P. Green, Sr., ed., *The Interlinear Bible: Hebrew-Greek-English*, 2d ed. (Grand Rapids, Michigan: Baker Book House, 1986), 893.
65. Friedrich, ed., *Theological Dictionary of the New Testament*, 8:512–13.
66. George G. Findlay, *The Expositor's Greek Testament* (Grand Rapids, Michigan: Eerdmans, 1942), 2:930, emphasis in original.
67. Kenneth S. Wuest, *The New Testament: An Expanded Translation* (Grand Rapids, Michigan: Eerdmans, 1983), 412, emphasis added.
68. Frederik W. Grosheide, *Commentary on the First Epistle to the Corinthians* (Grand Rapids, Michigan: Eerdmans, 1955), 372.
69. Daniel H. Ludlow, ed., *Encyclopedia of Mormonism* (New York: Macmillan, 1992), 1:97. For further reading on this subject see John A. Tvedtnes, "Baptism for the Dead in Early Christianity," in Donald W. Parry and Stephen D. Ricks, eds., *The Temple in Time and Eternity* (Provo, Utah: The Foundation for Ancient Research and Mormon Studies, 1999), 55–78.
70. *EM*, 4:1447.
71. Ibid., 4:1444; see also 4:1551; 2:455.
72. For further reading see Matthew B. Brown, *The Gate of Heaven: Insights on the Doctrines and Symbols of the Temple* (American Fork, Utah: Covenant Communications, 1999), 78–80, 126–27, 184–85.
73. See *EM*, 4:1444.
74. Ibid., 2:534.
75. See ibid., 4:1444, 1449.
76. See ibid., 2:455, 534.
77. See Brown, *The Gate of Heaven: Insights on the Doctrines and Symbols of the Temple*, 80–88, 127–31, 185–88.

78. See *EM*, 1:37; 2:455; 4:1444, 1447, 1449.
79. See Brown, *The Gate of Heaven: Insights on the Doctrines and Symbols of the Temple*, 6–8, 118, 123–24, 133–35, 138–39, 186–89.
80. *EM*, 3:1120.
81. See ibid., 1:37.
82. See ibid., 4:1449.
83. See Donald W. Parry, "Temple Worship and a Possible Reference to a Prayer Circle in Psalm 24," *BYUS*, vol. 32, no. 4, 1992, 57–62; John A. Tvedtnes, "Temple Prayer in Ancient Times," in Parry and Ricks, eds., *The Temple in Time and Eternity*, 79–98; Brown, *The Gate of Heaven: Insights on the Doctrines and Symbols of the Temple*, 124–26.
84. *EM*, 4:1445.
85. See Brown, *The Gate of Heaven: Insights on the Doctrines and Symbols of the Temple*, 135–38, 160, n. 153.

CHAPTER 4

The Restoration of Doctrine

When Joseph Smith was visited by the Father and the Son in the spring of 1820, he was informed by the Savior that men had so severely corrupted the doctrines of His gospel that they had become an "abomination in His sight" (JS–H 1:19). Joseph Smith was commissioned by the Lord to restore the doctrines of the gospel that had become either degraded or altogether lost during the preceding centuries.

Critics of Joseph Smith usually reject his claim to be a legitimate prophet of God because some of the doctrines that he introduced among the Latter-day Saints are foreign to their man-made creeds. The purpose of this chapter is to list some of the more distinctive doctrines of the LDS Church and demonstrate that they can be found among the beliefs of the ancient Israelites and early Christians.

THE NATURE OF GOD

It is the doctrine of the LDS Church that God the Father is an exalted, glorified, and perfected man. According to Doctrine and Covenants section 130 verse 22 "the Father has a body of flesh and bones as tangible as man's." Joseph Smith proclaimed that "God himself was once as we are now, and is an exalted man. . . . if you were to see Him today, you would see Him like a man in form–like yourselves in all the person, image, and very form [of] a man. . . . He was once a man like us. . . . God Himself, the Father of us all, dwelt on an earth, the same as Jesus Christ Himself did."[1] The vast majority of sectarian Christians believe that God is without body, parts, or passions. To this unscriptural concept the Prophet replied: "That which is without body or parts is nothing. There is no other God in heaven but that God who has flesh

17 And when he was gone forth into the way, there came one running, and kneeled to him, and asked him, Good master, what shall I doe that I may inherit eternall life?

18 And Jesus said unto him, Why callest thou me good? There is no man good, but one, *that is* God.

FIGURE 10. In this citation of Mark 10:17–18, from the 1611 edition of the King James Bible, Jesus Christ refers to God the Father as a man. This passage was rewritten in all subsequent editions of the King James translation.

and bones. . . . God the Father took life unto Himself precisely as Jesus did"[2] (cf. John 5:19–20, 26).

There is some biblical evidence to support the Prophet's doctrine. In Hosea 2:16 the Lord says his people will call him *ishi*. This Hebrew word can be translated as "man" or "male person."[3] The prophet Ezekiel, who saw a vision of God's throne in heaven, said that "upon the likeness of the throne was the likeness as the appearance of a *man* above upon it" (Ezekiel 1:26, emphasis added). According to Phillip Munoa "commentators have long noticed how Daniel 7:9 has built upon Ezekiel 1:26–27. What needs to be singled out especially is the description of God as a 'figure like that of a man.'"[4] In John 8:17–18 Jesus Christ clearly states that his Father is a man. In these verses we read: "It is also written in your law, that the testimony of two men is true. I am one that bear witness of myself, and the Father that sent me beareth witness of me." In the 1611 edition of the King James Bible, Mark 10:18 reads: "And Jesus said unto him, 'Why callest thou me good? There is no *man* good, but one, that is *God*.'"[5] The phrase "no man" was removed from every subsequent printing of the King James Bible even though the same Greek word that underlies the 1611 rendition [*oudeis*] is also translated as "no man" in Revelation 7:9 and 14:3.

Joseph Smith's teachings about the nature of God also find support among the Dead Sea Scrolls discovered in the caves of Qumran. Some of these texts, such as *1QM 12.2* and *1QM 19*, identify God as a "glorious man."[6] Torleif Elgvin, a professor at the Norwegian Lutheran School of Theology, believes that one of the texts from Qumran (*4Q416*, fragment 1) should be rendered to say that God is "a creature of flesh."[7]

An ancient Armenian apocryphal document entitled *Concerning the Creation of Adam* not only teaches that God is a man but also presents other concepts that are familiar to some Latter-day Saints.

> When Adam departed and was walking around in the garden, the serpent spoke to Eve and said, "Why do you taste of all the trees, but from this one tree which is beautiful in appearance you do not taste?" Eve said, "Because God said, 'When you eat of that tree, you shall die.'" But the serpent said, "God has deceived you, for formerly God was man like you. When He ate of that fruit, He attained this great glory.

> That is why He told you not to eat, lest [by] eating [it] you would become equal to God." When she heard the advice of the serpent, she wanted to become divine. She promptly picked and ate of the fruit. And immediately she became stripped [of the light]. Now Adam came and saw his wife stripped [of the light and] he turned and said, "What is this you have done? Why did you eat of that fruit and become stripped [of the light]?" Eve said, "This fruit is extremely sweet and tasty; you take also [and] eat". . . Adam said, "I cannot taste it and become like you". . . But Eve cried and begged him and said, "Eat and do not separate me from you. If we live, let us live together, and if we die, let us die together". . . Adam, because of his love for the woman, could not restrain himself and he ate of the fruit and stripped himself of the light.[8]

In a Christian gnostic work called the *Corpus Hermeticum* (10.25) we find the straightforward statement that "God in the heavens is an immortal man."[9] Those scholars who are familiar with the gnostic system of belief point out that the "gnostic speculations about 'Man' were anchored in the 'older Israelite mentality.'"[10]

In the Book of Moses, which is a lost scriptural text restored through the Prophet Joseph Smith, we learn that "Man" is one of God's names. Moses 6:57 says: "Man of Holiness is his name, and the name of his Only Begotten is the Son of Man" (see also Moses 7:35). In Exodus 15:3 "man" [*ish*] is likewise applied to God as a divine name. This concept can also be seen in John 1:49–51 where the title "Son of God" is equated with the title "Son of Man." John 5:25–27 makes the same equation: "Son of God" = "Son of Man." Thus, "God" = "Man." Such a name/title can also be found in a Christian gnostic work from the Nag Hammadi library known as the *Apocryphon of John* (14.14). There, God is referred to as "Man."[11]

What does God look like? Joseph Smith claimed that when he saw the Father and the Son together during the First Vision they "exactly resembled each other in features and likeness."[12] The teachings of Jesus Christ confirm this point. "If you have seen me," said the Savior, "you have seen the Father" (John 14:8–9). In Hebrews 1:3 the apostle Paul states that Jesus Christ is in the "express image of [God's] person." The New International Version of the Bible translates Hebrews 1:3 as "exact representation of [God's] being." Paul, in Philippians 2:5–6, states that Jesus Christ is "in the form [*morphē*, shape] of God." Again, Paul teaches that Christ is "the image [*eikōn*, resemblance] of the invisible [*aoratou*, unseen] God" (Colossians 1:15; see also Matthew 17:5).

Some biblical scholars are willing to acknowledge that the God of the Old Testament is depicted as "a human being," even a "living man."[13] Latter-day Saints believe that the God of the Old Testament was Jesus Christ in His premortal state.

According to Joseph Fielding Smith "all revelation since the fall has come through Jesus Christ, who is the Jehovah of the Old Testament. . . . The Father has never dealt with man directly and personally since the fall, and He has never appeared except to introduce and bear record of the Son."[14] Thus, when Old Testament passages speak of God being seen, it is the Son who is being manifested to mortals. The Son speaks as if He were the Father by divine investiture of authority (see D&C 29:1, 42; John 5:43). The scriptures listed below demonstrate that the God of the Old Testament was seen by mortals on several occasions.

- "And the Lord *appeared* unto [Abraham] in the plains of Mamre" (Genesis 18:1, emphasis added).
- "I have *seen God face to face*" (Genesis 32:30, emphasis added).
- "Moses . . . was afraid to *look upon God*" (Exodus 3:6, emphasis added).
- "I will come down in the *sight* of all the people" (Exodus 19:11, emphasis added).
- "Then went up Moses, and Aaron, Nadab, and Abihu, and seventy of the elders of Israel. And they *saw the God of Israel*: and there was under his *feet* as it were a paved work of a sapphire stone . . . . the nobles of the children of Israel . . . *saw God*" (Exodus 24:9–11, emphasis added).
- "And the Lord spoke unto Moses *face to face*, as a man speaketh to a friend" (Exodus 33:11, emphasis added).
- "My servant Moses . . . . with him will I speak *mouth to mouth* . . . and the similitude [*t*^{e}*munah*, shape, image, embodiment] of the Lord shall he *behold*" (Numbers 12:7–8, emphasis added).
- "The Lord talked with you *face to face* in the mount out of the midst of the fire" (Deuteronomy 5:4, emphasis added).
- "And there arose not a prophet since in Israel like unto Moses, whom the Lord knew *face to face*" (Deuteronomy 34:10, emphasis added).
- "And the Lord was angry with Solomon, because his heart was turned from the Lord God of Israel, which had *appeared unto him* twice" (1 Kings 11:9, emphasis added).
- "In the year that King Uzziah died *I saw* also *the Lord* sitting upon a throne, high and lifted up, and his train filled the temple. . . . *[M]ine eyes have seen the King, the Lord of hosts*" (Isaiah 6:1, 5, emphasis added).

- "And above the firmament that was over their heads was the likeness of a throne, and the appearance of a sapphire stone: and upon the likeness of the throne was the likeness as *the appearance of a man* above upon it" (Ezekiel 1:26, emphasis added). According to the New English Bible translation of this verse, the God of the Old Testament had "a form in human likeness."

One passage in the book of Acts makes it clear that under certain circumstances mortals can also see God the Father. "But [Stephen], being full of the Holy Ghost, looked up steadfastly into heaven, and saw the glory of God, and Jesus standing on the right hand of God. And said, 'Behold, *I* see *the heavens opened, and the Son of Man standing on the right hand of God*'" (Acts 7:55–56, emphasis added). Since this scripture plainly states that God *can* be seen, what is one to make of biblical passages that say that God *cannot* be seen? It is evident from Joseph Smith's work on the Bible that these scriptures were tampered with in the past to make them conform with men's notions about God. Following is a comparison between the King James Version (KJV) and the Joseph Smith Translation (JST).

King James Version	Joseph Smith Translation
"Thou [Moses] canst not see my face: for there shall [be] no man see me, and live. . . . my face shall not be seen" (Exodus 33:20, 23).	"Thou [Moses] canst not see my face *at this time, lest mine anger be kindled against thee* also, *and I destroy thee, and thy people*; for there shall [be] no man *among them* see me *at this time*, and live, *for they are exceeding sinful. And no sinful man hath at any time, neither shall there be any sinful man at any time, that shall* see *my face and live*. . . . my face shall not be seen *as at other times; for I am angry with my people Israel*" (JST Exodus 33:20, 23).
"No man hath seen God at any time" (John 1:18).	"No man hath seen God at any time; *except he hath borne record of the Son*" (JST John 1:19).
"No man hath seen God at any time" (1 John 4:12).	"No man hath seen God at any time, *except them who believe*" (JST 1 John 4:12).

It was Joseph Smith's teaching that nobody can see God unless they undergo a transfiguration by the power of the Spirit. "For no man has seen God at any time in the flesh, except quickened by the Spirit of God" (D&C 67:11). This doctrine conforms perfectly with Acts 7:55–56 where it is stated that the apostle Stephen was able to see the Father and the Son because he was "full of the Holy Ghost." Moses 1:11, which is part of the Joseph Smith Translation of the book of Genesis, says that the prophet Moses "saw God face to face, and he talked with him, and the glory of God was upon Moses; therefore Moses could endure his presence." In verse two of this same chapter, Moses provides a further explanation. "But now mine own eyes have beheld God; but not my natural, but my spiritual eyes, for my natural eyes could not have beheld; for I should have withered and died in his presence; but his glory was upon me; and I beheld his face, for I was transfigured before him." This is similar to a statement reportedly made by the apostle Peter in the *Clementine Homilies* (17.16). In this source Peter says the eyes of mortals cannot see the forms of the Father and the Son because those exalted beings are illuminated "by exceeding great light. . . . [He] who sees God cannot live [because] the excess of light dissolves the flesh of him who sees; unless by the secret power of God the flesh be changed into the nature of light, so that it can see light."[15] In conjunction with this, we read in the pseudepigraphical book known as the *Ascension of Isaiah* (9.37) that the prophet Isaiah could see God only because "the eyes of [his] spirit were open."[16]

THE NATURE OF THE GODHEAD

The LDS doctrine of the Godhead, which claims to be a doctrine restored in its purity, is distinct from what is believed among sectarian Christians. The Doctrine and Covenants contains this concise statement: "The Father has a body of flesh and bones as tangible as man's; the Son also; but the Holy Ghost has not a body of flesh and bones, but is a personage of Spirit" (D&C 130:22).

Then what about John 4:24 which, in the King James Bible, plainly states that "God is a spirit"? Let us analyze this passage carefully. First, the reader will notice that in the King James Bible the word "is" is italicized. This is because the King James translators have inserted it on their own—it is not present in the Greek text from which the translation was made. Second, the reader should be made aware that the indefinite article "a" is not present in the Greek text either and has also been added at the discretion of the translators.[17] This leaves us with only two Greek words: *theos pneuma*–"God spirit." Interestingly, the Joseph Smith Translation of this verse (JST John 4:26) incorporates these two words into what was apparently the original text. "For unto such hath *God* promised His *Spirit*" (emphasis added).

What of the concept of the Trinity? Isn't 1 John 5:7 proof that the early Christians believed that the Father, Son, and Holy Ghost are one substance with three different manifestations? Not hardly. Some modern Bible translations do not even include this verse anymore because it is not found in the earliest Greek manuscripts of the New Testament. It may simply be an unauthorized addition.[18] Jesus clearly explained that members of the Godhead are "one" because they are unified. As a multitude of scriptures testify, the three members of the Godhead are "one" in knowledge, purpose, glory, and power (see John 10:30; 17:11, 20–23; cf. Acts 4:32; 1 Corinthians 1:10; 2 Corinthians 13:11; 1 Peter 3:8).

Was the Trinitarian concept a part of original Christianity? No, it certainly was not. In fact, "the exact theological definition of the doctrine of the Trinity was the result of a long process of development, which was not complete till the fifth century or even later."[19] Needless to say, the doctrine of the Trinity "is not to be found in the New Testament." Indeed, the word Trinity "does not occur in the Bible. It is generally acknowledged that the church father Tertullian (ca. A.D. 145–220) either coined the term or was the first to use it with reference to God. The explicit doctrine was thus formulated in the post-biblical period."[20] Even Catholic scholars admit that "among the Apostolic Fathers, there had been nothing even remotely approaching such a mentality or perspective" as "one God in three Persons."[21] The Nicene Creed, which forcefully promoted the metaphysical dogma of the Trinity, "would probably have been unintelligible to the first disciples" of Jesus Christ in the meridian of time.[22]

A correct understanding of the nature of the Godhead can be easily gleaned from the texts of the New Testament. Following are some of the scriptures that plainly indicate that God the Father and His Son Jesus Christ are two separate individuals.

- The Father and Son were seen together as two separate beings (see Acts 7:55–56).
- Jesus Christ is the Father's Son (see Mark 9:7; John 3:16; 9:35–37; 17:1; 20:17, 21, 31; Romans 15:6; Ephesians 3:14; Hebrews 1:6; 5:5).
- The Father is Jesus Christ's God (see Matthew 27:46; Mark 15:34; John 20:17; 2 Corinthians 11:31; Ephesians 1:3, 17; 1 Peter 1:3; Revelation 3:12).

- The Father is greater than the Son (see John 10:29; 14:28; 1 Corinthians 15:28).
- Jesus Christ intercedes between God and man (see John 14:6; Romans 8:34; Hebrews 7:25; 1 Timothy 2:5).
- The Father and the Son have distinct wills (see Matthew 26:39–42; Luke 22:41–42; John 5:30).
- The Son teaches the Father's doctrine, not His own (see John 7:16–17; 8:27–28).
- Jesus Christ did not perform His own work but His Father's work (see Luke 2:49–50; John 17:3–4).
- Jesus Christ prayed unto the Father (see Matthew 6:6–9; 26:39; 27:46; Luke 3:34; John 12:27–28; 16:26; 17:5–11).
- Jesus Christ commanded others to pray unto the Father (see Matthew 6:6, 9; Luke 11:2; Colossians 3:17; Hebrews 7:25–26).
- The Father "sent" His Son to the earth (Mark 9:37; John 3:16; 5:24; 6:38; 7:28–29; 8:26, 29, 42; 12:44–45; 17:3–10, 18, 25; 20:21; 1 John 4:14).
- While upon the earth Jesus Christ spoke of His Father as being in heaven (see Matthew 5:48; 6:9; 10:33; 16:17; Luke 11:2; John 14:12; 20:17).
- The Father spoke to His Son from heaven before witnesses (see Matthew 3:17; 17:5; Mark 1:11; Luke 3:22; John 12:28–30).
- Jesus Christ returned to the Father after His resurrection (see John 14:12; 16:27–28, 30; 1 Peter 3:21–22).
- The Father has committed all judgment unto His Son (see John 5:17–20, 22–23, 27; Romans 2:16; 2 Timothy 4:1).

Jesus Christ is Jehovah

A correct understanding of the nature of the Godhead includes correctly understanding the identity of Jehovah. Latter-day Saints teach that Jesus Christ was the "Jehovah" of the Old Testament.[23] The LDS viewpoint on this issue is unique among Christian denominations even though the doctrine is plainly spelled out in the New Testament. In John 12:37–41, for instance, we read that the prophet Isaiah was seeing Jesus Christ in the vision recorded in Isaiah 6:1–10. This was a vision of Jehovah.

Some of the early Church fathers also taught that Jesus was the God of the Old Testament. Irenaeus (ca. A.D. 115–202), bishop of Lyons, said in his work called *Against Heresies* (4.7.2, 4) that "all who have known God from the beginning, and have foretold the advent of Christ, have received the revelation from the Son Himself . . . [T]he Son . . . [is] that God who spake in human shape to Abraham, and again to Moses."[24] According to Justin Martyr (ca. A.D. 163), in his *Dialogue with Trypho* (113), "it was Jesus who appeared to and conversed with Moses, and Abraham, and all the other patriarchs without exception, ministering to the will of the Father."[25] Eusebius, who served as the bishop of Caesarea around A.D. 339, wrote in his *History of the Church* that "it is obvious that [the patriarchs] knew God's Christ Himself, since He appeared to Abraham, instructed Isaac, spoke to [Jacob], and conversed freely with Moses and the prophets who came later."[26]

The following chart is designed to demonstrate, from Old and New Testament texts, that Jehovah and Jesus Christ are the same being.

JEHOVAH	JESUS CHRIST
I am (Exodus 3:14)	**I am** (John 8:56–59)
Every knee to bow before (Isaiah 45:23)	**Every knee to bow before** (Philippians 2:10–11)
Lord of Lords (Deuteronomy 10:17)	**Lord of Lords** (Revelation 17:14)
Judge (Psalms 96:13)	**Judge** (John 5:22)
Rock (Deuteronomy 32:3–4)	**Rock** (1 Corinthians 10:4)
Cornerstone (Psalms 118:22)	**Cornerstone** (Acts 4:10–12)
Creator (Isaiah 45:12)	**Creator** (Ephesians 3:9)
Almighty (Genesis 17:1)	**Almighty** (Revelation 1:8)
Savior (Isaiah 45:15)	**Savior** (1 John 4:14)
Redeemer (Isaiah 54:5)	**Redeemer** (Revelation 5:6–9)

JEHOVAH	JESUS CHRIST
Pierced One (Zechariah 12:9–10)	**Pierced One** (Revelation 1:7)
Holy One (Isaiah 43:3)	**Holy One** (Mark 1:24)
Light and Life (Psalms 36:9)	**Light and Life** (John 1:4, 9)
Bridegroom (Isaiah 62:5)	**Bridegroom** (Matthew 9:15)
Shepherd (Psalms 80:1)	**Shepherd** (John 10:14)
Living Water (Jeremiah 2:13)	**Living Water** (John 4:13–14)
The First and the Last (Isaiah 48:12)	**The First and the Last** (Revelation 22:13)

The Personage of the Holy Ghost

The Prophet Joseph Smith taught: "I have always declared God to be a distinct personage, Jesus Christ a separate and distinct personage from God the Father, and that the Holy Ghost was a distinct personage and a Spirit: and these three constitute three distinct personages, and three Gods."[27] Does the New Testament sustain the Prophet's doctrine that the Holy Ghost is a separate and distinct personage from the Father and the Son? Yes, it certainly does. The following scriptures demonstrate this point.

- All three personages were manifested at Jesus Christ's baptism (see Luke 3:22).
- All three personages are to be mentioned during the ordinance of baptism (see Matthew 28:19).
- Stephen was filled with the Holy Ghost and then saw the Father and the Son (see Acts 7:55–56).
- Paul spoke of "the grace of the Lord Jesus Christ, and the love of God, and the communion of the Holy Ghost" (2 Corinthians 13:14).
- God the Father gives the Holy Ghost to the obedient (see Luke 11:13; Acts 5:32).
- The Savior says that the Holy Ghost will give His disciples utterance (see Mark 13:11; Luke 12:12).

- The Father will send the Holy Ghost in Jesus Christ's name (see John 14:16, 26; 15:26).
- The Holy Ghost led the Lord Jesus Christ into the wilderness (see Luke 4:1).
- The Holy Ghost testifies of Jesus Christ (see John 15:26).
- God the Father anointed Jesus Christ with the Holy Ghost (see Acts 10:38).
- The Holy Ghost is "sent" down from heaven (1 Peter 1:12).
- Jesus Christ speaks through the Holy Ghost (see Acts 1:1–2).
- The Holy Ghost will "not speak of Himself" but He will repeat the words of Jesus Christ and also glorify Christ (John 16:13–14).

HEAVENLY MOTHER

One of the most interesting, and logical, doctrines of the LDS Church teaches that God the Father has a spouse. According to President Joseph F. Smith, it was the Father who revealed this concept to Joseph Smith.[28] The Prophet evidently first taught the Heavenly Mother doctrine to others in 1839 while consoling Zina D. Huntington after the death of her mother. Joseph told Zina that once she had passed through the veil between life and death she would not only be reunited with her earthly mother, but she would also become acquainted with her "eternal Mother, the wife of . . . Father in Heaven." Eliza R. Snow learned the Heavenly Mother doctrine from the Prophet at about this same time and several years later she included the concept in a poem entitled "O My Father."[29] In 1909 the First Presidency of the LDS Church officially explained that "all men and women are in the similitude of the universal Father and Mother, and are literally the sons and daughters of Deity"[30] Even though Latter-day Saints acknowledge the existence of a Heavenly Mother, they do not pray to her nor worship her in any way.[31]

A biblical precedent for the Heavenly Mother doctrine can be found in Genesis 1:26–27 where God, addressing an unidentified audience, says: "Let *us* make man in *our* image, after *our* likeness . . . So God created man in his own image, in the image of God created He him; *male and female* created He them" (emphasis added). In Genesis 5:1–2 we again read that "God created man, in the likeness of God made He him; *male and female* created He them" (emphasis added). We may deduce from these scriptures that the "likeness of God" is "male and female."

There are other hints of the existence of a Heavenly Mother to be found in the Bible. We read in Ephesians 3:15 of the "family in heaven" and the apostle Paul explains, in 1 Corinthians 11:11, that "neither is the man without the woman . . . in the Lord." We might also closely consider this intriguing passage in Genesis 2:23–24: "This is now bone of my bones, and flesh of my flesh: she shall be called woman, because she was taken out of man. Therefore shall a man leave his *father* and his *mother*, and shall cleave unto his wife: and they shall be one flesh" (emphasis added).

The Latter-day Saint belief in a Heavenly Mother is paralleled by the belief of the ancient Hebrews. According to Peter Hayman "many, perhaps the majority, of ancient Israelites," believed that God had a "female consort."[32] Some Jews, during a much later age, held a similar view. In the collection of Jewish writings known as the *Zohar* (3.12*a*), it is said that "the soul has a father and a mother, as the body has a father and a mother in this world. In fact, all things above and below proceed from Male and Female."[33]

And what of the early Christians? Did they believe God the Father had a spouse? Yes, some of them did. In what appears to be a ritual dialogue that followed an initiation ceremony, Melito, who served as the bishop of Sardis (ca. A.D. 170), speaks to a group of orthodox Christian "brides and bridegrooms" of "the Father" and "your Mother." Said Melito, "We hymn, we exalt (them) exceedingly, we holy ones."[34]

THE NATURE OF MANKIND

LDS doctrine proclaims that men and women are literally the sons and daughters of Deity (see Moses 6:36, 51). Biblical texts confirm this profound truth. The apostle Paul declared, through a revelation given by the Spirit, that "we are the children of God" (Romans 8:16). Man is created in the likeness [*d*^{e}*muth*] and image [*tselem*] of God (see Genesis 1:26–27). In Genesis 5:3 these exact same Hebrew words are used to describe Seth, the son of Adam. "And Adam . . . begat a son in his own likeness [*d*^{e}*muth*], after his image [*tselem*]; and called his name Seth." According to Acts 17:28-29 "we are the offspring [*genos*] of God." The Greek word *genos* is related to the Latin word *genus* which means "race." Hence, mankind is of the same "race" as God. And in Hebrews 12:9 we are informed that God is "the Father of [our] spirits."

Angels are Men

"Angels . . . are resurrected personages, having bodies of flesh and bones" taught the Prophet Joseph Smith (D&C 129:1).[35] Parley P. Pratt wrote that "Gods, angels, and men are all of one species, one race, one great family."[36] According to Elder Bruce R. McConkie, angels of God come "from among His offspring and are themselves pressing forward along the course of progression and salvation."[37] Joseph Smith emphatically taught that "an angel of God never has wings."[38] And biblical scholars confirm this point by stating that "Hebrew angels were men, and were not winged."[39] This idea is borne out by scriptures like Acts 10:3 and 30 where we read that the "angel of God" who appeared to Cornelius was a "man." Also, the angel who appeared to Joshua in the Old Testament (Joshua 5:13–15) is called a "man." The angel who showed Ezekiel the temple of God is likewise identified as a "man" (Ezekiel 40:3–4). And finally, the angel who showed the apostle John part of his vision explained that he was John's "fellowservant" and of his "brethren the prophets" (Revelation 19:10; 22:8–9).

Matthew 28:2–6 speaks of "the angel of the Lord" whose "countenance was like lightning, and his raiment white as snow." Mark 16:5 identifies this angel as "a young man . . . clothed in a long white garment." Luke 24:3–4, however, states that there were actually "two men . . . in shining garments" present at the Savior's sepulcher. In John 20:11–12 they are called "two angels in white." Hence, we gather that the "angels" at the garden tomb were "men." After the resurrection the twelve apostles saw the Savior ascend into heaven before their eyes. "And while they looked steadfastly toward heaven as he went up, behold, two men [i.e., angels] stood by them in white apparel" (Acts 1:10).

THE NATURE OF LUCIFER

What is the nature of Lucifer? Is he part animal, as so often depicted in sectarian Christian art? In latter-day scripture we learn that Lucifer is a son of God, albeit a very bad one. "Satan came among them, saying: 'I am also a son of God,'" says Moses 5:13. In the premortal life, Lucifer was "an angel of God who was in authority in the presence of God [but he] rebelled against the Only Begotten Son . . . [and] was thrust down from the presence of God and the Son" (D&C 76:25). Spencer W. Kimball referred to Lucifer as Christ's "brother."[40] In the book of Job, we read: "Now there was a day when the sons of God came to present themselves before the Lord, and Satan came also among them" (Job 1:6). The Joseph Smith Translation changes "sons" to "children," thus identifying Lucifer as a child of God.

Lactantius, an early Christian writer who lived A.D. 260–340, taught in his book *Divine Institutions* (2.9) that "before creating the world, God produced a spirit like Himself, replete with the virtues of the Father. Later he made another, in whom the mark of divine origin was erased, because this one was besmirched by the poison of jealousy and turned therefore from good to evil. . . . He was jealous of his older Brother who, remaining united with the Father, insured His affection unto himself. This being who from good became bad is called Devil by the Greeks." The Catholic scholar Giovanni Papini, in commenting on this statement says: "According to Lactantius, Lucifer would have been nothing less than the brother of the Logos. . . . The elder spirit, filled with every divine virtue and beloved by God above all other spirits, can easily be recognized as the Word, that is, the Son. But Lactantius' story leads one to think that the other spirit, also endowed with every grace, was the second son of the Father: the future Satan would be, no less, the younger brother of the future Christ."[41]

Both ancient and modern scripture speak of a premortal "war in heaven" when Satan and his followers were cast out and sent to the earth (Revelation 12:7–9; see also Moses 4:1–4; Abraham 3:23–28; D&C 29:36–38). According to the Prophet Joseph Smith, "the contention in heaven was [that] Jesus said there would be certain souls that would not be saved; and the devil said he could save them all, and laid his plans before the grand council, who gave their vote in favor of Jesus Christ. So the devil rose up in rebellion against God, and was cast down, with all who put up their heads for him."[42] This teaching finds confirmation in the words of the early Christian fathers. Origen (ca. A.D. 240) taught that "before the eons existed, all spirits were pure; demons, souls and angels alike, all served God and did what he commanded them. The devil was one of them. He had free will and wanted to set himself up against God, but God cast him down."[43]

PREMORTAL LIFE

Joseph Smith provided the world with several scriptural texts that teach the Lord "made . . . men before they were in the flesh" (Moses 6:51; see also 3:5). In D&C 93:29 it is related that "man was . . . in the beginning with God." And in the Book of Abraham, it is even stated that God selected some of his premortal children to serve in leadership capacities upon the earth (see Abraham 3:22–28). Is there any evidence to support Joseph Smith's claim that the doctrine of premortal existence was taught among the Israelites and Christians of former dispensations? Yes, there is plenty of evidence to support such a claim.

Old Testament and Jewish Evidence

There are hints of the doctrine of premortal life in Old Testament texts. In Job chapter 38 verses 4 and 7, for instance, we read that "the sons of God shouted for joy" when the foundations of the earth were laid. The book of Jeremiah, however, contains an even clearer reference to premortality. In chapter 1 verses 4 and 5, we find the following statement: "Then the word of the Lord came unto me, saying, 'Before I formed thee in the belly I knew thee; and before thou camest forth out of the womb I sanctified thee, and I ordained thee a prophet unto the nations.'" This is strikingly similar to Joseph Smith's teaching that "every man who has a calling to minister to the inhabitants of the world was ordained to that very purpose in the Grand Council of heaven before this world was."[44]

In an apocryphal text called *The Wisdom of Solomon* (8.19–20), which was included in almost every Christian Bible up through the seventeenth century, King Solomon is reported to have said that because he was "noble" in premortal times he "entered an undefiled body." In commenting on this verse, David Winston says that "we must conclude that the words 'I entered an undefiled body' are meant to suggest the pre-existence of souls of varying spiritual capacities, and that in the case of Solomon it was a noble soul that had taken the initiative of entering an undefiled body." Winston further states that "this verse is as clear a statement of the concept of preexistent souls as one could wish, and there is no need to explain it away as many commentators have done."[45] It is clear that the doctrine of the premortal life was widespread among the ancient Jews since "in the Talmud and Midrash, pre-existence is constantly taught."[46]

New Testament and Early Christian Evidence

The question posed in John 9:2 is prime evidence that the doctrine of the premortal existence was understood by the disciples of Jesus Christ. This passage reads: "And his disciples asked him, saying, 'Master, who did sin, this man, or his parents, that he was born blind?'" This question explicitly implies that the blind man had a conscious existence and the capacity to make choices prior to his mortal birth.

There are other New Testament scriptures that also suggest the premortal existence of human beings. In Ephesians 1:3–6, the apostle Paul addresses a group of Saints and says that God had chosen them "before the foundation of the world."[47] And in Titus 1:1–2, Paul states that God made the promise of eternal life "before the world began." In the *Clementine Recognitions* (1.28), the apostle Peter is represented as saying that the earth was created for man but the spirit of man is older than the earth.[48]

Some of the Christians who lived after the time of the apostles spoke of the doctrine of premortal life. Origen of Alexandria (ca. A.D. 185–254), for instance, said in *De Principiis* (4.1.23) that "everyone, accordingly, of those who descend to the earth is, according to his deserts, or agreeably to the position which he occupied there [i.e., the premortal sphere], ordained to be born in this world, in a different country, or among a different nation, or in a different mode of life, or surrounded by infirmities of a different kind, or to be descended from religious parents, or parents who are not religious."[49]

The doctrine of premortal life, like some of the other vital doctrines of the gospel, was discarded by those who no longer had authoritative leaders to guide their decisions. This belief was officially declared "anathema" by a council of bishops in A.D. 553 at Constantinople.

THE CREATION

Christian sects have inherited the belief that God created the universe and the earth *ex nihilo*, or "out of nothing." But Joseph Smith taught differently. According to the Prophet "this earth was organized or formed out of other planets which were broken up and remodeled and made into the one on which we live."[50] On another occasion he said: "You ask the learned doctors [of theology] why they say the world was made out of nothing; and they will answer, 'Doesn't the Bible say [God] *created* the world?' And they infer, from the word 'create,' that it must have been made out of nothing. Now, the word 'create' came from the [Hebrew] word *baurau* which does not mean to create out of nothing; it means to organize; the same as a man would organize materials and build a ship. Hence, we infer that God had materials to organize the world out of chaos—chaotic matter, which is element . . . . [These elements] may be organized and reorganized, but not destroyed."[51]

Joseph Smith's teachings on this subject are supported by the scriptures, by Jewish documents, and by early Christian texts. Colossians 1:16 states that "by [Jesus Christ] were all things created, that are in heaven, and that are in earth, visible and invisible . . . all things were created by him." The Greek word behind "created" is *ktizō* and it means "to fabricate."[52] A Jewish apocryphal document known as the *Wisdom of Solomon* (11.17), which is still today considered to be scripture by the Catholics, says of God: "your all-powerful hand . . . created the world out of formless matter."[53]

Christian documents tell the same story. In a document called *The Instructor* (3.12), Clement of Alexandria (A.D. 150–215) taught that "the universe" was created out of a "shapeless mass of matter" and the "ordered sphere" of the earth was formed from "a confused heap."[54] Justin Martyr (ca. A.D. 165) in his *First Apology* (10) indicated that it was the Christian doctrine of his day that "in the beginning [God] . . . create[d] all things out of unformed matter."[55] Jonathan Goldstein tells us that "medieval Jewish thinkers . . . held that the account of creation in Genesis could be interpreted to mean that God created from pre-existing formless matter, and ancient Jewish texts state that he did so."[56]

SALVATION

While many sectarian Christian groups teach that one's salvation is based solely upon their faith in Jesus Christ, the Prophet Joseph Smith taught that one's salvation is dependent upon a combination of faith and works. In the third Article of Faith, the Prophet wrote: "We believe that through the atonement of Christ, all mankind may be saved, by obedience to the laws and ordinances of the gospel." Does this mean that Latter-day Saints do not believe that they are saved by the grace of God? Certainly not. The Book of Mormon plainly teaches that "it is only in and through the grace of God that ye are saved" (2 Nephi 10:24). But we also find an important rejoinder in that book of scripture. In 2 Nephi 25:23 we read that "it is by grace that we are saved, after all we can do."

The LDS concept of salvation is consistent with the teachings of the Bible. In Revelation 20:12 the apostle John says, "And I saw the dead, small and great, stand before God; and the books were opened: and another book was opened, which is the book of life: and the dead were judged out of those things which were written in the books, according to their *works*" (emphasis added). The apostle James asked: "What doth it profit, my brethren, though a man say he hath faith, and have not works? Can faith save him?" (James 2:14). In verse 17 he answers the question. "Even so faith, if it hath not works, is dead, being alone." "For as the body without the spirit is dead, so faith without works is dead also" (v. 26). Righteous works, according to James, make one's faith "perfect" (v. 22). By works a man "is justified, and not by faith only" (v. 24).

Still, critics of the LDS faith may appeal to some biblical passages that they interpret as saying that salvation comes by grace alone. Such scriptures usually originate with the apostle Paul. A favorite text in this category is Ephesians 2:8–9 which reads: "For by grace are ye saved through faith; and that not of yourselves: it is the gift of God. Not of works, lest any man should boast." But biblical scholars have pointed out that the "works" spoken of in this passage are the "Old Testament commandments and Jewish customs." In other words, Paul is speaking here about the works of the Law of Moses that some of the Jewish converts to Christianity (i.e., Judaizers) were trying to impose upon the Gentile converts.[57] Similar scriptures, such as Romans 3:27–28, should also be approached from this perspective.

A statistical look at the Bible passages on salvation is most interesting. "The New Testament records 541 scriptural statements by over sixteen different biblical personalities that pertain directly or indirectly to the way salvation is achieved. The preponderance of evidence is clearly in favor of statements that indicate that man will be held accountable and judged on the basis of his works, deeds, acts, fruits, obedience, and so forth. Of the 541 New Testament scriptural statements 418 (or 77%) are supportive of works as a criterion in final judgment."[58] In studying the New Testament scriptures on salvation, one must keep in mind that Jesus Christ's words take precedence over all others. And He has said: "Not everyone that saith unto me, 'Lord, Lord' shall enter into the kingdom of heaven; but he that *doeth* the will of my Father which is in heaven" (Matthew 7:21, emphasis added). And on another occasion He declared: "For the Son of man shall come in the glory of his Father with his angels; and then he shall reward every man according to his *works*" (Matthew 16:17, emphasis added).

CONTINUOUS REVELATION

A basic belief of sectarian Christianity is that the heavens are now sealed; divine revelation has ceased. The Bible is the final word of God to mankind, they say. The Prophet Joseph Smith pointed out the obvious flaw in this belief. "It is nowhere said in that volume by the mouth of God that He would not, after giving what is there contained, speak again."[59]

Joseph Smith taught that divine revelation continues not only for the restored Church at large, but even for individual members of the Church who have the privilege of receiving revelations to govern their personal affairs. The Prophet said that "the [First] Presidency [is] over the Church; and revelations of the mind and will of God to the Church are to come through the [First] Presidency. This is the order of heaven, and the power and privilege of this Priesthood. It is also the privilege of any officer in this Church to obtain revelations, so far as relates to his particular calling and duty in the Church."[60] On another occasion the Prophet taught that "no man can receive the Holy Ghost without receiving revelations. The Holy Ghost is a revelator."[61] Revelation is vitally important to all, said Joseph, because "salvation cannot come without revelation; it is in vain for anyone to minister without it. No man is a minister of Jesus Christ . . . except he has the testimony of Jesus; and this is the spirit of prophecy [see Revelation 19:10]. Whenever salvation has been administered, it has been by testimony."[62]

The following New Testament scriptures support the doctrine of Joseph Smith that the heavens are not sealed. They unmistakably demonstrate that the members of the meridian Church were receiving divine revelation and guidance long *after* the Savior had ascended into heaven.

- "Ask, and it shall be given you; seek, and ye shall find; knock, and it shall be opened unto you. For everyone that asketh receiveth; and he that seeketh findeth; and to him that knocketh it shall be opened" (Matthew 7:7–8).
- "All that Jesus began both to do and teach, until the day in which he was taken up, after that he through the Holy Ghost had given commandments unto the apostles whom he had chosen" (Acts 1:1–2).
- "But God hath revealed them unto us by his Spirit: for the Spirit searcheth all things, yea, the deep things of God. . . . the Holy Ghost teacheth" (1 Corinthians 2:10, 13).

- "And in these days came prophets from Jerusalem unto Antioch. And there stood up one of them named Agabus, and signified by the Spirit that there should be great [famine] throughout all the world: which came to pass in the days of Claudius Caesar" (Acts 11:27–28).
- "Now there were in the church that was at Antioch certain prophets and teachers . . . . As they ministered to the Lord, and fasted, the Holy Ghost said, 'Separate me Barnabas and Saul for the work whereunto I have called them.' . . . So they, being sent forth by the Holy Ghost, departed" (Acts 13:1–4).
- "And . . . there came down from Judea a certain prophet named Agabus. And when he was come unto us, he . . . said, 'Thus saith the Holy Ghost . . .'" (Acts 21:10–11).
- "For to one is given by the Spirit . . . the word of knowledge" (1 Corinthians 12:8).
- "These things have I spoken unto you, being yet present with you. But the Comforter, which is the Holy Ghost, whom the Father will send in my name, he shall teach you all things" (John 14:25–26).
- "Howbeit when he, the Spirit of truth, is come, he will guide you into all truth: for he shall not speak of himself; but whatsoever he shall hear, that shall he speak: and he will show you things to come. He shall glorify me: for he shall receive of mine, and shall show it unto you" (John 16:13–14).
- "He that hath an ear, let him hear what the Spirit saith unto the churches." Notice that a good portion of the book of Revelation consists of Christ delivering revelations from heaven to His scattered churches through His authorized representative—an apostle" (Revelation 2:7; see Revelation 2:2–5).
- In 1 Corinthians 14:6 the apostle Paul indicates that it was expected that "revelation" would continue among Christ's disciples after his ascension. In Ephesians 1:17 Paul even prays that God the Father will grant "the spirit of . . . revelation" unto the Ephesian Saints.

THREE DEGREES OF GLORY

The seventy-sixth section of the Doctrine and Covenants records a series of divine visions shown to Joseph Smith and Sidney Rigdon on 16 February 1832. While viewing these visions, Joseph and Sidney learned that there are three degrees of glory that will be inherited by most of the sons and daughters of God after the resurrection. These glories, in descending order, are the Celestial, Terrestrial, and Telestial kingdoms. The concept of multiple heavens is foreign to the dogmatic systems of most Christian sects, but it was most definitely known among the ancient Israelites and the early Christians.

For an Israelite example we need only turn to a document known as the *Testament of the Twelve Patriarchs.* Within this text, the "Testament of Levi" purports to report the words of Levi who was the head of one of the twelve tribes of Israel. This document (2.5–3.4) states that Levi ascended through three heavens, accompanied by an angel of the Lord. The lowest or "first heaven" was "dark" because it "sees all the injustices of humankind." The "second heaven" was "much brighter and more lustrous" than the first. Finally, Levi ascended to "the uppermost heaven" which was even "more lustrous and beyond compare." In this place, which the angel called "the Holy of Holies," Levi saw God seated upon His throne.[63]

The Christians who lived during the generation of the Savior were also familiar with the concept of multiple heavens. In 2 Corinthians 12:2–4, the apostle Paul mentions the "third heaven" but in 1 Corinthians 15:40–42 he says much more. In "the resurrection of the dead," there is a "glory of the sun," and a "glory of the moon," and a "glory of the stars." In connection with these eternal abodes, the King James Version of the Bible refers to "the glory of the celestial" and "the glory of the terrestrial." This is almost an exact match with the information in the seventy-sixth section of the Doctrine and Covenants.

In Matthew 13:8–9 the Savior teaches the parable of the sower. He speaks of seeds bringing forth fruit; some a hundredfold, some sixtyfold, and some thirtyfold. Irenaeus (ca. A.D. 115–202), the bishop of Lyons, tied together the Lord's parable and the concept of three heavens in a work called *Against Heresies* (5.36.1–2). He reports that according to the Elders of the Church "those who are deemed worthy of an abode in heaven shall go there, others shall enjoy the delights of paradise, and others shall possess the splendor of the city . . . . [They say moreover], that there is this distinction between the habitation of those who produce an hundredfold, and that of those who produce sixtyfold, and that of those who produce thirtyfold: for the first will be taken up into the heavens, the second will dwell in paradise, the last will inhabit the city. . . . The [Elders, who were] the disciples of the apostles, affirm that this is the gradation and arrangement of those who are saved."[64]

GODHOOD

Joseph Smith taught the stunning, and inspiring, doctrine that men and women can literally become like the Savior by sharing in His divine attributes and powers (see D&C 76:54–58; 132:19, 37). According to President John Taylor, "man is a dual being, possessed of body and spirit, made in the image of God, and connected with Him and with eternity. He is a god in embryo and will live and progress throughout the eternal ages, if obedient to the laws of the Godhead."[65] President Lorenzo Snow said the Lord had revealed to him, independent of Joseph Smith, that "as God now is, man may be."[66] During his famous King Follett discourse, the Prophet taught: "You have got to learn how to be a god yourself . . . to be priests and kings as all gods [have] done."[67] This statement hints at the fact that such an exalted station can only be reached through participation in the ordinances of the temple.[68]

The root of the doctrine of godhood can be found in the book of Genesis where Adam and Eve became "as gods" by partaking of the Tree of Knowledge (Genesis 3:5), a fact confirmed by God Himself (see Genesis 3:22). In an early Jewish document (*Mid. Alpha Beta diR. Akiba, BhM* 3.32) the concept of deification can be found. "The Holy One . . . will in the future call all of the pious by their names, and give them a cup of elixir of life in their hands so that they should live and endure forever. . . . [and He will also] reveal to all the pious in the world to come the Ineffable Name with which new heavens and a new earth can be created, so that all of them should be able to create new worlds."[69]

And what of the Christians who lived during the time of Christ? Did they really believe they could become divine like their Lord? The Savior commanded his disciples in Matthew 5:48, "Be ye therefore perfect, even as your Father which is in heaven is perfect." The apostle Paul taught that the Saints are to be "changed into the same image [of Christ] from glory to glory, even as by the Spirit of the Lord" (2 Corinthians 3:18). And the apostle Peter taught that the Saints may be "partakers of the divine nature" (2 Peter 1:4; see also 2 Thessalonians 2:14; 1 Corinthians 2:7; Colossians 3:4; 2 Peter 1:3; Romans 8:17; cf. D&C 84:38; 76:58–60; 132:19–21).

The following chart serves to demonstrate that the early Christians expected to become like their Lord by living a life of holiness and righteousness.

	Jesus Christ	Saints
Crown	Revelation 14:14	James 1:12; Revelation 2:10; 4:4, 10
White Robe	Matthew 17:2; Mark 9:3; Luke 9:29	Revelation 6:11; 7:9–14
Scepter	Hebrews 1:8	Revelation 2:26–27
Throne	Revelation 3:21	Revelation 3:21
Heir of God	Romans 8:17	Romans 8:14–21; Galatians 4:1–7
Son Title	Hebrews 1:5, 5:5; John 3:1; Philippians 2:15; 2 Peter1:4	Romans 8:14, 16; John 1:12; 1 John 3:1–2; Galatians 3:26
King and Priest	John 1:49; Hebrews 3:1	Revelation 1:6; 5:10
Perfect	Matthew 5:48	Matthew 5:48
One with God	John 4:11; 17:20–21; 10:30	John 17:21–23
Equal with God	John 5:18; Philippians 2:6	John 17:22; Romans 8:29

The leaders of the Christian communities who lived after the time of the apostles often spoke of the divine nature of man. And they were not shy to utilize the word "god" in describing those who reached their full potential.

Irenaeus (ca. A.D. 115–202), bishop of Lyons, in his writings known as *Against Heresies* (4.38.4) said, "we have not been made gods from the beginning, but at first merely men, then at length gods."[70] Irenaeus also wrote in the same collection of writings (5.preface) that Jesus Christ "bec[a]me what we are, that He might bring us to be even what He is Himself."[71]

Tertullian (ca. A.D. 155–225), an elder in Carthage, wrote in his work called *Against Hermogenes* (5): "For we shall be even gods, if we shall deserve to be among those of whom He declared, 'I have said, ye are gods' [see John 10:34–36], and 'God standeth in the congregation of the gods' [see Psalms 82:1]. But this comes of His own grace, not from any property in us, because it is He alone who can make gods."[72]

Clement of Alexandria (A.D. 160–215), head of the theological school in Alexandria, Egypt, records in his *Stromata* (7.10) that in the "future life" we shall be among "gods . . . those who have become perfect . . . [and] become pure in heart. . . . [T]hey are called by the appellation of gods, being destined to sit on thrones with the other gods that have been first put in their places by the Savior."[73]

Justin Martyr (ca. A.D. 163), an educator in Rome, said in his *Dialogue with Trypho* (124) that "all men are deemed worthy of becoming 'gods,' and of having power to become sons of the Highest."[74] This phraseology is similar to that which is found in D&C 76:56–58. There we read that those who are made "priests and kings" after the order of the Only Begotten Son "are gods, even the sons of God."

Origen (ca. A.D. 185–251), head of the theological school in Alexandria, Egypt, states in his *Commentary on the Gospel of John* (2.2–3) that "the firstborn of all creation, who is the first to be with God . . . is a being of more exalted rank than the other gods beside Him, of whom God is the God, as it is written, 'The God of gods, the Lord, hath spoken and called the earth.' It was by the offices of the firstborn that they became gods, for He drew from God in generous measure that they should be made gods, and He communicated it to them according to His own bounty. . . . Now it is possible that some may dislike what we have said representing the Father as the one true God, but admitting other beings besides the true God, who have become gods by having a share of God. They may fear that the glory of Him who surpasses all creation may be lowered."[75]

Jerome (ca. A.D. 347–419), commenting on Psalms 82:6, said that God "made man for that purpose, that from men they may become gods." Jerome also informs us that when Psalms 136:2 says "'Give thanks to the God of gods' . . . [it is] referring to those gods . . . in the divine assembly. They who cease to be mere men, abandon the ways of vice and are become perfect, are gods and sons of the Most High."[76]

All of the preceding material helps to explain Paul's statement in 1 Corinthians 8:4–6. The vast majority of non-LDS biblical commentators believe that when Paul said "there be gods many and lords many," he was referring to pagan gods and lords. But Joseph Smith was emphatic about the proper interpretation of this passage. "I say there are Gods many and Lords many, but to us only one [God], and we are to be in subjection to that one. . . . Some say I do not interpret the scripture the same as they do. They say it means the heathen's gods. . . . I testify that Paul had no allusion to the heathen gods. I have it from God, and get over it if you can. I have a witness of the Holy Ghost, and a testimony that Paul had no allusion to the heathen gods in the text."[77] Joseph Smith's position is strengthened by scriptures such as Deuteronomy 10:17, Joshua 22:22, and Psalms 136:2–3 which explicitly state that "God is God of gods, and Lord of lords." Indeed, the Prophet placed these deities in the heavenly council. "The head God called together the Gods and sat in grand council to bring forth the world. The grand councilors sat at the head in yonder heavens and contemplated the creation of the worlds which were created at the time."[78] There are several scholarly translations of Paul's statement that bolster Joseph Smith's interpretation of it. These versions of the verse say that "there are indeed gods many and lords many."[79] Clement of Alexandria in his work known as *Stromata* (6.14) makes it clear that Paul is referring to heavenly Lords and Gods, not pagan ones. He says those who become "perfect . . . according to the image of the Lord . . . [will receive] the just inheritance of the lords and gods."[80]

Are Latter-day Saints the only modern Christians who believe that righteous men and women can achieve the status of godhood? Certainly not. The following quotation demonstrates that this is the goal of many of those who desire to be Christlike.

> Deification (Greek, *theosis*) is for Orthodoxy the goal of every Christian. Man, according to the Bible, is "made in the image and likeness of God" . . . . It is possible for man to become like God, to become deified, to become god by grace. This doctrine is based on many passages of both [the] Old Testament and New Testament (e.g., Psalms 82:6; 2 Peter 1:4), and it is essentially the teaching both of St. Paul, though he tends to use the language of filial adoption (cf. Romans 8:9–17; Galatians 4:5–7), and the Fourth Gospel (cf. John 17:21–23).
>
> The language of 2 Peter is taken up by St. Irenaeus, in his famous phrase, "if the Word has been made man, it is so that men may be made gods" (Adv. Haer V, Pref.), and becomes the standard in Greek [Orthodox] theology. In the fourth century St. Athanasius repeats Irenaeus almost word for word, and in the fifth century St. Cyril of Alexandria says that we shall become sons "by participation" (Greek methexis). Deification is the central idea in the spirituality of St. Maximus the Confessor, for whom the doctrine is the corollary of the Incarnation . . . and St. Symeon the New Theologian at the end of the tenth century writes, "He who is God

> by nature converses with those whom he has made gods by grace, as a friend converses with his friends, face to face." . . .
>
> Finally, it should be noted that deification does not mean absorption into God, since the deified creature remains itself and distinct. It is the whole human being, body and soul, who is transfigured in the Spirit into the likeness of the divine nature, and deification is the goal of every Christian.[81]

SUMMARY

Joseph Smith claimed that the Lord had commissioned him to restore the doctrines of the gospel of Jesus Christ in the latter days. The material that has been presented in this chapter demonstrates that the doctrines of the LDS Church were indeed had among the ancient Israelites and the early Christians. Therefore, the doctrines of the LDS Church qualify as an authentic restoration of ancient, orthodox beliefs. Well might one ask: "If a Church does not teach doctrines that were taught by the Lord's covenant people, then how can they claim to be the Lord's true Church?"

NOTES

1. *TPJS*, 345–46.
2. *WJS*, 60.
3. James Strong, *The New Strong's Exhaustive Concordance of the Bible* (Nashville: Thomas Nelson Publishers, 1996), Hebrew and Aramaic Dictionary of the Old Testament, 7, word #376.
4. Phillip B. Munoa, III, *Four Powers in Heaven* (Sheffield, England: Sheffield Academic Press, 1998), 99.
5. Alfred W. Pollard, *The Holy Bible: An Exact Reprint in Roman Type, Page for Page, of the Authorized Version Published in the Year 1611* (New York: Oxford University Press, 1985), Mark 10:18, emphasis added.
6. Munoa, III, *Four Powers in Heaven*, 103–04.
7. David L. Paulsen, "The Doctrine of Divine Embodiment: Restoration, Judeo-Christian, and Philosophical Perspectives," *Brigham Young University Studies*, vol. 35, no. 4, 1995–96, 47, n. 105.
8. William L. Lipscomb, *The Armenian Apocryphal Adam Literature* (Atlanta: Scholars Press, 1990), 262–64, emphasis added.
9. This work is cited in Munoa, III, *Four Powers in Heaven*, 102.
10. Ibid.
11. Søren Giversen, *Apocryphon Johannis* (Copenhagen: Prostant Apud Munksgaard, 1963), 73.
12. *Times and Seasons*, vol. 3, no. 9, 1 March 1842, 707.
13. Edmond Jacob, *Theology of the Old Testament* (New York: Harper and Brothers, 1958), 39.
14. Joseph Fielding Smith, *Doctrines of Salvation* (Salt Lake City: Bookcraft, 1954), 1:27.
15. Alexander Roberts and James Donaldson, eds., *Ante-Nicene Fathers* (Peabody, Massachusetts: Hendrickson Publishers, 1994), 8:322–23.
16. James H. Charlesworth, ed., *The Old Testament Pseudepigrapha* (Garden City, New York: Doubleday, 1985), 2:172.
17. See Leon Morris, *The Gospel According to John* (Grand Rapids, Michigan: Eerdmans, 1989), 271.
18. Joseph Smith said; "I believe the Bible as it read when it came from the pen of the original writers. Ignorant translators, careless transcribers, or designing and corrupt priests have committed many errors" (*TPJS*, 327).
19. John R. Dummelow, ed., *A Commentary on the Holy Bible* (New York: Macmillan, 1956), cxiii.
20. Paul J. Achtemeier, ed., *The Harper Collins Bible Dictionary* (San Francisco: Harper Collins, 1996), 1178–79.
21. John P. Whalen, ed., *New Catholic Encyclopedia* (New York: McGraw-Hill, 1967), 14:299.
22. Edwin Hatch, *The Influence of Greek Ideas on Christianity* (Gloucester, Massachusetts: Peter Smith, 1970), 1.
23. See D&C 110:1–4; 1 Nephi 17:30, 40; *EM*, 2:720–21; James E. Talmage, *Jesus the Christ* (Salt Lake City: Deseret Book, 1981), 32–41; *Improvement Era*, August 1916, 935.
24. Roberts and Donaldson, eds., *Ante-Nicene Fathers*, 1:470.

25. Ibid., 1:255.
26. Geoffrey A. Williamson, trans., *Eusebius: The History of the Church from Christ to Constantine* (New York: Dorset Press, 1984), 47.
27. *TPJS*, 370.
28. See *Deseret Evening News*, 9 February 1895, 9.
29. Susa Y. Gates, *History of the Young Ladies' Mutual Improvement Association* (Salt Lake City: Deseret News Press, 1911), 16. The words of the hymn "O My Father" (#292) were first published in Nauvoo, Illinois, in the *Times and Seasons*, 15 November 1845, vol. 6, no. 17, 1039.
30. James R. Clark, comp., *Messages of the First Presidency* (Salt Lake City: Bookcraft, 1970), 4:203; see also Joseph Fielding Smith, *Answers to Gospel Questions* (Salt Lake City: Deseret Book, 1960), 3:142–44; Bruce R. McConkie, *Mormon Doctrine*, 2d ed. (Salt Lake City: Bookcraft, 1979), 516–17; Daniel H. Ludlow, ed., *Encyclopedia of Mormonism* (New York: Macmillan, 1992), 2:961.
31. See Orson Pratt, *The Seer*, vol. 1, no. 10, October 1853, 159.
32. Peter Hayman, "Monotheism–A Misused Word in Jewish Studies?" *Journal of Jewish Studies*, vol. 42, no. 1, Spring 1991, 14.
33. Harry Sperling, Maurice Simon, and Paul P. Levertoff, trans., *The Zohar*, 2d ed. (New York: Soncino Press, 1984), 3:37.
34. Stuart G. Hall, ed., *Melito of Sardis on Pascha and Fragments* (Oxford: Clarendon Press, 1979), 85.
35. See also *HC*, 4:425; D&C 130:5.
36. Parley P. Pratt, *Key to the Science of Theology* (Salt Lake City: Deseret Book, 1978), 21.
37. McConkie, *Mormon Doctrine*, 35.
38. *TPJS*, 162.
39. George A. Buttrick, ed., *The Interpreter's Bible* (New York: Abingdon Press, 1956), 6:111.
40. Spencer W. Kimball, "Jesus of Nazareth," *Ensign*, December 1980, 5.
41. Giovanni Papini, *The Devil* (New York: E. P. Dutton and Co., 1954), 81–82.
42. *TPJS*, 357.
43. Jean Danielou, *Origen* (New York: Sheed and Ward, 1955), 214.
44. *TPJS*, 365.
45. David Winston, *The Wisdom of Solomon* (Garden City, New York: Doubleday, 1982), 26, 197–98.
46. James Hastings, ed., *A Dictionary of the Bible* (Edinburgh: T&T Clark, 1902), 4:63.
47. In this passage, and also in Romans 8:29–30, the King James translators make it look like the apostle Paul believed in predestination. But the Greek word translated in both instances as "predestinate" [*proorizō*] really means "foreordain" (see *Ensign*, December 1990, 29–31).
48. See Roberts and Donaldson, eds., *Ante-Nicene Fathers*, 8:85. See the footnote by the editors of this work which confirms that Peter is talking about "the pre-existence of souls." For further reading see Adolph Harnack, *History of Dogma* (New York: Russell and Russell, 1958), 1:318–32.
49. Roberts and Donaldson, eds., *Ante-Nicene Fathers*, 4:372–73.
50. *WJS*, 60.
51. *TPJS*, 350–52, emphasis in original.

52. Strong, *The New Strong's Exhaustive Concordance of the Bible*, Greek Dictionary of the New Testament, 52, word #2936.
53. Winston, *The Wisdom of Solomon*, 230.
54. Roberts and Donaldson, eds., *Ante-Nicene Fathers*, 2:296.
55. Ibid., 1:165.
56. Jonathan A. Goldstein, "The Origins of the Doctrine of Creation Ex Nihilo," *Journal of Jewish Studies*, vol. 35, no. 2, Fall 1984, 127. Goldstein also reminds us that "we have to wait until the second half of the second century [A.D.] to find unambiguous Christian statements of creation *ex nihilo*" (ibid., 132). For further reading see Keith Norman, "Ex Nihilo: The Development of the Doctrines of God and Creation in Early Christianity," *Brigham Young University Studies*, vol. 17, no. 3, Spring 1977, 291–318.
57. Markus Barth, *Ephesians 1–3* (Garden City, New York: Doubleday, 1974), 244–45.
58. Michael D. Adair, "The Doctrines of Salvation by Grace vs. Works: A New Look at an Old Controversy," in *A Symposium on the New Testament* (Salt Lake City: The Church of Jesus Christ of Latter-day Saints, 1980), 28–33; see also Daniel H. Ludlow, "The Relationship between Grace and Works," in *A Symposium on the New Testament: Supplement* (Salt Lake City: The Church of Jesus Christ of Latter-day Saints, 1984), 29–36; Robert E. Parsons, "What is the Role of Grace in LDS Theology?" *Ensign*, July 1989, 59–61.
59. *TPJS*, 61.
60. Ibid., 111.
61. Ibid., 328.
62. Ibid., 160.
63. James H. Charlesworth, *The Old Testament Pseudepigrapha* (Garden City, New York: Doubleday, 1983), 1:788–89.
64. Roberts and Donaldson, eds., *Ante-Nicene Fathers*, 1:567. Clement of Alexandria taught in his work called *Stromata* (6.14) that "there are various abodes" in heaven. "These chosen abodes, which are three, are indicated by the numbers in the gospel [of Matthew (13:8)]—the thirty, the sixty, the hundred" (ibid., 2:506).
65. *JD*, 23:65.
66. *Millennial Star*, vol. 54, no. 26, 27 June 1892, 404.
67. *WJS*, 357.
68. See Matthew B. Brown, *The Gate of Heaven: Insights on the Doctrines and Symbols of the Temple* (American Fork, Utah: Covenant Communications, 1999), 249–56.
69. Cited in Raphael Patai, *The Messiah Texts* (New York: Avon Books, 1979), 251.
70. Roberts and Donaldson, eds., *Ante-Nicene Fathers*, 1:522.
71. Ibid., 1:526.
72. Ibid., 3:480.
73. Ibid., 2:539.
74. Ibid., 1:262.
75. Ibid., 9:323.

76. Marie L. Ewald, trans., *The Homilies of Saint Jerome* (Washington, D.C.: The Catholic University of America Press, 1964), 1:106, 353.
77. *TPJS*, 371.
78. Ibid., 348–49.
79. Gordon D. Fee, *The First Epistle to the Corinthians* (Grand Rapids, Michigan: Eerdmans, 1987), 372. In another translation we find "indeed there are many 'gods' and many 'lords'" (Adelbert Denaux, "Theology and Christology in 1 Corinthians 8:4–6" in R. Bieringer, ed., *The Corinthian Correspondence* [Leuven, Belgium: University Press, 1996], 595). The rendering "and indeed" is likewise offered in Frederic L. Godet, *Commentary on First Corinthians* (Grand Rapids, Michigan: Eerdmans, 1977), 412–13. Robertson and Plummer tell us that "'granted that' is the meaning" of the Greek words that underlie this passage (Archibald Robertson and Alfred Plummer, *A Critical and Exegetical Commentary on the First Epistle to the Corinthians* [New York: Charles Scribner's Sons, 1911], 167). Finally, we will mention Green's literal translation which reads, "even as there are many gods, and many lords" (Jay P. Green, Sr., *Interlinear Greek-English New Testament*, 3d ed. [Grand Rapids, Michigan: Baker Books, 1996], 528). Hodge reminds us that "to make [Paul's statement] mean, there are *in the estimation of the heathen* many gods, is to insert something which is not in the text" (Charles Hodge, *An Exposition of the First Epistle to the Corinthians* [New York: Robert Carter and Brothers, 1857], 143, emphasis in original). Indeed, one must remember that Paul did not grant the title of "gods" to the idols of the heathens (see Galatians 4:8).
80. Roberts and Donaldson, eds., *Ante-Nicene Fathers*, 2:506.
81. Alan Richardson and John Bowden, eds., *A New Dictionary of Christian Theology* (London: SCM Press, 1983), 147–48. For further reading see Daniel C. Peterson, "'Ye are Gods': Psalm 82 and John 10 as Witnesses to the Divine Nature of Humankind," in Stephen D. Ricks, Donald W. Parry, and Andrew H. Hedges, eds., *The Disciple as Scholar: Essays on Scripture and the Ancient World in Honor of Richard Lloyd Anderson* (Provo, Utah: Foundation for Ancient Research and Mormon Studies, 2000), 471–594; Ernst W. Benz, "Imago Dei: Man in the Image of God," in Truman G. Madsen, ed., *Reflections on Mormonism: Judaeo-Christian Parallels* (Provo, Utah: BYU Religious Studies Center, 1978), 201–21; A. M. Allchin, *Participation in God: A Forgotten Strand in Anglican Tradition* (Wilton, Connecticut: Morehouse-Barlow, 1988); Panayiotis Nellas, *Deification in Christ: The Nature of the Human Person* (Crestwood, New York: St. Vladimir's Seminary, 1987); Georgios I. Mantzaridis, *The Deification of Man: Saint Gregory Palamas and Orthodox Tradition* (Crestwood, New York: St. Vladimir's Seminary, 1984); Seely J. Beggiani, *Early Syriac Theology* (Lanham, Maryland: University Press of America, 1983), 73–78; Jaroslav Pelikan, *The Christian Tradition*, 2 vols. (Chicago: University of Chicago Press, 1971, 1974), in both volumes see the index entries under "Salvation–defined as deification"; G. W. Butterworth, "The Deification of Man in Clement of Alexandria," *Journal of Theological Studies*, vol. 17, 1916, 157–69; Christoforos Stavropoulos, *Partakers of Divine Nature* (Minneapolis, Minnesota: Light and Life, 1976), 11, 17.

CHAPTER 5

The Restoration of Spiritual Gifts

Jesus Christ promised that certain "signs" would follow those who believed in Him (Mark 16:17). According to the apostle Mark, the Savior worked on a spiritual level with His disciples when they went out to preach His gospel by confirming the truth of their teachings "with signs following" (Mark 16:20). The New Testament records many instances of "signs and wonders" as they were manifested among the Lord's faithful followers.

When the Lord restored His Church in the dispensation of the fullness of times He stated once again that He would manifest "signs and wonders" among those of His disciples who exhibited faith in Him (D&C 35:8; see also 58:64; 63:9–11; 68:10; 84:65).[1] In speaking of these signs in the seventh Article of Faith, the Prophet Joseph Smith said: "We believe in the gift of tongues, prophecy, revelation, visions, healing, interpretation of tongues, and so forth." But the Prophet also taught that "these things cannot be enjoyed without the gift of the Holy Ghost . . . [because] the gift of tongues, and also the gift of prophecy are gifts of the Spirit, and are obtained through that medium."[2]

This chapter is designed to demonstrate that Latter-day Saints enjoy the same spiritual gifts that were had among the early Christians. Each section in this chapter will begin by providing biblical references for the gift under discussion and then proceed to cite examples of that gift as it has been manifested among the Latter-day Saints. This will serve to establish that the ancient blessings of the gospel have once more been restored.

SPEAKING IN TONGUES
(1 Corinthians 13:28)

The gift of tongues was manifested at an early stage of the Restoration. Joseph Smith reports:

> About the 8th of November [1832] I received a visit from Elders Joseph Young, Brigham Young, and Heber C. Kimball of Mendon, Monroe county, New York. They spent four or five days at Kirtland, during which we had many interesting moments. At one of our interviews, Brother Brigham Young and John P. Greene spoke in tongues, which was the first time I had heard this gift among the brethren; others also spoke, and I received the gift myself.[3]

After this time the gift of tongues was manifested on numerous occasions among the Latter-day Saints.[4]

In the *History of the Church*, Joseph Smith relates a vision that he had in 1836, in Kirtland, Ohio, that was tied to the gift of tongues. The Prophet said that he saw Brigham Young "in a strange land, in the far south and west, in a desert place, [standing] upon a rock in the midst of about a dozen men of color, who appeared hostile. He was preaching to them in their own tongue."[5] This vision seems to have been fulfilled when the Saints emigrated to the Utah territory, which was a desert place to the far south and west of Kirtland, Ohio. Caleb D. Brinton, who served as one of the early missionaries in the southern regions of Utah, swore to the following incident in an affidavit dated 15 September 1932. Elder Brinton certified that he was in Kanab, Utah when President Brigham Young visited the town in 1870. Brinton relates:

> Black Hawk, an Indian chief, also some other chiefs, were camped near there. Black Hawk and his followers had been on the "warpath" for some time, and President Young was desirous of meeting him with a view of coming to some understanding as to peaceful settling of the south part of the state.
>
> Jacob Hamblin, an Indian interpreter, was with the party, and while they were trying to parley with the chiefs, President Young commenced to talk to them in their own tongue, and continued to do so for a period of time estimated by me to be 20 or 30 minutes. This incident was quite a surprise to all of us, as we knew that President Young did not know their language.
>
> At the beginning of this talk, the Indians manifested considerable anger. However, at the conclusion of this parley the Indians seemed to be appeased; for shortly after this incident the Black Hawk War, as it was termed, ended.[6]

At the October 1934 General Conference of the LDS Church, Elder Alonzo A. Hinckley of the Quorum of the Twelve Apostles spoke of a time when he personally received the gift of tongues.

> When I first arrived in Holland to fill a mission in 1897, I was unable to learn the language. I wrote home to my father and asked him to call upon the Bishop of the Ward, the Patriarch of the Stake, and other men in whom he had confidence, and invite them to join him in praying to the Lord in my behalf that I might acquire the language and be able to deliver my message to the people.
>
> I had never sought for a sign because I was fearful of them, but I did seek the Spirit of the Lord to help me touch the hearts of men. I not only prayed to the Lord to assist me to learn the Dutch language, but I also studied it as faithfully as I could. I succeeded in learning two or three sentences which enabled me to deliver my literature from door to door.
>
> One day, when I was alone, visiting among the people at Rotterdam, it was my duty to go back to the homes in which I had left tracts and take up the literature. As I went to gather the booklets some power, that I cannot understand, possessed me until I quaked and trembled. I stood and looked at the house at which I was to call and felt as if I could not go to the door. But I knew my duty and so, with fortitude and determination, I went to the house, raised the knocker and dropped it. Almost instantly, the door opened and an irate woman stepped out and closed it behind her. She talked in a very loud, shrill voice, berating me most severely.
>
> I did not realize for the moment, that I was understanding Dutch as clearly as though she had been speaking English. I felt no supernatural power or influence, or feeling. I just knew every word she was saying. She spoke so loud that a carpenter, who was working across the street, building a porch on a little store, heard her and, I suppose, thought I was abusing the woman, for he came over to where we stood and brought his son with him and, greatly to my alarm, he carried a broadax. The man took his position near me and listened to the woman, who continued her tirade against me in a shouting voice.
>
> I did not grow angry because of the woman's abuse but, to the contrary, my soul was filled with a burning desire to speak her language and to testify of the divinity of the gospel of the Lord Jesus Christ. I thought, "If I could only explain to her the importance of my message and the good it would do her, she would not berate me as she does now."
>
> In a few moments she ceased her abuse and I began speaking. And I spoke the Dutch language. I defended the truth and bore testimony of the restoration of the gospel.
>
> I had forgotten the large man who stood near me with his ax and, as I looked at the woman and delivered my message of truth, he put his arm across my shoulders, and looking the woman in the face, said, "The Mormon Church may have its black sheep, but this is a man of God!"

Her bitterness now gone, the woman replied, "I know it!"

After the conversation, I went back home, hardly touching the ground. It dawned upon me that the prayers I had offered–and perhaps as a result in part, of the hard study I had made—and the prayers of those at home, had been answered in a moment, for I had spoken the Dutch language intelligently for the first time in my life.

In ecstasy, I rushed home to tell Brother Thatcher in the office, and to tell the president of the mission; but when I attempted to speak, to my great dismay, I was the same as before. I could not understand nor speak the language.

President Farrell asked me if I would go to meeting that night.

"Yes, President Farrell," I answered, "after a man has been blessed of the Lord as I have been, I will gladly go. But I beg of you not to call upon me to speak even if you call upon someone to translate what I say."

"Very well," he agreed, "I promise you, Brother Hinckley, that if you go you will not be asked to speak."

I went to meeting and everything progressed nicely, as I thought, until Brother DeBry, the Branch President, arose and contrary to Brother Farrell's promise announced, "We shall now hear from Elder Hinckley."

President Farrell stepped forward, greatly embarrassed, and addressing me asked, "Brother Hinckley, shall I interpret for you?"

I felt a power I cannot describe. "Wait, President Farrell," I said as I stood upon my feet. And then I began to speak, not in my native tongue, but in the Dutch language. And, then and there, I delivered the first discourse in my life in the tongue of that mission. The following morning I was sent to preside over the Amsterdam District.

I know that the Lord can give power to his servants, can equip the honest soul for his work and that the inspiration and power of the Spirit of God, with all the gifts and blessings that pertain to the gospel of Jesus Christ, as he himself established it anciently, are with the Latter-day Saints today.[7]

INTERPRETATION OF TONGUES
(1 Corinthians 13:28)

On 25 December 1934, President David O. McKay related the following incidents pertaining to the gift of the interpretation of tongues.

One of the most important events on my world tour of the missions of the Church was the gift of interpretation of the English tongue given to the Saints of New Zealand, at a session of their conference, held on the 23rd day of April, 1921, at Puketapu, Huntly, Waikato.

The service was held in a large tent, beneath the shades of which hundreds of earnest men and women gathered in anxious anticipation of seeing and hearing an Apostle of the Church, the first one to visit that land.

When I looked over that vast assemblage and contemplated the great expectations that filled the hearts of all who had met together, I realized how inadequately I might satisfy the ardent desires of their souls, and I yearned, most earnestly, for the gift of tongues that I might be able to speak to them in their native language.

Until that moment I had not given much serious thought to the gift of tongues, but on that occasion, I wished with all my heart, that I might be worthy of that divine power.

In other missions I had spoken through an interpreter but, able as all interpreters were, I nevertheless felt hampered, in fact somewhat inhibited, in presenting my message.

Now I faced an audience that had assembled with unusual expectations, and I then realized, as never before, the great responsibility of my office. From the depth of my soul I prayed for divine assistance.

When I arose to give my address I said to Brother Stuart Meha, our interpreter, that I would speak without his translating sentence by sentence what I said, and then, to the audience, I continued:

"I wish, oh, how I wish I had the power to speak to you in your own tongue, that I might tell you what is in my heart; but since I have not the gift I pray, and I ask you to pray, that you might have the spirit of interpretation, of discernment, that you may understand at least the spirit while I am speaking, and then you will get the words and the thought when Brother Meha interprets."

My sermon lasted forty minutes and I have never addressed a more attentive, a more respectful audience. My listeners were in perfect rapport–this I knew when I saw tears in their eyes. Some of them at least, perhaps most of them, who did not understand English, had the gift of interpretation.

Brother Sidney Christie, a native New Zealander who had been a student at Brigham Young University, at the close of my address, whispered to me, "Brother McKay, they got your message."

"Yes," I replied, "I think so, but for the benefit of some who may not have understood, we will have Brother Meha give a synopsis of it in their language."

During the translation some of the New Zealanders corrected him on some points, showing that they had a clear conception of what had been said in English.

Two subsequent experiences, one of which occurred on that memorable world tour, enabled me to realize more clearly how the spirit of interpretation may come.

On one occasion when I was addressing an audience at Aintab, Syria, I realized that Elder J. Wilford Booth, who was translating the Turkish language, had interpreted incorrectly a thought I had expressed and, although I did not then–and do not now–understand a word of Turkish, I stopped brother Booth in his translation and said, "That was the wrong interpretation, Brother Booth."

I then repeated my sentence.

"How did you know, Brother McKay?" he asked. "I gave the opposite meaning."

Later when I was called to preside over the European Mission, I was one day addressing an audience at Rotterdam. Brother Cornelius Zappei was interpreting and, on that occasion, I had an experience identical to that which occurred with Brother Booth. When I called Brother Zappei's attention to what I felt was not the correct interpretation, he laughingly said to the audience, before making the correction, "There is no need of my interpreting; Brother McKay understands Dutch."

I cite these two incidents merely to emphasize the fact that, although I did not realize when I was in New Zealand, how the spirit of interpretation operated on others, yet, I accepted it as a fact, as a truth that later was demonstrated to me by the Spirit of the Lord.[8]

HEALINGS
(1 Corinthians 12:9–30)

Jesus Christ taught that one of the signs that would follow His true disciples would be the ability to "*lay hands on the sick*, and they shall recover" (Mark 16:18, emphasis added). This process is explained in more detail in James 5:14–15 and Mark 6:13 where the following three elements of the rite are enumerated: (1) Elders of the Church performed the ordinance; (2) Anointing with oil was done in the name of the Lord; (3) A prayer of faith was offered over the sick and afflicted. It was the Savior Himself who delegated to his disciples the authority [*exousian*] "to heal all manner of sickness and all manner of disease" (Matthew 10:1) and then commanded them to go among the people and "heal the sick" (v. 8).

In New Testament times the sick were usually healed by the laying on of the hands of Christ and His representatives. In Mark 5:23 we read of a request that was made of the Savior. "My little daughter lieth at the point of death: I pray thee, come and *lay thy hands on* her, that she may be healed" (emphasis added). Again, in Mark 6:5 it is stated that Christ "*laid his hands upon* a few sick folk, and healed them" (emphasis added). In yet another instance we read of Jesus: "all they that had any sick with divers diseases brought them unto him; and he *laid his hands on* every one of them, and healed them" (Luke 4:40, emphasis added). And finally, we are told in Luke 13:13 that the Master "*laid his hands on* her: and immediately she was made straight, and glorified God" (emphasis added; see also Mark 8:23–25 and Mark 7:32 where one hand is mentioned). The Saints followed the pattern set by their Exemplar. In Acts

9:17 we read that Ananias healed Paul's blindness by the laying on of hands and in Acts 28:8 Paul heals Publius by the laying on of his hands.

The same pattern of healing that was practiced by the New Testament Saints is practiced in the LDS Church, by direct commandment of Jesus Christ. "And the elders of the Church, two or more, shall be called, and shall pray for and lay their hands upon them in my name," says the Lord in D&C 42:44. Joseph Smith asked: "What is the sign of the healing of the sick? The laying on of hands is the sign, or way, marked out by James [5:14–15] and the custom of the ancient Saints as ordered by the Lord and we should not obtain the blessing by pursuing any other course except the sign or way which God has marked out."[9]

There are several extraordinary incidents in the New Testament where the Savior accomplished healings simply by stating they would occur (see Matthew 8:5–13; John 4:46–53; 5:9). It is interesting to note that the Prophet Joseph Smith performed this same type of miracle by invoking the name of Jesus Christ.

> Ezra Booth, of Mantua, [Ohio,] a Methodist preacher of much more than ordinary culture, and with strong natural abilities, in company with his wife, Mr. and Mrs. Johnson, and some other citizens of [Hiram, Ohio], visited [Joseph] Smith at his home in Kirtland, in 1831. Mrs. Johnson had been afflicted for some time with a lame arm, and was not at the time of the visit able to lift her hand to her head. The party visited [Joseph] Smith partly out of curiosity, and partly to see for themselves what there might be in the new doctrine [of Mormonism].
>
> During the interview the conversation turned on the subject of supernatural gifts, such as were conferred in the days of the apostles. Someone said, "Here is Mrs. Johnson with a lame arm; has God given any power to men now on the earth to cure her?" A few moments later, when the conversation had turned in another direction, [Joseph] Smith rose, and walking across the room, taking Mrs. Johnson by the hand, said in the most solemn and impressive manner: "Woman, in the name of the Lord Jesus Christ, I command thee to be whole," and immediately left the room.
>
> The company were awe-stricken at the infinite presumption of the man, and the calm assurance with which he spoke. The sudden mental and moral shock—I know not how better to explain the well-attested fact—electrified the rheumatic arm. Mrs. Johnson at once lifted it up with ease, and on her return home the next day she was able to do her washing without difficulty or pain.[10]

Mark 7:32–37 relates the story of a man who was healed by the Savior of deafness and a speech impediment. A tale of a parallel occurrence was published in a non-LDS paper called *The Mertin* in Merthyr Tydfil, Wales. This amazing story was subsequently reprinted in the Church periodical called the *Millennial Star*.

> During the night of [22 September 1848], between the hours of eleven and twelve, a very extraordinary occurrence took place in Newport. A young man named Reuben Brinkworth was [the 2nd of July 1839] at Bermuda, on board the Terror, Commodore Franklin, in the Arctic expedition when, in the midst of a storm of thunder and lightning, he was suddenly deprived of both hearing and speech, and in this deplorable condition returned to Stroud, in England, of which place he was a native. He has since been residing with Mr. Naish—basket maker, Market Street, Newport—who, with several other persons, is attached to the community of people known as "Mormons." Persons of this denomination have been able to communicate their doctrines to Brinkworth by means of writing, signs, and the finger alphabet. His sad condition, they allege, excited their sympathy for his spiritual as well as temporal welfare; and their doctrines made [a] very considerable impression upon him—perhaps, more especially, because their creed was that God did perform miracles in these days as he did in the days of old, and a miracle might be wrought in his favor.
>
> On [22 September 1848] the young man was seized with a kind of fit, in which he continued some time; and on his recovery he was called upon, by sight, to believe in the Savior, that the healing power of God might be exercised in his behalf. He was, moreover, earnestly entreated to be baptized; but this was very strongly opposed by a person in the room. The deaf and dumb man, however, signified his acquiescence. He was taken to the canal and baptized in the name of our Savior; and immediately on coming up out of the water he cried out, "Thank the Lord, I can speak and hear again as well as any of you!" He now speaks fluently and hears distinctly; which miraculous circumstance is attributed to the power of Providence by the friends of the young man; who called at our office with him, and gave us the details.[11]

In Mark 8:22–26 we read of the Son of God giving sight to the blind. Healings of this nature have also been wrought among the Latter-day Saints. The following story tells of one incident involving President Joseph F. Smith.

> It was on the 7th day of August, 1906, that President Smith and party arrived in Rotterdam, having come in the boat from Antwerp two days before. There was living in that city a boy of eleven years of age, John Roothoff by name, who had suffered greatly for a number of years with his eyes. His mother was a faithful member of the Church as also was the boy, who was slowly losing his sight and was unable to attend school. The boy said to his mother: "The Prophet has the most power of any missionary on earth. If you will take me with you to [the] meeting and he will look into my eyes I believe they will be healed." According to his desire he was permitted to accompany his mother to the meeting. At the close of the meeting, as was the custom, President Smith moved towards the door and began to shake hands and

> speak encouragingly to the people as they passed from the hall. As John Roothoff approached him, led by his mother and his eyes bandaged, President Smith took him by the hand and spoke to him kindly. He then raised the bandage slightly and looked sympathetically into the inflamed eyes, at the same time saying something in English which the boy did not understand. However, he was satisfied. President Smith had acted according to the boy's faith; and according to his faith it came to pass. When he arrived home, he cried out with great joy: "Mama, my eyes are well; I cannot feel any more pain. I can see fine now, and far too." Following this event the boy was able to attend school again. When he had grown to young manhood he came to the United States, to the body of the Church, rejoicing in the restoration of his eyesight.[12]

In Acts 19:11–12, we are told that "God wrought special miracles by the hands of Paul, so that from his body were brought unto the sick handkerchiefs or aprons, and the diseases departed from them, and the evil spirits went out of them." Healings involving objects such as handkerchiefs are known among Latter-day Saints. In the early part of July 1839 many of the inhabitants of Nauvoo, Illinois, became sick from exposure and disease. The Elders of the Church administered to the sick and some were healed because of their faith. Then Joseph Smith became sick himself. After suffering for several days, he arose on the morning of July 22nd and administered to those of his household, commanding them in the name of Jesus Christ to be made whole and arise. The Prophet then started walking up the banks of the Mississippi River and healed all the sick that he found along his path, including some who were near the point of death. The Prophet then took some brethren with him across the river where they administered to, and healed, the sick they found in Montrose, Iowa. Wilford Woodruff reports:

> After healing the sick in Montrose, all the company followed Joseph to the bank of the river, where he was going to take the boat to return home. While waiting for the boat, a man from the West, who had seen that the sick and dying were healed, asked Joseph if he would not go to his house and heal two of his children who were very sick. They were twins and were three months old. Joseph told the man he could not go, but he would send someone to heal them. He told Elder Woodruff to go with the man and heal his children. At the same time he took from his pocket a silk bandanna handkerchief and gave [it] to Brother Woodruff, telling him to wipe the faces of the children with it, and they should be healed. . . . Elder Woodruff did as he was commanded, and the children were healed.[13]

PERSONAL REVELATION

(1 Corinthians 14:6; 2 Corinthians 12:1; Ephesians 1:17; 3:1–5)

Elder Matthias Cowley recounts an incident where personal revelation played a direct role in the calling of Wilford Woodruff to serve a mission.

> He wanted to go on a mission, but felt that he should be called, and yet he sincerely believed that the Lord would prompt those whose duty it was to bestow upon him such an honor, such a privilege. He retired to the woods in prayer. There upon his knees in humility and childlike simplicity, he told the Lord his wishes and his hopes. He asked Him, if it was within His holy will, that the way might be opened for him to preach the gospel in the world. "Before I arose from my knees," he says, "the Spirit of the Lord rested upon me and bore witness that my prayer was heard and should be answered upon my head. I arose very happy and walked through thick woods about forty rods into an open road. As I entered the roadway, I met Judge Elias Higbee. Brother Higbee was a high priest and a very faithful man, one of the noblest men of God in the last days. I had associated with him daily, but never mentioned to him my desire to preach the gospel. To my surprise, as soon as I approached him he said: 'Brother Wilford, the Spirit of the Lord tells me that you should be ordained to go and preach the gospel.'"[14]

President Joseph F. Smith was warned by a heavenly voice immediately before a terrible accident occurred on the train that he was riding. Bishop Charles W. Nibley relates what happened.

> While [Joseph F. Smith] was a hard-headed, successful businessman, yet very few in this dispensation have been more gifted with spiritual insight than he. As we were returning from an eastern trip some years ago on the train, just east of Green River, I saw him go out to the end of the car, on the platform, and immediately return and hesitate a moment, and then sit down in the seat just ahead of me. He had just taken his seat when something went wrong with the train. A broken rail had been the means of ditching the engine and had thrown most of the cars off the track. In the sleeper we were shaken up pretty badly, but our car remained on the track.
>
> The President immediately said to me that he had gone on the platform when he heard a voice saying, "Go in and sit down."
>
> He came in, and I noticed him stand a moment, and he seemed to hesitate, but he sat down.
>
> He said further that as he came in and stood in the aisle he thought, "Oh pshaw, perhaps it is only my imagination;" when he heard the voice again, "Sit down," and he immediately took his seat, and the result was as I have stated.

He, no doubt, would have been seriously injured had he remained on the platform of that car, as the cars were all jammed up together pretty badly. He said, "I have heard that voice a good many times in my life, and I have always profited by obeying it."[15]

On 30 October 1838 in Portland, New York, a congregation of Latter-day Saints received the startling news, by means of a unique revelation, that a massacre had just taken place at Haun's Mill in Missouri. Benjamin Brown tells the story of this remarkable manifestation.

One Sunday morning, while opening the meeting with prayer, the gift of tongues came upon me, but thinking of Paul's words, that it is sometimes wisdom not to speak in tongues unless one is present who can interpret, and forgetting that a sister possessing the gift of interpretation was present, I quenched the Spirit, and it left me.

Immediately after, another brother spoke in tongues, the interpretation of which was, that "The Lord knew we were anxious to learn of the affairs of our brethren in Missouri, and that if we would humble ourselves before Him, and ask, He would reveal unto us the desires of our hearts."

Missouri was some thousand miles from Portland. We accordingly bowed again in supplication before the Lord, and, after rising from our knees and re-seating ourselves, the same brother broke out singing in tongues in a low, mournful strain.

But judge our feelings when the interpretation was given, and was found to be some thirteen or fourteen verses of poetry, descriptive of affairs in Missouri, and the murder of our brethren there, telling us that just at that time—

"Our brethren lay bleeding on the ground,
With their wives and children weeping around."

We had so often proved the truth of similar communications, that we felt as assured of the truth of this shocking news as though our eyes actually beheld the horrid sight. Our hearts were filled with sorrow.

In a fortnight afterwards we received a letter from John P. Greene, a faithful Elder of the Church in Missouri, who was, at the time he managed to write, secreted in the woods. The letter detailed and confirmed all the events previously revealed in tongues, proving that on the very day we had been informed of the transactions occurring a thousand miles off, the bleeding corpses of our brethren lay stretched on the ground after the slaughter. It was either at or about this time, that the massacre at Haun's Mill took place.[16]

PROPHECY

(Acts 2:17–18; 21:8–9; Romans 12:6; 1 Corinthians 12:10; 13:2; 14:3)

Benjamin Brown relates that in September of 1848, when the Saints were desperately low on food, tools, clothing, and usable wagons, Elder Heber C. Kimball prophesied that "in a short time" the Saints would be able to obtain the supplies they needed, and even buy them cheaper in the Salt Lake valley than they would be able to back east. The Saints rightly felt that, under the circumstances, it would take a miracle for such a prophesy to be fulfilled. They were, after all, far away from civilization. Yet, just a few months later, gold was discovered in California and large companies of eastern merchants—with wagonloads of clothing, metallic implements, and food supplies—headed to the West Coast. Then something providential happened.

> When these companies arrived within a short distance of Salt Lake City, news reached them that ships had been dispatched from many parts of the world, fitted out with goods for California. This threatened to flood the market. So these companies brought their goods into the valley, and disposed of them for just what could be got–provisions, wagons, clothes, tools, almost for the taking away, at least at half the price for which the goods could have been purchased in the states.
>
> Many disposed of their wagons because the teams gave out, and could not get on any farther. Some sold almost all they had to purchase a mule or a horse to pack through with.
>
> Thus were the Saints amply provided, even to overflowing, with every one of the necessaries and many of the luxuries of which they had been so destitute, and thus was the prediction of the servant of the Lord fulfilled.[17]

When he was just a child, President Heber J. Grant was told, through the gift of tongues, that he would one day stand in the leading councils of the Church. "Eliza R. Snow, in the gift of tongues, promised him that he should be one of the leading men in the Church, the interpretation being given by Zina D. Young."[18] Heber C. Kimball issued an even more specific prophesy regarding him. President Grant's mother once asked him:

> Do you remember Heber C. Kimball picking you up when you were a young boy and putting you on a table and talking to you at a great dinner he was having for a lot of his friends? "Yes." Do you remember anything that he said? "No, I only remember that he had the blackest eyes I have ever looked into. I was frightened. That is all I can remember." He prophesied in the name of the Lord Jesus Christ

that you would become an Apostle of the Lord Jesus Christ and become a greater man in the Church than your own father, and your father, as you know, became one of the counselors to President Brigham Young.[19]

VISIONS
(Acts 9:10–12; 11:4–10; 16:9–10; 18:9–10; 22:17–21; 26:19; 2 Corinthians 12:1)

Joseph Smith had numerous visionary experiences, of which we might mention a few. When the angel Moroni first appeared unto the Prophet, he saw in vision the exact location where the golden plates of the Book of Mormon had been hidden.[20] On the night of 11 April 1839, Joseph Smith saw the future in vision and was shown that he would soon escape from his enemies, who had imprisoned him.[21] After some of the members of Zion's Camp died in Missouri, the Prophet saw their condition and reward in the post-mortal spirit world.[22] The Prophet learned by vision that he must travel to Missouri and designate the very spot for the building of the holy City of Zion.[23] And finally, Joseph Smith was shown a vision of the resurrection of the dead and learned that in the resurrection all the earthly losses of the faithful would be made up to them.[24]

Another Latter-day Saint who enjoyed the gift of visions was Jedediah M. Grant. Brother Grant was shown a vision of the location of Zion's Camp when he accidentally got lost in the wilderness and discovered that he was unable to return to it.

> In the year 1834, when Zion's camp was moving from Kirtland to Missouri, one day I left the camp and went out to hunt in the woods of Ohio, and strayed away from the camp some 10 or 11 miles. The camp kept moving on all the time, and I entirely lost the track, and having no compass, I knew not towards what point I should travel.
>
> I kept traveling on till the after part of the day. I then concluded I would pray, but I could not get any impression where the camp was. However, I soon after received an impression from the Spirit, the same Spirit we had in Kirtland, and the same Spirit we enjoy in [the Salt Lake Valley]; and immediately after receiving the impression I looked before me, and there was the camp moving on in regular order. I could see it just as clear as I did in the morning; there were the people, the wagons and horses, all in their places as I left them in the fore part of the day, and I supposed they were not more than 80 rods off.
>
> But after turning away for a moment, I again looked in the same direction, but all was gone. Still the Spirit told me to travel on in the same direction I had seen the

> camp. I did so, and after traveling some 8 or 10 miles, [I] came up with them. And when they first came in sight they looked just as I saw them in the vision.[25]

In 1835 Wilford Woodruff was serving a mission in the state of Kentucky. He had received a letter from Joseph Smith and Oliver Cowdery requesting him to stay in the area and take charge of Church affairs. Grateful for the encouraging words in the letter, Elder Woodruff knelt down to pray.

> While I was upon my knees praying, my room was filled with light. I looked up and a messenger stood by my side. I arose, and this personage told me he had come to instruct me. He presented before me a panorama. He told me he wanted me to see with my eyes and understand with my mind what was coming to pass in the earth before the coming of the Son of Man. He commenced with what the revelations say about the sun being turned to darkness, the moon to blood, and the stars falling from heaven. Those things were all presented to me one after another, as they will be, I suppose, when they are manifest before the coming of the Son of Man.
>
> Then he showed me the resurrection of the dead—what is termed the first and second resurrection. In the first resurrection I saw no graves, nor anyone raised from the grave. I saw legions of celestial beings, men and women who had received the gospel, all clothed in white robes. In the form they were presented to me, they had already been raised from the grave.
>
> After this, he showed me what is termed the second resurrection. Vast fields of graves were before me, and the Spirit of God rested upon the earth like a shower of gentle rain. And when that fell upon the graves they were opened, and an immense host of human beings came forth. They were just as diversified in their dress as we are here, or as they were laid down. This personage taught me with regard to these things. Among other things which he showed me were several lions like burnished brass placed in the heavens. I asked the messenger what they were for. He said they were representative of the different dispensations of the gospel of Christ to men, and they would all be seen in the heavens among the signs that would be shown. After this passed by me, he disappeared.[26]

DREAMS

(Matthew 1:20; 2:12, 19, 22)

At the beginning of George Q. Cannon's first mission, he and nine of his brethren were unable to set sail off the coast of California because of strong head winds. During their week-long delay, Elder Cannon had a vivid dream wherein he saw the Prophet Joseph Smith and was taught an important lesson pertaining to faith and prayer.

> I dreamed one night that this party of brethren were heaving at the windlass, having a rope attached to it reaching forward to the anchor at the bow of the vessel. We were working with all our might, endeavoring to raise the anchor, but seemingly we made but little progress.
>
> While thus engaged I thought the Prophet Joseph came from the [aft] part of the vessel dressed in his temple clothes, and tapping me on the shoulder told me to go with him. I went, and he climbed onto the forecastle which was higher than the main deck and on a level with the bulwarks, and there he knelt down, also telling me to kneel down with him. He prayed according to the order of prayer which is revealed.
>
> After prayer, he arose upon his feet. "Now," said he, "George, take hold of that rope"—the rope we had been pulling on with all our might. I took hold of it, and with the greatest ease and without the least effort, the anchor was raised. "Now," said he, "let this be a lesson to you; remember that great things can be accomplished through the power of prayer and the exercise of faith in the right way."[27]

Elder Heber C. Kimball learned through a symbolic dream that Jedediah M. Grant was going to pass away.

> About two weeks previous to the death of Brother Jedediah M. Grant, I dreamed that we were traveling, and we came to a beautiful stream of water. I thought I was going to cross it with him, and with the expectation and understanding that he would guard me across. He crossed the stream unobserved by me, and then I saw him running up the hill as fast as he could, and he got away from me and passed out of my sight. The stream kept rising and becoming more boisterous and apparently more dangerous; and so it continued till I awoke.[28]

While Wilford Woodruff was serving as a missionary in the state of Arkansas, he was granted a symbolic dream that pertained directly to his immediate future.

> I thought an angel came to us, and told us we were commanded of the Lord to follow a certain straight path, which was pointed out to us, let it lead us wherever it might. After we had walked in it awhile, we came to the door of a house, which was in the line of a high wall running north and south, so that we could not go around. I opened the door and saw the room was filled with large serpents, and I shuddered at the sight. My companion said he would not go into the room for fear of the serpents. I told him I should try to go through the room though they killed me, for the

Lord had commanded it. As I stepped into the room, the serpents coiled themselves up, and raised their heads some two feet from the floor, to spring at me. There was one much larger than the rest in the center of the room, which raised his head nearly as high as mine and made a spring at me. At that instant I felt as though nothing but the power of God could save me, and I stood still. Just before the serpent reached me, he dropped dead at my feet; all the rest dropped dead, swelled up, turned black, burst open, took fire and were consumed before my eyes; and we went through the room unharmed and thanked God for our deliverance.

I awoke in the morning and pondered upon the dream. We took breakfast and started on our journey on Sunday morning, to visit Mr. Akeman. I related to my companion my dream, and told him we should see something strange. We had great anticipations of meeting Mr. Akeman, supposing him to be a member of the Church. When we arrived at his house, he received us very coldly, and we soon found that he had apostatized. He brought railing accusations against the Book of Mormon and the authorities of the Church.

Word was sent through all the settlements on the river for twenty miles that two "Mormon" preachers were in the place. A mob was soon raised, and warning sent to us to leave immediately or we would be tarred and feathered, ridden on a rail and hanged. I soon saw where the serpents were. My companion wanted to leave; I told him no, I would stay and see my dream fulfilled.

There was an old gentleman and lady, named Hubbel, who had read the Book of Mormon and believed. Father Hubbel came to see us, and invited us to make our home with him while we stayed in the place. We did so, and labored for him some three weeks with our axes, clearing land, while we were waiting to see the salvation of God.

I was commanded of the Lord by the Holy Ghost to go and warn Mr. Akeman to repent of his wickedness. I did so, and each time he railed against me, and the last time he ordered me out of his house. When I went out he followed me and was very angry. When he came up to me, about eight rods from the house, he fell dead at my feet, turned black and swelled up, as I saw the serpents do in my dream.

His family, as well as ourselves, felt it was the judgment of God upon him. I preached his funeral sermon. Many of the mob died suddenly. We stayed about two weeks after Akeman's death and preached, baptized Mr. Hubbel and his wife, and then continued on our journey.[29]

BEHOLDING ANGELS AND SPIRITS

(Luke 1:26–38; Acts 5:19–20; 10:3–8; 12:6–11; 23:11; 27:22–24)

Frederick G. Williams and David Whitmer reported that they saw angels in the Kirtland Temple while it was being dedicated in March of 1836.[30] Heavenly beings were also observed at one of the dedicatory services of the Salt Lake Temple on 17

April 1893. On this day a member of the Tabernacle Choir named Andrew Smith, Jr. saw many heavenly visitors inside the sacred building.

> President George Q. Cannon announced that a certain brother would read the dedicatory prayer. When he did so, I concluded that I would keep my eyes open and look at him instead of closing them as I had done on previous occasions. On reflection I came to the conclusion that I would pay as strict attention to the prayer with my eyes open as I could when I kept them closed.
>
> A few moments after the apostle began to read, a scale seemed to remove from my eyes, and a bright light appeared above his head and from behind his shoulders upwards. This light remained in that position a few moments and then raised until I could see the face of a personage in the midst of it. It was the countenance of President Brigham Young. I turned my gaze away for a moment, as if to ascertain whether I was looking with my own eyes. On again looking toward the stand I beheld the entire person of President Young, clothed in robes. He soon retired toward the rear of the stand and disappeared behind President Wilford Woodruff.
>
> After he had vanished I again turned my attention to the Elder who was reading, when I saw a light similar to what had appeared previously, and then I beheld the person of President John Taylor, who seemed to be looking towards the reader. I also saw a personage whom I took to be Hyrum Smith, although he appeared to be more square in build than he is represented to be in his pictures; then Orson Pratt, whom I at once recognized: then there were three large men whom I could not identify. There were others of more slender build whom I also failed to recognize. There were, in all, about twelve men whom I saw during the dedicatory prayer. When the prayer was concluded, and just before and during the sacred Hosanna Shout, I noticed a bright halo of light surrounding several of the brethren, and the speakers during the same services were seemingly encircled by a brightness which appeared to emanate from their own persons.
>
> While President George Q. Cannon was making the concluding remarks during this session, I was overcome and wept for joy. Having my head bowed for a short time I saw nothing for a few moments. On raising it again I saw a brilliant light over the head of each member of the First Presidency while they sat upon the stand.
>
> Whichever way any of the speakers turned while addressing the people, the light followed every movement made by them.
>
> The number of personages seen by me during the services subsequent to the reading of the dedicatory prayer was about twelve, making as near as I can state, about twenty-four in all.
>
> At the afternoon session on the same day, I saw several personages, and immediately felt a desire to communicate the information of what I saw to Brother George Kirkman, who was sitting near me. The vision then became dim. I turned to him and told him of those appearances. On directing my gaze once more toward the Melchizedek stand, I could see nothing more, the vision having closed.[31]

A short time after John Parry had joined the LDS Church in England, in 1846, he was visited by an angel of God who taught him a valuable lesson about the nature of prayer.

> After joining the Church Elder Parry was often troubled in his sleep by evil spirits. Upon one occasion he enquired of the President of the Liverpool branch why it was that he was thus annoyed. The [President] replied that some persons were troubled more than others, and told him to use the following words in his prayers before retiring to rest: "O God, the Eternal Father, I ask thee in the name of thy Son, Jesus Christ, to give thine angels charge concerning me this night and allow not the powers of darkness to molest my spirit nor body."
>
> He did this, and was troubled with evil spirits no more, until one night, feeling very sleepy, he uttered a hasty, formal prayer and went to bed. During the night he was almost overcome by the power of evil spirits, which were visible. Unable to utter a word, he prayed fervently in his mind to the Lord to release him. In an instant the heavens appeared to him to open, and he saw an angel descend towards him. The personage took hold of him and raised him up a little, and immediately the powers of darkness disappeared.
>
> Elder Parry asked the angel why it was that the Lord permitted the evil one to abuse him in such a manner, to which he replied: "Because thou didst not pray from the heart, but with thy lips."[32]

PERFORMING MIRACLES
(Acts 6:8; 19:11; 1 Corinthians 12:10)

Miracles can be manifested in many forms. In this section we will mention only two–power over the elements and raising the dead.

Power Over the Elements

Jesus Christ possessed an astounding power over the elements. On one occasion He commanded the boisterous winds and the heaving seas to be calm, and they obeyed Him (see Matthew 8:23–27; Mark 4:35–41; Luke 8:22–25). Brigham Young was once enabled to perform a similar miracle. On 27 November 1839 Brother Brigham was traveling aboard a steamer vessel to Buffalo, New York, when it got caught in a storm. "About 1 o'clock [in the] morning the wind arose [and] Elder Brigham Young went on deck [and] prayed to the Father in the name of Jesus [Christ. He then] felt to command the wind and the waves to cease, and permit them to proceed on their journey in safety. The winds abated, and he gave glory, honor, and praise to the God who rules all things."[33]

Raising the Dead

The Lord Jesus Christ brought the dead back to life (see Matthew 9:23–26; Mark 5:35–43; Luke 7:11–17; John 11:1–45) and He commanded His authorized servants to also "raise the dead" (Matthew 10:5–8; see Acts 20:9–12).

Levi Carter relates a remarkable incident where the Prophet Joseph Smith participated in raising someone from the dead. The person involved certifies that his spirit did, in fact, leave his body.

> William D. Huntington, when in Nauvoo, lived with and worked for Joseph Smith and at the time the Prophet had such a wonderful success in administering to the sick, when nearly everybody was stricken down. He was among the afflicted and was one of those who were healed by divine power manifested through the Prophet and his brethren.
>
> He said he had been sick some weeks and kept getting weaker, until he became so helpless that he could not move. Finally, he got so low he could not speak but had perfect consciousness of all that was passing in the room. He saw friends come to the bedside, look at him a moment and commence weeping, then turn away.
>
> He further stated that he presently felt easy and observing his situation found that he was in the upper part of the room, near the ceiling. [He] could see the body he had occupied lying in the bed with weeping friends standing around, as he had witnessed in many cases where persons had died under his own observation.
>
> About this time Joseph Smith and two other brethren came into the room. Joseph turned to his wife, Emma, and asked her to get him a dish of clean water. This she did. The Prophet, with the two brothers accompanying him, washed their hands and carefully dried them. Then they stepped to the bed and laid their hands upon the head of [Huntington's] body, which at that time looked loathsome to [Huntington]; and as the three stretched out their hands to place them upon the head, [Huntington] by some means became aware that he must go back into that body and started to do so. The process of getting in [Huntington] could not remember, but when Joseph said "Amen," he heard and could see and feel with his body. The feeling for a moment was most excruciating, as though his body was pierced in every part with some sharp instruments.
>
> As soon as the brethren had taken their hands from his head, [Huntington] raised up in bed, sitting erect, and in a moment turned his feet off the bed. Joseph asked him if he had not better be careful, for he was very weak. He replied, "I never felt better in my life," almost immediately adding, "I want my pants."
>
> His pants were found and given to him, which he drew on, Joseph assisting him, although he said that he needed no help. Then he signified his intention to sit

> in a chair near the fireplace. Joseph took hold of his arm to help him along safely, but William declared his ability to walk alone, notwithstanding which the help continued.
>
> Astonishment had taken the place of weeping throughout the room. Every [onlooker] was ready to weep for joy; but none were able [or] felt inclined to talk.
>
> Presently, William said he wanted something to eat. Joseph asked him what he would like and he replied that he wanted a dish of bread and milk.
>
> Emma immediately brought what he called for. As one may easily comprehend, every hand was anxious to supply the wants of a man who, a few moments before, was dead—really and truly dead! Brother Huntington ate the bowl of bread and milk with as good a relish as he ever ate.
>
> In a short time all felt more familiar and conversation upon the scene that transpired followed. William related his experience and the friends theirs. Joseph listened to the conversation and in his turn remarked that they had just witnessed a great miracle—they had seen the dead brought to life.[34]

On 9 January 1935 President Heber J. Grant related an incident where his own brother was raised from the dead.

> My brother Hyrum had yellow jaundice that later turned to black jaundice. He became as black as my coat. He was so badly emaciated that he weighed slightly more than eighty-five pounds. The doctor, Van Cott by name as I remember, who attended him, announced that he was dead. "His pulse," he said, "has not been beating for four or five minutes. He is gone."
>
> Hyrum's son and son-in-law laid their hands upon his head and prayed to God that his spirit might return and that he might live to fulfill a promise made to him that he should preside over the Davis Stake of Zion. When they got through praying, my brother opened his eyes and said, "What is the matter with you folks, you look scared half to death?" He got well and did preside over the Davis Stake of Zion.[35]

Another well-documented case of raising the dead was published in the *Improvement Era* in September of 1929. This case involved a fifteen-year-old girl named Mary Ellen Jensen who lived in Brigham City, Utah. Ella, as she was nicknamed, had suffered from the effects of scarlet fever for several weeks. On 3 March 1891, at about four o'clock in the morning, Ella told a friend who had been attending her that Hans Jensen, her deceased uncle, had appeared to her and informed her that he and some other messengers were coming in the morning to conduct her into the spirit world.

Ella's parents believed that she was simply delirious but around ten o'clock the next morning her pulse stopped and she passed away. Around noontime Ella's father, Jacob Jensen, went into town and into the tabernacle where President Lorenzo Snow was speaking. Jacob passed a note to the pulpit; and after reading it, President Snow immediately excused himself, asked Rudger Clawson to accompany him, and headed toward Ella's home.

Lorenzo Snow had received his Patriarchal Blessing in Kirtland, Ohio, under the hands of Joseph Smith, Sr., the Prophet's father. In this blessing a prophecy was pronounced: "The dead shall rise and come forth at thy bidding." After arriving at the Jensen home, President Snow retrieved some consecrated oil and asked Brother Clawson to anoint Ella with it. Both men then laid their hands upon Ella's head. After the anointing ceremony was completed, President Snow sealed the anointing with the words: "Ella, I command you, in the name of the Lord, Jesus Christ, to come back and live; your mission is not yet ended."

After this administration was over President Snow turned to Ella's parents and said, "Now do not mourn or grieve anymore. It will be alright. Brother Clawson and I are busy and must go, we cannot stay, but you just be patient and wait, and do not mourn, because it will be alright."

Ella remained dead for an hour after the administration had taken place, making three hours in all since her pulse had stopped. Jacob Jensen relates: "We were sitting there watching by the bedside, her mother and myself, when all at once she opened her eyes. She looked about the room, saw us sitting there, but still looked for someone else, and the first thing she said was: 'Where is he? Where is he?' We asked, 'Who? Where is who?' 'Why, Brother Snow,' she replied. 'He called me back.'"[36]

CASTING OUT EVIL SPIRITS

(Matthew 17:14–21; Mark 1:34; 9:17–29; Acts 19:11–12)

In the New Testament the Savior states that one of the "signs" that would be manifested among His followers would be the ability to "cast out devils" in his name (Mark 16:17). In Matthew 10:1 it is recorded that Christ "gave" his twelve apostles authority [*exousian*] over "unclean spirits, to cast them out." This authority [*exousian*] over evil spirits is likewise mentioned in Mark 3:14–15 and Mark 6:7. We learn in Luke 10:17 that the Seventy subjected devils by invoking the name of Jesus Christ.

Following are a few examples of this authority being exercised among the Latter-day Saints. Between April 11 and June 9, 1830 Joseph Smith attended many Church meetings along with a man named Newel Knight. The Prophet had many serious discussions with Newel about man's eternal salvation; and he encouraged Newel to pray vocally during their meetings, even offering to assist him in doing so. But Newel declined, indicating that he would rather attempt to pray alone in the seclusion of the woods. The Prophet informs us that after retiring to the woods, Newel

> made several attempts to pray, but could scarcely do so, feeling that he had not done his duty, in refusing to pray in the presence of others. He began to feel uneasy, and continued to feel worse both in mind and body, until, upon reaching his own house, his appearance was such as to alarm his wife very much. He requested her to go and bring me to him. . . .
>
> I went and found him suffering very much in his mind, and his body acted upon in a very strange manner; his visage and limbs distorted and twisted in every shape and appearance possible to imagine; and finally he was caught up off the floor of the apartment, and tossed about most fearfully.
>
> His situation was soon made known to his neighbors and relatives, and in a short time as many as eight or nine grown persons had got together to witness the scene. After he had thus suffered for a time, I succeeded in getting hold of him by the hand, when almost immediately he spoke to me, and with great earnestness requested me to cast the devil out of him, saying that he knew he was in him, and that he also knew that I could cast him out.
>
> I replied, "If you know that I can, it shall be done"; and then almost unconsciously I rebuked the devil, and commanded him in the name of Jesus Christ to depart from him; when immediately Newel spoke out and said that he saw the devil leave him and vanish from his sight. This was the first miracle which was done in the Church, or by any member of it; and it was done not by man, nor by the power of man, but it was done by God, and by the power of godliness.[37]

The following incident of casting out evil spirits was related by Lena H. Heiselt in Salt Lake City, Utah, on 7 August 1934.

> In the Spring of 1879, I was living at Spanish Fork, Utah. In this settlement lived a young man by the name of Jim Peter. One day he was taken with a very strange affliction. After watching him and his actions for a few days, it became the common belief that he was possessed by an evil spirit.
>
> One morning when his family was having prayers, the person speaking asked that the evil spirit might be banished from the home. Immediately, the boy arose and left the house. He came directly to our home where he knew he would be wel-

come because of his association with our own children. He gave as his excuse for coming so early that he had been driven out of his own home.

We were just going to offer our morning prayer and he was asked to join us, which he did. In his supplication, my husband requested that the evil spirit might be driven from our home and, as soon as these words were spoken, the boy withdrew from our circle and went out of the house. In a short time he returned. When we asked him why he left, he replied that he could not do otherwise, since he was ordered out of the house.

His illness appeared in two peculiar forms. Most of the time he was a raving maniac. As the spells wore off he would drop in his tracks and would be so weak that he could neither move nor speak. When he was in this weakened condition, the Elders were often called to administer to him and, immediately he would fall asleep, but not for long. He would rest for only a short time and then he would awake with a start and be as bad as ever. When under the spell of this evil power, he would call himself "Murphy."

At last, Brother Zebedee Coltrin, of the same town, was sent for. He brought with him a Brother John Lewis, and invited twelve other brethren to join them at our house, where the boy was being cared for by his mother. When the brethren arrived, he was in a weakened condition, propped up in a chair. He was so exhausted that he could not speak. After all had knelt in prayer, he was administered to. Immediately, he spoke in a whisper and then, his voice could be heard across the room. He was healed instantly, and was never again troubled with that affliction.[38]

SUMMARY

The New Testament records that during, and shortly after, the mortal ministry of the Messiah, the Saints of God enjoyed the gifts of the Spirit in great abundance. These spiritual gifts are also found, in their fullness, among the Latter-day Saints. This fact stands as strong evidence that The Church of Jesus Christ of Latter-day Saints is a genuine restoration of ancient Christianity.

NOTES

1. For an exposition on the gifts of the Spirit among Latter-day Saints see Dallin H. Oaks, "Spiritual Gifts," *Ensign*, September 1986, 68–72.
2. *TPJS*, 243. Compare this statement with Moroni 10:17 which indicates that all spiritual gifts "come by the Spirit of Christ." See also Moroni 7:35–37; Mormon 9:7–9; D&C 46:8–29. The Prophet Joseph Smith taught, as a key to discerning between the true gifts of the Spirit and the manifestations of false spirits, that "there is nothing unnatural in the Spirit of God" (*TPJS*, 214; see also 202–07).
3. *HC*, 1:296–97. The Prophet taught the Saints "not to speak in tongues except there be an interpreter present." He also said that "the ultimate design of tongues is to speak to foreigners" (*TPJS*, 247). On another occasion he taught: "You may speak in tongues for your own comfort but I lay this down for a rule that if anything is taught by the gift of tongues, it is not to be received for doctrine" (ibid., 229).
4. See *HC*, 2:383, 428, 432.
5. Ibid., 2:381.
6. *Improvement Era*, July 1934, 433.
7. Jeremiah Stokes, *Modern Miracles*, 2d ed. (Salt Lake City: Bookcraft, 1945), 13–16.
8. Ibid., 64–66. Corroborative testimonies from witnesses to these events can be found on pages 67–70 of this same source.
9. *WJS*, 108.
10. *HC*, 1:215–16, footnote.
11. *Millennial Star*, vol. 10, no. 22, 15 November 1848, 349–50.
12. Joseph Fielding Smith, comp., *Life of Joseph F. Smith* (Salt Lake City: Deseret Book, 1969), 397.
13. *HC*, 4:3–5, footnote.
14. Matthias F. Cowley, *Wilford Woodruff: History of His Life and Labors* (Salt Lake City: Deseret News Press, 1909), 46–47.
15. Preston Nibley, *The Presidents of the Church* (Salt Lake City: Deseret Book, 1971), 213.
16. *Gems for the Young Folks: Fourth Book in the Faith-Promoting Series* (Salt Lake City: Juvenile Instructor Office, 1881), 67–68.
17. Ibid., 86–88.
18. Andrew Jenson, *Latter-day Saint Biographical Encyclopedia* (Salt Lake City: Deseret News Press, 1901), 1:150.
19. Bryant S. Hinckley, *The Faith of Our Pioneer Fathers* (Salt Lake City: Deseret Book, 1956), 69, 71.
20. See JS–H 1:42.
21. See *HC*, 3:316.
22. See ibid., 2:181, footnote.
23. See ibid., 2:254.
24. See ibid., 5:361–62.

25. *JD*, 3:9.
26. *Millennial Star*, vol. 67, no. 39, 28 September 1905, 612–13. In another recital of this incident, President Woodruff recalled that those who arose in the first resurrection were "clothed in the robes of the Holy Priesthood," and he said that there were seven lions seen by him (*Deseret Weekly*, vol. 38, 3 March 1889, 389).
27. *JD*, 22:289.
28. Ibid., 8:88.
29. *Leaves from My Journal: Third Book of the Faith-Promoting Series* (Salt Lake City: Juvenile Instructor Office, 1881), 13–15.
30. *HC*, 2:427.
31. *Millennial Star*, vol. 58, no. 13, 26 March 1896, 205–06.
32. *Early Scenes in Church History: Eighth Book of the Faith-Promoting Series* (Salt Lake City: Juvenile Instructor Office, 1882), 45. The Prophet Joseph Smith taught: "We may look for angels and receive their ministrations, but we are to try the spirits and prove them" (*TPJS*, 161; see D&C 129:1–9).
33. *HC*, 4:23.
34. Edwin F. Parry, *Stories about Joseph Smith the Prophet* (Salt Lake City: Deseret News Press, 1934), 108–12.
35. Stokes, *Modern Miracles*, 131.
36. *Improvement Era*, September 1929, 881–86; vol. 32, no. 12, October 1929, 972–80. See also the first-hand account of this incident in *Young Woman's Journal*, vol. 4, no. 4, January 1893, 164–65.
37. *HC*, 1:82–83.
38. Stokes, *Modern Miracles*, 34–35.

CHAPTER 6

The Restoration of Biblical Texts

The eighth Article of Faith of the LDS Church reads: "We believe the Bible to be the word of God as far as it is translated correctly." Why didn't Joseph Smith take the Bible at face value? Because, he said, "there are many things in the Bible which do not, as they now stand, accord with the revelations of the Holy Ghost to me."[1] The Prophet also said he believed the Bible "as it read when it came from the pen of the original writers. Ignorant translators, careless transcribers, or designing and corrupt priests have committed many errors."[2] From the various revelations he had received, Joseph Smith knew that "many important points touching the salvation of men had been taken from the Bible, or lost before it was compiled."[3]

One of the revelations that alerted Joseph Smith to the damaged nature of the Bible can be found in the Book of Mormon. In 1 Nephi 13:20–40 we read that around 600 B.C. the Israelite prophet Nephi was shown a vision by an angel of God, during which he beheld the Bible as it would exist after the mortal ministry of Jesus Christ. Nephi was informed during his vision that the biblical records contained "the fullness of the gospel" when the apostles of Jesus Christ first dispensed them. But sometime afterward the great and abominable church was formed among the Gentiles and "after the book [had] gone forth through the hands of the great and abominable church . . . there [were] many plain and precious things taken away from the book." In this diminished form, the texts of the Bible were disseminated throughout the nations of the earth. Because some of the vital knowledge of the gospel was "kept back" by the great and abominable church, the nations of the earth entered into an "awful state of blindness" which caused a great many to "stumble exceedingly." But Nephi also learned during his vision that in the last days Jesus Christ would restore the missing parts of his gospel by bringing forth the Book of Mormon and several "other books."[4]

THE CORRUPTION OF BIBLICAL TEXTS

If Joseph Smith was truly a prophet of God then there should be some verifiable evidence that his statement about the corruption of biblical texts is true. And, indeed, there is abundant evidence that confirms the Prophet's claim. The idea of "corrupt" biblical texts may be disturbing to some, but it must be remembered that "no 'original' biblical documents, such as Paul's letters, have survived . . . All we have are copies of copies of copies, and so forth. Because of mistakes in copying, later elaborations and even intentional alterations, surviving manuscripts contain numerous discrepancies."[5]

Professor Emmanuel Tov, in his examinations of the Hebrew manuscripts of the Old Testament, has come to the following conclusions. "Most of the [Old Testament] texts—ancient and modern—which have been transmitted from one generation to the next have been *corrupted* in one way or another." These corruptions include "*corrections* and *changes* inserted in the biblical text. . . . Such tampering with the text is evidenced in *all* textual witnesses." Tov further informs us that "during the textual transmission many complicated changes occurred, making it now almost impossible for us to reconstruct the original form of the text." The "pervasive changes in the biblical text," he says, should be ascribed to "editors who allowed themselves such massive changes in the formative stage of the biblical literature."[6]

Such tampering with the words of scripture even occurred during biblical times. Some translations of Jeremiah 8:8 read: "How can you say, 'We are wise, we have the law of the Lord,' when scribes with their lying pens have falsified it?"[7] And in the Joseph Smith Translation of Luke 11:52, we read that Christ accused the scribes [*nomikois*] of "tak[ing] away the key of knowledge, the fullness of the scriptures."

From biblical scholar Michael Fishbane, we learn that "theological changes [in the Old Testament] underscore the fact that those persons most responsible for maintaining the orthography of the texts tampered with their wording so as to preserve the religious dignity of these documents according to contemporary theological tastes. . . . [N]ot only do the old rabbinic lists preserve considerable older biblical traditions of scribal corrections, but there are also examples of theological corrections in the [Masoretic Text] unattested in rabbinic literature."[8] Other scholars concur by stating that "some liberal-minded scribes altered the text for both philological and theological reasons. . . .They supplemented and clarified the text by the insertion of additions and the interpolation of glosses from parallel passages."[9]

And what of the New Testament texts? Bruce Metzger informs us that "of the approximately five thousand Greek manuscripts of all or part of the New Testament that are known today, no two agree exactly in all particulars."[10] Why is this so? Because after A.D. 135 "recensions [of the New Testament texts] proliferated with a resultant textual diversity which reached a peak before the year [A.D.] 200." Thus, "between the years [A.D.] 150 and 250, the text of the first recensions acquired a host of new readings. They were a mixture of accidental carelessness, deliberate scribal corrections, involuntary mistakes, a translator's conscious departure from literalness, a reviser's more systematic alterations, and not least, contamination caused by harmonizing." As for the New Testament epistles, "it is . . . not possible to reconstitute with certainty the earliest text[s], even though there is no doubt about [their] having existed in written form from a very early date."[11]

Dionysius, the Christian bishop of Corinth (A.D. 168–177), testified that documents from Church leaders, and even scriptural texts, were being tampered with at an early date. "When my fellow-Christians invited me to write letters to them I did so. These the devil's apostles have filled with tares [see Matthew 13:24–26], taking away some things and adding others. For them the woe is reserved [see Revelation 22:18–19]. Small wonder then if some have dared to tamper even with the word of the Lord Himself, when they have conspired to mutilate my own humble efforts."[12]

Bart Ehrman, in his insightful book called *The Orthodox Corruption of Scripture*, forthrightly states that early Christian "scribes occasionally altered the words of their sacred texts to make them more patently orthodox and to prevent their misuse by Christians who espoused aberrant views."[13] There is early evidence to support this view. In A.D. 178 the non-Christian writer Celsus claimed that some Christians had "changed the original text of the Gospels three or four times or even more, with the intention of thus being able to destroy the arguments of their critics."[14] And Origen, who wrote sometime between ca. A.D. 185 and 251, stated: "It is an obvious fact today that there is much diversity among the manuscripts, due either to the carelessness of the scribes, or to the perverse audacity of some people in correcting the text, or again to the fact that there are those who add or delete as they please, setting themselves up as correctors."[15]

When did most of the damage to the Christian writings occur? It was the opinion of Frederick Scrivener that "the worst corruptions to which the New Testament has ever been subjected, originated within a hundred years after it was composed."[16] This statement is in remarkable agreement with the Book of Mormon prophecy found in 1 Nephi 13:24–29.

THE JOSEPH SMITH TRANSLATION

The Lord gave Moses a revelation "concerning this heaven, and this earth" and commanded Moses to record His words. But the Lord was also aware that the time would come when the children of men would not esteem His holy words and would remove "many of them" from the book Moses would write. Nevertheless, the Lord made Moses a promise, saying: "I will raise up another like unto thee; and [my words] shall be had again among the children of men" (Moses 1:40–41; 2:1). This promise was fulfilled with the publication of the Book of Moses in the Pearl of Great Price, which is actually a part of the Joseph Smith Translation. The Book of Moses is thus a restoration of lost biblical material.

The "translation" or correction of biblical scriptures was a divinely assigned branch of Joseph Smith's prophetic calling.[17] The Prophet was not educated in biblical languages when he undertook the majority of the JST and so he was under the necessity of depending upon heavenly help in his efforts. The revelatory element of the Joseph Smith Translation can be detected in several documents. The preface of Joseph Smith's reworking of the book of Matthew reads: "A translation of the New Testament, translated by the power of God."[18] This statement is in accordance with D&C 45:60–61 wherein the Lord says to the Prophet, regarding the New Testament, "*I give unto you* now that ye may translate it" (emphasis added). And the Prophet made another statement that points to the fact that at least parts of the translation were governed by God. Said Joseph: "I completed the translation and *receiving* of the New Testament, on the 2nd of February, 1833."[19]

Robert J. Matthews points out that even though the Lord had a hand in the production of the Joseph Smith Translation, we still do not fully understand the exact nature of this undertaking.

> To regard the New Translation as a product of divine inspiration given to Joseph Smith does not necessarily assume that it be a restoration of the original Bible text. It seems probable that the New Translation could be many things. For example, the nature of the work may fall into at least four categories.
>
> 1. Portions may amount to restorations of content material once written by the biblical authors but since deleted from the Bible.
>
> 2. Portions may consist of a record of actual historical events that were not recorded, or were recorded but never included in the biblical collection.
>
> 3. Portions may consist of inspired commentary by the Prophet Joseph Smith, enlarged, elaborated, and even adapted to a latter-day situation. This may be simi-

lar to what Nephi meant by "likening" the scriptures to himself and his people in their particular circumstance (see 1 Nephi 19:23–24; 2 Nephi 11:8).

4. Some items may be a harmonization of doctrinal concepts that were revealed to the Prophet Joseph Smith independently of his translation of the Bible, but by means of which he was able to discover that a biblical passage was inaccurate.[20]

Since at least some of the JST is attributable to revelation or inspiration it is fair to ask, "Has any of the material in the Joseph Smith Translation been verified by biblical scholarship?" The answer is yes, it has. On the pages that follow, the reader will find a substantial collection of examples. This section will not, however, address many of the historical elements of the JST that have been confirmed in the writings of LDS scholars.

Song of Solomon is not Scripture

In his copy of the King James Bible, Joseph Smith wrote: "The Songs of Solomon are not inspired writings." This statement is reproduced verbatim in the footnotes of the LDS edition of the King James Bible.

In A.D. 90 a council of Jewish rabbis gathered at Jamnia, in western Judea, so that they could debate which books should be included in the Old Testament canon. In this council, doubts were raised about the spiritual value of the Song of Solomon. Even in the second century A.D., there was still heated debate among the Jews about whether the Song of Solomon should have been included in the canon of scripture. Modern biblical scholars believe the Song of Solomon was ultimately included in the Old Testament canon for two reasons: (1) Tradition attributed the authorship of the text to King Solomon; and (2) There were those who interpreted the Song of Solomon in an allegorical manner and insisted that it represented the love of God for the nation of Israel. In recent times, however, many ancient Egyptian love songs have been discovered that contain "many parallels and similarities of language and imagery" with the so-called "Solomonic" biblical material. Therefore, "there is every reason to suspect that the Song [of Solomon] belonged to a particular genre of love lyrics in the ancient Near East."[21]

Gerson Cohen notes that "according to the reports of one of the earliest of the Tannaim: 'Originally Proverbs, Song of Songs, and Ecclesiastes were suppressed; since they were held to be mere parables and not part of the Holy Writings, (the religious authorities) arose and suppressed them; (and so they remained) until the men of

Hezekiah came and interpreted them.'" It should also be understood that "modern scholars of scripture . . . have unanimously dismissed the theory that the Song of Songs was originally a religious work."[22]

In light of the preceding comments, it would appear that Joseph Smith's statement about the status of the Song of Solomon is justified.

Hardening of Pharaoh's Heart

"And *I [the Lord] will harden Pharaoh's heart* . . . And *[the Lord] hardened Pharaoh's heart*" (Exodus 7:3, 13).

"And *Pharaoh will harden his heart* . . . And *Pharaoh hardened his heart*" (JST Exodus 7:3, 13).

Joseph Smith made this correction in each instance where the phraseology occurs in the story (see JST Exodus 4:21; 7:3, 13; 9:12; 10:1, 20, 27; 11:10; 14:8, 17). In commenting on the King James Version of Exodus 7:13, commentator Adam Clarke pointed out that the text is faulty since the identical Hebrew words are translated "and Pharaoh's heart was hardened" in Exodus 7:22. Clarke insists that verses 13 and 22 should be translated the same "lest the hardening, which was evidently the effect of [Pharaoh's] own obstinate shutting of his eyes against the truth, should be attributed to God."[23]

Other biblical scholars concur with Clarke's point of view. Thomas Scott, for example, writes that Exodus 7:13 should read, "'Pharaoh's heart was hardened;' for nothing is here said concerning any interposition of God in the case. The same [Hebrew] words are afterwards rendered [in verse 22 as] 'Pharaoh's heart was hard,' and this accords with the subsequent words of God [in verse 14], 'Pharaoh's heart is hardened.'"[24] The Jerusalem Bible translation of this passage reads: "Pharaoh's heart was stubborn."[25]

Temptation

"*Lead us not* into temptation, but deliver us from evil" (Matthew 6:13).

"And *suffer us not to be led* into temptation, but deliver us from evil" (JST Matthew 6:14).

The Contemporary English Version of the Bible renders this portion of the verse as "keep us from being tempted" and the Phillips Modern English Bible says "keep us clear of temptation."

Modern biblical scholars believe that "it is possible that the causative form of the Lord's Prayer is . . . not meant to be unmediated but has a permissive nuance: 'Let us not be brought into temptation (i.e., by the devil).' This interpretation is greatly strengthened if the word 'temptation' can be taken to mean 'trial or temptation that results in [a] fall'; and this appears to be required in two New Testament passages (Mark 14:38; Galatians 6:1)."[26]

This interpretation is more in keeping with James 1:13 which reads: "Let no man say when he is tempted, 'I am tempted of God: for God cannot be tempted with evil, neither tempteth he any man." Furthermore, Joseph Smith's reading is supported by other early Christian evidence. Augustine (A.D. 354–430), in speaking of the early Saints in *Our Lord's Sermon on the Mount* (2.9.30), said that "many parties in prayer express themselves thus, 'suffer us not to be led into temptation;' that is to say, explaining in what sense the word 'lead' is used. For God does not Himself lead, but suffers that man to be led into temptation whom He has deprived of His assistance."[27] Finally, we have the commentary of Adam Clarke on this verse. "*Bring us not in*, or *lead us not in*. This is a mere Hebraism: God is said to *do* a thing which he only *permits* or *suffers* to be done."[28]

Christ's Prayer on the Cross

"Then said Jesus, 'Father, forgive *them*; for they know not what they do'" (Luke 23:34).

"Then said Jesus, 'Father, forgive them; for they know not what they do' (*meaning the soldiers who crucified him*)" (JST Luke 23:35).

Joseph Smith's addition to this scripture seems to be verified in an early Christian text known as the *Clementine Homilies* (11.20). There we read: "For the Teacher Himself, being nailed to the cross, prayed to the Father that the sin of *those who slew Him* might be forgiven, saying, 'Father, forgive them their sins, for they know not what they do.'"[29]

Partial Judges

"Are ye not then partial in yourselves, and are become *judges of evil thoughts*?" (James 2:4).

"Are ye not then *in yourselves partial judges, and become evil in your thoughts*?" (JST James 2:4).

There are at least four Bible translations that render the Greek words underlying this verse as "judges with evil thoughts." These translations are the New King James Version, Revised Standard Version, New International Version, and New Revised Standard Version.

Two Sets of Tablets at Sinai

The biblical story of the stone tablets made by Moses at Mt. Sinai indicates that there was no difference between what was written on the first set and the second set (see Exodus 32:15–16, 19; 34:1). But the Joseph Smith Translation of this episode indicates that there was a major difference between the two sets of tablets.

> And the Lord said unto Moses, "Hew thee two other tables of stone, like unto the first, and I will write upon them also, the words of the law, according as they were written at the first on the tables which thou brakest; but it shall not be according to the first, for I will take away the priesthood out of their midst; therefore my holy order, and the ordinances thereof, shall not go before them; for my presence shall not go up in their midst, lest I destroy them.
>
> But I will give unto them the law as at the first, but it shall be after the law of a carnal commandment; for I have sworn in my wrath, that they shall not enter into my presence, into my rest, in the days of their pilgrimage. Therefore do as I have commanded thee, and be ready in the morning, and come up in the morning unto mount Sinai" (JST Exodus 34:1–2; see also JST Deuteronomy 10:2).

The ancient Jews preserved traditions that closely correspond to the knowledge provided by Joseph Smith. In the *Zohar*, for instance, we read that the first set of tablets "emanated from the tree of life" while the second set "came from the side of the tree of good and evil." And according to Jewish kabbalistic lore, the first set of tablets "were the light and doctrine of the Messiah, the outpouring of universal deliverance, the source of eternal life on earth" while the second set "represented the indirect or 'fragmented' manifestation of this light."[30]

Paul's Knowledge

"I know nothing *by* myself" (1 Corinthians 4:4).

"I know nothing *against* myself" (JST 1 Corinthians 4:4).

The word "against" has been introduced into the following modern translations of the Bible. The New King James Version, Revised Standard Version, New American Standard Bible, Amplified Bible, Contemporary Bible, and the New Revised Standard Version.

Abraham Rejoiced

"Then Abraham fell upon his face, and *laughed*" (Genesis 17:17).

"Then Abraham fell upon his face, and *rejoiced*" (JST Genesis 17:23).

Joseph Smith's rendition is verified by one Hebrew commentary on the book of Genesis which says that Abraham "*laughed.* Jubilantly; as *Onkelos* renders [the Hebrew], *and he rejoiced.* . . . Abraham had faith and *rejoiced.*"[31]

The Name "Jehovah"

"And I appeared unto Abraham, unto Isaac, and unto Jacob, by the name of God Almighty [see Genesis 17:1], but by my name JEHOVAH was I not known to them" (Exodus 6:1–3).

"And I appeared unto Abraham, unto Isaac, and unto Jacob. I am the Lord God Almighty; the Lord JEHOVAH. And was not my name known unto them?" (JST Exodus 6:3).

Despite the King James text of Exodus 6:3, biblical scholars assure us that the sacred name "YHWH" [sometimes translated as 'Jehovah'] was known to the patriarchs. . . . [There are] passages in Genesis where the patriarchs apparently knew and worshipped God under this name (Genesis 15:7; 28:13; etc.). . . . Therefore one need not doubt the biblical tradition that the use of this name was already ancient by the time of Moses (cf. Genesis 4:26; 9:26)."[32]

The Writing on the Wall

"And this is the writing that was written, MENE, MENE, TEKEL, UPHARSIN. . . . *PERES*; 'Thy kingdom is divided, and given to the Medes and Persians'" (Daniel 5:25, 28).

"And this is the writing that was written, MENE, MENE, TEKEL, UPHARSIN. . . . *UPHARSIN*; 'Thy kingdom is divided, and given to the Medes and Persians'" (JST Daniel 5:25, 28).

The text found in the New English Bible follows the change that was made by the Prophet Joseph Smith.[33]

Hold Me Not

"Jesus saith unto her, '*Touch* me not; for I am not yet ascended unto my Father'" (John 20:17).

"Jesus saith unto her, '*Hold* me not; for I am not yet ascended unto my Father'" (JST John 20:17).

Bible translations that incorporate the word "hold" include the New International Version, New Revised Standard Version, Today's English Version, New Century

Version, Contemporary English Version, Phillips Modern English, and Revised Standard Version. The New American Bible reads "stop holding on."

Along similar lines we find the word "cling" in the Jerusalem Bible, Revised English Bible, Amplified Bible, New English Bible, New Living Translation, and New King James Version. The New American Standard Bible has "stop clinging."

The Greek word that is being translated in all of these Bible versions is *haptou* which properly means "to *attach* oneself to."[34]

Punishment

". . . they that resist shall receive to themselves *damnation*" (Romans 13:2).

". . . they that resist shall receive to themselves *punishment*" (JST Romans 13:2).

The word "punishment" is utilized in the New English Bible, Living Bible, New Century Version, and New Living Translation. The Jerusalem Bible and Phillips Modern English version both read "bound to be punished" while the Contemporary English Version says "will be punished."

Faith

"Now faith is the *substance* of things hoped for, the evidence of things not seen" (Hebrews 11:1).

"Now faith is the *assurance* of things hoped for, the evidence of things not seen" (JST Hebrews 11:1).

Translations that incorporate the word "assurance" include the Revised Standard Version, New American Standard Bible, New Revised Standard Version, New Living Translation, and Amplified Bible. Vincent informs us that the word *assurance* "gives the true meaning" of *hupostasis*, which is the Greek word that underlies the English text.[35]

Similar translations include the New International Version and New Century Version, which read "being sure," and Today's English Version which says "to be sure."

Rulership

"Let your women keep silence in the churches: for it is not permitted unto them to *speak*" (1 Corinthians 14:34).

"Let your women keep silence in the churches: for it is not permitted unto them to *rule*" (JST 1 Corinthians 14:34).

Adam Clarke noticed the inconsistency between this remark and 1 Corinthians 11:5 where Paul acknowledges that women have the privilege of speaking in the

Christian congregations. Clarke solves this apparent problem by noting that from the context of the passage it is clear that Paul objects to women "*dictating* in the assemblies. It was permitted to any man to ask questions, to object, altercate, attempt to refute, etc., in the synagogue; but this liberty was not allowed to any woman. . . . All that the apostle opposes here is their questioning, finding fault, disputing, etc., in the Christian Church, as the Jewish men were permitted to do in their synagogues; together with the attempts to *usurp any authority* over the man, by setting up their judgment in opposition to them."[36]

Covenant

Throughout Hebrews 9:15–18 and 20 the Prophet Joseph Smith changed the word "testament" to "covenant." The Greek word that underlies the King James translation is *diathēkē* and it can, indeed, be properly rendered as "covenant."[37]

One popular research tool known as *The Interlinear Greek-English New Testament* makes the change from "testament" to "covenant" in every instance where Joseph Smith indicated that it should occur.[38]

Scripture

"*All scripture is given by inspiration of God*, and is profitable for doctrine, for reproof" (2 Timothy 3:16).

"And *all scripture given by inspiration of God*, is profitable for doctrine, for reproof" (JST 2 Timothy 3:16).

- American Standard Version: "Every scripture inspired by God is also profitable."
- Rheims New Testament: "All scripture, inspired by God, is profitable."
- New English Bible: "Every inspired scripture has its use."

Anger

"But I say unto you, that whosoever is angry with his brother *without a cause* shall be in danger of the judgment" (Matthew 5:22).

In the Joseph Smith Translation of Matthew 5:22 the words "without a cause" are deleted. The same deletion is found in 3 Nephi 12:22 where the Savior repeats the Sermon on the Mount to his Nephite disciples in the New World.

Since the words "without a cause" are missing in some of the early Greek manuscripts of the book of Matthew many Bible translations have deleted them. These three words have been removed from the New English Bible, Jerusalem Bible, Revised Standard Version, Amplified Bible, Rheims New Testament, Contemporary English Version, New Living Translation, New Century Version, New American Standard, New International Version, and New Revised Standard Version.[39]

The Kingdom of God

"For, behold, the kingdom of God *is within you*" (Luke 17:21).

"For, behold, the kingdom of God *has already come unto you*" (JST Luke 17:21).

In the footnotes of the LDS edition of the King James Bible, it is stated: "Many translations read 'among' because the pronoun 'you' is plural here in Greek." Those translations that read "among you" include the Jerusalem Bible, New English Bible, New American Bible, New Revised Standard Version, and New Living Translation.

Similar phraseology is found in the Contemporary English Version which reads "here with you." The Revised Standard Version reads "in the midst of you" while the New American Standard Bible has "in your midst."

Woman's Veil

"For this cause ought the woman to have *power* on her head because of the angels" (1 Corinthians 11:10).

"For this cause ought the woman to have *a covering* on her head because of the angels" (JST 1 Corinthians 11:10).

FIGURE 11. The Joseph Smith Translation of 1 Corinthians 11:10 is in agreement with several ancient versions of the passage which specify that under certain circumstances a woman should wear a veil upon her head.

The words "a covering" are employed in the Amplified Bible, Today's English Bible, and the New Living Translation while the Jerusalem Bible speaks of women "covering their heads." The Revised Standard Version says that a woman should "have a veil on her head." Adam Clarke notes that in some of the ancient manuscripts of 1 Corinthians chapter 11 verse 10 the word "covering" or "veil" is found.[40]

King of the Jews

"And Pilate asked him, 'Art thou the King of the Jews?' And he answering said unto him, '*Thou sayest it*'" (Mark 15:2).

"And Pilate asked him, 'Art thou the King of the Jews?' And he answering said unto him, '*I am, even as thou sayest*'" (JST Mark 15:4).

There are only two Greek words that underlie the King James text [*su legeis*]. These words translate literally as "you say." This short response has given rise to two different types of translations. In the first category are renditions where Christ offers an ambiguous response to the question. "You say so" (New American Bible, New Revised Standard Version); "It is you who say it" (Jerusalem Bible); "The words are yours" (New English Bible; Anchor Bible Series Translation); "Those are your words" (New Century Version, Contemporary English Version); "You have said so" (Revised Standard Version); "You say that I am" (Phillips Modern English). In the second category are renditions where Christ offers a forthright and affirmative response to the question. "Yes, it is as you say" (New International Version, New Living Translation); "It is as you say" (New King James Version, New American Standard Bible, Amplified Bible).

Decree of Caesar Augustus

"And it came to pass in those days, that there went out a decree from Caesar Augustus, that all *the world* should be taxed" (Luke 2:1).

"And it came to pass in those days, that there went out a decree from Caesar Augustus, that all *his empire* should be taxed" (JST Luke 2:1).

Joseph Smith's rendition is supported by the following translations:

- Today's English Version: "the Empire."
- New Living Translation: "the Roman Empire."
- Amplified Bible: "the whole Roman empire."
- New English Bible: "the Roman world."
- New International Version: "the entire Roman world."
- New Century Version: "the countries under Roman rule."

Unicorns

"And the *unicorns* shall come down with them" (Isaiah 34:7).

"And the *re'em* shall come down with them" (JST Isaiah 34:7).

In this instance Joseph Smith replaced "unicorns" with a Hebrew word for "wild bulls" or "wild oxen." Green renders this verse: "And wild oxen shall come down with them."[41] Kohlenberger and Stein also supply the words "wild oxen" in their translations.[42]

Afflictions

"My brethren, count it all joy when ye fall into *divers temptations*" (James 1:2).

"My brethren, count it all joy when ye fall into *many afflictions*" (JST James 1:2).

The New Century Version provides us with reading, "many kinds of troubles;" the New American Standard Bible, New King James Version, and Revised Standard Version say "various trials;" the New International Version and New English Bible both have "trials of many kinds."

Condemnation

"And he that doubteth is *damned* if he eat" (Romans 14:23).

"And he that doubteth is *condemned* if he eat" (JST Romans 14:23).

Those translations that have changed "damned" to "condemned" include the New American Standard Bible, New International Version, New King James Version, New Living Translation, Amplified Bible, Rheims New Testament, New Revised Standard Version, and the Jerusalem Bible.

Complaint

"He maketh *intercession* to God against Israel" (Romans 11:2).

"He maketh *complaint* to God against Israel" (JST Romans 11:2).

The Jerusalem Bible, New Living Translation, and Contemporary English Version of the scriptures all state that Elijah the prophet "complained to God" about the people of Israel while the Living Bible says that he was "complaining to God about the Jews."

Sin

"He that *committeth* sin is of the devil" (1 John 3:8).

"He that *continueth in* sin is of the devil" (JST 1 John 3:8).

The New Century Version of the Bible renders this passage: "anyone who continues to sin belongs to the devil." Today's English Version places "whoever continues to sin" in this category while the New Living Translation and the Contemporary English Version say it is those who "keep on sinning" who belong to the devil.

Moses' Childhood

"They saw he was a *proper* child" (Hebrews 11:23).

"They saw he was a *peculiar* child" (JST Hebrews 11:23).

The New Living Translation reads: "They saw that God had given them an unusual child." The New International Version says that Moses' parents "saw he was no ordinary child." Josephus (*Ant.*, 2.9.6–7) records that as a child Moses had a "divine form" that was so striking it caused those who saw him to stand still and stare.

Moses' Death

Deuteronomy 34:5–6 states that Moses died in the land of Moab "according to the word of the Lord. And [the Lord] buried him in a valley in the land of Moab, over against Beth-peor: but no man knoweth of his sepulcher unto this day." The Joseph Smith Translation changes verse 6 to read: "*For the Lord took him unto his fathers*, in a valley in the land of Moab, over against Beth-peor; *therefore* no man knoweth of his sepulcher unto this day."

In the Book of Mormon we read that "the saying went abroad in the Church that [Alma] was taken up by the Spirit, or buried by the hand of the Lord, even as Moses. But behold, the scriptures saith the Lord took Moses unto Himself" (Alma 45:19). The idea that Moses was translated into heaven without suffering physical death is also supported by Jewish tradition. The ancient historian Josephus (*Ant.*, 4.8.48) says that "as [Moses] was going to embrace Eleazar and Joshua, and was still discoursing with them, a cloud stood over him on the sudden, and he disappeared in a certain valley, although he wrote in the holy books that he died, which was done out of fear, lest they should venture to say that, because of his extraordinary virtue, he went to God."

Imposture

". . . so the last *error* shall be worse than the first" (Matthew 27:64).

". . . so the last *imposture* shall be worse than the first" (JST Matthew 27:64).

The New American Bible agrees with the Joseph Smith Translation by inserting the word "imposture." The Revised Standard Version, Jerusalem Bible, Amplified Bible, and Phillips Modern English version all supply the word "fraud" while the New International Version, New King James Version, New Revised Standard Version, New English Bible, and New American Standard Bible all say "deception."

Vine

"Thy mother is like a vine *in thy blood*, planted by the waters: she was fruitful and full of branches by reason of many waters" (Ezekiel 19:10).

The Joseph Smith Translation omits the words "in thy blood" from this passage. The Jerusalem Bible also removes this phrase and reads: "Your mother was like a vine planted beside the water, fruitful and leafy, because the water flowed so full." The JPS translation specifically singles out the words "in your blood" and notes that the meaning of the Hebrew words is uncertain.[43]

Freed From Sin

"For he that is *dead* is freed from sin" (Romans 6:7).

"For he that is *dead to sin* is freed from sin" (JST Romans 6:7).

Many biblical commentators take this verse literally and interpret it to mean that those who are physically dead are no longer capable of sinning. But the context of Paul's discourse points in a different direction. John Murray says of this verse:

> While it is not possible to be decisively dogmatic, yet the context would rather favour the view that the apostle is here again referring to the death of the believer with Christ through baptism into Jesus' death. At least this thought had been sufficiently stressed in the preceding verses (cf. vv. 2, 3, 5) that there is no necessity to consider verse 7 as other than a succinct statement of what had been developed in the preceding verses and introduced here by way of confirmation in support of the doctrine stated in verse 6. Furthermore, the first clause in verse 8, "But if we died with Christ" would suggest that verse 7 is to be interpreted in that sense.[44]

James Murdock's translation of the New Testament from the Syriac Peshitta demonstrates that Joseph Smith's rendition of Romans 6:7 is entirely plausible. "For he that is dead (to it), is emancipated from sin."[45]

Noah

In the Book of Moses, which is the Joseph Smith Translation of portions of Genesis, it is stated that giants "sought [Noah's] life" (Moses 8:18, 26). This detail is not found in the Genesis account but the Jewish historian Josephus (*Ant.*, 1.3.1) records that wicked men, who "did what resembled the acts of those whom the Grecians call giants," would not heed Noah's call to repentance and the patriarch "was afraid they would kill him."

Repentance

In the Joseph Smith Translation of the book of Genesis, we see the correction of an erroneous theological notion. Genesis 6:6 reads: "And *it repented the Lord* that he had made man on the earth, and it grieved him at his heart." In the Joseph Smith Translation of this verse (Moses 8:25) we read: "And *it repented Noah*, and his heart was pained that the Lord had made man on the earth, and it grieved him at the heart." On 15 October 1843 Joseph Smith publicly reiterated that Genesis 6:6 is a mistranslation which should read: "but it repented Noah that God made man."[46]

In several other biblical passages where it is claimed that the Lord "repented" (see Exodus 32:12, 14; 1 Samuel 15:11; 1 Chronicles 21:15; Jeremiah 26:19 and Amos 7:3, 6) Joseph Smith changed the wording in the JST. These reworked verses were brought into line with Numbers 23:19 which states that God is not like mortal men and therefore has no need to "repent." It is noted in the LDS edition of the King James Bible (Genesis 6:6, footnote *a*), that the Hebrew verb from which the word "repented" was translated [*nācham*] can also be rendered as "to be sorry."[47] Thus, God might have indeed been sorry that some of the men that He created chose wickedness over godliness, but He most certainly did not "repent" of the fact that He had created them.

Ships of the Sea

"And upon all the ships of Tarshish, and upon all pleasant pictures" (Isaiah 2:16).

"*And upon all the ships of the sea*, and upon all the ships of Tarshish, and upon all pleasant pictures" (JST Isaiah 2:16).

2 Nephi 12:16, which is a quotation of this passage from Isaiah, reads precisely the same as the JST. In the Greek Septuagint version of Isaiah 2:16 the additional phrase—"and upon every ship of the sea"—is present.[48]

Some of the changes in the Joseph Smith Translation appear to have been made so that modern readers could better understand archaic or unclear terms from the King James Bible. Following are a few examples of Joseph Smith's clarifications that find support in modern Bible translations.

Human Relations

"Let no man seek his own, but every man another's *wealth*" (1 Corinthians 10:24).

"Let no man seek his own, but every man another's *good*" (JST 1 Corinthians 10:24).

At least four different translations—the New American Standard Bible, New International Version, New Century Version, and Revised Standard Version—agree with Joseph Smith's rendition by saying that one should seek for the "good" of others.

Lips

"Behold, I am of *uncircumcised lips*, and how shall Pharaoh hearken unto me?" (Exodus 6:30).

"Behold, I am of *stammering lips, and slow of speech*; how shall Pharaoh hearken unto me?" (JST Exodus 6:29).

Both of these elements can be found in the translations of non-LDS scholars. In Thomson's rendition of the Septuagint we have, "Behold, I am a stammerer"[49] and in the Jerusalem Bible we find: "I am slow of speech."[50] Along similar lines, Kohlenberger renders this passage: "Since I speak with faltering lips, why would Pharaoh listen to me?"[51] while the JPS translation says, "I am of impeded speech; how then should Pharaoh heed me?"[52]

Conduct

In 1 Peter 3:1–2 and 16, the Prophet Joseph Smith changed the word "conversation" to "conduct," thus reflecting a more modern translation of the Greek word *anastrophē*. Bible translations that concur with the change made by the Prophet Joseph Smith include the New King James Version, Today's English Version, Twentieth Century New Testament, and New Revised Standard Version which all use the word "conduct." The New American Standard Bible and New International Version use the word "behavior," while the New American Bible and New English Bible use both "conduct" and "behavior."

The Savior's Retreat

"And when it was day, he departed and went into a *desert* place" (Luke 4:42).

"And when it was day, he departed and went into a *solitary* place" (JST Luke 4:42).

The New International Version confirms the Joseph Smith Translation by using the word "solitary." The New American Standard has "secluded," the Amplified Bible says "isolated," while the Jerusalem Bible, Revised Standard Version, and New

Century Version all have "lonely." The Contemporary English Version reads "a place where he could be alone."

Hindered

"I purposed to come unto you, but was *let* hitherto" (Romans 1:13).

"I purposed to come unto you, but was *hindered* hitherto" (JST Romans 1:13).

The American Standard Version agrees with the Joseph Smith Translation in that it uses the word "hindered." The Revised Standard Version, Phillips Modern English, New International Version, and Jerusalem Bible all utilize the word "prevented."

SUMMARY

The Prophet Joseph Smith claimed, in the 1830s, that the texts of the Bible had been tampered with both by careless and designing people. This concept seemed quite preposterous to those of his day, who felt the Bible was the complete and inerrant word of God. Modern scholarship, however, has provided substantial evidence for the Prophet's position on this matter.

Under the direction and inspiration of heaven, Joseph Smith restored and clarified some of the biblical texts that had been altered during centuries of abuse by copyists and clerics. Some of the corrections and clarifications that were made by the Prophet have now been vindicated by biblical scholars.

NOTES

1. *TPJS*, 310.
2. Ibid., 327. According to Brigham Young, the Prophet Joseph Smith "said the Bible was right in the main but, through the translators and others, many precious portions were suppressed and several other portions were wrongly translated" (*JD*, 8:224).
3. *TPJS*, 9–10. For further reading see Robert J. Matthews, "The Role of the Joseph Smith Translation of the Bible in the Restoration of Doctrine," in Stephen D. Ricks, Donald W. Parry, and Andrew H. Hedges, eds., *The Disciple as Witness: Essays on Latter-day Saint History and Doctrine in Honor of Richard Lloyd Anderson* (Provo, Utah: FARMS, 2000), 327–53.
4. For two articles on the role of the Book of Mormon in the restoration of Church organization and doctrine see Scott H. Faulring, "The Book of Mormon: A Blueprint for Organizing the Church," *Journal of Book of Mormon Studies*, vol. 7, no. 1, 1998, 60–69, 71; and John A. Tvedtnes, "The Role of the Book of Mormon in the Restoration of the Church," in John A. Tvedtnes, *The Most Correct Book* (Salt Lake City: Cornerstone Publishing, 1999), 291–316. Some LDS scholars believe that the "great and abominable church" spoken of by Nephi can be identified with the hellenized Christian church that arose shortly after the death of Christ's apostles. As Stephen E. Robinson puts it: "The historical abominable church of the devil is that apostate church that replaced true Christianity in the first and second centuries, teaching the philosophies of men mingled with scriptures" (Stephen E. Robinson, "Warring Against the Saints of God," *Ensign*, January 1988, 39).
5. Daniel N. Schowalter, "Lost in Translation," *Bible Review*, August 1995, 36.
6. Emanuel Tov, *Textual Criticism of the Hebrew Bible* (Minneapolis: Fortress, 1992), 8, 9, 177, 265–66, in that order, emphasis in original.
7. New English Bible. See also the Jerusalem Bible and the Revised Standard Version.
8. Michael Fishbane, *Biblical Interpretation in Ancient Israel* (Oxford: Clarendon Press, 1985), 67.
9. Roland K. Harrison, et al., *Biblical Criticism: Historical, Literary and Textual* (Grand Rapids, Michigan: Zondervan, 1978), 53–54.
10. Bruce M. Metzger, *A Textual Commentary on the Greek New Testament*, 3d ed. (Stuttgart, Germany: United Bible Societies, 1975), xxiv.
11. Leon Vaganay and Christian-Bernard Amphoux, *An Introduction to New Testament Textual Criticism*, 2d ed. (New York: Cambridge University Press, 1991), 98, 105–106, 97, in that order.
12. G. A. Williamson, trans., *Eusebius: The History of the Church from Christ to Constantine* (New York: Dorset Press, 1984), 185.
13. Bart D. Ehrman, *The Orthodox Corruption of Scripture: The Effect of Early Christological Controversies on the Text of the New Testament* (New York: Oxford University Press, 1993), xi. On page 4 of this same source it is again stated that Christian scribes "alter[ed] the words of scripture in order to make them more serviceable for the polemical task. Scribes modified their manuscripts to make them more patently 'orthodox' and less susceptible to 'abuse' by the opponents of orthodoxy."

14. Quoted by Origen in *Contra Celsum, SC*, 132.2.27, cited in Vaganay and Amphoux, *An Introduction to New Testament Textual Criticism*, 96.
15. Origen, *In Matthaeum*, 15.14 cited in Vaganay and Amphoux, *An Introduction to New Testament Textual Criticism*, 96.
16. Frederick H. Scrivener, *A Plain Introduction to the Criticism of the New Testament*, 3d ed. (Cambridge: Deighton, Bell and Co, 1883), 511.
17. See *HC*, 1:238.
18. For a picture of the actual manuscript page that carries this notation see Robert J. Matthews, *A Plainer Translation: Joseph Smith's Translation of the Bible* (Provo, Utah: Brigham Young University Press, 1975), 267.
19. *Times and Seasons*, vol. 5, no. 22, 1 December 1844, 723. See also D&C 35:20 (and footnote), and D&C 42:56 (and footnote), President George Q. Cannon wrote: "On the second day of February, 1833, the Prophet completed, for the time being, his inspired translation of the New Testament. No endeavor was made at that time to print the work. It was sealed up with the expectation that it would be brought forth at a later day with other of the scriptures. Joseph did not live to give the world an authoritative publication of these translations. But the labor was its own reward, bringing in the performance a special blessing of broadened comprehension to the Prophet and a general blessing of enlightenment to the people through his subsequent teachings. We have heard President Brigham Young state that the Prophet before his death had spoken to him about going through the translation of the scriptures again and perfecting it upon points of doctrine which the Lord had restrained him from giving in plainness and fullness at the time of which we write" (George Q. Cannon, *Life of Joseph Smith the Prophet* [Salt Lake City: Deseret Book, 1958], 147–48).
20. Matthews, *A Plainer Translation: Joseph Smith's Translation of the Bible*, 253.
21. John G. Snaith, *The New Century Bible Commentary: Song of Songs* (Grand Rapids, Michigan: Eerdmans, 1993), 3–5.
22. Gerson D. Cohen, "The Song of Songs and the Jewish Religious Mentality," in Sid Z. Leiman, ed., *The Canon and Masorah of the Hebrew Bible* (New York: Ktav Publishing House, 1974), 262–63.
23. Adam Clarke, *Clarke's Commentary* (Nashville: Abingdon, 1977), 1:324.
24. Thomas Scott, *Scott's Commentary on the Bible* (London: James Nisbet and Co., 1866), 1:2B1.
25. Alexander Jones, ed., *The Old Testament of the Jerusalem Bible* (Garden City, New York: Doubleday, 1966), 85.
26. Frank E. Gaebelein, ed., *The Expositor's Bible Commentary* (Grand Rapids, Michigan: Zondervan, 1984), 8:173.
27. Philip Schaff, ed., *Nicene and Post-Nicene Fathers*, first series (Peabody, Massachusetts: Hendrickson Publishers, 1994), 6:43.
28. Clarke, *Clarke's Commentary*, 5:87, emphasis in original.
29. Alexander Roberts and James Donaldson, eds., *Ante-Nicene Fathers* (Peabody, Massachusetts: Hendrikson Publishers, 1994), 8:289, emphasis added.

30. Leo Schaya, *The Universal Meaning of the Kabbalah* (London: George Allen and Unwin, 1971), 15–16.
31. Meir Zlotowitz, *Bereishis: Genesis*, 2d ed. (New York: Mesorah Publications, 1988), 1:577, emphasis in original. Hamilton acknowledges that "Speiser (*Genesis* p. 125) tones down *yishaq*, 'he laughed,' to 'he smiled' and notes 'that the concept of Abraham in a derisive attitude toward God would be decidedly out of keeping with P's character.' This may explain, if Speiser is correct, the absence of any rebuke to Abraham" (Victor P. Hamilton, *The Book of Genesis: Chapters 1–17* [Grand Rapids, Michigan: Eerdmans, 1990], 477).
32. Bromiley, ed., *The International Standard Bible Encyclopedia*, 2:507; see also Genesis 22:14; cf. Abraham 1:16; 2:8.
33. See Samuel Sandmel, ed., *The New English Bible with the Apocrypha: Oxford Study Edition* (New York: Oxford University Press, 1976), 953.
34. James Strong, *The New Strong's Exhaustive Concordance of the Bible* (Nashville: Thomas Nelson Publishers, 1996), Greek Dictionary of the New Testament, 12, word #680, emphasis in original.
35. Marvin R. Vincent, *Word Studies in the New Testament* (Grand Rapids, Michigan: Eerdmans, 1976), 4:510.
36. Clarke, *Clarke's Commentary*, 6:279, emphasis added.
37. Strong, *The New Strong's Exhaustive Concordance of the Bible*, Greek Dictionary of the New Testament, 22, word #1242.
38. Jay P. Green, Sr., ed., *The Interlinear Greek-English New Testament*, 3d ed. (Grand Rapids, Michigan: Baker Books, 1996), 679–80.
39. Metzger believes that it is "likely" the Greek word εἰκη, which is rendered as "without a cause" in the King James Version of Matthew 5:22, "was added by copyists in order to soften the rigor of the precept" of the passage sometime after the second century A.D. (Metzger, *A Textual Commentary on the Greek New Testament*, 13).
40. Clarke, *Clarke's Commentary*, 6:252.
41. Jay P. Green, Sr., ed., *The Interlinear Bible: Hebrew-Greek-English*, 2d ed. (Grand Rapids, Michigan: Baker Book House, 1986), 559.
42. John R. Kohlenberger III, *The NIV Interlinear Hebrew-English Old Testament* (Grand Rapids, Michigan: Zondervan, 1987), 4:67; David E. Sulomm Stein, ed., *JPS Hebrew-English Tanakh*, 2d ed. (Philadelphia: The Jewish Publication Society, 1999), 923.
43. Stein, ed., *JPS Hebrew-English Tanakh*, 1191.
44. John Murray, *The Epistle to the Romans* (London: Marshall, Morgan, and Scott, 1965), 222. On page 223 of this same source Murray states that "dying with Christ entails death to sin."
45. James Murdock, *The New Testament: Translated from the Syriac Peshito Version* (New York: Robert Carter and Brothers, 1869), 285.
46. *WJS*, 256.
47. Confirmation of this can be found in Strong, *The New Strong's Exhaustive Concordance of the Bible*, Hebrew and Aramaic Dictionary of the Old Testament, 92, word #5162.
48. Lancelot C. Brenton, ed., *The Septuagint with Apocrypha: Greek and English* (Grand Rapids, Michigan: Zondervan, 1980), 837.

49. Charles Thomson, ed., *The Septuagint*, as cited in Curtis Vaughan, ed., *Twenty-Six Translations of the Bible* (Chattanooga, Tennessee: AMG Publishers, 1985), 1:135.
50. Alexander Jones, ed., *The Jerusalem Bible* (London: Darton, Longman, and Todd, 1966), 85.
51. Kohlenberger III, *The NIV Interlinear Hebrew-English Old Testament*, 1:161.
52. Stein, ed., *JPS Hebrew-English Tanakh*, 124.

CHAPTER 7

Book of Mormon Evidences

Critics of the LDS Church have long been of the opinion that the Book of Mormon is nothing more than a fictional fraud. They deny that such a publication could be the revealed word of God since they believe that the heavens have been sealed since the time of Jesus Christ. In marked contrast to such an opinion is a direct revelation from Jesus Christ that forthrightly declares that Joseph Smith "has translated the [Book of Mormon], even that part which I have commanded him, and as your Lord and your God liveth it is true" (D&C 17:6). In this chapter the reader will be presented with some of the evidences that bolster the Book of Mormon's claim to be a genuine, ancient text.

Before we continue, it would be prudent to review the hierarchy of evidence in spiritual matters. Elder Dallin H. Oaks of the Quorum of the Twelve Apostles has pointed out that the issue of the historical authenticity of the Book of Mormon rests fundamentally in the realm of faith and revelation—since secular evidence, though worthy of attention, can neither prove nor disprove the Book of Mormon's claims.[1] As Moroni 10:3–5 so plainly states, God the Father will confirm the divine authenticity of the Book of Mormon, by the power of the Holy Ghost, to all those who seek for such a confirmation in the spirit of sincerity and faith.

So, the hierarchy of evidence is clear. The power of the Holy Ghost, said Elder B. H. Roberts, "must ever be the chief source of evidence for the truth of the Book of Mormon. All other evidence is secondary to this. . . . No arrangement of evidence, however skillfully ordered; no argument, however adroitly made, can ever take its place; for this witness of the Holy Spirit to the souls of men for the truth of the Nephite volume of scripture, is God's evidence to the truth." But, he reminds us, "secondary evidences in support of truth, like secondary causes in natural phenomena, may be of first-rate importance, and mighty factors in the achievement of God's purposes."[2]

With this in mind, let us now examine some of the secondary evidences that support the notion that the Book of Mormon is what it claims to be.

ADDING TO SCRIPTURE

One of the primary arguments used against the validity of the Book of Mormon runs something like this: "God no longer issues revelations; he does not need to since the Bible is the *complete*, and *final*, word of God." The primary proof-text for this argument is Revelation 22:18–19 which reads:

> For I testify unto every man that heareth the words of the prophecy of this book, if any man shall add unto these things, God shall add unto him the plagues that are written in this book. And if any man shall take away from the words of the book of this prophecy, God shall take away his part out of the book of life, and out of the holy city, and from the things which are written in this book.

Proponents of the closed-canon theory believe that this scriptural passage, which is found at the very end of the Bible, is proof positive that the scriptures cannot be added to. A careful reading of the passage, however, reveals that the warning applies only to the book of Revelation (i.e., "this book"), not to the entire Bible. Even though the book of Revelation has been placed at the end of the current collection of biblical books, scholars do not believe that it was the last book of the Bible to be written.[3] Thus the proposition that nothing can be added to scripture, because the last book of the Bible forbids it, simply cannot be sustained. The prohibition in the book of Revelation against adding to its text must be understood in proper context. A similar prohibition can be found in Deuteronomy 4:2 where the Lord says, "Ye shall not add unto the word which I command you, neither shall ye diminish ought from it, that ye may keep the commandments of the Lord your God which I command you" (see also Deuteronomy 12:32). The point of this divine directive is that *man* is forbidden from tampering with God's revelations. But there is no restriction, found anywhere in the Bible, that would prevent God from adding to His revealed word at any given time.

Another reason why the closed-canon theory is not valid is that the Bible was not created, and then closed to any additions, by divine decree. The Bible, as it is now constituted, did not even exist until several hundred years after the time of Jesus Christ. According to New Testament scholar David F. Payne, "it was not until the year A.D. 393 that a church council first listed the 27 New Testament books now universally recognized. There was thus a period of about 350 years during which the New Testament canon was in process of being formed."[4] Even after this council had made its selection of scriptural books there were still controversies over what constituted a scriptural text. Some Christian sects considered the Apocrypha to be worthy of inclusion in the canon of scripture while others did not. The Lord informed the Prophet Joseph Smith that the apocryphal books contained "many" things that were true but also "many" things that were not true, but which were "interpolations by the hands of men" (D&C 91:1–6).

What of the argument that the Bible contains the *complete* word of God and there is, therefore, no need for further scripture? The Bible itself provides clear evidence that it is not complete since it mentions scriptural texts that are now missing. The "lost" books of the Bible include:

- Book of the Covenant (Exodus 24:7)
- Book of the Wars of the Lord (Numbers 21:14)
- Book of Jasher (Joshua 10:13; 2 Samuel 1:18)
- Book of the Acts of Solomon (1 Kings 11:41)
- Book of the Manner of the Kingdom (1 Samuel 10:25)
- Book of Nathan the Prophet (1 Chronicles 29:29; 2 Chronicles 9:29)
- Book of Shemaiah the Prophet (2 Chronicles 12:15)
- Book of Jehu (2 Chronicles 20:34)
- Book of Samuel the Seer (1 Chronicles 29:29)
- Book of Gad the Seer (1 Chronicles 29:29; 2 Chronicles 2:29)
- Visions of Iddo the Seer (2 Chronicles 9:29; 12:15; 13:22)
- The Sayings of the Seers (2 Chronicles 33:19)
- Prophecy of Ahijah (2 Chronicles 9:29)
- Acts of Abijah (2 Chronicles 13:22)
- Acts of Uzziah (2 Chronicles 26:22)
- Lost Epistle to the Corinthians (1 Corinthians 5:9)
- Lost Epistle to the Ephesians (Ephesians 3:3)
- Lost Epistle to the Laodiceans (Colossians 4:16)
- Lost Epistle from Jude (Jude 1:3)
- Lost Book of Enoch (Jude 1:14–15)

In addition to these lost books of scripture, there is presently no biblical text that records the prophecy that Jesus Christ would be "called a Nazarene" (Matthew 2:23). Nor do we presently possess another important prophecy concerning the Son of God. "Thus it is *written*, that Christ should suffer and on the third day rise from the dead" (Luke 24:46, emphasis added). The apostle Luke informs us that before he penned his own book "*many* . . . eyewitnesses, and ministers of the word" had "taken in hand to set forth in order a declaration of those things which are most surely believed among us" (Luke 1:1, emphasis added). Where are these records? Does the Bible at least provide us with a *complete* record of Christ's earthly ministry? Certainly not. The apostle John informs us that "there are also *many* other things which Jesus did, the which, if they should be written every one, I suppose that even the world itself could not contain the books that should be written" (John 21:25, emphasis added; see also John 20:30). And what of the Savior's post-resurrection teachings. The Bible testifies that Jesus spent 40 full days, after He had arisen from the grave, instructing His disciples on things "pertaining to the kingdom of God" (Acts 1:3). Where are the records of these important truths?

Is it accurate to say that the Bible contains the *final* word of God? No, certainly not. In the Book of Mormon the Lord lays out the fallacy of such an idea. "Thou fool, that shall say: 'A Bible, we have got a Bible, and we need no more Bible.' . . . Wherefore murmur ye, because ye shall receive more of my word? . . . And because I have spoken one word ye need not suppose that I cannot speak another; for my work is not yet finished . . . Wherefore because that ye have a Bible ye need not suppose that it contains all my words; neither need ye suppose that I have not caused more to be written. For I command all men . . . that they shall write the words which I speak unto them" (2 Nephi 29:6, 8–11).

THE STICKS OF EZEKIEL

Not only is it allowable for the Lord to add to the scriptural corpus whenever He pleases, but it appears from one Old Testament text that He foretold of a time when He would do just that. In the King James Version of Ezekiel 37:15–20 we read:

> The word of the Lord came unto me, saying,
> "Moreover, thou son of man, take thee one stick, and write upon it, 'For Judah,

and the children of Israel his companions': then take another stick, and write upon it, 'For Joseph, the stick of Ephraim, and for all the house of Israel his companions':

And join them one to another into one stick; and they shall become one in thine hand.

And when the children of thy people shall speak unto thee, saying, 'Wilt thou not show us what thou meanest by these?'

Say unto them, 'Thus saith the Lord God; Behold, I will take the stick of Joseph, which is in the hand of Ephraim, and the tribes of Israel his fellows, and will put them with him, even with the stick of Judah, and make them one stick, and they shall be one in mine hand.'

And the sticks whereon thou writest shall be in thine hand before their eyes."

In this passage Ezekiel is commanded by the Lord to write [*kātab*, inscribe, engrave] certain words upon two pieces of wood [*ᶜēṣ*]. What kind of wood did Ezekiel use? A possible answer arises when one remembers that Ezekiel was an exile in Babylon when the Lord spoke to him about these pieces of wood. Ancient textual and artistic evidence indicates that the Babylonians and other ancient peoples wrote upon wax-filled writing boards or wooden tablets. These tablets were hinged on one edge so that two or more of them could be connected together and folded shut.[5] Thus, it is possible, in context, to interpret Ezekiel's "sticks" as two wax-filled writing boards that were to be written upon and then hinged to each other.

A set of wax-filled writing boards, belonging to the ancient king Sargon, was discovered in Assyria in 1953. The outermost board of this set had an inscription on its outside surface that identified the content of the record.[6] With this physical evidence at hand, the translators of the New English Bible rendered Ezekiel 37:15–19 in the following manner.

FIGURE 12. Some biblical scholars believe that the "sticks" of Ezekiel 37:15–20 were the wax-filled writing boards of the ancient Near East. This is a logical conclusion since the Lord commanded Ezekiel to "write" upon them.

> These were the words of the Lord to me: "Man, take one leaf of a *wooden tablet* and write on it, 'Judah and his associates of Israel.' Then take another leaf and write on it, 'Joseph, the leaf of Ephraim, and all of his associates of Israel.' Now bring the two together to form one tablet; then they will be a folding tablet in your hand. When your fellow-countrymen ask you to tell them what you mean by this, say to them, 'These are the words of the Lord God: I am taking the leaf of Joseph, which belongs to Ephraim and his associate tribes of Israel, and joining to it the leaf of Judah. Thus I shall make them *one* tablet, and they shall be *one* in my hand'" (emphasis added).

In the verses that follow this passage the Lord explains that the "sticks" of Joseph and Judah represent the divided kingdom of Israel ("Stick of Joseph"—Northern Kingdom; "Stick of Judah"—Southern Kingdom). The Lord states in verses 21 and 22 of Ezekiel 37 that the joining together of the inscribed "sticks" is symbolic of the gathering together of Israel's scattered children and their reunification as "one nation." When will this gathering occur? In a day when the Lord's temple stands once again among the covenant people (vv. 26–28).

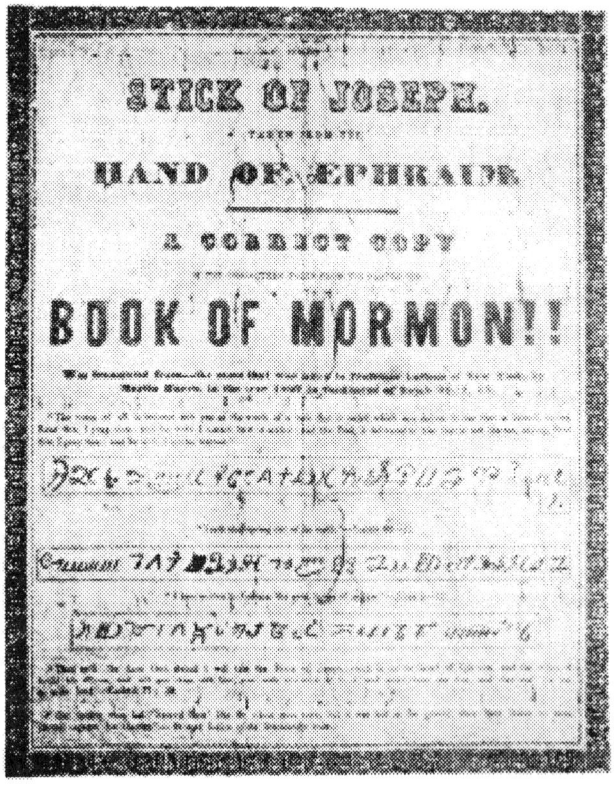

FIGURE 13. This placard (ca. 1844), from the collection of Hyrum Smith, identifies the Book of Mormon with the "Stick of Joseph" that is mentioned in Ezekiel 37:19.

In a revelation issued in August 1830 the Lord said that He had committed unto Moroni "the keys of the record of the stick of Ephraim" (D&C 27:5).[7] This passage clearly implies that the "stick of Ephraim" (or "stick of Joseph") is the Book of Mormon and also that the "sticks" of Ezekiel are symbolic of records. This helps to explain why LDS Church leaders were teaching in print, as early as 1832, that the "stick of Judah" referred to the Bible and the "stick of

Joseph" referred to the Book of Mormon.[8] This interpretation finds additional support in 2 Nephi 3:11–12 and JST Genesis 50:30–31. Even though they are two separate texts, these passages both record an identical revelation that was given by the Lord to Joseph of Egypt.

> A seer [i.e., Joseph Smith] will I raise up out of the fruit of thy loins, and unto him will I give power to bring forth my word [i.e., the Book of Mormon] unto the seed of thy loins; and not to the bringing forth of my word only, saith the Lord, but to the convincing them of my word, which shall have already gone forth among them in the latter days [i.e., the Bible].
>
> Wherefore the fruit of thy loins shall write [i.e., the Book of Mormon], and the fruit of the loins of Judah shall write [i.e., the Bible]; and that which shall be written by the fruit of thy loins, and also that which shall be written by the fruit of the loins of Judah, shall *grow together* unto the confounding of false doctrines, and laying down of contentions, and establishing peace among the fruit of thy loins, and bringing them to a knowledge of their fathers in the last days; and also to a knowledge of my covenants, saith the Lord (emphasis added).

Another Book of Mormon passage strengthens the Stick of Joseph/Book of Mormon interpretation even further. Nephi, the son of Lehi, was shown a vision of the future by an angel of God and saw several books during the manifestation. Nephi reports:

> And it came to pass that the angel of the Lord spake unto me, saying: "Behold, saith the Lamb of God, after I have visited the remnant of the house of Israel—and this remnant of whom I speak is the seed of thy father—wherefore, after I have visited them in judgment, and smitten them by the hand of the Gentiles, and after the Gentiles do stumble exceedingly, because of the most plain and precious parts of the gospel of the Lamb which have been kept back by that abominable church, which is the mother of harlots, saith the Lamb—I will be merciful unto the Gentiles in that day, insomuch that I will bring forth unto them, in mine own power, much of my gospel, which shall be plain and precious, saith the Lamb.
>
> "For, behold, saith the Lamb: I will manifest myself unto thy seed, that they shall write many things which I shall minister unto them, which shall be plain and precious [i.e., Book of Mormon]; and after thy seed shall be destroyed, and dwindle in unbelief, and also the seed of thy brethren, behold, these things shall be hid up, to come forth unto the Gentiles, by the gift and power of the Lamb.
>
> "And in them shall be written my gospel, saith the Lamb, and my rock and my salvation.
>
> "And blessed are they who shall seek to bring forth my Zion at that day, for they shall have the gift and the power of the Holy Ghost; and if they endure unto the end

they shall be lifted up at the last day, and shall be saved in the everlasting kingdom of the Lamb; and whoso shall publish peace, yea, tidings of great joy, how beautiful upon the mountains shall they be."

And it came to pass that I beheld the remnant of the seed of my brethren, and also the book of the Lamb of God, which had proceeded forth from the mouth of the Jew [i.e., the Bible], that it came forth from the Gentiles [i.e., Christian immigrants to the New World] unto the remnant of the seed of my brethren [i.e., the Lamanites].

And after it had come forth unto them I beheld *other books* [Book of Mormon, Doctrine and Covenants, Pearl of Great Price?], which came forth by the power of the Lamb, from the Gentiles unto them, unto the convincing of the Gentiles and the remnant of the seed of my brethren, and also the Jews who were scattered upon all the face of the earth, that the records of the prophets and of the twelve apostles of the Lamb are true.

And the angel spake unto me, saying: "These *last records,* which thou hast seen among the Gentiles, shall establish the truth of the first [i.e., the Bible], which are of the twelve apostles of the Lamb, and shall make known the plain and precious things which have been taken away from them; and shall make known to all kindreds, tongues, and people, that the Lamb of God is the Son of the Eternal Father, and the Savior of the world; and that all men must come unto Him, or they cannot be saved.

"And they must come according to the words which shall be established by the mouth of the Lamb; and the words of the Lamb shall be made known in the *records* of thy seed [i.e., Book of Mormon], as well as in the *records* of the twelve apostles of the Lamb [i.e., Bible]; wherefore they both shall be *established in one;* for there is one God and one Shepherd over all the earth" (1 Nephi 13:34–41, emphasis added).[9]

MIRACULOUS PRODUCTION OF THE TEXT

Joseph Smith stated that the angel Moroni gave him the golden plates of the Book of Mormon on 22 September 1827.[10] It is of great interest, and probably planned significance, that this date marked the Israelite holy day called *Rosh ha-Shanah,* also known as the Day of Remembrance, the Feast of Trumpets, and the Feast of Ingathering. This was the day when the ancient Israelites prayed for God to remember His covenant with the house of Israel. Since the final harvest of the agricultural season was also celebrated on this day, the children of Israel also prayed that God would gather (i.e., harvest) his scattered people (cf. D&C 4:4).

On this very day, in Old Testament times, the temple priest Ezra restored a true understanding of God's words to the Israelites after they had returned from their Babylonian exile (see Nehemiah 8:1–12). Trumpets were blown on this festival to signify the sounding of God's revelations or proclamations of truth (cf. Exodus 19:16; D&C 24:12). The trumpet blast was also seen as God's final warning to repent before the impending day of judgment (symbolized by *Yom Kippur*). Latter-day Saints can easily see the parallels between the typology of the Feast of Trumpets and the Restoration of the Gospel.[11] It is also of more than passing interest that a statue of the angel Moroni stands atop the highest spire of many LDS temples, trumpet in hand, symbolically sounding the message of the Restoration to the nations of the earth.

FIGURE 14. The Lord commanded the ancient Israelites to make two silver trumpets for the service of His Tabernacle. These trumpets were blown to announce important events and also to summon the children of Israel to the House of the Lord (see Numbers 10:1–8).

There are many other evidences of a divine governing hand in the coming forth of the Book of Mormon. We can learn about some of them through a series of questions and answers.

What was Joseph Smith's age, social circumstance, and level of education at the time that the Book of Mormon text was produced?

When Joseph Smith produced the Book of Mormon text he was only 23 years old. His family lived in near poverty on a rural farm in the upper part of New York state. At this point in his life, Joseph Smith had only a meager amount of education. Orson Pratt informs us that the Prophet's "advantages for acquiring scientific knowledge were exceedingly small, being limited to a slight acquaintance with two or three of the common branches of learning. He could read without much difficulty, and write a very imperfect hand; and had a very limited understanding of the elementary rules of arithmetic. These were his highest and only attainments; while the rest of those branches, so universally taught in the common schools throughout the United States, were entirely unknown to him."[12]

The Prophet's distinct lack of formal schooling strengthens the proposition that he was not capable of producing the Book of Mormon as a fraudulent text. David Whitmer expounded on the Prophet's low level of learning. "In translating the characters [on the Book of Mormon plates Joseph] Smith, who was illiterate and but little versed in biblical lore, was ofttimes compelled to spell the words out, not knowing the correct pronunciation." Furthermore, said Whitmer, at the time of the translation the Prophet "did not even know that Jerusalem was a walled city. [Oliver] Cowdery, however, being a school teacher, rendered invaluable aid in pronouncing hard words and giving their proper definition."[13]

Emma Smith, the wife of the Prophet, likewise spoke of her husband's "limited education while he was translating the Book of Mormon . . . [S]he was scribe at the time, [and relates that] 'He could not pronounce the word Sariah.' And one time while translating, where it speaks of the walls of Jerusalem, he stopped and said, 'Emma, did Jerusalem have walls surrounding it?' When I informed him it had, he replied, 'O, I thought I was deceived.'"[14]

When Joseph Smith's oldest son reached adulthood he asked his mother what she thought about the origin and authenticity of the Book of Mormon. The Prophet's wife testified: "My belief is that the Book of Mormon is of divine authenticity–I have not the slightest doubt of it. I am satisfied that no man could have dictated the writing of the manuscript unless he was inspired: for, when I was his scribe, your father would dictate to me hour after hour; and when returning after meals, or after interruptions, he would at once begin where he had left off, without either seeing the manuscript or having any portion of it read to him. It would have been improbable that a learned man could do this; and, for one so ignorant and unlearned as he was, it was simply impossible."[15]

There seems to have been a divine purpose in Joseph Smith's accentuated lack of worldly education. The Lord said to the Prophet in a revelation dated 19 January 1841: "I raised you up, that I might show forth my wisdom through the weak things of the earth" (D&C 124:1). The Prophet's educational credentials stand as a strong witness that he simply was not capable of producing the Book of Mormon text on his own. He required assistance from an outside source. The Prophet testified that the outside source was the Lord.

How was the text of the Book of Mormon produced and how long did the translation process take?

The text of the Book of Mormon was produced by dictation as Joseph Smith read aloud the English text that he saw in either the Nephite "Interpreters" or in his personal seerstone. The Prophet would sometimes place his seerstone in the crown of a hat so that he could exclude all exterior light and thus have a better view of the writing that appeared on the stone. Scribes would repeat back the text that Joseph Smith had seen and spoken; and, if correct, another word or sentence would appear in the stone and the dictation would continue.[16]

The Book of Lehi (otherwise known as the lost 116 pages)[17] was translated between 12 April 1828 and 14 June 1828. Between 22 September 1828 and March of 1829, the Prophet translated only a few pages of manuscript with his wife acting as a scribe. The bulk of the Book of Mormon text, as it presently stands (531 pages), was translated between 7 April 1829 and 30 June 1829. The available evidence suggests that during the period of translation (65–75 days total) Joseph Smith, with Oliver Cowdery as the main scribe, produced approximately eight pages of text per day. But they also had to accomplish many other tasks during this time period.

> They also took time to eat, to sleep, to seek employment (once, to work for money when supplies ran out), to receive the Aaronic and Melchizedek Priesthoods, to make at least one (and possibly two) trips to Colesville thirty miles away, to convert and baptize Hyrum and Samuel Smith (who came to Harmony at that time), to receive and record thirteen revelations that are now sections of the Doctrine and Covenants, to move on buckboard from Harmony to Fayette, to acquire the Book of Mormon copyright, to preach a few days and baptize several people near Fayette, to experience manifestations with the Three and Eight Witnesses, and to begin making arrangements for the Book of Mormon's publication.[18]

What is really amazing in all of this is that the first draft of the Book of Mormon was also the last. After the text had been dictated, there was no editing (other than to add punctuation and capitalization), rearranging, correcting, or excising. The Book of Mormon text stands today exactly as it was dictated by an uneducated farmboy who was staring, day after day, into the bottom of a hat.

Did Joseph Smith have access to research materials that could have assisted him in creating a fraudulent text?

No, he did not. In fact, there is no evidence that there was a library anywhere close to Harmony, Pennsylvania, where the translation took place. The production of the Book of Mormon occurred in a resource desert. Joseph Smith could not have checked how the material in his manuscript squared with reputable biblical and ancient Near Eastern scholarship even if he had wanted to.[19]

Did the Prophet have any manuscripts to read from during the production of the Book of Mormon text?

Emma Smith answered this question in an interview with one of her sons.

> In writing for your father I frequently wrote day after day, often sitting at the table close by him, he . . . dictat[ed] hour after hour with nothing between us.
>
> [Question] Had he not a book or manuscript from which he read or dictated to you?
>
> [Answer] He had neither manuscript or book to read from.
>
> [Question] Could he not have had [a book or manuscript] and you not know it?
>
> [Answer] If he had anything of the kind he could not have concealed it from me. . . .
>
> [Question] Could not father have dictated the Book of Mormon to you, Oliver Cowdery and the others who wrote for him, after having first written it, or having first read it out of some book?
>
> [Answer] Joseph Smith . . . could neither write nor dictate a coherent and well-worded letter; let alone dictating a book like the Book of Mormon.[20]

David Whitmer confirms this point. He "was present very frequently during the writing of this manuscript [and] affirms that *Joseph Smith had no book or manuscript before him from which he could have read* as is asserted by some that he did, he (Whitmer) having every opportunity to know."[21]

Is there any evidence that Joseph Smith was simply reciting sentences that he had memorized?

No, there is not. In fact, Martin Harris, who acted as one of the scribes for the Book of Mormon, relates an incident where he tried to determine if the Prophet was not simply reciting memorized material. "Martin said [that] after continued translation they would become weary, and would go down to the river and exercise by throwing stones out on the river, etc. While so doing on one occasion, Martin found a stone resembling the one used for translating, and on resuming their labor of translation, Martin put in place the stone that he had found. He said the Prophet remained silent, unusually and intently gazing in darkness, no traces of the usual sentences appearing. Much surprised, Joseph exclaimed, 'Martin! What is the matter? All is as dark as Egypt!' Martin's countenance betrayed him, and the Prophet asked Martin why he had done so. Martin said, to stop the mouths of fools, who had told him that the Prophet had learned those sentences and was merely repeating them."[22]

Another evidence that Joseph Smith was being assisted by divine means in the translation process comes from Emma Smith who recalled, "he dictated each sentence, word for word, and when he came to proper names he could not pronounce, or long words, he spelled them out; and while I was writing them, if I made a mistake in spelling, he would stop me and correct my spelling, although it was impossible for him to see how I was writing them down at the time."[23]

Does the original manuscript of the Book of Mormon show any signs that it was produced by any other means than by dictation, as the Prophet said it was?

No, it does not. There are no signs on the original manuscript that the text was produced by a collaborative committee; no signs of development after conducting research. There is no evidence that modern expressions were changed in order to make them sound more archaic. There are no signs of rethinking, revising, or rewriting. There is no indication that any thoughts were reformulated to make them sound more believable. There are no signs of copying from outside sources. And there is no punctuation, capitalization, or paragraphs, just one continuous block of writing. The original manuscript of the Book of Mormon supports the claim that Joseph Smith dictated a text and his scribes simply wrote down what he said.[24]

THE TESTIMONY OF WITNESSES

One of the strongest evidences that Joseph Smith's account of the angel and the plates is true is that God allowed others to see both the angel and the plates and they verified the Prophet's story. Two of the prophets whose writings appear in the Book of

Mormon foretold that "three witnesses" would be allowed by the Lord to view the golden plates (see Ether 5:2–4; 2 Nephi 27:12–14). In a latter-day revelation the Lord verified that He would allow such an occurrence to take place (see D&C 17:1–5). The men who were chosen for this choice experience were Oliver Cowdery, David Whitmer, and Martin Harris. The testimony of these Three Witnesses is recorded in the introduction to the Book of Mormon. This testimony reads, in part:

> Be it known unto all nations, kindreds, tongues, and people, unto whom this work shall come: That we, through the grace of God the Father, and our Lord Jesus Christ, have seen the plates which contain this record, which is a record of the people of Nephi, and also of the Lamanites, their brethren, and also of the people of Jared, who came from the tower of which hath been spoken. And we also know that they have been translated by the gift and power of God, for His voice hath declared it unto us; wherefore we know of a surety that the work is true. And we also testify that we have seen the engravings which are upon the plates; and they have been shown unto us by the power of God, and not of man. And we declare with words of soberness, that an angel of God came down from heaven, and he brought and laid before our eyes, that we beheld and saw the plates, and the engravings thereon; and we know that it is by the grace of God the Father, and our Lord Jesus Christ, that we beheld and bear record that these things are true. And it is marvelous in our eyes. Nevertheless, the voice of the Lord commanded us that we should bear record of it; wherefore, to be obedient unto the commandments of God, we bear testimony of these things.

From the recollections of David Whitmer, the experience of the Three Witnesses can be reconstructed as follows. On the day of this experience, in late June of 1829,

FIGURE 15. Oliver Cowdery, David Whitmer, and Martin Harris (l-r) each bore witness, throughout their lives, that an angel of God showed them the golden plates of the Book of Mormon. They also testified that during this manifestation they heard the voice of the Lord declare that the translation of the plates was correct and true.

the Prophet reminded Cowdery, Harris, and Whitmer that the Lord had promised a manifestation of the plates to three witnesses and informed them that the time had come for it to occur. At about 11 A.M. Joseph and his friends walked to a secluded spot near the Whitmer family farm. After they had engaged in prayer a glorious light overshadowed them and spread out around them. This light increased in brightness until an angel, dressed in white, appeared about five or six feet from the group with a table in between them. On the table were the Book of Mormon plates, the Brass Plates, the plates of the Book of Ether, other ancient records, the breastplate, the Interpreters or "Urim and Thummim," the Liahona or Director, and the sword of Laban. The angel turned the unsealed portion of the Book of Mormon plates over one at a time so that the Three Witnesses could see the engravings on both sides of them. While this was taking place, the voice of the Lord spoke from heaven and confirmed that the record was a true one, that the translation was correct, and that it had been accomplished by the gift and power of God. This voice also commanded the Witnesses to bear their testimony of these things to the world; and then the manifestation ended, disappearing in the same manner that it had appeared.[25]

David Whitmer testified that he "heard the voice of the angel, and saw the engravings on the plates. . . . The messenger brought the several [sets of] plates and laid them on the table before our eyes, and we saw them, and bore testimony of them, and our testimony is true. And if these things are not true then there is no truth, and if there is no truth there is no God, and if there is no God there is no existence. But I know there is a God, for I have heard His voice and witnessed the manifestation of His power."[26]

After the Three Witnesses had seen the angel and the plates, the Prophet told his father and mother: "You do not know how happy I am: the Lord has now caused the plates to be shown to three more besides myself. They have seen an angel, who has testified to them, and they will have to bear witness to the truth of what I have said, for now they know for themselves, that I do not go about to deceive the people, and I feel as if I was relieved of a burden which was almost too heavy for me to bear, and it rejoices my soul that I am not any longer to be entirely alone in the world."[27]

Shortly after the Three Witnesses saw the angel and the plates, the Lord allowed eight other witnesses—Christian Whitmer, Jacob Whitmer, Peter Whitmer, Jr., John Whitmer, Hiram Page, Joseph Smith, Sr., Hyrum Smith, and Samuel H. Smith—to see and handle the golden plates without any supernatural display. The testimony of the Eight Witnesses reads:

> Be it known unto all nations, kindreds, tongues, and people, unto whom this work shall come: That Joseph Smith, Jr., the translator of this work, has shown unto us the plates of which hath been spoken, which have the appearance of gold; and as many of the leaves as the said Smith has translated we did handle with our hands; and we also saw the engravings thereon, all of which has the appearance of ancient work, and of curious workmanship. And this we bear record with words of soberness, that the said Smith has shown unto us, for we have *seen and hefted,* and know of a surety that the said Smith has got the plates of which we have spoken. And we give our names unto the world, to witness unto the world that which we have seen. And we lie not, God bearing witness of it.[28]

The great strength of the testimonies of the official Book of Mormon witnesses is that none of them ever denied what they said, even though several of them became embittered against Joseph Smith and the Church.[29]

In addition to the three and eight official witnesses, there were also others who saw both the angel Moroni and the golden plates, or otherwise handled the plates, and could therefore vouch for their existence.

Oliver Cowdery, one of the Three Witnesses, was shown the plates by the Lord around February of 1829. The Prophet reports that the Lord "appeared unto a young man by the name of Oliver Cowdery and showed unto him the plates in a vision, and also the truth of the work, and what the Lord was about to do through me, his unworthy servant."[30]

Mary Musselman Whitmer, mother of David Whitmer, was shown the plates by an angel at her farm where the Book of Mormon translation was taking place. She was told that she was given such a witness of the truth so that her faith might be strengthened. The angel turned over the unsealed plates one at a time and pointed out the engravings on them.[31]

Lucy Harris, wife of Martin Harris, saw an unidentified personage, in a dream, who showed her the golden plates. Because of this experience she was able to describe the Book of Mormon record in minute detail.[32]

Harrison G. Burgess relates the following story:

> In July, 1832, when I first heard the fullness of the gospel proclaimed by Elder Simeon Carter, I was convinced that the scriptures were true and that the Book of Mormon was divine revelation from heaven. I was baptized . . . On the third Sabbath in May, while speaking to a congregation, I declared that I knew that the Book of Mormon and the work of God were true. The next day while laboring in the field something seemed to whisper to me, 'Do you know the Book of Mormon

> is true?' My mind became perplexed and darkened, and I was so tormented in spirit that I left my work and retired into the woods. The misery and distress that I there experienced cannot be described. The tempter all the while seemed to say, 'Do you know the Book of Mormon is true?' I remained in this situation about two hours. Finally I resolved to know, by exercising faith similar to that which the brother of Jared possessed, whether I had proclaimed the truth or not, and commenced praying to the God of heaven for a testimony of these things. Suddenly a glorious personage clothed in white stood before me and exhibited to my view the plates from which the Book of Mormon was taken.[33]

Emma Smith, though not privileged to actually see the plates, did feel them as they lay wrapped in a linen cloth upon a table in her home. "The plates often lay on the table without any attempt at concealment, wrapped in a small linen tablecloth, which I had given [the Prophet] to fold them in," said Emma. "I once felt of the plates, as they lay on the table, tracing their outline and shape. They seemed to be pliable like thick paper, and would rustle with a metallic sound when the edges were moved by the thumb, as one does sometimes thumb the edges of a book."[34]

Heber C. Kimball, although he did not see the plates, stated that he was visited by the angel Moroni just prior to his death and was informed by that heavenly messenger that his earthly mission was complete.[35]

HISTORICAL PLAUSIBILITY

Since the Book of Mormon claims to be an historical narrative about peoples who migrated to the New World from the ancient Near East it is fair to ask whether the historical details associated with the book can be substantiated.

In this section of the book the reader will find that the basic historical aspects of the Book of Mormon story are well supported.

Arabian Map

The Book of Mormon's central account claims that, at the Lord's command, a small group of Israelites left Jerusalem around 600 B.C. and traveled "by the borders near the shore of the Red Sea" (1 Nephi 2:5). Continuing on in "nearly a south-southeast direction . . . in the borders near the Red Sea" (1 Nephi 16:13–14) this colony arrived at "the place which was called Nahom" (1 Nephi 16:34) where they buried a deceased member of their group. At that point the band of sojourners turned "nearly

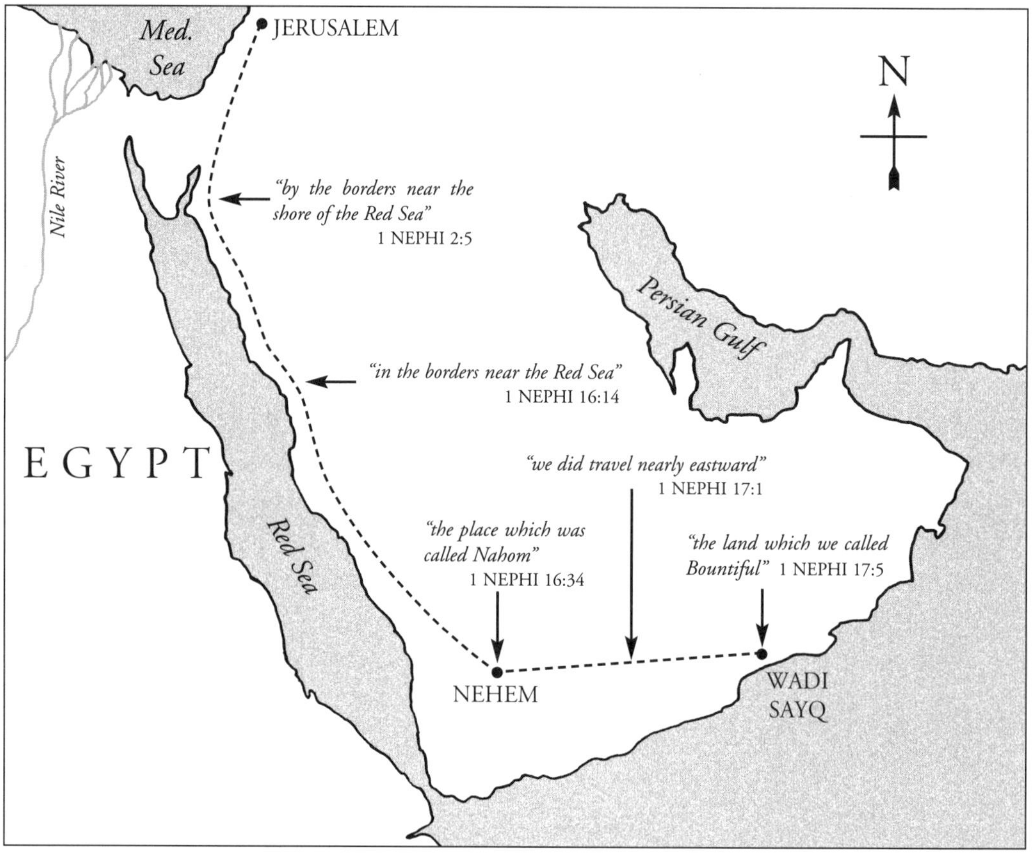

FIGURE 16. Possible route of Lehi's colony as they journeyed from Jerusalem to the eastern coast of the Arabian Peninsula.

eastward" (1 Nephi 17:1) and traveled until they arrived at an oasis by the sea which they named "Bountiful" (1 Nephi 17:5).

In general, this description follows the ancient trade routes of the Arabian peninsula. What is striking, however, is that there is a location in the southern part of the peninsula that has been known from ancient times as *nhm* and which is now known as Nehem. A route taken from there "nearly eastward" leads one to a small, but lush, oasis on Oman's Dhofar coast. This fertile oasis, called Khor Karfot, appears to meet the criteria of the Book of Mormon "Bountiful" to a remarkable degree. For instance:

1. Both Khor Karfot and Bountiful are nearly due east from Nehem/Nahom.
2. Both sites are/were located on the coast and accessible from the desert.
3. Both locations are/were fertile and vegetated.

4. Both sites are/were suitable for long-term occupation and for constructing a large boat.
5. Both locations have/had the type of timber necessary for building a sea-worthy vessel.
6. Both locations have/had a constant fresh water supply.
7. Both locations have/had a nearby mountain.
8. Both locations have/had dangerous cliffs on the seashore.
9. Both locations have/had iron ore nearby for making tools.
10. Both locations have/had flint available for starting fires.
11. Both locations are/were uninhabited.
12. Both locations have/had adequate winds and currents for sailing a sizable ship.

Noel B. Reynolds points out that the Book of Mormon account of the journey taken by Lehi's party is not only plausible in a historical sense but it also ran counter to prevailing beliefs about Arabia in the days of Joseph Smith.

> Critics of the Book of Mormon who believe that Joseph Smith or a contemporary author created the story of Lehi out of his own imagination have much to explain. How did Joseph Smith know that Lehi's party had to follow an inland route to reach southern Arabia? How did he know that the direction should shift from south by southeast to east at a place bearing the Semitic name *nhm?* How did he know that this was an appropriate place for the burial of an important person like Ishmael? How did he know that a group traveling due east from *nhm* would meet the sea at a uniquely fertile and hospitable spot that was suitable for building and launching a ship? How did he know that Oman had ample resources for ship building and sailing, and that there were mountains and cliffs on the sea shore itself?
>
> These important details run directly counter to all knowledge of Arabia in Joseph Smith's day and to most popular belief about Arabia even today. The simplest and most reasonable explanation is that Joseph Smith and his contemporaries did not know these things; they truthfully said that the account was written by Nephi, who had experienced these things firsthand, and was given to Joseph Smith by divine intervention.[36]

Transoceanic Voyage

Once Lehi's colony had built a ship after the pattern the Lord had revealed unto them, they set sail across the ocean toward the New World. The Book of Mormon also describes the undertaking of such long trips by the Jaredites and Mulekites. Were transoceanic voyages feasible during the times of Jared, Mulek, and Lehi? Critics of the Book of Mormon think not, insisting that the knowledge and the technology necessary for these trips was simply not available during this early period of human history.

Yet, modern man has demonstrated that such trips were plausible by constructing primitive watercraft and making successful open-ocean voyages of several thousand miles' duration. In addition, some scholars have amassed a large amount of "diffusionist" evidence that supports the premise that there was contact across the oceans in premodern times. This evidence is gleaned from ethnological, linguistic, and archeological data on both sides of the seas. Even though this is an area of ongoing debate among academics, it is clear that pre-Columbian transoceanic travel was at least possible.[37]

Mesoamerican Map

The Book of Mormon, which is an abridgment of several ancient records, clearly identifies the New World as the location where its main activities took place. But this record, as it now stands, does not specify exactly where in the New World those activities occurred. Unfortunately, there is also no official Church declaration, nor divine revelation, that pinpoints the precise location of Book of Mormon events.[38]

Despite the lack of certainty on this issue there are scores of theories about where Book of Mormon activities took place, some more imaginative than others.[39] Several LDS scholars have recognized that even though the Book of Mormon does not spell out the exact location of its activities there are enough statements, clues, and allusions scattered throughout its texts to enable any reader to reconstruct a tentative map. Based upon the physical characteristics of this internal map, and other relevant evidence, many of these researchers have theorized that the Book of Mormon story took place in the region of Mesoamerica.[40] Some of the evidence that supports this conclusion includes the fact that the book of Alma mentions oppressive heat at New Year's time (see Alma 51:33; 52:1). Furthermore, there is no mention of snow, ice, or cold in Book of Mormon texts that describe the climate. These facts tend to point away from North America as a location for the events that are described in the Book of Mormon narrative.

Strong support for the Mesoamerican geographical model comes from the time of Joseph Smith. While the Prophet was serving as the managing editor of the *Times and Seasons* newspaper in Nauvoo, Illinois, an editorial was printed which stated that the Nephites "lived about the narrow neck of land, which now embraces Central America." A few pages after this statement another editorial claimed that Lehi's colony

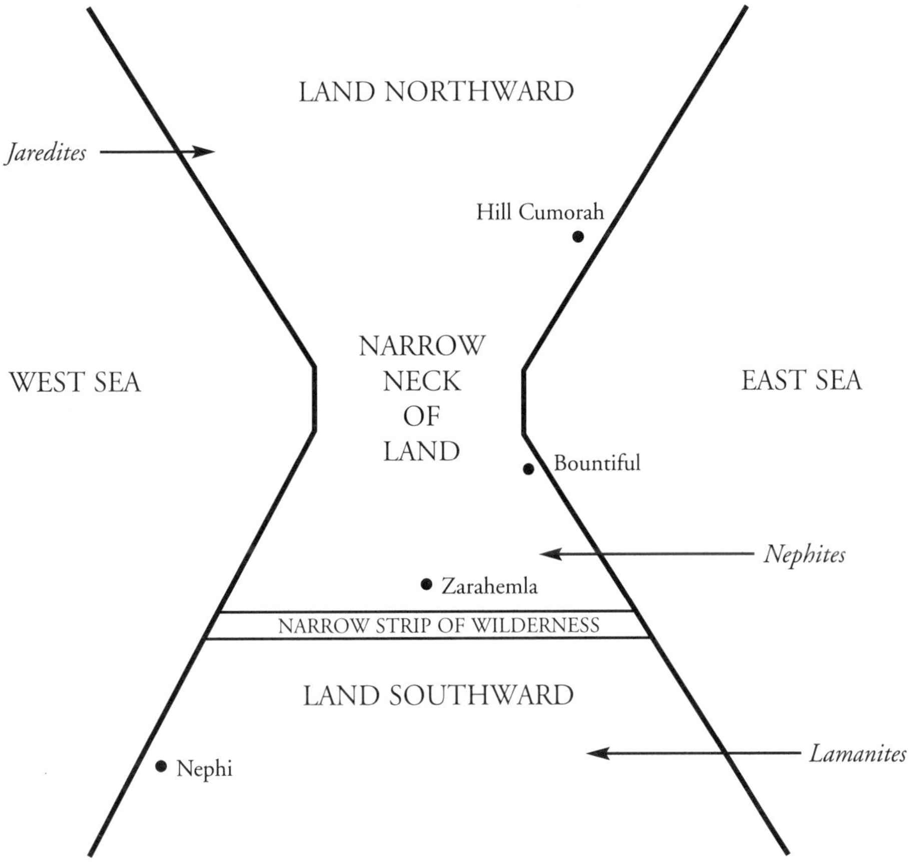

FIGURE 17. This model of Book of Mormon geography is based solely upon unambiguous material that is found within the text itself.

"landed a little south of the Isthmus of Darien," meaning the vicinity of Panama in Mesoamerica.[41] Another editorial, published the following month in the *Times and Seasons*, declared that "Central America, or Guatemala, [which] is situated north of the Isthmus of Darien and once embraced several hundred miles of territory from north to south" was where "the city of Zarahemla . . . stood."[42] Even though these statements do not qualify as revelations from the Lord, they do indicate that at least some members of the LDS faith, who lived in Nauvoo in 1842, believed in a Mesoamerican geographical model for Book of Mormon events.

Some may argue that a Mesoamerican model for the Book of Mormon makes no sense since Moroni hid up the golden record of the Nephites in the hill called "Cumorah" in New York state. This sounds logical until one remembers that after the final battle at the hill Cumorah, when the Nephites were almost completely wiped out, Moroni wandered the earth for 35 years. This would have been plenty of time for Moroni to deliver the golden plates to what would, in the future, become the state of New York. Once there, Moroni could have named the North American hill where he hid the plates "Cumorah," in commemoration of the Mesoamerican hill where the other records of the Nephite nation were hidden (see Mormon 6:6; Ether 15:11).

The Stone Box and Golden Plates

When the angel Moroni first visited Joseph Smith on 21 September 1823, he showed young Joseph a clear and distinct vision of the place where the Book of Mormon plates had been hidden.[43] The Prophet reported that "convenient to the village of Manchester, Ontario county, New York, stands a hill of considerable size, and the most elevated of any in the neighborhood. On the west side of the hill, not far from the top, under a stone of considerable size, lay the plates, deposited in a stone box. . . . The box in which [the plates] lay was formed by laying stones together in some kind of cement."[44] The stone box was not conjured up by an overactive imagination. Joseph Smith took David Whitmer and Oliver Cowdery to see this relic.[45] Persons who were not affiliated with the LDS Church also went to the hill and saw the receptacle where the plates had been placed.[46] The stone box, though a minor detail, qualifies as a physical evidence of the reality of the Prophet's story.[47]

The Prophet provided a fairly detailed description of the golden plates of the Book of Mormon.

> These records were engraven on plates which had the appearance of gold, each plate was six inches wide and eight inches long, and not quite so thick as common tin. They were filled with engravings, in Egyptian characters, and bound together in a volume as the leaves of a book, with three rings running through the whole. The volume was something near six inches in thickness, a part of which was sealed. The characters on the unsealed part were small, and beautifully engraved. The whole book exhibited many marks of antiquity in its construction, and much skill in the art of engraving. With the records was found a curious instrument, which the ancients called "Urim and Thummim," which consisted of two transparent stones set in the rim of a bow fastened to a breastplate. Through the medium of the Urim and Thummim I translated the record by the gift and power of God.[48]

Are the elements of Joseph Smith's description historically plausible? Yes, they certainly are. In Joseph Smith's day the idea of ancient records being written upon golden plates sounded quite absurd. Yet, since the time of the Prophet there have been numerous discoveries of ancient documents engraved on metallic plates. In the 1920s and 1930s, several discoveries were made of gold plates that were deposited in the stone foundation boxes of ancient Persian palaces. These tablets bore inscriptions that related the majesty of Persia's kings such as Darius I (515 B.C.), Ariaramnes, Arsames, Artaxerxes II, and Darius II.[49] Did the Hebrews, and other Semites, write upon metallic plates during Book of Mormon times? Yes, they certainly did. Some of the more pertinent examples are the Copper Scroll (found in the Dead Sea caves) and also two silver scrolls that were discovered in Jerusalem in 1980 during an archeological excavation. These silver scrolls, dating close to the time of Lehi, are inscribed with religious texts, thus paralleling the content of the metallic plates of the Book of Mormon.[50]

Critics of Joseph Smith assume that he made a fatal error when he said that the Book of Mormon plates—measuring six inches wide, eight inches long, and six inches thick—were made of gold. If a set of plates of that size were made of 24 karat gold they would have weighed between 100 and 200 pounds. Yet, historical records report that Joseph Smith ran through the woods with them to avoid a mob, Emma Smith moved them around while cleaning house, and the Eight Witnesses all "hefted" them. Joseph Smith's brother William, Martin Harris, and Willard Chase estimated that the set of plates only weighed 40 to 60 pounds. These figures make good sense if it is granted that the plates, which the Prophet only said had the "appearance of gold," were made from the Mesoamerican gold/copper alloy known as "tumbaga." Interestingly, William Smith, the Prophet's brother, said the Book of Mormon plates were "a mixture of gold and copper." If the Book of Mormon plates were made of the tumbaga alloy, then the whole set would have only weighed about 53 pounds.[51]

The Anthon Transcript

The Book of Mormon writers stated that they spoke Hebrew but wrote their records in "altered" Egyptian characters that they called "reformed Egyptian." This course of action was taken so they could conserve space on the plates they were writing upon (see Mormon 9:32, 34). This information raises several questions.

Is there any historical evidence that the ancient Egyptians altered or 'reformed' their writing system? Yes, there certainly is. The Egyptian hieroglyphic system, which was used essentially as a script for monuments, was modified for use in formal documents that were written upon papyrus. This new, or reformed, system of writing was

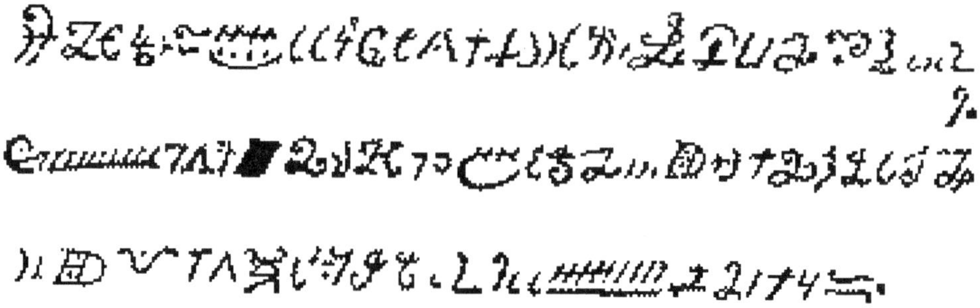

FIGURE 18. Joseph Smith copied several lines of "reformed Egyptian" characters from the Book of Mormon plates and then sent them with Martin Harris to Professor Charles Anthon in New York City. Joseph Smith said that Harris' meeting with Anthon fulfilled the "sealed book" prophecy that is found in Isaiah 29:11–12. The "Anthon Transcript" characters can be matched with the symbols of Egyptian and Mesoamerican writing systems.

known as "hieratic." A further modification took place in the creation of the "demotic" Egyptian script, which was cursive in nature.[52] Both of these scripts were in use during the time when Lehi's colony left Jerusalem and both could rightly be referred to as "reformed Egyptian" scripts.

Is there any historical evidence of ancient Hebrew or other Semitic texts being written in Egyptian script? Yes, there is. *Papyrus Amherst 63* is one example. This second century B.C. document, discovered in Thebes, Egypt, is written in the Egyptian demotic script but the underlying language is Aramaic. This document includes a heathenized rendition of Psalms 20:2–6. Of further relevance is the fact that evidence has now been recovered at archeological sites in Israel that indicates that some of the Israelites of Lehi's time were being schooled both in Hebrew and Egyptian hieratic scripts.[53] Thus, the claim that Lehi—an Israelite from Jerusalem—knew the Egyptian language is entirely plausible (see 1 Nephi 1:2; Mosiah 1:3–4).

Did Joseph Smith ever indicate what the characters on the Book of Mormon plates looked like? Yes, he did. In fact, he made a copy of some of these characters. The paper that the characters were transcribed onto became known as the Anthon Transcript because in 1828 the Prophet gave the paper, and a partial translation of the characters on it, to Martin Harris who exhibited them to Professor Charles Anthon of New York City. After certifying, in writing, to Harris that the characters were genuine, and the translation of them correct, Anthon asked to have the Book of Mormon plates brought to him so he could translate them himself. Harris relates: "I informed him that a part of the plates were sealed, and that I was forbidden to bring them. He replied, 'I cannot read a sealed book'" (JS–H 1:62–65). Joseph Smith reports that this encounter between Anthon and Harris, and his own subsequent translation of the plates, were a direct fulfillment of the prophecy that is found in Isaiah 29:11–12.[54]

Do the Anthon Transcript characters correspond to any Egyptian scripts? Yes, they do. It has been demonstrated by one researcher that each of the Anthon Transcript characters can be matched to various Egyptian symbols.[55] It is also of great interest that some of the characters on the Anthon Transcript match characters that have been found on two Mesoamerican cylinder seals[56] and also the script of Old Southern Arabia.[57]

LITERARY EVIDENCES

There are many literary devices in the Book of Mormon text that provide evidence that it is indeed a multi-authored volume that was composed by those who had an intimate knowledge of the Hebrew language. In perusing the section that follows, it should be kept in mind that Joseph Smith did not study biblical languages until many years after the Book of Mormon had been published.

Wordprints

Critics of the LDS faith insist that either Joseph Smith was the sole creator of the Book of Mormon text or he must have collaborated in the effort with some of his contemporaries such as Oliver Cowdery. Another argument is that the Prophet plagiarized an existing text, such as Solomon Spaulding's *Manuscript Found*, and then simply claimed to have translated an ancient book.

Such claims were difficult to dispute until the age of the computer dawned. Every author writes in their own distinctive style and that style creates a unique type of "wordprint." If a sufficient block of writing is available from a known author, then a distinctive wordprint can be established for that person. Since computers can distinguish between the wordprints of individual writers, they can help to determine who likely wrote an anonymous work of literature.

In 1980 a group of statisticians at Brigham Young University analyzed the Book of Mormon text using an early wordprinting technique. The study carried out by this group concluded that, from a statistical standpoint, it could be demonstrated that Joseph Smith and his contemporaries were not the authors of the Book of Mormon.

In addition, they concluded that the Book of Mormon showed clear signs of multiple authorship, just as the book itself claimed.[58]

It was immediately noted by some scholars that the methodology used in this wordprint study had its weaknesses. And so, a decade later, John L. Hilton published the findings of a second research group that was composed of both LDS and non-LDS scientists from Berkeley, California. Using a more refined set of stylometric measurements, this latter group concluded: "By using a new wordprint measuring methodology which has been verified, we show that it is statistically indefensible to propose Joseph Smith or Oliver Cowdery or Solomon Spaulding as the author of the 30,000 words from the Book of Mormon manuscript texts attributed to Nephi and Alma. Additionally these two Book of Mormon writers have wordprints unique to themselves and measure statistically independent from each other in the same fashion that other uncontested authors do. Therefore, the Book of Mormon measures multi-authored, with authorship consistent to its own internal claims. These results are obtained even though the writings of Nephi and Alma were 'translated' by Joseph Smith."[59]

Ancient Hebrew Structures

There are numerous ancient literary patterns that can be found in the Book of Mormon. Following is a small sample of these ancient structures and their Book of Mormon counterparts.[60] Keep in mind that these sometimes complex patterns were dictated to a scribe and were not even noticed until long after the Book of Mormon had been published.

Hebrew Idioms

"And Moses fled *from before* it" (Exodus 4:3).
"And they fled *from before* my presence" (1 Nephi 4:28).

"To fulfill the word of the Lord *by the mouth of* Jeremiah" (2 Chronicles 36:21).
". . . spoken *by the mouth of* all the holy prophets" (1 Nephi 3:20).

". . . but he *stiffened his neck*" (2 Chronicles 36:13).
". . . they at Jerusalem will *stiffen their necks* against him" (2 Nephi 10:5).

". . . and will *multiply thee exceedingly*" (Genesis 17:2).
"And we *multiplied exceedingly*, and spread upon the face of the land" (Jarom 1:8).

"... she *vowed a vow*" (1 Samuel 1:11).
"... I have *dreamed a dream*" (1 Nephi 8:2).

"... *after that* the city was smitten" (Ezekiel 40:1).
"... *after that* I am gone to the Father" (3 Nephi 28:1).

"... bear a son, and shall *call his name* Immanuel" (Isaiah 7:14).
"... we did *call the name* of the place Shazer" (1 Nephi 16:13).

CLIMACTIC PARALLELISM

"Behold, he created
Adam, and by
Adam came
the fall of man. And because of
the fall of man came
Jesus Christ, even the Father and the Son; and because of
Jesus Christ came the
redemption of man. And because of the
redemption of man, which came by Jesus Christ, they are
brought back into the presence of the Lord" (Mormon 9:12–13).

SYNONYMOUS PARALLELISM

"*Wo unto him* that spurneth at *the doings of the Lord*; yea,
wo unto him that shall deny the *Christ and his works*" (3 Nephi 29:5).

"... *pray* unto him continually *by day*, and
give thanks unto his holy name *by night*" (2 Nephi 9:52).

"... *they* were brought near even to be *carried out of this time to meet their God*;
yea, *their* grey hairs were about to be *brought down to lie low in the dust*;
yea, even *they* were near to be *cast with sorrow into a watery grave*" (1 Nephi 18:18).

ALTERNATING LINE PARALLELISM

A for the *preacher*
B was no *better than the hearer,*
A neither was the *teacher*
B any *better than the learner* (Alma 1:26).

Nevertheless, I have received a commandment of the Lord
A that I should make *these plates,* for the special purpose that there should be an account engraven
B of the *ministry* of my people.
C Upon the *other plates* should be engraven
D an account of the *reign of the kings,*
E and the *wars*
F and *contentions of my people;*
A wherefore *these plates*
B are for the more part of the *ministry;*
C and the *other plates*
D are for the more part of the *reign of the kings*
E and the *wars*
F and *contentions of my people* (1 Nephi 9:3–4).

REPEATED ALTERNATE PARALLELISM

A The God of Jacob, yieldeth himself,
B *according to the words of* the angel,
A as a man, into the hands of wicked men, to be *lifted up,*
B *according to the words of* Zenock,
A and to be *crucified,*
B *according to the words of* Neum,
A and to be buried in a sepulcher,
B *according to the words of* Zenos (1 Nephi 19:10).

Word Pairs

"Then thou scarest me with *dreams*, and terrifiest me through *visions*" (Job 7:14).
"Behold I have dreamed a *dream*; or, in other words, I have seen a *vision*" (1 Nephi 8:2).

"A *thousand* shall fall at thy side, and *ten thousand* at thy right hand" (Psalms 91:7).
". . . ye are surrounded with *thousands* of those, yea, and *tens of thousands*" (Alma 60:22).

"When *pride* cometh, then cometh shame: but with the lowly is *wisdom*" (Proverbs 11:2).
"See that ye are not lifted up unto *pride*; yea, see that ye do not boast in your own *wisdom*" (Alma 38:11).

"How goodly are thy tents, O *Jacob*, and thy tabernacles, O *Israel*" (Numbers 24:5).
"And they shall assist my people, the remnant of *Jacob*, and also as many of the house of *Israel* as shall come" (3 Nephi 21:23).

". . . but the Lord would not *hearken* to your voice, nor *give ear* unto you" (Deuteronomy 1:45).
"Wherefore, *hearken*, O my people, which are of the house of Israel, and *give ear* unto my words" (2 Nephi 25:4).

Chiasmus

The Book of Mormon contains dozens of examples of an ancient literary form known as chiasmus. In a chiastic passage certain words or concepts are arranged in a series and then repeated in reverse order. This style of writing is used to place emphasis on specific ideas, particularly the ones found at the turning point of the chiasm. The following example of chiasmus is found in Isaiah 40:28–31.

A the everlasting God, the Lord, the Creator of the ends of the earth, *fainteth* not,
  B neither is *weary*, there is no searching of his understanding.
    C He giveth *power* to the faint;
      D and to them that have no might he increaseth *strength*.
        E Even the *youths* shall faint and be weary,

E and the *young* men shall utterly fall:
D But they that wait upon the Lord shall renew their *strength*;
C they shall *mount up with wings* as eagles;
B they shall run, and not be *weary*;
A and they shall walk, and not *faint*.

The following example of the chiastic literary device can be found in the fifth chapter of the book of Mosiah, verses 10–12.

A whosoever shall not take upon him the *name* of Christ
B must be *called* by some other name;
C therefore, he findeth himself on the *left hand of God*.
D ye should *remember* also
E that never should be *blotted out*
F except it be through *transgression*;
F therefore, take heed that ye do not *transgress*,
E that the name be not *blotted out* of your hearts.
D ye should *remember* to retain the name
C that ye are not found on the *left hand of God*
B know the voice by which ye shall be *called*
A the *name* by which he shall call you.

Non-biblical Personal Names

There are several personal names found in the Book of Mormon that seemed anomalous in Joseph Smith's day but which have since been justified.

Alma. In Joseph Smith's day "Alma" was commonly believed to be a feminine name of Latin origin. But this name is used extensively in Book of Mormon texts to refer to a Hebrew man (see Mosiah 17:1–2). Critics have picked up on this seeming blunder by the Prophet and claimed that such an inconsistency is evidence of a fraudulent text. But in the twentieth century, a cache of Hebrew letters dating to about A.D. 130 was discovered in the Bar Kokhba caves in Israel. One of these documents contains the name *'lm'* in the title Alma ben Yehudah (Alma, son of Yehudah).[61] Since the Bar Kokhba discovery, other texts have also come to light that confirm Alma as an ancient male name. On the Ebla cuneiform tablets that were discovered in 1975 in northwestern Syria, one finds the Semitic personal name *al*$_6$*-ma* applied to a merchant from Mari, most likely a male.[62]

Sariah. This name is given to the Israelite wife of the prophet Lehi, who lived about 600 B.C. (see 1 Nephi 2:5). Because this female personal name is not found in any biblical text it might be seen as an invention by Joseph Smith. However, the female Hebrew name *śry[h br]t hwš*^{c} (Sariah daughter of Hoshea) has been found in fifth century B.C. Aramaic documents from Elephantine, Egypt. The Elephantine Papyri were discovered between 1900–1903 while Joseph Smith dictated the name Sariah to a scribe sometime in 1828 or 1829.[63]

Mosiah. This is the name of a king in the Book of Mormon (see Omni 1:12). This Hebrew word [*môšîa*^{c}] underlies the texts of Deuteronomy 22:27, 28:29, Judges 12:3, Psalms 18:41, and Isaiah 5:29; but since it was not transliterated in any of these passages, Joseph Smith could not have been aware that it was an authentic Hebrew word. Non-LDS scholars believe that this word designated an office or position along the lines of a champion, advocate, liberator, redeemer, or savior. The deliverance achieved by the *môšîa*^{c} was usually nonviolent, such as by negotiation. The *môšîa*^{c} provided an escape from injustice. This is precisely the role played by king Mosiah I in the Book of Mormon. He was divinely appointed to help the Lord's people escape from a hostile set of circumstances (see Omni 1:12–14).[64]

Shule. The name Shule is listed as the name of one of the Jaredite kings from the tower of Babel period (see Ether 1:30–31). It is interesting to note that *Shulgi* is attested as the name of a king who reigned in Sumeria from 2094–2045 B.C.[65]

Zarahemla. Even though this is the name of a Nephite capital city it was originally the personal name of a descendant of Mulek, the only son of king Zedekiah to escape from Jerusalem when it was besieged by king Nebuchadnezzar of Babylon (see Omni 1:12–15; Mosiah 25:2; Helaman 6:10; 8:21). It seems probable that this name is the combination of two Hebrew words–*zera*^{c} (seed/child) and *hemlāh* (compassion).[66]

Aha, Josh, and ***Jarom.*** The name "Aha" (Alma 16:5) is attested as *'h'* on bronze arrowheads from Israel, Lebanon, and Jordan dating from the eleventh to eighth centuries B.C. Israeli scholars believe this old Canaanite/Hebrew name was pronounced as *'aha'*. The name "Josh" (Mormon 6:14) is attested as *y'š* on seal impressions and pottery fragments dating from around 600 B.C. "Jarom" (Jarom 1:1) is also an attested Israelite name. It reads as *yrm* on a Hebrew pottery fragment which dates to between the seventh to sixth centuries B.C. In the cases of both "Josh" and "Jarom" the Hebrew "y" is pronounced as a "j."[67]

Abish and ***Luram.*** There are ancient Hebrew equivalents for these Book of Mormon names. Abish (see Alma 19:16) is paralleled by a name on a seal that dates to before 587 B.C.–*'bš'*. The name Luram (see Moroni 9:2) is attested in the second element of a 720 B.C. seal found at Hamath, Syria—*'dn-Lrm.*[68]

Non-biblical Place Names

Several non-biblical place names in the Book of Mormon can be verified as having ancient Near Eastern backgrounds.

Nahom. When Ishmael died he "was buried in the place which was called Nahom" (1 Nephi 16:34), a place that was already in existence when Lehi's colony arrived there. Dr. Hugh W. Nibley notes that "the Arabic root *nhm* has the basic meaning of 'to sigh or moan' . . . At this place, we are told, 'the daughters of Ishmael did mourn exceedingly,' and [we] are reminded that among the desert Arabs, mourning rites are a monopoly of the women."[69]

Jershon. Jershon is a land in the Book of Mormon narrative that is associated several times with the concept of "inheritance." In Alma 27:22 we read: "and this land Jershon is the land which we will give unto our brethren for an inheritance." In Alma 27:24 it is said that "they may inherit the land Jershon." And in Alma 35:14 we read: "they have lands for their inheritance in the land of Jershon." The word Jershon may very well come from the Hebrew root *yrš* which means "to inherit." In the transliteration process, the Hebrew "y" is replaced by the English "j" and the *š* is sounded as *sh*–the word root would thus read *jrsh*. The suffix *-ôn* was used anciently to denote Hebrew place names. We find such examples in Hebron (Joshua 10:36), Gibeon (Joshua 9:3), and Hammon (Joshua 19:28). The word *jrsh-ôn* could thus be translated quite literally as "land of inheritance."[70]

Cumorah. A plausible explanation for this word is that it consists of the Hebrew verb *qûm* (arise) and the Hebrew noun *'ôrāh* (light).[71] This would be an appropriate name for a hill from which arose the light of the gospel of Jesus Christ (D&C 45:9, 28).

Non-biblical Objects

There are at least three non-biblical objects in Book of Mormon texts whose names have parallels in the ancient world.

Deseret. The Jaredites "did also carry with them deseret, which, by interpretation, is a honey bee" (Ether 2:3). The red crown worn by the pharaohs of ancient Egypt had a large bee antenna protruding from its front surface. The name of this unique crown was *deshret.*[72]

Liahona. The liahona was a divinely delivered brass ball of curious workmanship that acted as a compass to guide Lehi's colony through the wilderness (see 1 Nephi 16:10). Dr. Hugh W. Nibley prefers to read this word as "*le-yah-hōn-na,* literally, 'to God is our commanding,' i.e., 'God is our guide,' since *hōn hwn,* is the common late Egyptian word for 'lead, guide, take command.'"[73] Nibley also notes that Professor Jonathan Shunary, "upon first opening the Book of Mormon, identified the word Liahona with a Jewish *gematria* designating the leader of a swarm of migrating bees in the desert."[74]

Sheum. This is a type of grain mentioned in Mosiah 9:9. This happens to be the Old Assyrian name for wheat [*she'um*] and the Akkadian/Babylonian name for barley.[75]

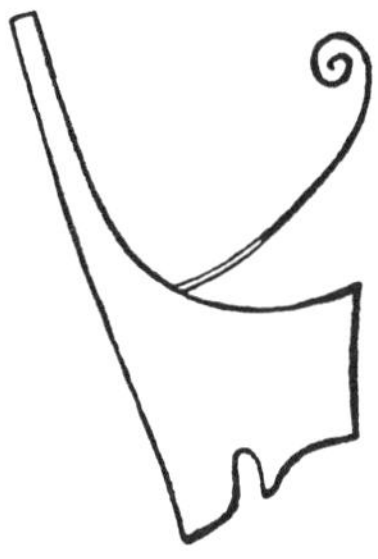

FIGURE 19. The Jaredites referred to the honey bee by the peculiar name *deseret* (see Ether 2:3). It is of great interest to Latter-day Saints that the name of the Egyptian Pharaoh's red crown—which sported a bee antenna on its front face—was *deshret.*

ARCHEOLOGICAL EVIDENCES

David Whitmer said "that when [the Three Witnesses] were first commanded to testify of [the Book of Mormon], they demurred and told the Lord the people would not believe them for the book, concerning which they were to bear record, told of a people who were educated and refined, dwelling in large cities; whereas all that was then known of the early inhabitants of this country was the . . . [unsophisticated Indians] that were roaming over the land. [But, said Whitmer,] 'The Lord told us, in reply, that he would make it known to the people that the early inhabitants of this land had been just such a people as they were described in the book, and he would lead them to discover the ruins of the great cities, and they shall have abundant *evidence* of the truth of that which is written in the book. All of which . . . has been fulfilled to the very letter.'"[76] Perhaps Whitmer is here referring to the new archeological discoveries that were made known to the public in the 1840s. In 1841, a book was published by John L. Stephens entitled *Incidents of Travel in Central America, Chiapas and Yucatan.* In the book were numerous pictures of the newly discovered Mayan cities of Mesoamerica. In 1842 the *Times and Seasons* newspaper in Nauvoo, Illinois, quoted extensively from Stephens' book; and then the editor of the paper stated that

"Mr. Stephens' great developments of antiquities are made bare to the eyes of all the people by reading the history of the Nephites in the Book of Mormon." He also said: "It will not be a bad plan to compare Mr. Stephens' ruined cities with those in the Book of Mormon."[77]

The Book of Mormon speaks of several animals and objects that, in Joseph Smith's day, were not attested in archeological records—and thus scoffed at by the critics of the LDS Church. But science is beginning to make discoveries that lend credence to the Book of Mormon account.

Elephants

Elephants are only mentioned in the Book of Mormon by the Jaredites who immigrated to the New World around 2,500 B.C. (see Ether 9:19). Paleontologists acknowledge that several different types of elephantine creatures once roamed the New World, but the majority of them believe that they became extinct about 25,000 years ago.

There are three different types of evidence to support the claim that elephants lived alongside man in the pre-Columbian New World. First, there are the traditions of the native Americans. Widely separated native American tribes had similar traditions of seeing and hunting a huge animal that had a big head, large ears, and "teeth" long enough to pierce seven men. This creature fed upon the leaves of trees, slept by leaning against upright objects, and left behind large round tracks as it walked. The most interesting detail in the description of this beast is that it had "a fifth leg rooted between its shoulders;" a "sort of arm which comes out of [its] shoulder;" a "long nose with which [it] hit people." This appendage was referred to among some of the Indian tribes as "a lip as long as seven paces." This creature, said the Indians, could use its "long nose" to uproot trees.[78]

The second type of evidence consists of archeological remains. Archeological digs that pair New World elephants and human artifacts are not uncommon. By 1950 Macgowan had listed no less than 27 instances.[79] In this category we have the complete mastodon skeleton found in 1928 in Quito, Ecuador that had lesions on its skull that could only have been inflicted by men who were attacking or butchering it. This skeleton had also been burned in several areas by fire. Man-made tools were found close to this mastodon's body and about 150 pieces of pottery surrounded it. The finer pieces of pottery were like "the fine Maya pots of the oldest Cuenca culture" and one had a design painted upon it "in Mayoid style."[80] The pottery pieces dated to between

150 and 350 years *after* the time of Jesus Christ.[81] Mammoth bones uncovered in 1887 in Attica, New York, were also found in association with a few fragments of charcoal. These artifacts were discovered twelve inches higher than many other pieces of charcoal and a fragment of pottery. "The associated human evidence found with or beneath the Attica mastodon bones," says Charles Schuchert, "is a positive hint that should open our minds to the possibility that man was associated in America with *Mammut Americanum*."[82]

We cannot fail to mention that a Carbon-14 date for mastodon remains in Richmond, Indiana, has been set at 3344 B.C., ± 400 years.[83] This is very close, geologically speaking, to the time frame of the Jaredite elephants. Finally, we will note that it was the considered opinion of Professor William B. Scott, "the doyen of American paleontologists," that mammoths may have still been living in the interior of the New World when the first Spanish explorers arrived.[84]

The third type of evidence for the contemporary existence of men and elephants in the pre-Columbian New World consists of artistic representations. Some "sculptures and paintings of Mayan and Aztec origin" have long thin noses that curve either

FIGURE 20. Some scholars are of the opinion that several of the ancient Mayan *Chac* sculptures, such as the one depicted here, resemble trumpeting elephants. Theodore A. Willard says of this particular artwork: "The step typifies the nose; the circles at the side thereof, the eyes; the ornamental squares, the ears; and the carved scrolls below represent the teeth."

up or down and "they appear to portray elephants. In most cases," notes John Thompson, "these supposed elephants' trunks are the snouts of the long-nosed rain gods [or Chacs], and are clearly of ophidian origin, but in one or two cases the trunks are clearly very elephantine. The explanation is probably to be found . . . in a half-forgotten tradition of the mastodon. Recent discoveries have now shown that the mastodon lingered on for many centuries as a contemporary of man in the New World, and there is some evidence that in Ecuador one was slain by man not more than 3000 years ago, as the polychrome pottery associated with it attests."[85] Some people have interpreted the long noses on the Mayan Chac masks to be highly stylized representations of tapir snouts but scholars who have studied these masks in detail reject this interpretation.[86]

Horses

In 1 Nephi 18:25, we read that when Lehi's colony arrived in the New World they "did find upon the land of promise . . . the horse." Thus, the Book of Mormon reports an indigenous population of horses in the New World around 600 B.C.

The conventional wisdom among archeologists and paleontologists is that the horse became extinct in the New World around the end of the glacial period (25,000 years ago) and was not reintroduced until after A.D. 1492 by the Spaniards. Yet, there are some scientists who are willing to admit that "there is no theoretical reason why a herd of . . . horses . . . could not have survived in some small refuge until . . . even 4,000 years ago" or 2,000 B.C.[87] Others are willing to grant dates of survival as recent as 3,000 B.C.[88] and 6,000 B.C.[89]

Some distinguished paleontologists, however, are of the opinion that "the horse never became extinct in America."[90] Dr. Edgar Howard, for example, was one of those scientists inclined to believe that the horse never entirely died out in the New World.[91] If this were indeed the case then it would help to explain why "there is a body of evidence . . . from the mainland of Central America . . . tending to show

FIGURE 21. This Peruvian representation of the *Strombus Galeatus* monster, from the Mochica Period (ca. A.D. 400–1000), hints that the horse was known to some of the Pre-Columbian natives of the New World.

that the horse may have been known to man in the Americas before the coming of the Spaniards."[92] Pictographic evidence, such as the illustration that accompanies this section, demonstrates convincingly that at least some of the natives of the pre-Columbian New World were familiar with the horse.

Wheels

The Book of Mormon mentions the combination of horses and chariots (see Alma 18:9–10, 12; 20:6; 3 Nephi 3:22), thus implying that the wheel was known in the New World in pre-Columbian times.

FIGURE 22. This Pre-Columbian wheeled "cart" from Popocatepetl, Mexico, indicates that some of the inhabitants of the New World were aware of the wheel before the arrival of the Spaniards.

Up until the 1940s, it was common for scholars to claim that the wheel was unknown among the pre-Columbian natives of the New World. But as reputable archeologists began to find "wheeled toys" in their excavations it became clear that the concept of the wheel was known to at least some of the pre-Columbian Indians.[93] Some of the wheeled objects that have been found are miniature models of carts. One of these objects is obviously a representation of a vehicle because it has a man sitting on top of it.[94] Thus, the Book of Mormon's implication that there were wheeled "chariots" in the pre-Columbian New World is entirely plausible.

Barley

Domesticated barley is mentioned in Book of Mormon passages such as Mosiah 7:22 and Alma 11:7. Up until December of 1983, there was no evidence for pre-Columbian domesticated barley in the Americas. But then archeologists uncovered what appears to be cultivated pre-Columbian barley at a Hohokam site in Phoenix, Arizona. The Hohokam culture extended from about 300 B.C. to about A.D. 1450. The barley samples from the Phoenix site have been generally dated to around A.D. 900. Some LDS scholars wonder if, perhaps, the Phoenix barley might be somehow related to Nephite barley since the Book of Mormon mentions that Hagoth took his departure from the narrow neck of land and sailed northward (see Alma 63:6–10).[95]

Cement

Around 46 B.C. the Book of Mormon records that some Nephites "became exceedingly expert in the working of cement." They built houses and other buildings out of a combination of wood and cement (Helaman 3:7–11).

President Heber J. Grant once related a conversation that he had with a well-educated man who could not accept the divine authenticity of the Book of Mormon because it spoke of some of the ancient Americans using cement for building purposes.

> I have often said, and desire to repeat here, that when I was a young unmarried man, another young man who had received a doctor's degree ridiculed me for believing in the Book of Mormon. He said he could point out two lies in that book. One was that the people had built their homes out of cement and that they were very skillful in the use of cement. He said there had never been found, and never would be found, a house built of cement by the ancient inhabitants of this country, because the people in that early age knew nothing about cement. He said that should be enough to make one disbelieve the book. I said: "That does not affect my faith one particle. I read the Book of Mormon prayerfully and supplicated God for a testimony in my heart and soul of the divinity of it, and I have accepted it and believe it with all my heart." I also said to him, "If my children do not find cement houses, I expect that my grandchildren will."[96]

And, indeed, evidence of pre-Columbian cement has now been discovered at Teotihuacan, El Tajin, Chichen Itza, Tula, Copan, Palenque, Tikal, Uxmal, and Cerro de Texcotzingo. This cement, which appears suddenly in the archeological record around the time specified by the Book of Mormon, has a remarkably high structural quality and was even used to form the large roofs of buildings.

Some LDS scholars have deduced (based upon Helaman 3:7–11) that, since cement has not been discovered outside of the southwest areas of North America, it is reasonable to assume that the Book of Mormon lands of Zarahemla and Desolation are not far south of sites where the cement has been found (i.e., the Valley of Mexico and the Maya regions of southern Mexico).[97]

Bearded Figures

When the Spanish arrived in the New World they noticed that, for the most part, the males of the indigenous populations did not grow beards. The Spaniards referred to native American men as *imberbes* (beardless).

The Book of Mormon claims that three Semitic groups from the ancient Near East (Jaredites, Mulekites, Nephites/Lamanites) migrated to New World locations. Thus, bearded populations would have been injected into beardless populations.

There is abundant evidence that bearded men inhabited the regions of Mesoamerica in pre-Columbian times. In A.D. 1559 Vincente Patatino de Curzola recorded an intriguing tradition from the Yucatan peninsula which claimed that numerous ruins in that area had been built by a group of bearded strangers. These foreigners, according to the tradition, were eventually exterminated by the Mayans in military confrontations.

Many pre-Columbian artifacts have been discovered throughout the Mesoamerican region that depict heavily bearded individuals. Some of the people who are pictured on these artifacts also have other Semitic facial traits.[98] Alexander von Wuthenau, who studied pre-Columbian terracotta figurines extensively, discovered that the "earliest figures" depicted included "all kinds of white people, especially Semitic types with and without beards . . . What is considered to be genuine Indian only developed, so far as I am able to judge on the strength of these terracotta representations, in early and middle Classic times," about A.D. 300.[99] This conclusion is most interesting when one remembers that according to the Book of Mormon, the Nephite civilization collapsed through military defeat about A.D. 385.

FIGURE 23. The native inhabitants of the Pre-Columbian New World did not grow beards. Yet, the Mesoamerican god Kukulcan (a.k.a. Quetzalcoatl)—who is described as a white man—is depicted on a temple pillar in Chichen-Itza with a long beard. This Semitic attribute is interesting because after His resurrection, Jesus Christ told His Old World disciples that He had "other sheep" He must visit (John 10:16). He informed the Nephites in the New World that they were those "other sheep" (3 Nephi 15:21).

ANCIENT PATTERNS

Israelite Festivals

The Book of Mormon informs us that the Nephites not only knew the details of the Law of Moses, which were recorded on the Brass Plates (see 1 Nephi 4:16), but they were also careful to keep the commandments of that Law (see 2 Nephi 5:10; 25:24; Jarom 1:5; Alma 30:3). Under the Law of Moses, the children of Israel were required to celebrate certain festivals throughout the course of the year. These festivals included Passover, Pentecost, and the Feast of Tabernacles. There are passages within the Book of Mormon that imply that these festivals were also kept by the Nephites.

Passover.[100] The festival of Passover commemorates the season when God delivered the children of Israel from the bondage of Egypt. As part of the Passover celebration Israelite fathers were to gather their sons together and provide them with certain types of instruction (see Exodus 10:2). Alma, in like manner, also gathered his sons to instruct them (see Alma 35:16). Once the Israelite father gathered his sons, a series of questions and answers followed. Three Passover questions are mentioned in Old Testament texts. Each of these questions came to be associated, in Jewish tradition, with three different types of sons. Alma's conversation with his three sons follows this ancient pattern.

The wise son asked: "What is the meaning of the testimonies, and the statutes, and the judgments, which the Lord our God hath commanded you?" (Deuteronomy 6:20). As Alma spoke to Helaman, his wise son, he mentioned "wisdom" no less than eight times. He also told Helaman of God's laws and testimonies. Jewish tradition held that while the Israelite father presented his answers to his son's questions he was to use "allegorical interpretations" as he spoke to "future generations." Interestingly, Alma does in fact employ allegorical interpretations (see Alma 37:45) and in Alma 37:19 mention is made of "future generations."

The wicked son asked: "What mean ye by this service?" (Exodus 12:26). Jewish tradition depicts this son as being one who had become an outcast because of his social crimes. This type of son also believed false doctrines. Alma's son Corianton had become alienated from his ministry (see Alma 39:3), had been the cause of social problems (see Alma 39:11), and had accepted false doctrines (see Alma 41:9).

The uninformed son asked: "What is this?" (Exodus 13:14). This type of son, in Jewish tradition, needed instruction in God's law in order for him to keep from breaking it. In correspondence to this, we see Alma teaching his son Shiblon a code of conduct (see Alma 38:11–14) and admonishing him to be diligent (see Alma 38:10).

In addition to the three sons pattern there are also several other Passover themes that can be seen in chapters 35 through 42 of the book of Alma.

Passover Theme	Old Testament	Book of Mormon
Crying out for deliverance	Deuteronomy 26:6–7	Alma 36:3, 18, 27
Bitter suffering	Exodus 12:8	Alma 36:18, 21
Hardness of heart	Exodus 11:10	Alma 35:15
Three days and nights of darkness	Exodus 10:22	Alma 36:16

Pentecost.[101] The festival of Pentecost was held fifty days after Passover. This springtime festivity was also known as Firstfruits and was held, in part, to remember the bounteous harvest (see Numbers 28:26). This festival also commemorated the time when God gave the Israelites his law at Mount Sinai. In ancient times admonitions were offered during the festival of Pentecost to keep the Lord's law.

There are some clues in the book of Mosiah that support the idea that Abinadi may have delivered his speech during the festival of Pentecost. The interesting thing to notice in the Book of Mormon narrative is that Abinadi has reversed some of the themes.

1. Pentecost was meant to be a time of rejoicing over the firstfruits that God had so graciously bestowed upon the Israelites. But Abinadi cursed the crops in a manner reminiscent of the curses that came upon Egypt (see Mosiah 12:6).

2. Pentecost celebrated the bounty that came after Egyptian bondage. But Abinadi, using the language of the Egyptian episode, prophesied captivity and burdens upon those disobedient to the Lord's counsel (see Mosiah 11:21, 23; 12:2, 5; cf. Exodus 1:11).

3. Abinadi recited the commandments God had delivered at Mount Sinai (see Mosiah 12:33).

4. Abinadi's "face shone with exceeding luster, even as Moses' did while in the mount of Sinai, while speaking with the Lord" (Mosiah 13:5; cf. Exodus 34:29–30).

5. Both the Sinai recital and Abinadi's speech employ "furnace" imagery (see Mosiah 12:3; cf. Exodus 19:18).

6. Pentecost appears to have been celebrated for three days (see Exodus 19:11) while Abinadi's trial was put off for three days, possibly because of the Pentecost celebration (see Mosiah 17:6).

7. Psalm 50 has been identified by biblical scholars as a Pentecost Psalm. There are several parallels between Psalm 50 and Abinadi's speech.

• God shall come	(Psalms 50:3/Mosiah 15:1)
• God prefers thanksgiving over sacrifice	(Psalms 50:13–14/Mosiah 13:11)
• Keep the law of God	(Psalms 50:16/Mosiah 11:23)
• Condemnation of the wicked	(Psalms 50:18/Mosiah 12:29)

Feast of Tabernacles.[102] There are many concepts in the Book of Mormon that parallel the Israelite Sukkot or Feast of Tabernacles.

FEAST OF TABERNACLES	OLD TESTAMENT	BOOK OF MORMON
Temple location	Deuteronomy 31:11	Mosiah 2:1
Booths/Tents	Leviticus 23:41–44	Mosiah 2:5–6
Speaker on platform	Nehemiah 8:4	Mosiah 2:7
God as Creator	Nehemiah 9:5–6	Mosiah 2:20–21
Commandments of God	Exodus 24:3–4	Mosiah 6:1–3
Covenant with God	Exodus 24:7	Mosiah 5:5
Blood of the covenant	Exodus 24:8	Mosiah 3:11
Blessings/Curses	Deuteronomy 27:14–26	Mosiah 2:22, 33
Sacrifice	Numbers 29:12–34	Mosiah 2:3
Those who understand	Nehemiah 10:28–29	Mosiah 2:40
Falling to the ground	Nehemiah 8:6	Mosiah 4:1–2, 6–7
Names recorded	Nehemiah 9:38	Mosiah 6:1–3

Jubilee Celebration.[103] Parallels can be detected between the Jubilee year celebration in ancient Israel and some of the material that is recorded in the book of Mosiah.

JUBILEE	OLD TESTAMENT	BOOK OF MORMON
Return of possessions	Leviticus 25:10	Mosiah 4:28
No injury to one another	Leviticus 25:14, 17	Mosiah 4:13
Render what is due	Leviticus 25:15–16, 50	Mosiah 4:13, 28
Prosperity follows obedience	Leviticus 25:18–19	Mosiah 2:22

Jubilee	Old Testament	Book of Mormon
Help the poor	Leviticus 25:35	Mosiah 4:16, 26
Use of riches	Leviticus 25:35–37	Mosiah 4:21
Peace in the land	Leviticus 26:6	Mosiah 2:31
Covenant with God	Leviticus 26:9	Mosiah 5:5–6
The Lord's dwelling	Leviticus 26:11	Mosiah 2:37
Lord with His people	Leviticus 26:11–12	Mosiah 2:36
Disobedient cursed	Leviticus 26:14–33	Mosiah 2:38, 3:25–27
Walk/Go contrary	Leviticus 26:21, 27	Mosiah 2:33, 36

Kingship

Another of the striking parallels that exists between the Book of Mormon and the Bible is the royal coronation pattern.[104] Notice that even though the elements of the pattern are scattered throughout the texts of the Bible, they are all mentioned in Book of Mormon texts.

Coronation	Old Testament	Book of Mormon
Temple setting	2 Kings 11:14	Mosiah 1:18
Platform	2 Chronicles 6:13	Mosiah 2:7
Insignia	2 Kings 11:12	Mosiah 1:15–16
Anointing	1 Kings 1:39	Mosiah 6:3/Jacob 1:9
Presentation	1 Kings 1:34, 39	Mosiah 2:30
Throne name	2 Kings 24:17	Jacob 1:10–11
Divine adoption	2 Samuel 7:14	Mosiah 5:6–12

Covenant Renewal

The formal structure of the Old Testament treaty/covenant pattern can be clearly seen in the record of the Nephites.[105]

Covenant	Old Testament	Book of Mormon
Preamble	Exodus 19:3; 20:1	Mosiah 2:9 [1:1–2:9]
Antecedent history	Exodus 19:4; 20:2	Mosiah 2:9–21, 23–24, 25–30
Terms of the covenant	Exodus 19:5–6; 20:3–23:19	Mosiah 2:22, 24, 31–41; 4:6–30

Covenant	Old Testament	Book of Mormon
Formal witness	Exodus 19:8; 24:3	Mosiah 5:2–8
Blessings and curses	Exodus 19:5; 23:20–33	Mosiah 5:9–15 [3:24–27]
Recital of the covenant and deposit of the text	Exodus 19:7; 24:4–8	Mosiah [2:8–9] 6:1–3, 6

Farewell Address

In 1985 William S. Kurz published an article in the *Journal of Biblical Literature* that outlined twenty typical attributes of ancient farewell speeches (both political and religious). With the exception of one of those elements, King Benjamin's speech in the Book of Mormon fits the pattern exactly.[106]

Kurz's Pattern	Book of Mormon
1. Summons	Mosiah 1:9–10
2. Description of speaker's mission	Mosiah 2:12–14, 18
3. Declaration of mission fulfillment	Mosiah 2:15, 27–28
4. Declaration of impending death	Mosiah 2:26, 28; 1:9
5. Exhortation	Mosiah 4:9–10; 2:9, 40–41; 5:12
6. Warnings and final injunctions	Mosiah 4:29–30; 2:32, 36–37, 39; 3:12
7. Blessings	Mosiah 2:22, 24, 31, 36, 41; 3:16
8. Farewell gestures	Mosiah 2:28; cf. 2 Nephi 9:44
9. Tasks for successors	Mosiah 1:15; 6:3
10. Theological review of history	Mosiah 3:13–15
11. Revelation of the future	Mosiah 3:1–2, 5–10
12. Promises	Mosiah 4:11–16; 2:22, 31; 5:9, 15
13. Appointment of successor	Mosiah 1:15–16; 2:31; 6:3
14. Bewailing the loss	Mosiah 4:2
15. Future degeneration	Mosiah 3:24–25
16. Covenant renewal / sacrifices	Mosiah 2:3; 5:1–7
17. Providing for survivors	Mosiah 4:14–26; 6:3
18. Consolation to inner circle	Mosiah 1; 4:4
19. Didactic speech	(many virtues expounded)
20. Approach to death	(–not found–)

Olive Tree Allegory

In summarizing the substantial amount of research that has been conducted on Zenos's olive tree allegory from chapter 5 of the book of Jacob, Dr. Daniel C. Peterson states:

FIGURE 24. The Book of Mormon accurately describes ancient olive tree horticulture in detail that would have been unknown to the Prophet Joseph Smith. This stands as one of many evidences that Joseph Smith did indeed translate an ancient text.

> A group of horticulturists (specialists in tree culture) looked at the account of olive culture and olive production in the Book of Mormon in Jacob 5 and found that in virtually every detail, it matches what we actually know about how olive trees are treated, how they are grown, cultivated, and cared for.
>
> Now, it has to be understood that olive trees do not grow in New York State. Joseph Smith probably didn't ever see any. He certainly wouldn't have known much about olive trees and olive cultivation, and olive cultivation is very, very different from the kinds of trees he would have known. So where did he get this information from? It seems to me that the most conservative notion, the best explanation, is that whoever wrote the parable of the olive tree in Jacob 5 knew olive cultivation at first hand. He knew how it was done. It's a very detailed account, a very rich account, because of course it's an account of the history of the world (in the past and on into the future) using the olive tree as a metaphor for the house of Israel. You have graftings in and cuttings off and the dispersion of branches of the olive tree into the farthest parts of the vineyard, and so on. And it's all accurate down to the last detail—with one notable exception. And that is that in the account in Jacob 5, it said that graftings from wild olive trees—or little pieces of wild olive trees—are grafted into the main olive tree, the domesticated olive tree, and then they produce tame fruit. Now, that doesn't happen. A wild olive branch, even if grafted into a tame olive tree, will still produce wild fruit. It will survive, but it won't produce tame fruit simply because it's grafted into a tame olive tree. So, is this an error on the part of the Book of Mormon? No, not really.
>
> One of the articles [from the book on Jacob 5 by the Foundation for Ancient Research and Mormon Studies]—an article that I was involved with . . . uncovered evidence that in the ancient Mediterranean world, they were aware of the possibility that miraculously, a wild olive branch grafted into a tame olive tree could produce tame fruit. It doesn't happen naturally, but it can happen miraculously. And the

prophetic figures of the ancient Mediterranean, specifically Greek thinkers and so on, saw this as a sign from God. It was a miraculous intervention from God, something that contravened the normal laws of olive cultivation and production.

Well, what does it stand for in that account of the Book of Mormon? It stands for the conversion of Gentiles into people of the house of Israel. It's a miraculous transformation, exactly what the Book of Mormon would have it to be. And this is a remarkable thing. It's a very long, a seventy-seven-verse long, description of olive culture. This is certainly enough rope for Joseph Smith to have hanged himself if he were making it up, but he didn't. He got it right, and on the one detail which seems to be wrong, it again has precedent in the ancient Near Eastern world and in the ancient Eastern Mediterranean.[107]

INTERNAL COMPLEXITY

Another point in favor of the ancient authenticity of the Book of Mormon is that even though the text is quite complex it never stumbles over itself. Noel B. Reynolds makes the following relevant points.

• The book has three independent dating systems that are maintained accurately throughout. Different writers tracked time from when Lehi left Jerusalem, from the initiation of the reign of the judges, or from the day the sign was given for the birth of Jesus Christ. Yet no confusion results, and dating sequences can always be reconstructed precisely.

• The Book of Mormon contains a complex system of religious teachings. These are presented in unique ways by different prophets in their own times and contexts. Lehi reports a vision of the tree of life. Nephi presents the gospel of Jesus Christ in conjunction with the vision of Christ's baptism. Jacob reports Zenos' allegory of the olive tree. Benjamin gives a great temple sermon. Alma teaches that the word of God is a seed that must be planted and nourished. Jesus gives the Nephites a modified version of his sermon on the mount. Each of these enrich understanding of the basic teachings; they never confuse them or contradict one another.

• The book's authors refer to a huge and complex set of source materials, including official records, sermons, letters, journals, monument inscriptions, church records, and ancient Israelite scriptures not known today. Yet these writers always manage to maintain a consistent relationship between the sources and the final text.

• Subtle and complex political traditions evolve early in the text and surface in a variety of forms in later sections, always plausibly and consistently. The complaints of Laman and Lemuel raised against Nephi in their earliest murmuring evolve into a national ideology that is still invoked 500 years later to justify Lamanite efforts to subjugate their Nephite brethren.

• The book describes various ebbs and flows of ethnic interaction without ever losing track of even the most minor groups.

• Hundreds of individual characters and place names are successfully introduced and tracked coherently.[108]

There are a few internal quotations within Book of Mormon texts that call for consideration. Alma 36:22, for instance, quotes 1 Nephi 1:8; and Helaman 14:12 is a citation of Mosiah 3:8. If Joseph Smith were simply making up the Book of Mormon text as he recited it to his scribes, how did he manage to accurately quote material that had been dictated many pages, and many days, before? Melvin J. Thorne points out that the Book of Mormon text:

> . . . presents complex geographical data that is internally consistent, so that places are always in the same relationship with each other. The book itself is structurally complex; for example, there are complicated sets of prefaces and summaries before and after a large number of significant sections, in which the editor gives the reader a forecast of what is coming and then summarizes what has been read. It is unlikely that an uneducated farmboy could, while dictating, keep in mind what he had promised in the prefaces and then remember to close off the sections with summaries. This intricate structure is much more compatible with the claims in the Book of Mormon itself that the record was made by ancient writers working with written materials over long periods of time.[109]

SUMMARY

Joseph Smith claimed that the Book of Mormon was an ancient record of an Israelite colony living in the New World. He also declared that he had been given this record by an angel of God and translated it through the gift and power of the Almighty. The material in this chapter has demonstrated that Joseph Smith's claims for the book can be solidly substantiated by a great deal of evidence. Noel B. Reynolds reminds us that:

> Empirical evidences never prove anything absolutely. They can be used only to refute or confirm theories. But to the extent that human knowledge generally depends on empirical evidence, this evidence does provide the same kind of proof we use to support accepted scientific theories.
>
> Because the Book of Mormon exists as an empirical phenomenon, the relevant theories are those which attempt to explain that existence. There are really only two such theories: (1) that the book is a fraudulent attempt to concoct an ancient text, and (2) that the divine intervention of God brought a previously written account of his dealings with men back into circulation.
>
> Inasmuch as the first theory fails repeatedly in the best scholarly studies, the second theory is left alone as the only remaining plausible hypothesis.[110]

NOTES

1. Dallin H. Oaks, "The Historicity of the Book of Mormon," FARMS transcript.
2. Brigham H. Roberts, *New Witnesses for God* (Salt Lake City: Deseret Book, 1950), 2:7–8.
3. Dummelow believes that of John's writings alone (Gospel, Epistles, Revelation), the book of Revelation may have been the first written (see John R. Dummelow, ed., *A Commentary on the Holy Bible* [New York: Macmillan, 1956], 772, 1053, 1060, 1069).
4. F. F. Bruce, ed., *The International Bible Commentary*, rev. ed. (Grand Rapids, Michigan: Zondervan, 1986), 1005.
5. See footnote *a* for Ezekiel 37:16 in the LDS edition of the King James Bible.
6. Keith Meservy, "Ezekiel's Sticks and the Gathering of Israel," *Ensign*, February 1987, 4–13. For non-LDS scholars who feel the "sticks" of Ezekiel 37 represent wax-filled writing boards, see Daniel I. Block, *The Book of Ezekiel: Chapters 25–48* (Grand Rapids, Michigan: Eerdmans, 1998), 399–405; Moshe Greenberg, *Ezekiel 21–37* (New York: Doubleday, 1997), 753; Walther Zimmerli, *Ezekiel* (Philadelphia: Fortress Press, 1983), 2:273; George A. Buttrick, ed., *The Interpreter's Dictionary of the Bible* (Nashville: Abingdon Press, 1962), 4:917.
7. Verses 1–4 of D&C 27 were received in Harmony, Pennsylvania, about 1 August 1830 while verses 5–18 were received in Fayette, New York on 4 September 1830 (see Lyndon W. Cook, *The Revelations of the Prophet Joseph Smith* [Salt Lake City: Deseret Book, 1985], 38–39).
8. This equation is made in such places as the *Evening and Morning Star*, vol. 1, no. 6, November 1832, 41–42; ibid., vol. 1, no. 8, January 1833, 57; *Messenger and Advocate*, vol. 3, no. 5, February 1837, 450; *Times and Seasons*, vol. 3, no. 6, 15 January 1842, 658; ibid., vol. 3, no. 8, 15 February 1842, 690; *HC*, 6:24; *JD*, 13:175. An editorial entry in the *Encyclopedia of Mormonism* states: "For Latter-day Saints, the 'Stick of Joseph' and the 'Stick of Ephraim' refer to the Book of Mormon. Both phrases appear in the book of the prophet Ezekiel (37:16, 19). The view that the Stick of Joseph consists of a scriptural record receives support from the Book of Mormon and the Doctrine and Covenants (1 Nephi 13:35–40; 2 Nephi 3:11–12, 18–21; D&C 27:5). Articles [in the *Encyclopedia of Mormonism*] that deal with this subject are Book of Mormon, Biblical Prophecies about; Ezekiel, Prophecies of; Joseph of Egypt: Writings of Joseph; and 'Voices from the Dust'" (*EM*, 3:1418).
9. See also verses 20–37 wherein Nephi sees "the book of the Lamb of God" or the Bible in his vision of the future. The angel also tells Nephi that his descendants will write the Book of Mormon which will be "hid up, to come forth unto the Gentiles, by the gift and power of the Lamb" (vv. 35–36).
10. See JS–H 1:59.
11. See Lenet H. Read, "Joseph Smith's Receipt of the Plates and the Israelite Feast of Trumpets," *Journal of Book of Mormon Studies*, vol. 2, no. 2, Fall 1993, 110–20. A shorter version of this article has been published as Lenet H. Read, "The Golden Plates and the Feast of Trumpets," *Ensign*, January 2000, 25–29.

12. Orson Pratt, *Remarkable Visions* (Liverpool, England: R. James, 1848), 1. Joseph Smith was the first to admit that he was "an unlearned boy" (*TPJS*, 371). On one occasion the Prophet said that the children of his family "were deprived of the benefit of an education. Suffice it to say I was merely instructed in reading, writing, and the ground [rules] of arithmetic which constituted my whole literary acquirements" (Dean C. Jessee, ed., *The Personal Writings of Joseph Smith* [Salt Lake City: Deseret Book, 1984], 4). George A. Smith indicated that "Joseph Smith [was] a ploughboy . . . one who cultivated the earth, and had scarcely education enough to read his Bible" (*JD*, 7:111). Charles C. Rich said that he was "an illiterate, unlearned boy" (*JD*, 19:28). Wilford Woodruff testified that Joseph "was an illiterate youth" (*JD*, 18:118), "an illiterate boy" (*JD*, 16:266) who "did the best he could in his illiterate state; he was, as it were, but a mere plow-boy" (*JD*, 2:196–97). Orson Pratt said that the Prophet "was uneducated; he had not been to college; he was . . . merely a country boy" (*JD*, 14:140). He was, said Pratt, simply a "young, unlettered boy" (*JD*, 13:66). He "was not a learned man, and in fact was scarcely in possession of an ordinary common school education. He could write a little, but was by no means an expert penman" said Pratt (*JD*, 12:357). Again, Pratt informs us that "the Prophet was a slow and awkward writer" (Letter, Orson Pratt to John Christensen, 2 September 1878, Orson Pratt Letter Box, LDS Church Archives, Salt Lake City, Utah). Finally, we have the following assessments from John Taylor. "At that time he was a feeble youth, inexperienced, without a knowledge of the learning of the day" (*JD*, 20:175). Joseph Smith was "born in the backwoods of America–a farmer's son, without any particular educational advantages" (*JD*, 5:239). "Joseph Smith was quite an uneducated man. He was uneducated when he was a boy. He was brought up in the Green Mountains of Vermont, and he did not have any of the advantages of what we call an education" (*JD*, 25:213). The Prophet was "an unlettered youth" (*JD*, 18:210).
13. Lyndon W. Cook, ed., *David Whitmer Interviews A Restoration Witness* (Orem, Utah: Grandin Book, 1991), 174.
14. Ibid., 126–27.
15. *The Saints' Herald*, 1 October 1879, 290.
16. See Stephen D. Ricks, "Translating the Book of Mormon: Interpreting the Evidence," *Journal of Book of Mormon Studies*, vol. 2, no. 2, Fall 1993, 201–06; Royal Skousen, "Translating the Book of Mormon: Evidence from the Original Manuscript," in Noel B. Reynolds, ed., *Book of Mormon Authorship Revisited: The Evidence for Ancient Origins* (Provo, Utah: Foundation for Ancient Research and Mormon Studies, 1997), 61–93. Perhaps something that helped Joseph Smith in translating the Book of Mormon was the fact that he had become personally familiar with those persons who had written it. Wilford Woodruff stated that the Prophet "brought forth [the Book of Mormon] according to the *dictation* of Moroni, Nephi, and Lehi, the angels of God who administered to him" (*JD*, 16:266, emphasis added). Perhaps this piece of information fits together with the report that "at times angels were in the room" in David Whitmer's house where the Book of Mormon was being translated ("History of the Life of Oliver B. Huntington," typescript, Special Collections, Harold B. Lee Library, Brigham Young University, Provo, Utah, 49–50).

17. The "Book of Lehi" designation can be found in the introduction to D&C 3. See also the comments in *JD*, 23:184. The 116 pages of the Book of Lehi were evidently burned by the person who had stolen them (see Dan Vogel, ed., *Early Mormon Documents* [Salt Lake City: Signature Books, 1998], 2:149).
18. John W. Welch and Tim Rathbone, "How Long Did it Take to Translate the Book of Mormon?" in John W. Welch, ed., *Reexploring the Book of Mormon* (Salt Lake City: Deseret Book and FARMS, 1992), 4.
19. *Insights*, FARMS Update, no. 92, January 1994, 2.
20. "Last Testimony of Sister Emma," *Saints' Advocate*, vol. 2, no. 4, October 1879, 50–52, emphasis added.
21. *St. Louis Republican*, 16 July 1884, emphasis added, cited in Cook, 139–40.
22. *Millennial Star*, vol. 44, no. 6, 6 February 1882, 87.
23. Edmund C. Briggs, "A Visit to Nauvoo in 1856," *Journal of History*, vol. 9, January 1916, 454.
24. John W. Welch, "What the Original Book of Mormon Manuscript is Not," in John W. Welch and Melvin J. Thorne, eds., *Pressing Forward with the Book of Mormon* (Provo, Utah: Foundation for Ancient Research and Mormon Studies, 1999), 293–95. There is some evidence that after a portion of the Book of Mormon text had been written down the Prophet's scribe would read the words back so that any errors in the recording process might be detected (see Skousen, "Translating the Book of Mormon: Evidence from the Original Manuscript," 82–84).
25. This manifestation has been reconstructed from information found in Cook, ed., *David Whitmer Interviews: A Restoration Witness*, 10–11, 15, 17, 18–23, 25–26, 33–34, 57, 63, 75, 86, 108, 127, 152, 167, 181, 184, 187–88, 192–93, 213, 245, 247. Joseph Smith reports that after he and the Three Witnesses had made an unsuccessful attempt to obtain the promised manifestation Martin Harris voluntarily withdrew himself from the group and the angel soon made his appearance. The Prophet then sought out Harris, who was "fervently engaged in prayer," and together they prevailed upon the Lord to allow them to see the angel and the plates also. It appears that Harris was not permitted to see the angel and the plates during the group's first attempt because he had not yet sufficiently repented of losing the first 116 pages of the Book of Mormon manuscript (*HC*, 1:54–55).
26. Ibid., 98.
27. Preston Nibley, ed., *History of Joseph Smith by His Mother, Lucy Mack Smith* (Salt Lake City: Bookcraft, 1958), 152.
28. This document is printed in the "Introduction" to the Book of Mormon, emphasis added.
29. See Richard L. Anderson, *Investigating the Book of Mormon Witnesses* (Salt Lake City: Deseret Book, 1981), 181–91.
30. Dean C. Jessee, ed., *The Personal Writings of Joseph Smith* (Salt Lake City: Deseret Book, 1984), 8.
31. See *Millennial Star*, vol. 40, no. 49, 9 December 1878, 773; ibid., vol. 55, no. 13, 27 March 1893, 214–15; *Juvenile Instructor*, vol. 24, no. 1, 1 January 1889, 22–23; see also Cook, ed., *David Whitmer Interviews: A Restoration Witness*, 33, 182, 214, 216, 218.
32. Nibley, ed., *History of Joseph Smith by His Mother, Lucy Mack Smith*, 116–17.

33. *Labors in the Vineyard: Twelfth Book in the Faith-Promoting Series* (Salt Lake City: Juvenile Instructor Office, 1884), 65–66.
34. *The Saints' Herald*, 1 October 1879, 290.
35. See *Deseret News*, Church Section, 12 February 1938, 8.
36. Noel B. Reynolds, "Lehi's Arabian Journey Updated," in Reynolds, ed., *Book of Mormon Authorship Revisited: The Evidence for Ancient Origins*, 387–88. For further reading see Warren P. Aston, "The Arabian Bountiful Discovered?: Evidence for Nephi's Bountiful," *JBMS*, vol. 7, no. 1, 1998, 5–11.
37. For reading in this area see John L. Sorenson, "Transoceanic Crossings," in Monte S. Nyman and Charles D. Tate, Jr., eds., *The Book of Mormon: First Nephi, The Doctrinal Foundation* (Provo, Utah: BYU Religious Studies Center, 1988), 251–70; John L. Sorenson and Martin H. Raish, *Pre-Columbian Contact with the Americas Across the Oceans: An Annotated Bibliography*, 2 vols., rev. ed. (Provo, Utah: Research Press, 1996); Marc K. Stengel, "The Diffusionists Have Landed," *Atlantic Monthly*, January 2000, 35–48; Stephen C. Jett, "Resist-Dyeing as a Possible Ancient Transoceanic Transfer," and Carl L. Johannessen, "Pre-Columbian American Sunflower and Maize Images in Indian Temples: Evidence of Contact Between Civilizations in India and America," in Davis Bitton, ed., *Mormons, Scripture, and the Ancient World: Studies in Honor of John L. Sorenson* (Provo, Utah: Foundation for Ancient Research and Mormon Studies, 1998), 307–50 and 351–89, respectively.
38. See *EM*, 1:176–79.
39. See John L. Sorenson, *The Geography of Book of Mormon Events: A Source Book*, rev. ed. (Provo, Utah: Foundation for Ancient Research and Mormon Studies, 1992).
40. See John L. Sorenson, *Mormon's Map* (Provo, Utah: The Foundation for Ancient Research and Mormon Studies, 2000), 1–128; John L. Sorenson, *An Ancient American Setting for the Book of Mormon* (Salt Lake City: Deseret Book and FARMS, 1985), 1–48.
41. *Times and Seasons*, vol. 3, no. 22, 15 September 1842, 915, 922.
42. Ibid., vol. 3, no. 23, 1 October 1842, 927.
43. JS–H 1:42.
44. Ibid., 1:51–52.
45. Cook, ed., *David Whitmer Interviews: A Restoration Witness*, 173, 248; see also 7, 20–23.
46. Ibid., 74.
47. For Oliver Cowdery's description of the stone box see *Messenger and Advocate*, vol. 2, no. 1, October 1835, 196–97.
48. *HC*, 4:537.
49. See H. Curtis Wright, "Ancient Burials of Metal Documents in Stone Boxes," in John M. Lundquist and Stephen D. Ricks, eds., *By Study and Also By Faith* (Salt Lake City: Deseret Book and FARMS, 1990), 2:273–334.
50. See William J. Hamblin, "Sacred Writings on Bronze Plates in the Ancient Mediterranean," FARMS preliminary report, 1994, 3–11; William J. Adams, Jr., "Lehi's Jerusalem and Writing on Metal Plates," *JBMS*, vol. 3, no. 1, Spring 1994, 204–06.

51. All citations are found in Robert F. Smith, "The 'Golden' Plates," in Welch, ed., *Reexploring the Book of Mormon*, 275–77; see also Roy W. Doxey, "What was the approximate weight of the gold plates from which the Book of Mormon was translated?" *Ensign*, December 1986, 65.
52. See William J. Hamblin, "Reformed Egyptian," FARMS Criticism Paper, 1995. For examples of hieratic and demotic Egyptian scripts see FARMS Staff, "Martin Harris' Visit with Charles Anthon: Collected Documents on Short-Hand Egyptian," FARMS, preliminary report, 1985, appendixes 11, 13–20. For further discussion on the hieratic style, see John Gee, "Two Notes on Egyptian Script," *JBMS*, vol. 5, no. 1, Spring 1996, 162–76.
53. See John A. Tvedtnes and Stephen D. Ricks, "Jewish and Other Semitic Texts Written in Egyptian Characters," *JBMS*, vol. 5, no. 2, 1996, 156–63.
54. See Dean C. Jessee, ed., *The Papers of Joseph Smith* (Salt Lake City: Deseret Book, 1989), 1:9. Compare Isaiah 29:11–12 and 2 Nephi 27:15–21. The angel Moroni quoted Isaiah 29:11 to the Prophet Joseph Smith during their first meeting on 21 September 1823 and explained its relationship to the Restoration (see Kent P. Jackson, "Moroni's Message to Joseph Smith," *Ensign*, August 1990, 16; JS–H 1:41). For further reading see David E. Sloan, "The Anthon Transcripts and the Translation of the Book of Mormon: Studying It Out in the Mind of Joseph Smith," *JBMS*, vol. 5, no. 2, 1996, 57–81.
55. See Ariel L. Crowley, *About the Book of Mormon* (Salt Lake City: Deseret News Press, 1961), 23–26, 34; Ariel L. Crowley, "The Anthon Transcript," *Improvement Era*, January 1942, 14–15, 58–60; February 1942, 76–80, 124–25; March 1942, 150–51, 182–83. Charles Anthon reportedly confirmed to Martin Harris that some of the characters copied off of the golden plates by Joseph Smith were "Egyptian" (JS–H 1:64).
56. See Carl H. Jones, "The 'Anthon Transcript' and Two Mesoamerican Cylinder Seals," *Newsletter and Proceedings of the Society for Early Historic Archaeology*, no. 122, September 1970, 1–8; "'Anthon Transcript' Writing Found?" *JBMS*, vol. 8, no. 1, 1999, 68–70.
57. See "Similarities Between the Anthon Transcript and Old South Arabian," *JBMS*, vol. 8, no. 2, 1999, 83. It should be noted here that Charles Anthon reportedly said that the characters that were shown to him by Martin Harris included "Arabic" (JS–H 1:64).
58. See Wayne A. Larsen, Alvin C. Rencher, and Tim Layton, "Who Wrote the Book of Mormon? An Analysis of Wordprints," *Brigham Young University Studies*, vol. 20, no. 3, Spring 1980, 225–51; see also Wayne A. Larsen, Alvin C. Rencher, and Tim Layton, "Multiple Authorship in the Book of Mormon," *New Era*, November 1979, 10–13.
59. John L. Hilton, "On Verifying Wordprint Studies: Book of Mormon Authorship," in Reynolds, ed., *Book of Mormon Authorship Revisited: The Evidence for Ancient Origins*, 241.
60. The material in this section has been drawn from Royal Skousen, "The Original Language of the Book of Mormon: Upstate New York Dialect, King James English, or Hebrew?" *JBMS*, vol. 3, no. 1, Spring 1994, 28–38; John A. Tvedtnes, "The Hebrew Background of the Book of Mormon," in John L. Sorenson and Melvin J. Thorne, eds., *Rediscovering the Book of Mormon* (Salt Lake City: Deseret Book and FARMS, 1991), 77–91; Hugh W. Pinnock, *Finding Biblical Hebrew and Other Ancient Literary Forms in the Book of Mormon* (Provo, Utah: Foundation for Ancient Research and

Mormon Studies, 1999); Paul Cracroft, "A Clear Poetic Voice: The Book of Mormon Bears the Unmistakable Mark of Ancient Hebrew Literary Forms," *Ensign*, January 1984, 28–31; Donald W. Parry, *The Book of Mormon Text Reformatted According to Parallelistic Patterns* (Provo, Utah: Foundation for Ancient Research and Mormon Studies, 1992); John W. Welch, "Chiasmus in the Book of Mormon," in John W. Welch, ed., *Chiasmus in Antiquity*, repr. ed. (Provo, Utah: Research Press, 1998), 198–210; Donald W. Parry, "Hebrew Literary Patterns in the Book of Mormon," *Ensign*, October 1989, 58–61; Sidney B. Sperry, "Hebrew Idioms in the Book of Mormon," *JBMS*, vol. 4, no. 1, Spring 1995, 218–25; Donald W. Parry, "Power Through Repetition: The Dynamics of Book of Mormon Parallelism," in Reynolds, ed., *Book of Mormon Authorship Revisited: The Evidence for Ancient Origins*, 295–309; Kevin L. Barney, "Poetic Diction and Parallel Word Pairs in the Book of Mormon," *JBMS*, vol. 4, no. 2, Fall 1995, 15–81.

61. Paul Y. Hoskisson, "Alma as a Hebrew Name," *JBMS*, vol. 7, no. 1, 1998, 72–73.
62. Terrence L. Szink, "Further Evidence of a Semitic Alma," *JBMS*, vol. 8, no. 1, 1999, 70.
63. See Jeffrey R. Chadwick, "Sariah in the Elephantine Papyri," in Welch and Thorne, eds., *Pressing Forward with the Book of Mormon*, 6–10.
64. See John W. Welch, "What Was a 'Mosiah'?" in Welch, ed., *Reexploring the Book of Mormon*, 105–07.
65. See E. Jan Wilson, "Inside a Sumerian Temple: The Ekishnugal at Ur," in Donald W. Parry and Stephen D. Ricks, eds., *The Temple in Time and Eternity* (Provo, Utah: Foundation for Ancient Research and Mormon Studies, 1999), 319.
66. See James Strong, *The New Strong's Exhaustive Concordance of the Bible* (Nashville: Thomas Nelson Publishers, 1996), Hebrew and Aramaic Dictionary of the Old Testament, 39, word #2233 and 44, #2551.
67. This information can be found in the newsletter of The Foundation for Ancient Research and Mormon Studies, *Insights: A Window on the Ancient World*, December 1999, 2.
68. See John A. Tvedtnes, John Gee, and Matthew Roper, "Book of Mormon Names Attested in Ancient Hebrew Inscriptions," *Journal of Book of Mormon Studies*, vol. 9, no. 1, 2000, 41–51.
69. Hugh W. Nibley, *Lehi in the Desert / The World of the Jaredites / There Were Jaredites* (Salt Lake City: Deseret Book and FARMS, 1988), 79; see also Alan Goff, "Mourning, Consolation, and Repentance at Nahom," in Sorenson and Thorne, eds., *Rediscovering the Book of Mormon*, 92–99; Warren P. Ashton and Michaela K. Aston, *In the Footsteps of Lehi: New Evidence for Lehi's Journey across Arabia to Bountiful* (Salt Lake City: Deseret Book, 1994), 3–25.
70. Stephen D. Ricks and John A. Tvedtnes, "The Hebrew Origin of Some Book of Mormon Place Names," *JBMS*, vol. 6, no. 2, 1997, 257–58.
71. William E. Vine, Merrill F. Unger, and William White, Jr., *Vine's Complete Expository Dictionary of Old and New Testament Words* (Nashville: Thomas Nelson Publishers, 1996), Old Testament Words, 6, 136. See also the alternative etymologies presented in Stephen D. Ricks and John A. Tvedtnes, "The Hebrew Origin of Some Book of Mormon Place Names," *JBMS*, vol. 6, no. 2, 1997, 255–57.

72. Manfred Lurker, *The Gods and Symbols of Ancient Egypt: An Illustrated Dictionary* (London: Thames and Hudson, 1980), 44. See also *EM*, 1:370–71.
73. Hugh W. Nibley, *Since Cumorah*, 2d ed. (Salt Lake City: Deseret Book and FARMS, 1988), 479, n. 80.
74. Hugh W. Nibley, *Abraham in Egypt*, 2d ed. (Salt Lake City: Deseret Book and FARMS, 2000), 643, n. 87.
75. John W. Welch, "Weighing and Measuring in the Worlds of the Book of Mormon," *JBMS*, vol. 8, no. 2, 1999, 43; *Review of Books on the Book of Mormon*, vol. 6, no. 1, 1994, 338.
76. Cook, ed., *David Whitmer Interviews: A Restoration Witness*, 98, emphasis added. "When we were first told to publish our statement [regarding the truthfulness of the Book of Mormon], we felt sure the people would not believe it, for the book told of a people who were refined and dwelt in large cities; but the Lord told us that he would make it known to the people, and people should discover the ruins of the lost cities and abundant *evidence* of the truth of what is written in the book" (ibid., 96, emphasis added). During the October 1946 General Conference of the LDS Church, Bishop LeGrand Richards related a story that he heard from Elder Charles A. Callis. Elder Callis is reported to have said that "when Joseph Smith received the plates he got down on his knees before the Lord and said, 'O God, what will the world say?' And the voice of God came to him, 'Fear not, I will cause the earth to testify of the truth of these things'" (*CR*, October 1946, 125).
77. *TS*, vol. 3, no. 22, 15 September 1842, 915; ibid., vol. 3, no. 23, 1 October 1842, 927. On page 922 of the 15 September 1842 issue the editor identifies the Mesoamerican cities in Stephens' book as "the remains and ruins of those mighty people" in the Book of Mormon. He then says, "we cannot but think the Lord has a hand in . . . proving the Book of Mormon true in the eyes of all the people. . . . It will be as it ever has been, the world will prove Joseph Smith a true prophet by circumstantial evidence." Unfortunately, the author of these editorials cannot be positively identified since Joseph Smith acted as the managing editor of the newspaper but John Taylor served as the production editor. It should be noted, however, that both of the articles contain extensive quotations from Stephens' book and it is known that Joseph Smith was sent a copy of this volume, by John Bernhisel, on 8 September 1841. In a letter dated 16 November 1841 the Prophet, with John Taylor acting as scribe and signer of the document, thanked Bernhisel for the book and said that "it unfolds and develops many things that are of great importance to this generation and corresponds with and supports the testimony of the Book of Mormon. . . . [O]f all the histories that have been written pertaining to the antiquities of this country it is the most correct, luminous, and comprehensive" (Jessee, ed., *The Personal Writings of Joseph Smith*, 501–02).
78. Ludwell H. Johnson, III, "Men and Elephants in America," *Scientific Monthly*, October 1952, 215–21; William D. Strong, "North American Indian Traditions Suggesting a Knowledge of the Mammoth," *American Anthropologist*, vol. 36, no. 1, January-March 1934, 81–88.
79. See Kenneth Macgowan, *Early Man in the New World* (New York: Macmillan, 1950), 137–39, 142.

80. George F. Carter, "Uhle's Mastodon," *Anthropological Journal of Canada*, vol. 6, no. 2, 1968, 21–24.
81. Josef Augusta, *The Age of Monsters, Prehistoric and Legendary* (London: Paul Hamlyn, 1966), 11–12.
82. Charles Schuchert, "Mammut Americanum in Connecticut," *American Journal of Science*, vol. 187, no. 220, April 1914, 328–29.
83. See Stephen Williams, "The Island 35 Mastodon: Its Bearing on the Age of Archaic Cultures in the East," *American Antiquity*, vol. 22, no. 4, April 1957, 368.
84. M. F. Ashley Montagu, "An Indian Tradition Relating to the Mastodon," *American Anthropologist*, vol. 46, no. 4, October-December 1944, 568. For further reading see John L. Sorenson, "Animals in the Book of Mormon: An Annotated Bibliography," FARMS paper, 1992, 2–3, 5–6, 10, 12, 14, 23–25, 31–35, 38–39; John L. Sorenson and Martin H. Raish, *Pre-Columbian Contact with the Americas Across the Oceans: An Annotated Bibliography*, 2d ed., rev. (Provo, Utah: Research Press, 1996), 1:45–46, 310, 349, 413, 426, 437, 443, 487, 520; 2:3, 104, 171, 209, 339, 385, 420, 422–23, 454.
85. John E. Thompson, *Mexico Before Cortez* (New York: Charles Scribner's Sons, 1933), 290. An artwork that may be relevant to this discussion can be found among the eighth century A.D. Mayan murals from the Temple of the Frescoes in Bonampak, Chiapas. A color reconstruction of these murals, in Mexico City's National Museum of Anthropology, shows an animal head that some observers take to be an elephant since it has a long trunk and a thin, white protrusion beneath the trunk that resembles a tusk (see Jill L. Furst and Peter T. Furst, *Pre-Columbian Art of Mexico* [New York: Abbeville Press, 1980], 71).
86. Kowalski states that the theoretical "identification of the mask snouts as modeled on the tapir's trunk is probably incorrect" (Jeff K. Kowalski, *The House of the Governor: A Maya Palace at Uxmal, Yucatan, Mexico* [Norman: University of Oklahoma Press, 1987], 193). Kowalski concludes that "there is compelling evidence that the principal model for the masks . . . with their pendulous, downcurving snouts, is long-snouted god B of the [Mayan] codices, [i.e.,] the Yucatec rain god Chac" (ibid., 202). This conclusion is important to keep in mind when considering other theoretical identifications of the masks since Mayan representations of Chac (see Peter Schmidt, Mercedes de la Garza, and Enrique Nalda, eds., *Maya* [New York: Rizzoli, 1998], 240, 242; Timothy Laughton, *The Maya: Life, Myth, and Art* [New York: Stewart, Tabori, and Chang, 1998], 77) do not resemble Mayan representations of either peccaries (see Laughton, *The Maya: Life, Myth, and Art*, 52) or anteaters (see Schmidt, Garza, and Nalda, eds., *Maya*, 521).
87. Paul S. Martin, "The Discovery of America," *Science*, vol. 179, no. 9, March 1973, 969–74.
88. See S. David Webb, ed., *Pleistocene Mammals of Florida* (Gainesville, Florida: University of Florida, 1974), 132, 144.
89. See Paul S. Martin and H. E. Wright, Jr., eds., *Pleistocene Extinctions* (New Haven: Yale University Press, 1967), 183, 186.
90. Montagu, "An Indian Tradition Relating to the Mastodon," 568, n. 1.

91. Loren C. Eiseley, "Indian Mythology and Extinct Fossil Vertebrates," *American Anthropologist*, vol. 47, no. 2, 1945, 318–20.
92. Ivan T. Sanderson, *Living Treasure* (New York: Viking, 1941), 39–40. For further reading see John L. Sorenson, "Once More: The Horse" in Welch, ed., *Reexploring the Book of Mormon*, 98–100; Sorenson, *An Ancient American Setting for the Book of Mormon*, 395, n. 63; John L. Sorenson, "Animals in the Book of Mormon: An Annotated Bibliography, FARMS paper, 1992, 2, 6–7, 10, 23–24, 28, 31; Sorenson and Raish, *Pre-Columbian Contact with the Americas Across the Oceans: An Annotated Bibliography*, 1:347, 366, 468; 2:57, 106, 421.
93. See John L. Sorenson, "Wheeled Figurines in the Ancient World," FARMS preliminary report, 1983. See also the picture of two ancient Near Eastern wheeled figurines in *Biblical Archaeology Review*, September/October, 1996, 80.
94. See John L. Sorenson, *Images of Ancient America: Visualizing Book of Mormon Life* (Provo, Utah: Research Press, 1998), 59.
95. See John L. Sorenson and Robert F. Smith, "Barley in Ancient America," in Welch, ed., *Reexploring the Book of Mormon*, 130–32.
96. *CR*, April 1929, 129.
97. See John L. Sorenson, "Digging Into the Book of Mormon: Part 2," *Ensign*, October 1984, 19 (see the color picture on page 22); Matthew G. Wells and John W. Welch, "Concrete Evidence for the Book of Mormon," in Welch, ed., *Reexploring the Book of Mormon*, 212–14.
98. See Kirk A. Magleby, "A Survey of Mesoamerican Bearded Figures," FARMS preliminary report, 1983.
99. Alexander von Wuthenau, *The Art of Terracotta Pottery in Pre-Columbian Central and South America* (New York: Crown Publishers, 1969), 49.
100. See Gordon C. Thomasson and John W. Welch, "The Sons of the Passover," in Welch, ed., *Reexploring the Book of Mormon*, 196–98.
101. See John W. Welch, Gordon C. Thomasson, and Robert F. Smith, "Abinadi and Pentecost," in Welch, ed., *Reexploring the Book of Mormon*, 135–38.
102. See John A. Tvedtnes, "King Benjamin and the Feast of Tabernacles," in John M. Lundquist and Stephen D. Ricks, eds., *By Study and Also By Faith* (Salt Lake City: Deseret Book and FARMS, 1990), 2:197–237; see also Terrence L. Szink and John W. Welch, "King Benjamin's Speech in the Context of Ancient Israelite Festivals," in John W. Welch and Stephen D. Ricks, eds., *King Benjamin's Speech: "That Ye May Learn Wisdom"* (Provo, Utah: Foundation for Ancient Research and Mormon Studies, 1998), 147–223.
103. See Tvedtnes, "King Benjamin and the Feast of Tabernacles," 226.
104. See Stephen D. Ricks, "Kingship, Coronation, and Covenant in Mosiah 1–6," in Welch and Ricks, eds., *King Benjamin's Speech: "That Ye May Learn Wisdom,"* 244–54.
105. See Stephen D. Ricks, "The Treaty/Covenant Pattern in King Benjamin's Address (Mosiah 1–6)," *BYUS*, vol. 24, no. 2, Spring 1984, 151–62.
106. See John W. Welch and Daryl R. Hague, "Benjamin's Sermon as a Traditional Ancient Farewell Address," in Welch and Ricks, eds., *King Benjamin's Speech: "That Ye May Learn Wisdom,"* 89–117.

107. Daniel C. Peterson, "A Scholar Looks at Evidences for the Book of Mormon, talk transcript, (Provo, Utah: Foundation for Ancient Research and Mormon Studies, 1995), 21–22. For further reading see Stephen D. Ricks and John W. Welch, eds., *The Allegory of the Olive Tree: The Olive, the Bible, and Jacob 5* (Salt Lake City: Deseret Book and FARMS, 1994).
108. Noel B. Reynolds, "Shedding New Light on Ancient Origins: Scholars Illuminate Book of Mormon Authorship," *Brigham Young Magazine*, Spring 1998, 40.
109. Melvin J. Thorne, "Complexity, Consistency, Ignorance, and Probabilities," in Reynolds, ed., *Book of Mormon Authorship Revisited: The Evidence for Ancient Origins*, 181.
110. Noel B. Reynolds, John L. Sorenson, Arthur Wallace, and Paul R. Cheesman, "External Evidences of Scripture: A Panel," in Paul R. Cheesman and C. Wilfred Griggs, eds., *Scriptures for the Modern World* (Provo, Utah: BYU Religious Studies Center, 1984), 127.

CHAPTER 8

Witnesses of the Restoration

The Lord has decreed that the Law of Witnesses be utilized in the establishment of truth (see Matthew 18:16; John 8:17; 2 Corinthians 13:1). This law is especially relevant when it comes to establishing the truthfulness of Joseph Smith's teachings and claims. If Joseph Smith did indeed see the Father and the Son in the Spring of 1820, and did indeed receive a commission from them to restore religious precepts, then it stands to reason that God would verify to others that these things were true.

And this is the case. Millions of Latter-day Saints have received a witness, for themselves, that Joseph Smith told the truth. This confirmation can come in a variety of ways; sometimes in a subtle manner, sometimes in miraculous ways. On the following pages the reader will find a few stories that demonstrate that the Lord has sustained the words of His prophet.

SPIRITUAL CONFIRMATIONS

In a previous chapter of this book, it was mentioned that the Lord allowed Oliver Cowdery, Martin Harris, and David Whitmer to have the golden plates of the Book of Mormon shown unto them by an angel. Perhaps it is a little less known that two of the Three Witnesses also had other encounters with the divine that convinced them of the truthfulness of Joseph Smith's claims. Joseph Smith wrote that around December of 1827 "the Lord appeared unto [Martin Harris] in a vision and showed unto him His marvelous work which He was about to do." This manifestation was granted, said the Prophet, "because of his faith."[1] The Prophet also reports that the "Lord appeared unto a young man by the name of Oliver Cowdery and showed unto him the plates in a vision and also the truth of the work and what the Lord was about to do through me his unworthy servant."[2]

Joseph Smith also reports that another well-known figure from Church history received a testimony of the Restoration's reality. On 9 June 1830 Newel K. Whitney, with others present, saw a heavenly vision of the future. "All of a sudden, a vision of the future burst upon him. He saw there represented the great work which through my instrumentality was yet to be accomplished."[3]

As a young boy John Taylor, who later became the third President of the Church, "saw, in vision, an angel in the heavens, holding a trumpet to his mouth, sounding a message to the nations. The import of this vision he did not understand until later in life."[4] The image of the angel with a trumpet is now commonly found on the spires of LDS temples.

Lorenzo Snow recounts a divine experience that occurred a short time after he had been baptized and confirmed as a member of the LDS Church.

> One evening, a few days after this, when alone, engaged in earnest prayer, the heavens were opened, the veil was rent from my mind, and then and there I received the most wonderful manifestations, grand and sublime, I believe as man was ever permitted to receive, and beyond the power of language fully to describe. It was shown me in that vision that there truly existed a Son of God, that Joseph Smith was really a prophet of God.
>
> The first intimation of the approach of that marvelous vision was a sound just above my head like the rustling of silken robes, when immediately the Holy Spirit descended upon me, enveloping my whole person, filling me from the crown of my head to the soles of my feet, which was a complete baptism, as tangible an immersion in a heavenly principle or element—the Holy Ghost—infinitely more real, physical in its effects upon every part of my system, than was the immersion when I was baptized in water. That night after retiring to rest the same wonderful manifestations were repeated, and continued to be for several successive nights.[5]

Wilford Woodruff tells a wonderful story about Robert Mason who, in 1800, had a vision of the coming Restoration of the gospel.

> There was one aged man in Connecticut . . . by the name of Robert Mason, who did not believe like the rest of the people. He believed it was necessary to have prophets, apostles, dreams, visions and revelations in the Church of Christ the same as they had who lived in ancient days; and he believed the Lord would raise up a people and a Church, in the last days, with prophets, apostles and all the gifts,

power, and blessings which it ever contained in any age of the world. The people called this man the old prophet Mason. He frequently came to my father's house when I was a boy, and taught me and my brothers those principles; and I believed them. This prophet prayed a great deal, and he had dreams and visions, and the Lord showed him many things, by visions, which were to come to pass in the last days.

I will here relate one vision, which he related to me. The last time I ever saw him, he said: "I was laboring in my field at mid-day when I was enwrapped in a vision. I was placed in the midst of a vast forest of fruit trees; I was very hungry, and walked a long way through the orchard searching for fruit to eat; but I could not find any in the whole orchard, and I wept because I could find no fruit. While I stood gazing at the orchard, and wondering why there was no fruit, the trees began to fall to the ground upon every side of me, until there was not one tree left standing in the whole orchard; and while I was marveling at the scene, I saw young sprouts start up from the roots of the trees which had fallen, and they opened into young thrifty trees before my eyes. They budded, blossomed, and bore fruit until the trees were loaded with the finest fruit I ever beheld, and I rejoiced to see so much fine fruit. I stepped up to a tree and picked my hands full of fruit, and I marveled at its beauty, and as I was about to taste of it, the vision closed, and I found myself in the field in the same place I was at the commencement of the vision.

I then knelt down upon the ground, and prayed unto the Lord, and asked him, in the name of Jesus Christ, to show me the meaning of the vision. The Lord said unto me: 'This is the interpretation of the vision; the great trees of the forest represent the generation of men in which you live. There is no Church of Christ, or kingdom of God upon the earth in your generation; there is no fruit of the Church of Christ upon the earth; there is no man ordained of God to administer in any of the ordinances of the gospel of salvation upon the earth in this day and generation. But, in the next generation, I the Lord will set up my kingdom and my Church upon the earth, and the fruits of the kingdom and Church of Christ, such as have followed the prophets, apostles and Saints in every dispensation, shall again be found in all their fullness upon the earth. You will live to see the day, and handle the fruit; but will never partake of it in the flesh.'"

When the old prophet had finished relating the vision and interpretation, he said to me, calling me by my Christian name: "I shall never partake of this fruit in the flesh; but you will, and you will become a conspicuous actor in that kingdom"; and then turned and left me, these being the last words he ever spoke to me on earth.

This was a very striking circumstance, as I had spent my hours and days, during twenty years, with this old Father Mason, and he had never [related] this vision before to me. But at the beginning of this last conversation, he told me that he felt impelled by the Spirit of the Lord to relate it to me. He had this vision about A.D. 1800, and he related it to me in 1830—the same spring that this Church was organized. This vision, with his other teaching to me, made a great impression upon my mind, and I prayed a great deal to the Lord to lead me by His Spirit, and prepare me for His Church when it did come.

> In 1832 I left Connecticut and traveled with my eldest brother to Oswego county, New York; and in the winter of 1833 I saw, for the first time in my life, an Elder of The Church of Jesus Christ of Latter-day Saints. He preached in a school house near where I lived. I attended the meeting, and the Spirit of the Lord bore record to me that what I heard was true. I invited the Elder to my house and next day I, with my eldest brother, went down into the water and was baptized. We were the first two baptized in Oswego county, New York. When I was baptized I thought of what the old prophet had said to me.
>
> In the Spring of 1834, I went to Kirtland, saw the Prophet Joseph Smith, and went with him and more than two hundred others in Zion's Camp, up to Missouri. When I arrived at my journey's end, I took the first opportunity and wrote a long letter to Father Mason, and told him I had found the Church of Christ that he had told me about. I told him about its organization and the coming forth of the Book of Mormon; that the Church had prophets, apostles, and all the gifts and blessings in it, and that the true fruit of the kingdom and Church of Christ were manifest among the Saints as the Lord had shown him in his vision. He received my letter, and read it over many times, and handled it as he had handled the fruit in the vision; but he was very aged, and soon died. He did not live to see any Elder to administer the ordinances of the gospel unto him. The first opportunity I had, after the doctrine of baptism for the dead was revealed, I went forth and was baptized for him.[6]

Solomon Chamberlain, one of the first missionaries of the LDS Church, recounts how he learned of the Restoration of the Lord's gospel from a heavenly source.

> In the year 1816 . . . the Lord showed me in a vision that there were no people on the earth that were right, and that faith was gone from the earth, excepting a few, and that all churches were corrupt. I further saw in vision that He would soon raise up a Church that would be after the Apostolic Order, that there would be in it the same powers and gifts that were in the days of Christ, and that I should live to see the day, and that there would [be] a book come forth, like unto the Bible, and the people would be guided by it, as well as the Bible.

In 1829, as Chamberlain was disembarking from a boat near Palmyra, New York, he felt prompted by the Spirit to travel south. He walked three miles until he ended up near Joseph Smith's family home. After hearing the story of the golden plates from the inhabitants of the area, Chamberlain decided to visit the Smith home.

> As I entered the door, I said, "Peace be to this house." [Hyrum Smith] looked at me as one astonished, and said, "I hope it will be peace." I then [asked], "Is there anyone here that believes in visions or revelations?" He said, "Yes, we are a visionary house." I said, "Then I will give you one of my pamphlets, which [is] visionary, and

> of my own experience." They then called the people together, which consisted of five or six men who were out at the door. Father Smith was one and some of the Whitmers.
>
> They then sat down and read my pamphlet. Hyrum read first, but was so affected he could not read it. He then gave it to a man which I learned was Christian Whitmer. He finished reading it. I then opened my mouth and began to preach to them, in the words that the angel had made known to me in the vision, that all churches and denominations on the earth had become corrupt, and no Church of God [was] on the earth. But . . . [God] would shortly [raise] up a Church that would never be confounded nor brought down and be like the Apostolic Church.
>
> They wondered greatly who had been telling me these things for, said they, "We have the same things [written] down in our house, taken from the gold record, that you are preaching to us." I said, "The Lord told me these things a number of years ago." I then said, "If you are a visionary house, I wish you would make known some of your discoveries, for I think I can bear them." They then made known to me that they had obtained a gold record, and just finished translating it [there]. Now the Lord revealed to me by the gift and power of the Holy Ghost that this was the work I had been looking for. Here I stayed two days and they instructed me in the manuscripts of the Book of Mormon.[7]

Hamilton G. Park, like many converts, learned that family members can sometimes become hostile to the concept of conversion. But he also learned that God supports and comforts those who sacrifice and obey.

> I joined the Church [in 1861] when I was fifteen years old. My mother was very much opposed to it and said to me: "Hamilton, you have brought disgrace on the family. You have brought a greater sorrow to me than your father's death." This grieved me very much, and set me to crying, for I loved my mother. I distinctly remember going out into the orchard and prostrating myself upon the grass; I prayed to die.
>
> While there I heard a voice which said to me: "Hamilton, what you have done is well pleasing to your Father in heaven. The young man, Joseph Smith, is a prophet, is without spot or blemish, chosen in heaven and ordained of God. If you will be faithful to the end, God will give you an everlasting inheritance in His celestial kingdom where God and Christ dwell." This has been my testimony throughout all my days. My mother afterward joined the Church and came to [America], crossing the plains with a handcart, and finally died a faithful Latter-day Saint in her 93rd year.[8]

Cleveland R. Keith, like so many others who seek the truth, was provided with a heaven-sent confirmation of the prophetic calling of Joseph Smith. The following story was related to Elliot J. Roberts on 21 February 1944.

> A few nights ago I became quite cold . . . [so] I pulled the covers [of my bed] up over my head . . . when someone called me by name. I pulled the covers off my head and was surprised to find the room filled with light and four personages standing by my bed, three at the foot and one at the head. The one at the head of my bed was the spokesman and began talking to me. He said, "You have been praying for a long time for wisdom and knowledge and to know whether Joseph Smith was a prophet of God. We are messengers of God, sent from His presence to tell you that God has heard your prayers and has looked with mercy upon your afflictions. We have been instructed to tell you that Joseph Smith was selected before the world was, at the same time that Abraham and all the other prophets were selected, to open this last dispensation; that he was, is, and always will be a prophet of the living God and that the Church called the Mormon Church is the right Church, the one that was established by Jesus Christ."[9]

A. Ramseyer tells the story of a missionary, identified only as Brother H., who was called to serve in the Bern, Switzerland mission around 1886. This young man was an honest seeker of truth but also:

> . . . keenly sensed his lack of knowledge; he wanted to know of a surety that this was the true Church of Christ, and he prayed very earnestly to the Lord for light and knowledge, and for a testimony of the truth. One morning, as this brother was lying in bed, calling upon the Lord for the testimony he so much longed to receive, an angel appeared by his bedside; at first awe filled his soul, but the divine messenger dissipated his fears, and asked him what he desired. The missionary asked him whether this Church was the true Church; to which the angel answered, "Yes, it is."[10]

About 1823 Daniel Tyler's father and grandfather studied the scriptures and came to the conclusion that since the signs that accompanied ancient Christianity were no longer to be found upon the earth then the true Church of Jesus Christ must not be upon the earth either. Daniel's grandfather "prophesied that he would die" without seeing Christ's true Church but also said that Daniel's "father would live to see the true Church organized with all the apostolic gifts and blessings."

Daniel's grandfather died in February of 1829 without finding the true Church of Jesus Christ. But in the spring of 1832, Samuel H. Smith (one of the eight witnesses who had handled the Book of Mormon plates) and Elder Orson Hyde came to Daniel's neighborhood to preach the gospel. Daniel's father was informed by these missionaries that the LDS Church enjoyed the same spiritual gifts that were spoken of in the New Testament. Some of Daniel's family believed the message of the missionaries; but the father, still skeptical, threatened to disown any members of his family who might be baptized into the LDS faith. After Hyrum Smith preached in the same neighborhood in December of 1832, Daniel's sister decided to proceed with baptism despite her father's negative response to the message of the gospel. Soon after this baptism, reports Daniel, his "grandfather appeared to [his] father in a dream, and told him that this was the people he prophesied of while living." Daniel's parents then entered the waters of baptism and joined themselves with the Saints.[11]

Francis A. Hammond was baptized into The Church of Jesus Christ of Latter-day Saints on 31 December 1847. He relates what happened shortly thereafter.

> After I was baptized, I commenced to worry about the Book of Mormon. The Bible was all right. The evil one got hold of me, and I could not understand so well about the Book of Mormon, and in my perplexity I told my dear, good friend, "Aunt" Matty Pell, of my trouble. As I was about to leave, she took me kindly by the hand, and calling me by name, said if I was sincere and really honest and desired to know the truth, and would go before the Lord and ask Him in faith, He would give me a testimony of the truth of the Book of Mormon. Accordingly when I returned to my lodgings in my desire to know, I took the Book of Mormon, opened it, knelt down by the side of my bunk, and asked the Lord, in the name of Jesus, if that book was true, and what it purported to be. I used but a very few words in my petition, yet before the words were fairly uttered from my lips a sheet of flame or fire commenced to descend upon me, not very warm at the first, but shock after shock succeeded till my whole frame seemed [like it was] literally being consumed with fire; and yet it was not like the fire that we use daily, and if we touch it will immediately give great pain; this was heavenly fire, and filled me with joy unspeakable. My pen [and my] tongue cannot express the peace, joy, and happiness that I experienced at this time. It continued till in the fullness of my soul I cried out, "Enough, Lord," when it gradually departed, leaving me the happiest mortal alive. This was as satisfactory to me as though an angel had appeared and told me the book was true. . . . With this testimony came the knowledge that Joseph Smith, the great modern Prophet, was sent of God to usher in the dispensation of the fullness of times.[12]

Newel K. Whitney and his wife, Elizabeth Whitney, saw a vision in the Fall of 1830 that helped prepare them to receive the restored gospel when the Church located its headquarters in Kirtland, Ohio. Elizabeth relates the story.

> We had been praying . . . to know from the Lord how we could obtain the gift of the Holy Ghost. My husband, Newel K. Whitney, and myself, were Campbellites. We had been baptized for the remission of our sins, and believed in the laying on of hands and the gifts of the Spirit. But there was no one with authority to confer the Holy Ghost upon us.

> We were seeking to know how to obtain the Spirit and the gifts bestowed upon the ancient Saints. Sister Eliza Snow was also a Campbellite. We were acquainted before the restoration of the gospel to the earth. She, like myself, was seeking for the fullness of the gospel. She lived at the time in Mantua.
>
> One night—it was midnight—as my husband and I, in our house at Kirtland, were praying to the Father to be shown the way, the Spirit rested upon us and a cloud overshadowed the house. It was as though we were out of doors. The house passed away from our vision. We were not conscious of anything but the presence of the Spirit and the cloud that was over us. We were wrapped in the cloud. A solemn awe pervaded us. We saw the cloud and we felt the Spirit of the Lord. Then we heard a voice out of the cloud saying: "Prepare to receive the word of the Lord, for it is coming!" At this we marveled greatly; but from that moment we knew that the word of the Lord was coming to Kirtland.[13]

James Bullock, who lived in Offchurch, Warwickshire, England, in the early part of the nineteenth century reports:

> In the year 1848, having returned home from a journey, my brother Thomas handed me the Book of Mormon and asked me to read it. I promised him I would, and having a desire to understand the truth, I commenced to read it. One day while reading it, a strange feeling came over me, and it seemed that I was enveloped in fire from my head to my feet, and a voice said to me: "This book was written by holy men inspired of God, and the Latter-day Saints are the people of God, and they have the gospel of Jesus Christ."

James pondered upon this experience continually and petitioned the Lord for further guidance. In 1851 he received another communication. This time a voice told him that he should travel some forty miles to the city of Brighton. In obedience to this divine directive, James walked to Brighton and there found a group of Latter-day Saints. Shortly thereafter he was baptized into the Church.[14]

Annie H. Free was baptized as a member of the LDS Church on 17 January 1855 in London, England. Her parents belonged to the Church of England and were not pleased with her decision to convert. She relates:

> Shortly after my baptism, before I had been confirmed, my relatives sent me a terrible book against the Mormons, marking it in many places for me to read. The tales were so wicked, I was afraid I had done wrong and decided to ask the Lord to direct me aright, never doubting that I would be answered. I fervently pleaded with our Father to answer my prayer that night as my confirmation was to take place the following morning.

> I immediately was comforted by a wonderful dream. A large book, the Book of Life, was opened before me and the leaves were turned in rapid succession until the page with my record was found. A loud, clear voice spoke to me saying, "This is the way; walk ye in it." I was overjoyed at this revelation and have never doubted the gospel from that time on. You may be assured I was confirmed the next day.[15]

When Benjamin Brown was twenty-five years old, he was shown a "vision" of his long-deceased brother who was in the act of praying. Benjamin reports that he heard his brother's voice "clearly and distinctly" as he prayed.

> In the course of his prayer, he referred to a great work to be done on the earth during the last days, quoting several scriptures. I did not, however, fully comprehend the meaning of them until, coming into The Church of Jesus Christ of Latter-day Saints, years after, I saw the applicability of his words to the views of that people, with regard to the restoration of the gospel gifts, the great work of gathering the Saints of all nations in the last days, and the fullness of the latter-day glory, for he particularly prayed for the hastening of those things.

Later on in life Benjamin received a divine revelation wherein he learned

> that the ancient gifts of the gospel—speaking in tongues, the power to heal the sick, the spirit of prophecy, etc.—were just about to be restored to the believers in Christ. The revelation was a perfect knowledge of the fact, so sure and certain that I felt as though the truth had been stereotyped upon me. I knew it from the crown of my head to the sole of my foot—in the whole of my system, being filled with the Holy Ghost! I can compare it to nothing better than the change made on a clean sheet of paper by a printing press, leaving an indelible impression behind.[16]

THE WITNESS OF THE HOLY GHOST

Every child of God who has an honest and sincere desire to know whether The Church of Jesus Christ of Latter-day Saints is "the only true and living Church upon the face of the whole earth" (D&C 1:30) can obtain a witness of that fact through the power of the Holy Ghost.

President Spencer W. Kimball has taught that:

> A testimony is obtained by earnest seeking. Now, it is a good question which has been asked by millions since Joseph Smith phrased it: "How am I to know which

> of all, if any, of the [religious] organizations is authentic, divine, and recognized by the Lord?". . . You may *know.* You need not be in doubt. Follow the prescribed procedures, and you may have an absolute knowledge that these things are absolute truths. The necessary procedure is: study, think, pray, and do. Revelation is the key. God will make it known to you once you have capitulated and have become humble and receptive. Having dropped all pride of your mental stature, having acknowledged before God your confusion, having subjected your egotism, and having surrendered yourself to the teaching of the Holy Spirit, you are ready to begin to learn. With preconceived religious notions stubbornly held, one is not teachable. The Lord has promised repeatedly that He will give you a knowledge of spiritual things when you have placed yourself in a proper frame of mind. He has counseled us to seek, ask, and search diligently.[17]

How does one go about seeking a testimony?

The very same principle that sparked the Restoration applies to all those who desire to have a testimony of its truthfulness. "If any of you lack wisdom, let him ask of God, that giveth to all men liberally, and upbraideth not; and it shall be given him. But let him ask in faith, nothing wavering" (James 1:5). This same basic principle of action is taught by the Lord Jesus Christ in Matthew 7:7–8. "Ask, and it shall be given you; seek, and ye shall find; knock, and it shall be opened unto you. For everyone that asketh receiveth; and he that seeketh findeth; and to him that knocketh it shall be opened."

What mechanism does God employ in the bestowal of a testimony?

The New Testament teaches that the Holy Ghost acts in the capacity of a Witness (see Acts 5:32; 20:23; Hebrews 10:15). What does the Holy Ghost bear witness to? Only the truth, for "the Comforter is . . . the Spirit of *truth* . . . [and] he shall testify" of that which is genuine and right (John 15:26, emphasis added). "It is the Spirit that beareth witness, because the Spirit is *truth*" (1 John 5:6, emphasis added). And "the Spirit of *truth*," said the Savior, "will guide you into all *truth*" (John 16:13, emphasis added; cf. Moroni 10:5).

How does the Holy Ghost bear testimony?

Every mortal has a spirit within them (see Job 32:8) and "the Spirit . . . beareth witness with our spirit" (Romans 8:16). The apostle Paul taught that the Spirit of God reveals things of a spiritual nature only to those who are spiritually minded (1 Corinthians 2:10–14).

What does it feel like when the Holy Ghost bears witness of the truth?

There are two different types of sensations that can attend the presence of the Spirit. The first type of sensation is physical in nature. One can be literally "filled with the Holy Ghost" (Acts 2:4; see also Luke 1:15, 35, 41; Acts 4:8; 9:17; 13:52). What does it feel like when one is thus filled? Like one's soul is enflamed. In Matthew 3:11 and Acts 2:3–4, the Holy Ghost is closely associated with heavenly "fire."[18] The second type of sensation is emotional in nature. "The fruit of the Spirit," says Galatians 5:22, is "joy [and] peace" (cf. Romans 14:17). The Holy Ghost is also referred to in scripture as the "Comforter" (see John 14:26; 15:26; 16:7; Acts 9:31), thus hinting at what it feels like to be under His heavenly influence.

SUMMARY

The foundational claims of The Church of Jesus Christ of Latter-day Saints have been verified by the Lord to independent witnesses on countless occasions. Millions of mortals know, beyond doubt, that Joseph Smith's testimony is true. Any individuals who are willing to approach God in humility and sincerity can obtain this same assurance for themselves by the power of the Holy Ghost.

NOTES

1. Dean C. Jessee, ed., *The Personal Writings of Joseph Smith* (Salt Lake City: Deseret Book, 1984), 7.
2. Ibid., 8.
3. *HC*, 1:85.
4. B. H. Roberts, *The Life of John Taylor* (Salt Lake City: Bookcraft, 1963), 28.
5. *The Young Woman's Journal*, vol. 4, no. 5, February 1893, 217.
6. *Juvenile Instructor*, vol. 2, no. 1, 1 January 1867, 14.
7. Solomon Chamberlain, *A Short Sketch of the Life of Solomon Chamberlain*, 11 July 1858, 2–4, LDS Church Archives, Salt Lake City, Utah.
8. *Deseret News*, Church Section, 27 May 1933, 6.
9. Ibid., 24 June 1944, 12.
10. *Improvement Era*, November 1916, 58–59.
11. *Classic Experiences and Adventures* (Salt Lake City: Bookcraft, 1969), part 3, 22–26.
12. Campus Education Week Staff, comps., *Voices from the Past: Diaries, Journals, and Autobiographies* (Provo, Utah: Brigham Young University Press, 1980), 42–43.
13. Edward W. Tullidge, *The Women of Mormondom* (New York: Tullidge and Crandall, 1877), 41–42.
14. *Millennial Star*, vol. 68, no. 10, 8 March 1906, 157.
15. Kate B. Carter, comp., *Our Pioneer Heritage* (Salt Lake City: Daughters of the Utah Pioneers, 1961), 5:184.
16. Benjamin Brown, *Testimonies for the Truth: A Record of Manifestations of the Power of God, Miraculous and Providential* (Liverpool, England: S. W. Richards, 1853), 4, 7.
17. Edward L. Kimball, ed., *Teachings of Spencer W. Kimball* (Salt Lake City: Bookcraft, 1998), 63, emphasis in original. Along the lines of what President Kimball has said, one should consider the words of Alma. "Behold, I testify unto you that I do know that these things whereof I have spoken are true. And how do ye suppose that I know of their surety? Behold, I say unto you they are made known unto me by the Holy Spirit of God. Behold, I have fasted and prayed many days that I might know these things of myself. And now I do know of myself that they are true; for the Lord God hath made them manifest unto me by His Holy Spirit; and this is the *spirit of revelation* which is in me" (Alma 5:45–46, emphasis added).
18. The Lord instructed Oliver Cowdery: "study it out in your mind; then you must ask me if it be right, and if it is right I will cause that your bosom shall *burn* within you; therefore, you shall feel that it is right" (D&C 9:8, emphasis added). The burning in the heart was also experienced by two of the Lord's disciples as they were taught the truths of the scriptures by Him (see Luke 24:13–35).

CONCLUSION

Latter-day Saint doctrine declares the same message as the New Testament scriptures: there is only "one faith" (Ephesians 4:5; cf. D&C 1:30). Christ is not divided (see 1 Corinthians 1:13); yet Christianity has fragmented into numerous denominations, each teaching its own version of the Lord's eternal gospel. This dire state of division was one of the primary reasons for the Restoration. The Church of Jesus Christ of Latter-day Saints proclaims that there is only one true Church and that it, alone, is the Church of the Savior restored to its original form; complete with legitimate priesthood authority, uncontaminated doctrinal beliefs, correct organizational structure, and valid ordinances.

This book has presented some of the many evidences that support the claim of the LDS Church to be a legitimate restoration of the ancient Church of Jesus Christ. It is the belief of the author that the material within this volume justifies the following eight conclusions.

1. The New Testament Saints clearly understood that before the Second Coming of Jesus Christ there would be an apostasy from the true Christian faith. This falling away was to be followed by a restoration of the gospel in its pure form.

2. There is abundant evidence to sustain Joseph Smith's claim to be a genuine prophet of God. This claim finds especially strong support in the fact that there were independent witnesses to his visions, visitations, and revelations.

3. The organizational structure, practices, and ordinances of the LDS Church are the same as those found in the early Christian Church.

4. The doctrines of the LDS Church are the same as the doctrines taught among the early followers of Christ.

5. The spiritual gifts enjoyed by the early Christian Saints are now enjoyed by the Latter-day Saints in all their particulars.

6. Joseph Smith's claim that the texts of the Bible have been corrupted has been overwhelmingly confirmed. Some of the corrections made in the Joseph Smith Translation of the Bible have now been verified by non-LDS scholars.

7. There is a substantial, and growing, body of evidence that the Book of Mormon is an authentically ancient scriptural record of Israelites in the New World.

8. Joseph Smith's claim to be a prophet of God, who was divinely directed to restore Christ's Church in its undefiled condition, has been verified on countless occasions by revelation from heaven, sometimes in very direct ways.

While the evidences presented in this book do not necessarily "prove" that the LDS Church is the true Church of Jesus Christ, they do demonstrate that such a claim is well within the limits of plausibility. An absolute confirmation of the truthfulness of the restored gospel can only be obtained through faithful prayer. And when that confirmation comes, through the power of the Holy Ghost, one may have absolute confidence in it since God is the "God of truth" (Deuteronomy 32:4) and "cannot lie" (Titus 1:2; see also Hebrews 6:18).

ILLUSTRATION SOURCES

Introduction

Figure 1, page vii. President Joseph F. Smith in the Sacred Grove. Photographer unknown. © by Intellectual Reserve, Inc. Courtesy of Museum of Church History and Art. Used by permission.

Chapter 2: *The Divine Calling of Joseph Smith*

Figure 2, page 33. Portrait of Joseph Smith by Danquardt A. Weggeland (1872–1918). © by Intellectual Reserve, Inc. Courtesy of Museum of Church History and Art. Used by permission.

Figure 3, page 37. Joseph Smith as Lieutenant General of the Nauvoo Legion. Painting by T. Hafen (1887). Photograph #13631. Courtesy of the Utah State Historical Society. Used by permission. All rights reserved.

Figure 4, page 38. Parallel columns showing Joseph of Egypt's prophecies as they appear in JST Genesis 50:24–33 and 2 Nephi 3:6–15. Graphic by Matthew B. Brown.

Figure 5, page 39. Five parallels between the *Messiah ben Joseph* legends and scriptural materials produced by Joseph Smith. Chart by Matthew B. Brown.

Figure 6, page 59. President Brigham Young. Photograph #14205. Courtesy of the Utah State Historical Society. Used by permission. All rights reserved.

Figure 13, page 188. "Stick of Joseph" placard. Joseph Fielding Smith, *Essentials in Church History* (Salt Lake City: Deseret News Press, 1922), 63.

Figure 14, page 191. Israelite temple priest blowing a trumpet. Louis C. Fillion, *Atlas d'Histoire Naturelle de la Bible* (Paris: Librairie Briday, 1884), plate 81, figure 1.

Figure 15, page 196. Engravings of the Three Witnesses of the Book of Mormon by Charles B. Hall. © by Intellectual Reserve, Inc. Courtesy of Museum of Church History and Art. Used by permission.

Figure 16, page 200. Route Lehi's colony may have taken from Jerusalem to the east coast of the Arabian Peninsula. Drawing by Jessica A. Warner and Matthew B. Brown.

Figure 17, page 203. Model of Book of Mormon geography based solely upon unambiguous information from the text. Drawing by Matthew B. Brown.

Figure 18, page 206. Anthon Transcript characters as published in the New York periodical *The Prophet,* no. 31, 12 December 1844, 2.

Figure 19, page 215. The Red Crown of Lower Egypt. John Kitto, ed., *The Cyclopaedia of Biblical Literature,* 10th ed. (Chicago: S. C. Griggs and Co., 1854), 1:498.

Figure 20, page 217. Stairway from Kabah in the Mayan region of Mesoamerica. Drawing by Matthew B. Brown based upon the illustration found in Theodore A. Willard, *The Lost Empires of the Itzaes and Mayas* (Glendale, California: The Arthur H. Clark Co., 1933), 115.

Figure 21, page 218. The Strombus Galeatus monster. Rafael L. Hoyle, "A Culture Sequence for the North Coast of Peru," in Julian H.

SELECTED BIBLIOGRAPHY

BOOKS

Agus, Aharon. *The Binding of Isaac and Messiah* (Albany, New York: State University of New York Press), 1988.

Anderson, Richard L. *Investigating the Book of Mormon Witnesses* (Salt Lake City: Deseret Book), 1989.

Babbs, Arthur V. *The Law of the Tithe* (New York: Fleming H. Revell Co.), 1912.

Backman, Milton V., Jr. *Joseph Smith's First Vision*, 2d ed. (Salt Lake City: Bookcraft), 1980.

Bauer, Walter, William F. Arndt, and F. Wilbur Gingrich, eds., *A Greek-English Lexicon of the New Testament and Other Early Christian Literature*, 2d. ed. (Chicago: The University of Chicago Press), 1979.

Black, Matthew. *The Scrolls and Christian Origins* (New York: Charles Scribner's Sons), 1961.

Brown, Matthew B. *The Gate of Heaven: Insights on the Doctrines and Symbols of the Temple* (American Fork, Utah: Covenant Communications), 1999.

Bruce, F. F. *Biblical Exegesis in the Qumran Texts* (Den Haag, Netherlands: Uitgeverij van Keulen N. V.), 1959.

Chadwick, Henry. *The Early Church*, rev. ed. (New York: Penguin), 1993.

Clarke, Adam. *Clarke's Commentary*, 6 vols. (Nashville: Abingdon), 1977.

Cohn-Sherbock, Dan. *The Jewish Messiah* (Edinburgh: T&T Clark), 1997.

Cook, Lyndon W., ed. *David Whitmer Interviews: A Restoration Witness* (Orem, Utah: Grandin Book), 1991.

Cote, Wolfred N. *The Archaeology of Baptism* (London: Yates and Alexander), 1876.

Cowley, Matthias F. *Wilford Woodruff: History of His Life and Labors* (Salt Lake City: Deseret News Press), 1909.

Crowley, Ariel L. *Statements of Beliefs of The Church of Jesus Christ of Latter-day Saints* (Salt Lake City: Deseret Book), 1963.

Davies, John G. *The Early Christian Church* (New York: Anchor Books), 1965.

Ehat, Andrew F. and Lyndon W. Cook. *The Words of Joseph Smith* (Orem, Utah: Grandin Book), 1994.

Ehrman, Bart D. *The Orthodox Corruption of Scripture: The Effect of Early Christological Controversies on the Text of the New Testament* (New York: Oxford University Press), 1993.

Fishbane, Michael. *Biblical Interpretation in Ancient Israel* (Oxford: Clarendon Press), 1988.

Fox, Robin L. *Pagans and Christians* (New York: Penguin Books), 1986.

Furst, Jill L. and Peter T. Furst. *Pre-Columbian Art of Mexico* (New York: Abbeville Press), 1980.

Ginzberg, Louis. *The Legends of the Jews*, 7 vols. (Philadelphia: The Jewish Publication Society of America), 1937.

Grant, Robert M. *Second-Century Christianity* (London: Society for Promoting Christian Knowledge), 1946.

Green, Jay P., Sr. *Interlinear Greek-English New Testament*, 3d ed. (Grand Rapids, Michigan: Baker Books), 1996.

Greenstone, Julius H. *The Messiah Idea in Jewish History* (Philadelphia: The Jewish Publication Society of America), 1906.

Hall, Stuart G. *Doctrine and Practice in the Early Church* (London: SPCK), 1991.

Harnack, Adolph. *The Mission and Expansion of Christianity in the First Three Centuries* (New York: Harper and Brothers), 1962.

Harrison, Roland K., et al. *Biblical Criticism: Historical, Literary and Textual* (Grand Rapids, Michigan: Zondervan), 1978.

Hatch, Edwin. *The Influence of Greek Ideas on Christianity* (Gloucester, Massachusetts: Peter Smith), 1970.

Hinckley, Bryant S. *The Faith of Our Pioneer Fathers* (Salt Lake City: Deseret Book), 1956.

Holbrook, Clyde A. *The Iconoclastic Deity: Biblical Images of God* (London: Associated University Presses), 1984.

Horsley, A. Burt. *Peter and the Popes* (Provo, Utah: BYU Religious Studies Center), 1989.

Jacob, Edmond. *Theology of the Old Testament* (New York: Harper and Brothers), 1958.

Jessee, Dean C., ed. *The Personal Writings of Joseph Smith* (Salt Lake City: Deseret Book), 1984.

Kelly, J. N. D. *Early Christian Doctrines* (New York: Harper and Brothers), 1958.

Kimball, Edward L., ed. *Teachings of Spencer W. Kimball* (Salt Lake City: Bookcraft), 1998.

Liddell, Henry G. and Robert Scott. *A Greek-English Lexicon*, rev. ed. (Oxford: Clarendon Press), 1968.

Ludlow, Daniel H., ed. *Encyclopedia of Mormonism*, 4 vols. (New York: Macmillan), 1992.

MacGowan, K. *Early Man in the New World* (New York: Macmillan), 1950.

Martin, Paul S. and H. E. Wright, Jr., eds. *Pleistocene Extinctions* (New Haven: Yale University Press), 1967.

Matthews, Robert J. *A Plainer Translation: Joseph Smith's Translation of the Bible* (Provo, Utah: Brigham Young University Press), 1975.

McConkie, Bruce R. *Mormon Doctrine*, 2d ed. (Salt Lake City: Bookcraft), 1979.

Metzger, Bruce M. *A Textual Commentary on the Greek New Testament*, 3d ed. (Stuttgart, Germany: United Bible Societies), 1975.

Mounce, William D. *The Analytical Lexicon to the Greek New Testament* (Grand Rapids, Michigan: Zondervan), 1993.

Mowinckel, Sigmund. *He That Cometh* (New York: Abingdon Press), 1954.

Mullen, E. Theodore, *The Assembly of the Gods* (Chico, California: Scholars Press), 1980.

Munoa, Philip B. *Four Powers in Heaven: The Interpretation of Daniel 7 in the Testament of Abraham* (Sheffield, England: Sheffield Academic Press), 1998.

Nibley, Preston. *The Presidents of the Church* (Salt Lake City: Deseret Book), 1971.

Odeberg, Hugo, ed. *3 Enoch or The Hebrew Book of Enoch* (New York: Ktav Publishing), 1973.

Parry, Donald W. *The Book of Mormon Text Reformatted According to Parallelistic Patterns* (Provo, Utah: Foundation for Ancient Research and Mormon Studies), 1992.

_____. ed. *Temples of the Ancient World: Ritual and Symbolism* (Salt Lake City: Deseret Book and FARMS), 1994.

_____. and Stephen D. Ricks, eds. *The Temple in Time and Eternity* (Provo, Utah: The Foundation for Ancient Research and Mormon Studies), 1999.

Parry, Edwin F., comp. *Stories about Joseph Smith the Prophet* (Salt Lake City: Deseret News Press), 1934.

Patai, Raphael. *The Messiah Texts* (New York: Avon Books), 1979.

Pinnock, Hugh W. *Finding Biblical Hebrew and Other Ancient Literary Forms in the Book of Mormon* (Provo, Utah: Foundation for Ancient Research and Mormon Studies), 1999.

Pratt, Parley P. *Key to the Science of Theology* (Salt Lake City: Deseret News Press), 1874.

Reynolds, Noel B., ed. *Book of Mormon Authorship: New Light on Ancient Origins* (Provo, Utah: BYU Religious Studies Center), 1982.

_____. ed. *Book of Mormon Authorship Revisited: The Evidence for Ancient Origins* (Provo, Utah: Foundation for Ancient Research and Mormon Studies), 1997.

Ricks, Stephen D. and John W. Welch, eds. *The Allegory of the Olive Tree: The Olive, the Bible, and Jacob 5* (Salt Lake City: Deseret Book and FARMS), 1994.

Roberts, Brigham H. *The Life of John Taylor* (Salt Lake City: Bookcraft), 1963.

_____. *The Rise and Fall of Nauvoo* (Salt Lake City: Bookcraft), 1965.

Rogers, Cleon L., Jr. and Cleon L. Rogers, III. *The New Linguistic and Exegetical Key to the Greek New Testament* (Grand Rapids, Michigan: Zondervan), 1998.

Scrivener, Frederick H. *A Plain Introduction to the Criticism of the New Testament*, 3d ed. (Cambridge: Deighton, Bell and Co.), 1883.

Shiel, James. *Greek Thought and the Rise of Christianity* (London: Longmans, Green and Co.), 1968.

Smith, Joseph. *History of the Church of Jesus Christ of Latter-day Saints*, 7 vols., 2d ed. (Salt Lake City: Deseret Book), 1959.

Smith, Joseph Fielding, comp. *The Teachings of the Prophet Joseph Smith* (Salt Lake City: Deseret Book), 1989.

_____. *Answers to Gospel Questions*, 5 vols. (Salt Lake City: Deseret Book), 1998.

Sorenson, John L. *The Geography of Book of Mormon Events: A Source Book* (Provo, Utah: Foundation for Ancient Research and Mormon Studies), 1990.

_____. and Melvin J. Thorne, eds. *Rediscovering the Book of Mormon* (Salt Lake City: Deseret Book and FARMS), 1991.

_____. *An Ancient American Setting for the Book of Mormon* (Salt Lake City: Deseret Book and FARMS), 1996.

_____. *Images of Ancient America: Visualizing Book of Mormon Life* (Provo, Utah: Research Press), 1998.

_____. *Mormon's Map* (Provo, Utah: The Foundation for Ancient Research and Mormon Studies), 2000.

Stokes, Jeremiah. *Modern Miracles*, 2d ed. (Salt Lake City: Bookcraft), 1945.

Strong, James. *The New Strong's Exhaustive Concordance of the Bible* (Nashville: Thomas Nelson Publishers), 1996.

Stuy, Brian H., ed. *Collected Discourses*, 5 vols. (Burbank, California: B. H. S. Publishing), 1987.

Taylor, Mark H., ed. *Witness to the Martyrdom: John Taylor's Personal Account of the Last Days of the Prophet Joseph Smith* (Salt Lake City: Deseret Book), 1999.

Thayer, Joseph H. *Thayer's Greek-English Lexicon of the New Testament*, rev. ed. (Grand Rapids, Michigan: Baker Book House), 1987.

Tov, Emmanuel. *Textual Criticism of the Hebrew Bible* (Minneapolis: Fortress), 1992.

Vaganay, Leon and Christian-Bernard Amphoux. *An Introduction to New Testament Textual Criticism*, 2d ed. (Cambridge: Cambridge University Press), 1991.

Vine, William E., Merrill F. Unger, and William White, Jr. *Vine's Complete Expository Dictionary of Old and New Testament Words* (Nashville: Thomas Nelson Publishers), 1996.

Welch, John W. *Reexploring the Book of Mormon* (Salt Lake City: Deseret Book and FARMS), 1992.

Williamson, Geoffrey A., trans. *Eusebius: The History of the Church from Christ to Constantine* (New York: Dorset Press), 1984.

ARTICLES

Adair, Michael D. "The Doctrines of Salvation by Grace vs. Works: A New Look at an Old Controversy," in *A Symposium on the New Testament* (Salt Lake City: The Church of Jesus Christ of Latter-day Saints, 1980), 28–33.

Anderson, Richard L. "Circumstantial Confirmation of the First Vision Through Reminiscences," *Brigham Young University Studies*, vol. 9, no. 3, Spring 1969, 373–404.

_____. "The Restoration of the Sacrament," Part 1, *Ensign*, January 1992, 40–46; Part 2, *Ensign*, February 1992, 11–17.

_____. "Joseph Smith's Testimony of the First Vision," *Ensign*, April 1996, 10–21.

Barney, Kevin L. "Poetic Diction and Parallel Word Pairs in the Book of Mormon," *Journal of Book of Mormon Studies*, vol. 4, no. 2, Fall 1995, 15–81.

Brown, S. Kent. "Whither the Early Church?" *Ensign*, October 1988, 7–10.

_____. "'The Place That Was Called Nahom': New Light from Ancient Yemen," *Journal of Book of Mormon Studies*, vol. 8, no. 1, 1999, 66–68.

Cannon, Brian Q. and BYU Studies Staff. "Priesthood Restoration Documents," *Brigham Young University Studies*, vol. 35, no. 4, 1995–96, 163–207.

Cracroft, Paul. "A Clear Poetic Voice: The Book of Mormon Bears the Unmistakable Mark of Ancient Hebrew Literary Forms," *Ensign*, January 1984, 28–31.

Esplin, Ronald K. "Joseph, Brigham and the Twelve: A Succession of Continuity," *Brigham Young University Studies*, vol. 21, no. 3, Summer 1981, 301–41.

Garr, Arnold K. "A Great and Marvelous Work. Part One: 1350–1805, Preparing for the Restoration," *Ensign*, June 1999, 34–45.

Hamblin, William J. "Basic Methodological Problems with the Anti-Mormon Approach to the Geography and Archaeology of the Book of Mormon," *Journal of Book of Mormon Studies*, vol. 2, no. 1, Spring 1993, 161–97.

_____. "Sacred Writings on Bronze Plates in the Ancient Mediterranean," FARMS preliminary report, 1994.

Hilton, John L. "On Verifying Wordprint Studies: Book of Mormon Authorship," in Noel B. Reynolds, ed., *Book of Mormon Authorship Revisited: The Evidence for Ancient Origins* (Provo, Utah: Foundation for Ancient Research and Mormon Studies, 1997), 225–53.

Hoskisson, Paul Y. "Alma as a Hebrew Name," *Journal of Book of Mormon Studies*, vol. 7, no. 1, 1998, 72–73.

Jackson, Kent P. "Early Signs of the Apostasy," *Ensign*, December 1984, 8–16.

_____. "'Watch and Remember': The New Testament and the Great Apostasy," in John M. Lundquist and Stephen D. Ricks, eds., *By Study and Also By Faith* (Salt Lake City: Deseret Book and FARMS, 1990), 1:81–117.

_____. "Moroni's Message to Joseph Smith," *Ensign*, August 1990, 13–16.

Johnson, Ludwell, H. "Men and Elephants in America," *Scientific Monthly*, October 1952, 215–21.

Jorgensen, Lynn W. and BYU Studies Staff. "The Mantle of the Prophet Joseph Passes to Brother Brigham: A Collective Witness," *Brigham Young University Studies*, vol. 36, no. 4, 1996–97, 125–204.

Ludlow, Daniel H. "The Relationship Between Grace and Works," in *A Symposium on the New Testament: Supplement* (Salt Lake City: The Church of Jesus Christ of Latter-day Saints, 1984), 29–36.

Magleby, Kirk A. "A Survey of Mesoamerican Bearded Figures," FARMS preliminary report, 1983.

Marsh, W. Jeffrey. "Training from the Old Testament: Moroni's Lessons for a Prophet," *Ensign*, August 1998, 10–17.

Matthews, Robert J. "The Role of the Joseph Smith Translation of the Bible in the Restoration of Doctrine," in Stephen D. Ricks, Donald W. Parry, and Andrew H. Hedges, eds., *The Disciple as Witness: Essays on Latter-day Saint History and*

Doctrine in Honor of Richard Lloyd Anderson (Provo, Utah: Foundation for Ancient Research and Mormon Studies, 2000), 327–53.

Maxwell, Neal A. "Discipleship and Scholarship," *Brigham Young University Studies*, vol. 32, no. 3, Summer 1992, 5–9.

Meservy, Keith. "Ezekiel's Sticks and the Gathering of Israel," *Ensign*, February 1987, 4–13.

Nelson, William O. "Is the LDS View of God Consistent With the Bible?" *Ensign*, July 1987, 56–59.

Oaks, Dallin H. "Spiritual Gifts," *Ensign*, September 1986, 68–72.

_____. "The Historicity of the Book of Mormon," FARMS transcript, 1993.

Parry, Donald W. "Hebrew Literary Patterns in the Book of Mormon," *Ensign*, October 1989, 58–61.

Parsons, Robert E. "What is the Role of Grace in LDS Theology?" *Ensign*, July 1989, 59–61.

Paulsen, David L. "The Doctrine of Divine Embodiment: Restoration, Judeo-Christian, and Philosophical Perspectives," *Brigham Young University Studies*, vol. 35, no. 4, 1995–96, 7–94.

Peterson, Daniel C. and Stephen D. Ricks. "Comparing LDS Beliefs with First-Century Christianity," *Ensign*, March 1988, 7–11.

_____. "Is the Book of Mormon True? Notes on the Debate," in Noel B. Reynolds, eds. *Book of Mormon Authorship Revisited: The Evidence for Ancient Origins* (Provo, Utah: Foundation for Ancient Research and Mormon Studies, 1997), 141–77.

_____. "Mounting Evidence for the Book of Mormon," *Ensign*, January 2000, 18–24.

_____. "'Ye are Gods': Psalm 82 and John 10 as Witnesses to the Divine Nature of Humankind," in Stephen D. Ricks, Donald W. Parry, and Andrew H. Hedges, eds., *The Disciple as Scholar: Essays on Scripture and the Ancient World in Honor of Richard Lloyd Anderson* (Provo, Utah: Foundation for Ancient Research and Mormon Studies, 2000), 471–594.

Peterson, H. Donl. "Moroni: Joseph Smith's Tutor," *Ensign*, January 1992, 22–29.

Porter, Larry C. "The Restoration of the Aaronic and Melchizedek Priesthoods," *Ensign*, December 1996, 30–47.

Pratt, John P. "The Restoration of Priesthood Keys on Easter 1836," Part 1, *Ensign*, June 1985, 59–68; Part 2, *Ensign*, July 1985, 55–64.

Read, Lenet H. "Joseph Smith's Receipt of the Plates and the Israelite Feast of Trumpets," *Journal of Book of Mormon Studies*, vol. 2, no. 2, Fall 1993, 110–20.

_____. "The Golden Plates and the Feast of Trumpets," *Ensign*, January 2000, 25–29.

Reynolds, Noel B., et al. "External Evidences of Scripture: A Panel," in Paul R. Cheesman and Wilfred C. Griggs, eds., *Scriptures for the Modern World* (Provo, Utah: BYU Religious Studies Center, 1984), 121–35.

_____. "Shedding New Light on Ancient Origins: Scholars Illuminate Book of Mormon Authorship," *Brigham Young Magazine*, Spring 1998, 37–45.

Ricks, Stephen D. "Translating the Book of Mormon: Interpreting the Evidence," *Journal of Book of Mormon Studies*, vol. 2, no. 2, Fall 1993, 201–06.

_____. and John A. Tvedtnes. "The Hebrew Origin of Some Book of Mormon Place Names," *Journal of Book of Mormon Studies*, vol. 6, no. 2, 1997, 255–59.

_____. "Kingship, Coronation, and Covenant in Mosiah 1–6," in John W. Welch and Stephen D. Ricks, eds., *King Benjamin's Speech: "That Ye May Learn Wisdom"* (Provo, Utah: Foundation for Ancient Research and Mormon Studies, 1998), 89–117.

Skousen, Royal. "The Original Language of the Book of Mormon: Upstate New York Dialect, King James English, or Hebrew?" *Journal of Book of Mormon Studies*, vol. 3, no. 1, Spring 1994, 28–38.

Sorenson, John L. "Wheeled Figurines in the Ancient World," FARMS preliminary report, 1983.

_____. "Animals in the Book of Mormon: An Annotated Bibliography," FARMS paper, 1992.

_____. and Robert F. Smith, "Barley in Ancient America," in John W. Welch, ed., *Reexploring the Book of Mormon* (Salt Lake City: Deseret Book and FARMS, 1992), 130–32.

Sperry, Sidney B. "Hebrew Idioms in the Book of Mormon," *Journal of Book of Mormon Studies*, vol. 4, no. 1, Spring 1995, 218–25.

Szink, Terrence L. "Further Evidence of a Semitic Alma," *Journal of Book of Mormon Studies*, vol. 8, no. 1, 1999, 70.

_____. and John W. Welch. "King Benjamin's Speech in the Context of Ancient Israelite Festivals," in John W. Welch and Stephen D. Ricks, eds., *King Benjamin's Speech: "That Ye May Learn Wisdom"* (Provo, Utah: Foundation for Ancient Research and Mormon Studies, 1998), 147–223.

Thorne, Melvin J. "Complexity, Consistency, Ignorance, and Probabilities," in Noel B. Reynolds, ed., *Book of Mormon Authorship Revisited: The Evidence for Ancient Origins* (Provo, Utah: Foundation for Ancient Research and Mormon Studies, 1997), 179–93.

Torrey, Charles C. "The Messiah Son of Ephraim," *Journal of Biblical Literature*, vol. 66, 1947, 253–77.

Tvedtnes, John A. "King Benjamin and the Feast of Tabernacles," in John M. Lundquist and Stephen D. Ricks, eds., *By Study and Also By Faith* (Salt Lake City: Deseret Book and FARMS, 1990), 2:197–237.

_____. "The Hebrew Background of the Book of Mormon," in John L. Sorenson and Melvin J. Thorne, eds., *Rediscovering the Book of Mormon* (Salt Lake City: Deseret Book and FARMS, 1991), 77–91.

_____. and Stephen D. Ricks. "Jewish and Other Semitic Texts Written in Egyptian Characters," *Journal of Book of Mormon Studies*, vol. 5, no. 2, 1996, 156–63.

_____. "Baptism for the Dead in Early Christianity," in Donald W. Parry and Stephen D. Ricks, eds., *The Temple in Time and Eternity* (Provo, Utah: The Foundation for Ancient Research and Mormon Studies, 1999), 55–78.

_____. John Gee, and Matthew Roper. "Book of Mormon Names Attested in Ancient Hebrew Inscriptions," *Journal of Book of Mormon Studies*, vol. 9, no., 1, 2000, 41–51.

Welch, John W. "The Power of Evidence in the Nurturing of Faith," in *Nurturing Faith Through the Book of Mormon* (Salt Lake City: Deseret Book, 1995), 149–86.

_____. "What Does Chiasmus in the Book of Mormon Prove?" in Noel B. Reynolds, ed., *Book of Mormon Authorship Revisited: The Evidence for Ancient Origins* (Provo, Utah: Foundation for Ancient Research and Mormon Studies, 1997), 199–224.

_____. "Chiasmus in the Book of Mormon," in John W. Welch, ed., *Chiasmus in Antiquity*, repr. ed. (Provo, Utah: Research Press, 1998), 198–210.

_____. and Daryl R. Hague. "Benjamin's Sermon as a Traditional Ancient Farewell Address," in John W. Welch and Stephen D. Ricks, eds., *King Benjamin's Speech: "That Ye May Learn Wisdom"* (Provo, Utah: Foundation for Ancient Research and Mormon Studies, 1998), 89–117.

Wright, H. Curtis. "Ancient Burials of Metal Documents in Stone Boxes," in John M. Lundquist and Stephen D. Ricks, eds., *By Study and Also By Faith* (Salt Lake City: Deseret Book and FARMS, 1990), 2:273–334.

INDEX